DAY HIKING

Olympic
Peninsula

Monkeyflowers add a little yellow to the emerald South Fork Hoh River valley.

Previous page: Deserted beach at South Indian Island County Park

Piper's Bellflower, an Olympic Peninsula endemic species

New Dungeness Lighthouse on Dungeness Spit

Tarn in upper Royal Basin, Olympic National Park

Blooming beargrass and Lake Crescent from Mount Muller

Autumn colors in the Grand Valley, Olympic National Park

Red sky at night, winter evening at Abbey Island

Oyster Lake and Mount Appleton

Larkspur on the side of Maynard Mountain

DAY HIKING

Olympic 2nd edition
Peninsula

national park · coastal beaches
southwest washington

Craig Romano

MOUNTAINEERS
BOOKS

Mountaineers Books is the publishing division of The Mountaineers, an organization founded in 1906 and dedicated to the exploration, preservation, and enjoyment of outdoor and wilderness areas.

MOUNTAINEERS BOOKS

1001 SW Klickitat Way, Suite 201, Seattle, WA 98134
800.553.4453, www.mountaineersbooks.org

Printed in the United States of America

First edition, 2007. Second edition: first printing 2016, second printing 2018, third printing 2019

Copy Editor: Julie Van Pelt
Cover and Book Design: Mountaineers Books
Layout: Jennifer Shontz, www.redshoedesign.com
Cartographer: Pease Press Cartography
Cover photograph: *Mount Constance from ridge above Silver Lakes, Buckhorn Wilderness*
Frontispiece: *Browns Point at Kalaloch Beach, Olympic National Park*

Library of Congress Cataloging-in-Publication Data
Romano, Craig.
Day hiking Olympic Peninsula : national park/ coastal beaches/
  southwest Washington / Craig Romano.
Olympic Peninsula
Second Edition. | Seattle, WA : Mountaineers Books, [2016]
LCCN 2016015116 (print) | LCCN 2016025263 (ebook) |
  ISBN 978-1-59485-961-8 (paperback : alk. paper) | ISBN 978-1-59485-962-5 (ebook)
LCSH: Hiking—Washington (State)—Olympic Peninsula—Guidebooks. |
  Olympic Peninsula (Wash.)—Guidebooks.
LCC GV199.42.W22 O527 2016 (print) | LCC GV199.42.W22 (ebook)
  | DDC 796.5109797—dc23
LC record available at https://lccn.loc.gov/2016015116

The background maps for this book were produced using the online map viewer CalTopo. For more information, visit caltopo.com.

Printed on FSC®-certified paper

ISBN (paperback): 978-1-59485-961-8
ISBN (ebook): 978-1-59485-962-5

Table of Contents

Olympic Peninsula: Northeast

Olympic Peninsula: North

Olympic Peninsula: West

Olympic Peninsula: Coast

LEGEND

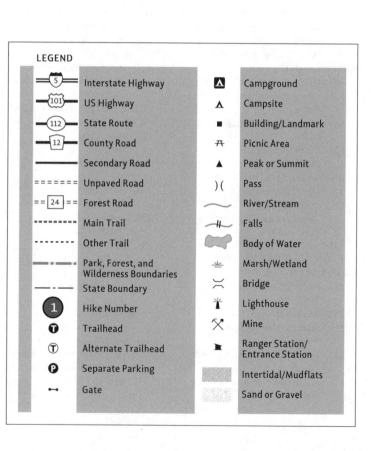

5	Interstate Highway
101	US Highway
112	State Route
12	County Road
——	Secondary Road
=======	Unpaved Road
== 24 ==	Forest Road
---------	Main Trail
--------	Other Trail
—··—··—	Park, Forest, and Wilderness Boundaries
—··—··—	State Boundary
1	Hike Number
T	Trailhead
T	Alternate Trailhead
P	Separate Parking
•—•	Gate
◬	Campground
▲	Campsite
■	Building/Landmark
⅋	Picnic Area
▲	Peak or Summit
)(	Pass
～	River/Stream
⎯∦⎯	Falls
⬭	Body of Water
⁂	Marsh/Wetland
≍	Bridge
⚲	Lighthouse
⚒	Mine
◣	Ranger Station/Entrance Station
	Intertidal/Mudflats
	Sand or Gravel

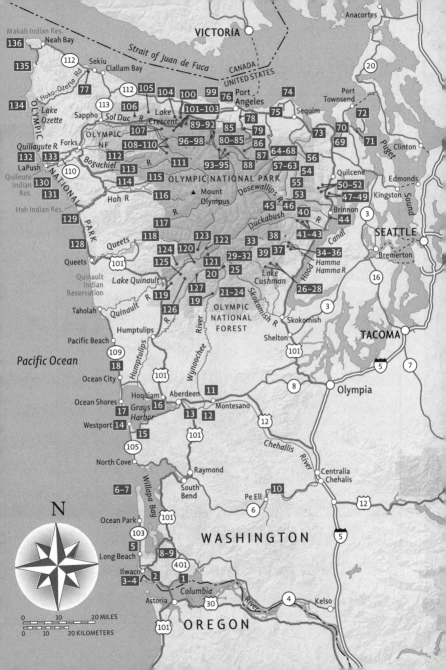

Hikes at a Glance

HIKE	DISTANCE: RT UNLESS NOTED	DIFFI-CULTY	HIKABLE ALL YEAR	KID-FRIENDLY
SOUTHWEST WASHINGTON				
1. Julia Butler Hansen Refuge for the Columbian White-Tailed Deer	2 miles	1	•	•
2. Scarborough Hill	2.4 miles	2	•	•
3. Cape Disappointment State Park: North Head	3.6 miles	2	•	•
4. Cape Disappointment State Park: Coastal Forest Loop	1.4 miles	1	•	•
5. Lewis and Clark Discovery Trail	8.2 miles one-way	2	•	•
6. Leadbetter State Park: Dune Forest Loop	2.9 miles	1	•	•
7. Willapa National Wildlife Refuge: Leadbetter Point	10.6 miles	2		•
8. Willapa National Wildlife Refuge: Salmon Art Trail	1.2 miles	2	•	•
9. Willapa National Wildlife Refuge: Long Island	5.8 miles	3	•	•
10. Rainbow Falls State Park	Up to 3 miles	1	•	•
11. Lake Sylvia State Park	2.2/2.7 miles	1/2	•	•
12. Friends Landing	1.7 miles	1	•	•
13. Chehalis River Surge Plain	7 miles	1	•	•
14. Westport Light Trail	4.4 miles	1	•	•
15. Johns River State Wildlife Area	2 miles	1	•	•
16. Bowerman Basin	1.9 miles	1	•	•
17. Damon Point	4.5 miles	1	•	•
18. Copalis River Spit	4 miles	1	•	•
OLYMPIC PENINSULA: SOUTH				
19. Wynoochee Lake	13.2 miles	3		
20. Wynoochee Pass and Lake Sundown	11.8 miles	4		
21. Spider Lake	2 miles	1	•	•
22. Pine Lake	5.8 miles	2	•	•
23. Church Creek and Satsop Lakes	6.4 miles	3		
24. Lower South Fork Skokomish River	10.2 miles	3	•	•
25. Upper South Fork Skokomish River	16.4 miles	5		

DOG-FRIENDLY	WILD-FLOWERS	BEACH HIKING	OLD GROWTH	BIRD-WATCHING	HISTORICAL	CAR CAMPING NEARBY	BACK-PACKING
				•	•	•	
•			•		•		
•			•		•		
•			•			•	
•		•		•	•	•	
•		•		•			
		•		•			
				•			
			•	•			•
•			•		•	•	
•					•	•	
•				•		•	
•				•	•		
•		•		•	•	•	
•				•			
				•			
		•		•			
•		•		•			
•			•			•	
			•				•
•			•	•			
•			•				
•			•	•			
•			•			•	•
	•		•				•

HIKE	DISTANCE: RT UNLESS NOTED	DIFFI-CULTY	HIKABLE ALL YEAR	KID-FRIENDLY
OLYMPIC PENINSULA: EAST				
26. Big Creek	4.3 miles	2	•	•
27. Mount Ellinor	6.6 miles	4		
28. Mount Rose	6.7 miles	5		
29. Dry Creek	12.6 miles	4		
30. Copper Creek	4.3 miles	4		
31. Wagonwheel Lake	5.8 miles	5		
32. Staircase Rapids	2 miles	1	•	•
33. North Fork Skokomish River and Flapjack Lakes	11/15.4 miles	2/4		•
34. Living Legacy Trail	1.8 miles	1	•	•
35. Elk Lakes	4.9 miles	2	•	•
36. Jefferson Ridge	6.6 miles	4		
37. Lena Lakes	6/14 miles	2/5		•
38. Lake of the Angels	7.4 miles	5		
39. Mildred Lakes	9 miles	5		
40. Mount Jupiter	14 miles	5		
41. Ranger Hole	1.9 miles	1	•	•
42. Duckabush River and Big Hump	10.6 miles	3	•	•
43. Murhut Falls	1.6 miles	1	•	•
44. Dosewallips State Park	3.6 miles	2	•	•
45. Dosewallips River Road	11 miles	3	•	•
46. Lake Constance	12.6 miles	5+		
47. Mount Walker	5 miles	3	•	
48. Elbo Creek	4.6 miles	3	•	•
49. Falls View Canyon	1.5 miles	1	•	•
50. Quilcene Ridge and Notch Pass	8.4 miles	4		•
51. Lower Big Quilcene River	10.2 miles	2		•
52. Tunnel Creek	9.4 miles	3		•
53. Marmot Pass	10.6 miles	4		•
OLYMPIC PENINSULA: NORTHEAST				
54. Mount Townsend	8.2 miles	4		
55. Silver Lakes	10.8 miles	4		
56. Mount Zion	4.8 miles	3		
57. Dirty Face Ridge	7.8 miles	4		
58. Tubal Cane Mine and Buckhorn Lake	12.4 miles	3		•
59. Upper Dungeness River	7 miles	2		•

DOG-FRIENDLY	WILD-FLOWERS	BEACH HIKING	OLD GROWTH	BIRD-WATCHING	HISTORICAL	CAR CAMPING NEARBY	BACK-PACKING
•						•	
	•		•				
	•					•	
•			•			•	•
			•		•	•	
			•			•	
			•		•	•	
			•		•	•	
•					•	•	
•			•	•		•	
•			•		•	•	
•			•			•	
	•						
	•		•				•
•	•						
•					•	•	
•			•			•	•
•						•	
•				•	•	•	
•							•
•							•
	•				•	•	
•					•	•	
•						•	
•	•				•		
•			•		•		•
•			•		•		
•	•		•				
•	•						
•	•						•
•	•				•		
•	•						
•	•					•	•
•			•		•		•

HIKE	DISTANCE: RT UNLESS NOTED	DIFFI-CULTY	HIKABLE ALL YEAR	KID-FRIENDLY
OLYMPIC PENINSULA: NORTHEAST (continued)				
60. Baldy	10.4 miles	5		
61. Royal Basin	14.4 miles	4		
62. Lower Dungeness River	13 miles	3		
63. Gold Creek	14.2 miles	4		•
64. Lower Gray Wolf River	7 miles	2	•	•
65. Ned Hill	2.2 miles	2		
66. Slab Camp Creek and Upper Gray Wolf River	5.6 miles	3		•
67. Deer Ridge	9.8 miles	4		
68. Three Forks	10 miles	5		
69. Gibbs Lake	2.8 miles	1	•	•
70. Anderson Lake	2.3 miles	1	•	•
71. South Indian Island	4 miles	1	•	•
72. Fort Flagler	5.6 miles	2	•	•
OLYMPIC PENINSULA: NORTH				
73. Miller Peninsula and Thompson Spit	7.7 miles	2	•	
74. Dungeness Spit	11 miles	3	•	•
75. Robin Hill Farm	1.9 miles	1	•	•
76. Striped Peak	5.4 miles	3	•	
77. Cowan Ranch	3 miles	1	•	•
78. Peabody Creek	5.9 miles	2	•	•
79. Heart O'the Forest	4.6 miles	2	•	•
80. Lake Angeles	7 miles	3		•
81. Heather Park	10 miles	4		
82. Klahhane Ridge	5.2 miles	4		
83. Sunrise Ridge	5.2 miles	2		•
84. Hurricane Hill	3.2/6 miles	2/4		•
85. Little River	7 miles	2	•	•
86. PJ Lake	1.8 miles	3		
87. Grand Ridge	7.4 miles one-way	3		
88. Grand Valley	9.4 miles	4		•
89. Cascade Rock	4.5 miles	3	•	
90. Griff Creek	5.6 miles	4		
91. West Elwha Trail	5 miles	3	•	•
92. Glines Canyon and Smoky Bottom	2.2/4 miles	2/2	•	•
93. Wolf Creek	16 miles	4		

DOG-FRIENDLY	WILD-FLOWERS	BEACH HIKING	OLD GROWTH	BIRD-WATCHING	HISTORICAL	CAR CAMPING NEARBY	BACK-PACKING
•	•		•				
	•		•				•
•			•		•		•
•			•				
•			•				
•	•				•		
•	•		•				
	•					•	
	•		•			•	•
•							
•	•						
•		•					
•		•			•	•	
•		•		•			
		•		•		•	
•					•		
•		•	•	•	•	•	
•					•		
•						•	
			•			•	
						•	•
	•					•	•
	•						
	•						
	•						
			•		•		
	•						
	•					•	•
	•						•
	•					•	
	•					•	
			•			•	
			•		•	•	
	•		•			•	

HIKE	DISTANCE: RT UNLESS NOTED	DIFFI-CULTY	HIKABLE ALL YEAR	KID-FRIENDLY
OLYMPIC PENINSULA: NORTH (continued)				
94. Geyser Valley	8.1 miles	2	•	•
95. Elwha River and Lillian River	13.4 miles	3	•	
96. Happy Lake	10 miles	4		
97. Boulder Lake	12 miles	4		•
98. Appleton Pass and Oyster Lake	15.2 miles	5		
99. Olympic Discovery Trail: Adventure Route	7 miles	2	•	
100. Spruce Railroad Trail	8.2 miles	2	•	•
101. Marymere Falls and Barnes Creek	1.8/8 miles	1/3	•	•
102. Mount Storm King	3.8 miles	4		
103. Aurora Ridge and Sourdough Mountain	12 miles	5		
104. Pyramid Mountain	7 miles	4		
105. Mount Muller	12.7 miles	4		
106. Kloshe Nanitch and Snider Ridge	6.4 miles	4		
107. Aurora Ridge and Eagle Lakes	12.2 miles	3		
108. North Fork Sol Duc River	12.4 miles	3		
109. Sol Duc Falls Loop	5.5 miles	1		•
110. Mink Lake and Little Divide	5.2/10.6 miles	2/4		•
111. Deer Lake and Bogachiel Peak	7.4/16.2 miles	3/5		
OLYMPIC PENINSULA: WEST				
112. North Snider–Jackson Trail	6 miles	3		
113. Bogachiel River	12 miles	3	•	•
114. South Snider–Jackson Trail	10.4 miles	4		
115. Hoh Rain Forest and Five Mile Island	10.6 miles	2	•	•
116. South Fork Hoh River and Big Flat	8.2 miles	2	•	•
117. Queets River	10.6 miles	4		
118. Sams River Loop	2.9 miles	1	•	•
119. Quinault National Recreation Trails	3.9 miles	2	•	•
120. Fletcher Canyon	3.8 miles	3	•	
121. East Fork Quinault River and Pony Bridge	5 miles	2	•	•
122. North Fork Quinault River and Halfway House	10.2 miles	3	•	•
123. Irely Lake and Three Lakes	2.4/14 miles	1/4		•
124. Kestner Homestead	1.5 miles	1	•	•
125. Colonel Bob Peak	14.6 miles	5		
126. Petes Creek and Colonel Bob Peak	8.2 miles	4		
127. West Fork Humptulips River	18.7 miles one-way	3		

DOG-FRIENDLY	WILD-FLOWERS	BEACH HIKING	OLD GROWTH	BIRD-WATCHING	HISTORICAL	CAR CAMP-ING NEARBY	BACK-PACKING
					•	•	•
			•		•	•	•
	•						•
			•				•
	•		•				•
•	•						
•				•	•		
			•				
			•				
	•		•				•
			•		•		
•	•						
•	•				•	•	
			•				•
			•		•		•
			•		•	•	
			•			•	•
	•		•			•	•
			•		•		•
			•		•	•	•
			•		•	•	
			•			•	•
			•			•	•
			•		•	•	•
			•		•	•	
•			•	•	•	•	
•			•				
			•			•	
			•		•	•	•
	•		•	•		•	•
					•		
•	•		•				•
•	•		•			•	
•			•			•	•

HIKE	DISTANCE: RT UNLESS NOTED	DIFFI-CULTY	HIKABLE ALL YEAR	KID-FRIENDLY
OLYMPIC PENINSULA: COAST				
128. Kalaloch and Browns Point	4 miles	1	•	•
129. Ruby Beach	6 miles	2	•	•
130. Second Beach	4 miles	2	•	•
131. Third Beach	3.6 miles	2	•	•
132. Hole-in-the-Wall	3.4 miles	1	•	•
133. Quillayute River Slough	1.8 miles	1	•	•
134. Ozette Triangle	9.4 miles	3	•	•
135. Shi Shi Beach and Point of the Arches	8.8 miles	3	•	
136. Cape Flattery	1.5 miles	2	•	•

DOG-FRIENDLY	WILD-FLOWERS	BEACH HIKING	OLD GROWTH	BIRD-WATCHING	HISTORICAL	CAR CAMP-ING NEARBY	BACK-PACKING
•		•				•	
•		•					
		•		•			
		•		•			
		•		•		•	
			•	•		•	
		•	•	•	•	•	•
		•		•		•	•
				•	•		

Acknowledgments

Researching and writing the second edition of *Day Hiking Olympic Peninsula* was fun, exciting, and a lot of hard work. I couldn't have finished this project without the help and support of the following people. A huge thank-you to all the wonderful people at Mountaineers Books, especially publisher Helen Cherullo, project managers Mary Metz and Lisa Wogan, and editor in chief Kate Rogers. A huge thank-you to copy editor Julie Van Pelt: It was great to once again work with you. I value your commanding use of the English language and your expert Olympic hiking insight as well.

Big thanks to Jay Thompson, Evan Brown, Douglas Romano, Jeff Romano, Ted Evans, Nicky Ducommun, Brad Stone, and Bret Wirta for accompanying me on so many great hikes during my research! And a big *grazie*, too, to Kevin Hinchen and Carol Zahorsky for shuttling me to a few trailheads.

I want to also once again thank God for watching over me while I hiked throughout the Olympic Peninsula, keeping me safe and healthy. And lastly, but most importantly, I want to thank my loving wife, Heather, for supporting me while I worked on yet another guidebook. Thanks for hiking with me, too, to some of the special places in this book and providing me with more precious memories, including of our son Giovanni's first Olympic adventures. I can't wait for us to take him on many more hikes throughout the Olympics and beyond!

Opposite: Hiking along a ridge of beargrass on the Putvin Trail (Hike 38)

Hamma Hamma River (Hike 34)

Introduction

The Olympic Peninsula is home to incredible biological diversity. With a rugged and undeveloped coastline (one of the largest wilderness coastlines in the continental United States), some of the largest tracts of unbroken old-growth forest in the Pacific Northwest, the largest undeveloped estuary on the Pacific coast, and some of the last free-flowing rivers in Washington, it's an area of superlatives in grandeur and ecological importance. Temperate rain forests, glacier-covered mountains, sprawling alpine meadows, and crystal-clear lakes are all found here. Nearly a million acres of this special landscape have been protected as a national park and recognized as a United Nations Biosphere Reserve. While eastern parks like the Great Smoky Mountains and the Everglades lay claim to the most biodiversity, no park comes close to the Olympics when it comes to biomass. You've never seen so much living matter until you've taken a stroll up an Olympic rainforest valley.

Day Hiking Olympic Peninsula focuses on the best trails you can hike in a day throughout the Olympic Peninsula, Grays Harbor area, and Long Beach Peninsula. You'll find short nature walks and all-day treks deep into wilderness areas, some with overnight backpacking options. Hikes to beaches, islands, riversides, lakefronts, old-growth forests, alpine meadows, and mountaintops. Hikes perfect for kids, dogs. Popular hikes and remote ones. New trails, historic trails, and revitalized trails. Where to find wildlife, where to escape crowds, and where to get the best bang for your boot.

You'll find trails rich in human history as well—along hunting and trade routes favored by First Peoples and on routes used by European explorers, merchants, and pioneers and homesteaders from the East. Retrace famous expeditions and hike to old townsites, fire lookout sites, mines, and Native villages. All of this is included in this packed-with-adventure, updated, and expanded volume. This book aims to help you find your own discoveries in the incredibly beautiful and diverse landscapes of the Olympic Peninsula region.

USING THIS BOOK

This user-friendly guidebook provides clear directions and enough detail to help you explore a region but leaves plenty of room for you to make your own discoveries. I have hiked every mile of trail described in this book, so you can follow my directions and advice with confidence. Conditions do change, however. More on that later in this introduction.

What the Ratings Mean

Each hike starts with detailed trail facts. The **overall rating** of 1 to 5 stars is based on a hike's general appeal, and the numerical **difficulty score** of 1 to 5 measures how challenging the hike is. These ratings are purely subjective, based on my impressions of each route, but they do follow a formula of sorts.

The **overall rating** is based on scenic beauty, natural wonder, and other unique qualities, such as the potential for solitude and wildlife-viewing opportunities.

***** Unmatched hiking adventure—
bucket-list hike!

**** Excellent experience that ranks
among the best hikes

*** A great hike that is sure to
impress and inspire

** May lack exceptional scenery
or unique trail experiences, but
offers a lot of little moments
to enjoy

* Worth doing as a refreshing
walk, especially if you're in
the neighborhood

The **difficulty score** is based on trail
length, cumulative elevation gain, steepness,
and trail conditions. Generally, trails rated
more difficult (4 or 5) are longer and steeper
than average. But it's not a simple equation.
A short, steep trail over uneven surfaces and
ledges may be rated 5, while a long, smooth
trail with little elevation gain may be rated 2.

5 **Extremely difficult:** excessive
elevation gain and/or long
distance for a day hike and
possibly rough conditions

4 **Difficult:** Some steep sections,
possibly rough trail or poorly
maintained trail

3 **Moderate:** A good workout but
no real problems

2 **Moderately easy:** Minimal
elevation gain or short route
with good tread

1 **Easy:** A relaxing stroll in
the woods

Other trail details follow, to help explain
these ratings and help you choose a hike.
Round-trip mileage (or loop or one-way)
gives you the hike's distance. While I have
measured most of the trails using GPS and
have consulted maps and land managers,
the distance noted may not always be exact,

but it'll be pretty close. **Elevation gain** sums
the *cumulative* ups and downs on the route
(including the return trip for all but one-way
hikes), accounting for all significant changes
in elevation along the way, not merely the
difference between the highest and lowest
points. As to the **high point** given, it's worth
noting that not all high points are at the end
of the trail—a route may run over a high ridge
before dropping to a lake basin, for instance.
The **season** listed tells you when a route is
hikable. Many trails can be enjoyed from the
time they lose their winter snowpack right
up until they're buried in fresh snow the following fall. But snowpacks vary from year to
year, so the hiking season for each trail is an
estimate. Always contact land managers for
current conditions.

To help with trip planning, each hike next
tells you which **maps** cover the route, typically Green Trails and Custom Correct maps,
which are based on the standard 7.5-minute
USGS topographical maps. Green Trails
maps are available at most outdoor retailers
in the state; Custom Correct, at many outlets
on the peninsula. Both are often available at
National Park Service and US Forest Service
visitors centers. I have also listed some specialty or online maps when these are more
appropriate for a hike. The **contact** line
gives a hike's land manager, whose complete
contact information you'll find in Appendix
I. Check with the agency for current road
and trail conditions. **Notes** tell you what
permits and entrance fees are required, if
any (if you choose to extend your day outing to an overnight, note that all overnight
stays in Olympic National Park require a
backpacking permit). Campfire and group-
size restrictions apply in both national park
and national forest wilderness areas. You'll
also find specifics on road or trail closures,

wheelchair-accessibility, whether dogs are permitted, and any special hazards or concerns (such as difficult routefinding, river fords, animal concerns, etc.). Finally, **GPS coordinates** for each trailhead will help get you to the trail.

The route descriptions themselves provide an overview of what you might find on your hike, driving directions to get you to the trailhead, and in some cases additional highlights to entice you to extend your trip or explore other nearby trails and attractions. Icons at the beginning of each hike description are an additional planning tool.

 Kid-friendly

 Dog-friendly (leash may be required)

 Exceptional wildflowers (in season, of course)

 Beach hiking (note that it's unlawful to remove living organisms from many beaches; leave them in place for the health of our coastal ecosystems and for others to enjoy)

 Exceptional old-growth forest

 Historical significance

 Endangered trail (threatened with loss or closure due to lack of maintenance, motorized encroachment, abandonment, or other detrimental conditions)

 Saved trail (formerly threatened or abandoned trail, now revived and restored)

PERMITS AND REGULATIONS

It's important that you know, understand, and abide by the rules that apply to the hikes in this book. As our public lands have become increasingly popular, and as both federal and state funding has declined, regulations and permits have become necessary components in managing our natural heritage. To help keep our wilderness areas wild and our trails safe and well maintained, land managers—especially the National Park Service and US Forest Service—have implemented a sometimes complex set of rules and regulations governing the use of these lands.

Generally, any developed trailhead in Washington's national forests (Oregon too) fall under the Region 6 forest pass program. In order to park legally at these designated national forest trailheads, you must display a Northwest Forest Pass. These sell for $5 per day or $30 for an annual pass, good throughout Washington and Oregon (which constitute Region 6).

In Olympic National Park, several areas (Staircase, Hurricane Ridge, Elwha Valley, Sol Duc Valley, Lake Ozette, and the Hoh Rain Forest) require an entrance fee, currently $30 for a one-week pass (good for vehicle and all occupants) or $55 for an annual pass. Your best bet if you hike a lot in both national parks and forests is to buy an annual America the Beautiful Pass (also known as the Interagency Pass) for $80. This pass grants you and three other adults in your vehicle (children under sixteen are admitted free) access to all federal recreation sites that charge a fee. These include national parks, national forests, national wildlife refuges, and Bureau of Land Management areas, not only here in Washington, but throughout the country. You can purchase passes at national

WHOSE LAND IS THIS?

Nearly all of the hikes in this book are on public land. They belong to you, me, and the rest of the citizenry. What's confusing is who is in charge of this public trust. Several different governing agencies manage lands described in this guide. The largest of the agencies, and managing most of the hikes in this book, are the National Park Service and US Forest Service. There's an Olympic National Park and an Olympic National Forest. Don't confuse them; they are two different entities with two different objectives.

The Park Service, a division of the Department of the Interior, manages over 922,000 acres as Olympic National Park. A national park's primary objective is "to conserve the scenery and natural and historic objects and the wildlife therein and to provide for the enjoyment of the same in such a manner and by such means as will leave them unimpaired for the enjoyment of future generations." In other words, the primary focus of the Park Service is preservation.

Contrast that with the Forest Service, a division of the Department of Agriculture, which strives to "sustain the health, diversity, and productivity of the Nation's forests and grasslands to meet the needs of present and future generations." The agency purports to do this under the doctrine of "multiple-use"—the greatest good for the greatest number. However, supplying timber products, managing wildlife habitat, and developing motorized and nonmotorized recreation options have a tendency to conflict with each other. Some of these uses may not exactly sustain the health of the forest either.

Olympic National Forest manages over 628,000 acres of land on the national park's periphery. Much has been heavily logged. Five areas within the forest, however, have been afforded stringent protections as federal wilderness areas (see the "Untrammeled Olympics" sidebar on page 118).

Other public lands you'll encounter in this book are Washington State Parks, managed for recreation and preservation; Washington State Department of Natural Resources lands, managed primarily for timber harvesting, with units of natural area preserves and natural conservation areas; national wildlife refuges, established to protect wildlife and their habitat; Washington State Department of Fish and Wildlife lands, established for wildlife habitat and set aside for hunting and fishing; and county parks, managed for recreation.

It's important that you know who manages the land you'll be hiking on, for each agency has its own fees and rules. Confusing? Yes, but it's our land and we should understand how it's managed for us. And remember that we have a say in how our lands are managed and can let the agencies know whether we like what they're doing or not.

park and forest visitors centers as well as at many outdoor retailers.

Washington State Parks, Washington State Department of Natural Resources, and Washington State Department of Fish and Wildlife properties require a Discover Pass, currently $10 per day or $30 for an annual pass (good for two vehicles). This pass is available online (www.discoverpass.wa.gov), at some parks, and at most sporting-goods outlets.

The Makah Tribe requires a recreation pass to hike the trails and beaches on their reservation, currently $10 for an annual pass. It can be purchased at several businesses and at the museum on the reservation.

If you plan to backpack in Olympic National Park, backcountry permits are required, currently $5 per person per night (no charge for youths fifteen years of age and under) or $35 annually (good for frequent wilderness visitors). Popular areas such as the High Divide and Cape Alava require reservations (May 1–September 30) and permits are limited. Visit Olympic National Park online for details (www.nps .gov/olym/planyourvisit/wilderness-permits .htm) or contact the Wilderness Information Center in Port Angeles (see Appendix I).

WEATHER

Mountain weather in general is famously unpredictable, but in the Olympic range— with its multitude of microclimates—you'll be completely baffled (or intrigued). For the most part, the Olympic Peninsula enjoys a moderate maritime climate, influenced by the ocean. Temperature fluctuates little between the seasons, thanks in part to the Pacific jet stream. Still, it's not uncommon to have below-freezing temperatures in the winter and periods of hot weather in the summer months. Alpine areas, of course, are subject to more severe conditions, including long periods of below-freezing tempera- tures accompanied by heavy snowfall.

The entire region is prone to heavy pre- cipitation, predominantly as rainfall. Rarely does it snow below 2000 feet. When it does, accumulations are usually gone within days. Winter sees the heaviest amount of rainfall, particularly in the western valleys of the Olympic Mountains: the rain forests. Along the coast, low clouds can roll right over, making for drier conditions than just 20 miles inland, where the hills begin trapping and wringing out moisture from the clouds.

The eastern slopes of the Olympics, particularly the northeastern corner of the peninsula, enjoy a rainshadow effect. High mountains to the west trap clouds moving eastward, forcing them to release much of their precipitation. These clouds then build up again, collecting moisture farther east to be trapped once more along the western slopes of the Cascades. Locales such as Sequim see as little as 17 inches of rain annually, while the Quinault Valley in the west "enjoys" over 140 inches of annual precipitation.

Bottom line: always prepare for rain and wet conditions while hiking in the Olympics. Being caught in a sudden storm without adequate clothing can lead to hypothermia (loss of body temperature), which is deadly if not immediately treated. Most hikers who have died of exposure (hypothermia) did so, not in winter, but during the milder months when caught unaware by a sudden change of temperature accompanied by winds and rain. Always carry extra clothing layers, including rain and wind protection.

While snow blankets the high country primarily from October to May, it can occur any time of year. Be prepared. Lightning is rare in the Olympics, but it does occasion- ally happen. If you hear thunder, waste no time getting off of summits and away from water. Take shelter, but not under big trees or rock ledges. If caught in an electrical storm, crouch down—making minimal contact with the ground—and wait for the boomer to pass.

River and creek crossings can be extremely dangerous after periods of heavy rain or snowmelt. Always use caution and

Hiker at Grandview Pass looking over Grand Valley (Hike 88)

sound judgment when fording. And be aware of snowfields left over from the previous winter's snowpack. Depending on the severity of the past winter, and the weather conditions of the spring and early summer, some trails may not melt out until well into summer, if at all. The winter of 1999 left most of the Olympic high country blanketed all summer. Obstruction Point Road never opened beyond the Waterhole that year, a distinct contrast to the winter of 2015, when the road opened in May. In addition to treacherous footing and difficulties in routefinding, lingering snowfields can be prone to avalanches or slides. Use caution crossing them.

The Olympics enjoy plenty of sunshine too. Midsummer to early autumn is often graced with prolonged dry periods, and it's not unusual to a have a dry week or two in the winter as well.

ROAD AND TRAIL CONDITIONS

In general, trails change little year to year. But change can and does occur, and sometimes very quickly. A heavy storm can cause a river to jump its channel, washing out sections of trail (or access road) in moments. Windstorms can blow down trees by the hundreds, making trails unhikable. And snow can bury trails well into the summer. Avalanches, landslides, and forest fires can also bring serious damage and obliteration to our trails.

Lack of adequate funding is also responsible for trail neglect and degradation. Before setting out, be sure you contact the appropriate land manager to check on current trail and road conditions. On the topic of trail conditions, it's vital that we thank the countless volunteers who donate tens of thousands of hours to trail maintenance each year. The Washington Trails Association

LEAVE NO TRACE

All of us who recreate in Washington's natural areas have a moral obligation and responsibility to respect and protect our natural heritage. Everything we do on the planet has an impact, and we should strive to minimize our negative impact. The Leave No Trace Center for Outdoor Ethics (www.lnt.org) is an educational, nonprofit, apolitical organization that was developed for responsible enjoyment and active stewardship of the outdoors. Its programs educate outdoor enthusiasts about their recreational impacts as well as how to prevent and minimize such impacts, following these seven principles:

1. Plan ahead and prepare
2. Travel and camp on durable surfaces
3. Dispose of waste properly
4. Leave what you find
5. Minimize campfire impacts
6. Respect wildlife
7. Be considerate of other visitors

(WTA) alone coordinates upward of one hundred thousand hours of volunteer trail work each year. But there's always a need for more. Our trail system faces ever-increasing threats, including lack of adequate funding, inappropriate trail uses, and conflicting land management policies and practices.

As timber harvesting has all but ceased on much of our federal forests, one of the biggest threats to our trails is now access. Many roads once used for hauling timber are also used by hikers to get to trailheads. Many of these roads are no longer being maintained and are becoming downright dangerous to drive, if they're drivable at all. While I support the decommissioning of many trunk roads that go "nowhere" as both economically and environmentally prudent, I'm deeply disturbed by the number of main trunk roads that are falling into disrepair. Once a road has been closed for several years, the trails radiating from it often receive no maintenance, in turn often making those trails unhikable

With this in mind, this guide includes trails that are threatened and in danger of becoming unhikable: Endangered Trails,

marked with a special icon. On the other hand, we've had some great trail successes in recent years, thanks in large part to the WTA. These Saved Trails are marked too, to illustrate that individual efforts do make a difference. As you enjoy these Saved Trails, consider becoming involved with the WTA or other trails groups.

WILDERNESS ETHICS

To ensure the long-term survival of our trails—and more specifically the wildlands they cross—we must embrace and practice a sound wilderness ethic. A strong, positive wilderness ethic includes making sure you leave the wilderness as good (or even better) as when you found it. This goes deeper than simply picking up after ourselves when we go for a hike. We need to ensure that our elected officials and public land managers recognize and respond to our wilderness needs and desires. Get involved with groups and organizations that safeguard, watchdog, and advocate for land protection. And let land managers and public officials know how important protecting lands and trails is to you.

TRAIL ETIQUETTE

Many of the trails in this book are open to an array of uses, and we need to be sensitive to other trail users. Some trails are hiker-only, but others allow equestrians and mountain bikers too (only a couple of hikes in this book are open to motorbikes). When you encounter other trail users, follow the Golden Rule of Trail Etiquette: exercise common sense and simple courtesy. That and the following will make everyone's trip more enjoyable:

- **Moving off-trail.** When meeting other trail users (like bicyclists and horseback riders), the hiker should move off the trail. Hikers are more mobile and flexible than other users, making it easier for them to step off the trail.
- **Encountering horses.** When meeting horseback riders, the hiker should step off the downhill side of the trail unless the terrain makes this difficult or dangerous. Make yourself visible so as not to spook the big beastie, and talk in a normal voice to the riders. This calms the horses. If hiking with a dog, keep your buddy under control.
- **Stay on trails**, and practice minimum impact. Don't cut switchbacks, take shortcuts, or make new trails. If your destination is off-trail, stick to snow and rock when possible so as not to damage fragile alpine meadows. Spread out when traveling off-trail to minimize the chance of compacting thin soils and crushing delicate plant environments.
- **Obey the rules** specific to the trail you're visiting. Many trails are closed to certain types of use, including hiking with dogs and mountain bikes.
- **Hiking with dogs.** Dogs are prohibited on Olympic National Park trails except (leashes required) for Kalaloch beaches, Rialto Beach to Ellen Creek, Peabody Creek Trail, and the Spruce Railroad Trail. Dogs are allowed on state park trails but must be leashed. In Olympic National Forest, dogs are generally allowed on trails. Hikers who take dogs on trails should have their dog on a leash or under very strict voice command at all times. And if leashes are required, this *does* apply to you. One of the most contentious issues in hiking circles is dogs on the trails. Far too many hikers have had negative encounters with dogs (or with the dog owners). Many hikers are not fond of dogs on the trail, and some are actually afraid. Respect their right to not be approached by your darling pooch. A well-behaved leashed dog, however, can certainly help warm up these hikers to your buddy.
- **Avoid disturbing wildlife.** Observe from a distance, resisting the urge to move closer to wildlife (use your telephoto lens). This not only keeps you safer, but it prevents the animal from having to exert itself unnecessarily as it flees from you.
- **Take only photographs.** Leave all natural things, features, and historical artifacts as you found them, for others to enjoy.
- **Never roll rocks off trails or cliffs.** You risk endangering lives below you.

While these rules don't address every situation, you can avoid problems by always remembering that *common sense and courtesy are in order*. This includes cleanup and backcountry bathroom etiquette.

When **washing your hands**, rinse off as much as you can in plain water first. If you still feel the need for a soapy wash, collect a pot of water from a lake or stream and move at least 200 feet away. Apply a small amount of biodegradable soap to your hands and lather up. Use a bandanna or towel to wipe away most of the soap; then rinse with the water in the pot.

The defecation proclamation, the first rule of backcountry bathroom etiquette, says that if an outhouse exists, use it. When there's no privy, the key factor to consider is location. Choose a site at least 200 feet from water, campsites, and the trail. Dig a cat hole (a trowel comes in handy). Once you're done, bury your waste with organic duff and place a "Microbes at Work" sign over it (as in some crossed sticks marking the spot).

WATER
As a general rule, treat all backcountry water sources to help prevent contracting *Giardia* (a waterborne parasite) and other aquatic nasties. Assume that all water is contaminated. Treating water can be as simple as boiling it, chemically purifying it (adding tiny iodine tablets), or pumping it through a water filter and purifier.

WILDLIFE
Bears
The Olympic Peninsula is home to a healthy population of black bears, and your chances of eventually seeing one are good. Your ursine encounters will most likely be of a bear's behind. But occasionally the bruin may want to get a look at *you*. In very rare cases, a bear may act aggressively (usually during berry failures, causing the bear to be hungry and malnourished; or if a sow feels that her cubs are threatened).

To avoid an un-*bear*-able encounter, practice bear aware prudence. Always keep a safe distance. If you encounter a bear at

close range, remain calm, do not look it in the eyes, talk in a low voice, and do not run from it. Hold your arms out to appear as big as possible. Slowly move away upwind from the animal. The bear may bluff-charge—do not run. If it does charge, lie down and play dead, protecting your head and neck. Usually the bear will leave once it perceives that you're no threat. If the bear does attack, fight back using fists, rocks, trekking poles, or bear spray if you're carrying it.

Cougars
Washington supports a healthy population of the shy and solitary *Felix concolor*. While cougar encounters are extremely rare, they do occur. Cougars are cats—they're curious. They will follow hikers, but rarely (almost never) do they attack adult humans. Minimize contact by not hiking or running alone and avoiding carrion. If you do encounter a cougar, remember that the cats look for prey that can't or won't fight back. Do not run, as this may trigger the animal's attack instinct. Stand up and face it. If you appear aggressive, the cougar will probably back down. Wave your arms, trekking poles, or a jacket over your head to appear bigger, and maintain eye contact with it. Pick up children and small dogs, and back away slowly if you can safely do so without breaking eye contact. If the cougar attacks, throw things at it. Shout loudly. If it gets close, whack it with your trekking pole and fight back aggressively.

Mountain goats
Olympic mountain goats are nonnative (see "Really Getting My Goat," page 133) and tend to be more aggressive than their Cascades' counterparts. Always keep a safe distance from them (at least 150 feet). Never follow or

Endemic Olympic marmot on Hurricane Hill

crowd them. If a goat approaches you, slowly move away allowing for it to safely pass. If it displays aggressive behavior or continues to approach you, yell at it and throw rocks. Goats love salt—never feed them or let them lick your skin or gear. Urinate far away from trails and campsites.

Hunting

Hikers should be aware that many of our public lands are opened to hunting. Open-season dates vary, but generally big-game hunting begins in early August and ends in late November. While hiking in areas frequented by hunters, it's best to make yourself visible by donning an orange cap and vest. If hiking with a dog, your buddy should wear an orange vest too. If being around outdoors-people who are schlepping rifles is unnerving to you, stick to hiking in Olympic National Park and Washington State Parks, where hunting is prohibited.

GEAR

While gear is beyond the scope of this book, it's worth noting a few points. No hiker should venture far up a trail without being properly equipped. Starting with the feet, a good pair of boots can make all the difference between a wonderful hike and a blistering affair. Every hiker will swear by different brands and types of boots, so your best bet is to get a professional fit and try a bunch out—see what works for you.

For clothing, wear whatever is most comfortable, unless it's cotton. When cotton gets wet, it stays wet and lacks any insulation value. In fact, wet cotton sucks away body heat, leaving you susceptible to hypothermia. Think synthetics and layering.

Make sure you have a good, well-fitting pack too. And while the list of what you bring will vary, you should include the Ten Essentials in your pack on every trip.

THE TEN ESSENTIALS

1. **Navigation (map and compass):** Carry a topographic map of the area you plan to be in and knowledge of how to read it. Likewise a compass or GPS unit.

2. **Sun protection (sunglasses and sunscreen):** Even on wet or cloudy days, carry sunscreen and sunglasses; you never know when the clouds will lift. At higher elevations your exposure to UV rays is much more intense than at sea level. You can easily burn on snow and near water.

3. **Insulation (extra clothing):** Storms can and do blow in rapidly. Carry raingear, wind protection, and extra layers.

4. **Illumination (flashlight/headlamp):** Carry extra batteries too.

5. **First-aid supplies:** At the very least, your emergency kit should include tape, gauze, bandages, scissors, tweezers, pain relievers, antiseptics, and perhaps a small how-to manual. Consider first-aid training through a program such as MOFA (Mountaineering Oriented First Aid).

6. **Fire (firestarter and matches):** Be sure you keep your matches dry. Plastic baggies do the trick.

7. **Repair kit and tools (including a knife):** A knife is helpful; a multitool is better. A basic repair kit should include such things as nylon cord, a small roll of duct tape, some 1-inch webbing and extra webbing buckles (to fix broken pack straps), and a small tube of superglue. Safety pins can do wonders too.

8. **Nutrition (extra food):** Always pack more food than what you need for your hike. Energy bars work well for emergency pick-me-ups.

9. **Hydration (extra water):** Carry two full water bottles, unless you're hiking entirely along a water source. Carry iodine tablets or a filter too.

10. **Emergency shelter:** This can be as simple as a garbage bag or something more efficient, such as a reflective space blanket. A poncho can double as an emergency tarp.

TRAILHEAD CONCERNS

Sadly, the topic of trailhead and trail crime must be addressed. While violent crime is extremely rare, theft and car prowls are far too common at many trailheads. Our trails are fairly safe places—far safer than most city streets. Common sense and vigilance, however, are still in order. Be aware of your surroundings at all times. Leave your itinerary with someone back home. If something doesn't feel right, it probably isn't. Take action by leaving the place or situation immediately.

To help thwart car break-ins, don't leave anything of value in your vehicle while you're out hiking. Take your wallet, smartphone, and listening devices with you; or don't bring them in the first place. Consider taking your car registration with you too. Don't leave anything in your car that may appear valuable. A duffle bag on the back seat may contain dirty T-shirts, but a thief may think there's a laptop in it. Save yourself the hassle of returning to a busted window by not giving criminals a reason to clout your car.

If you arrive at a trailhead and someone looks suspicious, don't discount your intuition. Take notes on the person and his or her vehicle. Record the license plate and report the behavior to the authorities. Don't confront the person. Leave and go to another trail.

While most car break-ins are crimes of opportunity by drug addicts looking for loot to support their fix, organized gangs intent on stealing IDs have also been known to target parked cars at trailheads. Some trailheads are regularly targeted and others rarely if at all. There's no foolproof way of preventing a break-in other than being dropped off at the trailhead or taking the bus (rarely an option either way). But you can make your car less of a target by not leaving anything of value in it. And contact your government officials and demand that law enforcement be a priority on our public lands. We taxpayers have a right to recreate safely in our parks and forests.

Pacific rhododendron

CARRYING ON AN OUTDOOR LEGACY

I grew up in rural New Hampshire and was introduced to hiking and the great outdoors at a young age. I grew to admire the men and women responsible for saving and protecting many of our trails and wilderness areas as I became more aware of the often tumultuous history behind such preservation efforts.

When I moved to Washington in 1989, I immediately gained a respect for Harvey Manning and Ira Spring through their pioneering *100 Hikes* guidebooks. They introduced me to and I fell in love with the Washington backcountry. I joined The Mountaineers, the Washington Trails Association, and other local trail and conservation organizations so that I could help protect these places and carry on this legacy to future generations.

I believe 100 percent in what Ira Spring termed *green bonding*. We must, in Ira's words, "get people onto trails. They need to bond with the wilderness." This is essential in building public support for trails and trail funding. When hikers get complacent, trails suffer.

While I often chuckled at Harvey Manning's tirades and diatribes as he lambasted public officials' short-sighted and misguided land practices, I tacitly agreed with him in many instances. Sometimes I thought Harvey was a bit combative, a tad too polarizing, and perhaps even risked turning off potential allies. But sometimes you have to raise a little hell to get results.

As you get out and hike the trails you find described here, consider that many would have long ago ceased to exist without the phenomenal efforts of people like Ira Spring, Harvey Manning, Louise Marshall, Robert Wood, and Greg Ball, not to mention the scores of hikers who joined them in their push for wildland protection, trail funding, and strong environmental stewardship programs.

Take a page from their playbook and write a letter to your congressperson or state representative, asking for better trail funding. If you're not already a member, consider joining an organization devoted to wilderness, backcountry trails, or other wild-country issues. Organizations like The Mountaineers, Washington Trails Association, Volunteers for Outdoor Washington, Great Peninsula Conservancy, North Olympic Land Trust, Washington's National Park Fund, and countless others leverage individual contributions and efforts to help ensure the future of our trails and the wonderful wilderness legacy we've inherited. Buy a specialty license plate for Washington's national parks or state parks and let everybody on the way to the trailhead see what you value and are willing to work for.

I am well aware of the dilemma of getting too many boots on the ground, but I also understand that we can't and shouldn't turn people away from our trails. Instead, we should turn these people into good stewards of the land, defenders of the land, and promoters of healthy lifestyles and conservation. Many hikers will perhaps seek less explored places and thus disperse trail impacts. This book highlights many trails that get very little use—check them out.

Our trails and wild places face many challenges. Many outdoor folks view wilderness differently today than in the past. Some want to open up wilderness areas to mountain bikes. People have a lot of gadgets, and they take them into the wilderness. Smartphones are ubiquitous, and the annoying buzz of drones violating your privacy and peace of mind is a new and growing threat that needs to be addressed. The explosion of social media has created flash hikes and mob events in the wilderness, often with no regard to conservation ethics, wilderness regulations, and wilderness values. Through education, enlightenment, and perhaps a little self-control, we can have quality trail time and a healthy environment with strong wilderness protections. I trust you will do the right thing.

ENJOY THE TRAILS

Most importantly, be safe and enjoy the trails in this book. They exist for our enjoyment, and for the enjoyment of future generations. We can use them and protect them at the same time if we're careful with our actions, as well as forthright with our demands on Congress and state legislators to continue protecting our wildlands.

Throughout the last century, wilderness lovers helped secure protection for many of the lands we enjoy today. President Theodore Roosevelt was visionary in establishing the national forest system and in greatly expanding our public lands (over 40 million acres). President Franklin D. Roosevelt was ingenious in stimulating infrastructure on our public lands and in expanding our parks and preserves.

Democrats, Republicans, Independents, city dwellers, country folks, Americans of all walks of life have helped establish and protect our open spaces and wilderness areas. As we cruise into the twenty-first century, we must see to it that these protections continue and that the last bits of wildland are preserved for the enjoyment of future generations.

Unfortunately, many of our fellow humans may never experience the outdoors. These people have chosen a different path, leading them far from the redeeming qualities of nature. As the world continues to urbanize and as our society grows more sedentary, materialistic, and disconnected from the natural world, life has become less meaningful for many. Nature may need us to protect it, but we need nature to protect us from an encroaching world of meaningless consumption and pursuits.

Henry David Thoreau proclaimed, "In wildness is the preservation of the world." And I would add, "In wildness is the salvation of our souls, the meaning of life, and the preservation of our humanness." So shun the mall, turn off the TV and smartphone, and hit the trail. I've lined up 136 magnificent hikes for you to celebrate nature, life, the increible landscapes of the Olympic Peninsula, and you. Yes, you—go take a hike,

celebrate life, and come back a better and more content person.

And if I'm preaching to the choir, help me introduce new disciples to the sacred world of nature. Though we might relish our solitude on the trail, we need more like-minded souls to help us keep what little wildlands remain. Help nature by introducing family members, coworkers, your neighbors, children, and politicians to our wonderful trails. I'm convinced that a society that hikes is not only good for our wild and natural places (people will be willing to protect them) but also good for us (as we live in a healthy and connected way).

Enjoy this book. I've enjoyed writing it. I believe that we can change our world for the better, one hike at a time.

Happy hiking!

A NOTE ABOUT SAFETY

Safety is an important concern in all outdoor activities. No guidebook can alert you to every hazard or anticipate the limitations of every reader. Therefore, the descriptions of roads, trails, routes, and natural features in this book are not representations that a particular place or excursion will be safe for your party. When you follow any of the routes described in this book, you assume responsibility for your own safety. Under normal conditions, such excursions require the usual attention to traffic, road and trail conditions, weather, terrain, the capabilities of your party, and other factors. Because many of the lands in this book are subject to development and/or change of ownership, conditions may have changed since this book was written that make your use of some of these routes unwise. Always check for current conditions, obey posted private property signs, and avoid confrontations with property owners or managers. Keeping informed on current conditions and exercising common sense are the keys to a safe, enjoyable outing.

—*Mountaineers Books*

Opposite: Long Island, Willapa National Wildlife Refuge (Hike 9)

southwest washington

Columbia River

Entering Washington's northeast corner and exiting at its southwest corner, the mighty Columbia River snakes across the Evergreen State, threading two-thirds of its land mass into one massive watershed. A sustaining life force to the region's First Peoples, the Columbia also allowed explorers, settlers, and sailors access to the Pacific Northwest.

A transportation corridor, power provider, and irrigation source for thousands of acres, the Columbia has changed much since its most famous visitors, Captains Meriwether Lewis and William Clark and their Corps of Discovery, plied it over two hundred years ago. But while much of the countryside that clings to the river's shorelines has been radically altered since Boston merchant Robert Gray named the river after his vessel in 1792, wild stretches do still exist.

No dams or large settlements mar the waterway near the Columbia's mouth on the Pacific. And though the legendary salmon runs have sadly yielded to "progress," another kind of progress is being made in restoring some of the area's rich estuaries and bottomland forests. The Vancouver-based Columbia Land Trust has been instrumental in this ecosystem recovery.

Much of the hilly riverbanks are owned by private timber firms, but a few public parcels grace the lower Columbia. On your hikes to these places, imagine the past. Native peoples, explorers, and hardscrabble farmers and fishermen have all left their signatures on this fascinating corner of Washington State.

1 Julia Butler Hansen Refuge for the Columbian White-Tailed Deer

RATING/ DIFFICULTY	ROUNDTRIP	ELEV GAIN/ HIGH POINT	SEASON
**/1	2 miles	None/ 10 feet	Year-round

White-Tail Trail at Julia Butler Hansen Refuge

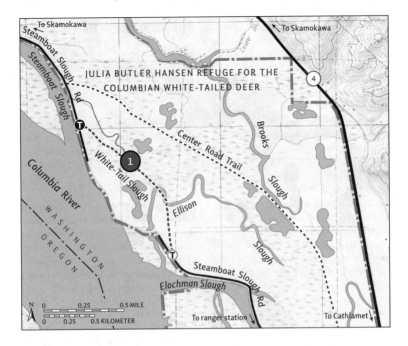

Map: Refuge brochure and map available at refuge headquarters; **Contact:** Julia Butler Hansen Refuge for the Columbian White-Tailed Deer; **Notes:** Dogs prohibited. Open to mountain bikes; **GPS:** N 46 15.255, W 123 26.111

Hike this perfectly flat trail along the teeming-with-wildlife White-Tail Slough on the Columbia River. Look toward the river for waterfowl and look to the rich bottomlands for the rare and federally endangered Columbian white-tailed deer.

GETTING THERE

From Kelso, travel west on State Route 4 for 25 miles to Cathlamet. Proceed west for another 6.4 miles to Skamokawa, turning left onto Steamboat Slough Road. Continue 1.4 miles to the parking area near the trailhead (elev. 10 ft).

ON THE TRAIL

The Julia Butler Hansen Refuge for the Columbian White-Tailed Deer was established in 1972 to protect habitat for its endangered namesake deer. The refuge includes bottomland forests, open pastures, river islands, and lazy sloughs that may make you feel like you're in the American South rather than the Pacific Northwest.

In 1988, the refuge name was changed to honor Julia Butler Hansen from nearby Cathlamet (about 10 miles to the south). Hansen served twenty-two years in the state legislature and fourteen years in Congress, where she became the first woman to head an appropriations subcommittee. She was instrumental in establishing the now 6000-acre refuge.

From the parking area, pass the trailhead for the Center Road Trail and walk 0.1 mile on the road to the gated White-Tail Trail. Officially opened in May 2015, this trail—more of a service road—follows the northern shore of the newly created White-Tail Slough. The trail and slough were developed after the failing Steamboat Slough Road was breached.

Take your time walking this easy path, looking for wildlife. When the tide is in, waterfowl fill the slough. When it's out, waders take to the mud. Look for nesting killdeers along the ground, look in the spruces and alders for raptors, and catch views of the Columbia River not too far from where Captain Clark (of Lewis and Clark fame) exclaimed, "Ocian in view!" He was a little premature, but not that far off. At 1 mile, come to the southeast trailhead. Return the way you came.

EXTENDING YOUR TRIP

The Center Road Trail is a gated and grassy service road that marches 2.5 miles across pasture and wetlands through the middle of the refuge, offering plenty of opportunities for spotting a few of the three hundred shy Columbian white-tailed deer that reside here. Elk, coyotes, otters, herons, eagles, kingfishers, and ospreys are also frequent visitors, if you come up short in the deer department. The trail is only open from June to September. With access to a boat, you can head to the refuge's Tenasillahee Island (which is actually in Oregon), where you can hike around on a 6.5-mile trail that follows an old dike.

2 Scarborough Hill

RATING/ DIFFICULTY	ROUNDTRIP	ELEV GAIN/ HIGH POINT	SEASON
**/2	2.4 miles	630 feet/ 780 feet	Year-round

Map: Adventure Maps NW Coast Trail Map and Guide; **Contact:** Fort Columbia State Park; **Notes:** Discover Pass required. Dogs permitted on-leash; **GPS:** N 46 15.177, W 123 55.096

 *Grunt up Scarborough Hill through a coastal old-growth Sitka spruce forest. Admire big trees and enjoy window views of the mouth of the Columbia River. Then snoop around the well-preserved early twentieth-century historical structures of Fort Columbia.*

GETTING THERE

From Kelso, follow State Route 4 west for 56 miles to Naselle. Turn left onto SR 401, proceeding 12 miles to US Highway 101 at the Astoria–Megler Bridge. Continue north on US 101 for 2.5 miles, turn left (after emerging from small tunnel), and circle around into Fort Columbia State Park. Continue 0.3 mile to the trailhead (elev. 150 ft) located east of the interpretive center and vacation rentals. (From Ilwaco, follow US 101 south for 8.4 miles to the Fort Columbia turnoff.)

ON THE TRAIL

Fort Columbia State Park sits on a scenic bluff at the mouth of the Columbia River. Established in 1899, the fort was one of several defense installations designed to protect the Columbia from enemy attack. Never fired upon, the fort preserves a piece of our history and a good chunk of

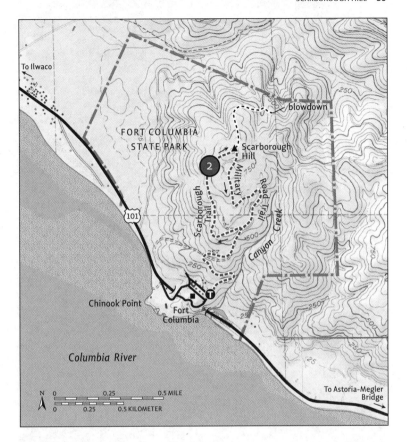

old-growth forest. Much of the surrounding coastal hills were heavily logged, but within this 593-acre park, stately giant Sitka spruce trees still stand—trees that were old when Lewis and Clark paddled by over two hundred years ago.

Two trails lead through these centuries-old sentinels. They wind their way up and above the tidy historical military base to 780-foot Scarborough Hill. And while the arboreal giants are the main attraction,

occasional gaps in the forest canopy provide satisfying views of the massive mouth of the Columbia—its ocean-lancing jetties, New England–like Astoria, Oregon, and lumpy Saddle and Neahkahnie mountains rising behind it.

From the parking area, walk a short distance on pavement to the Military Road trailhead, passing the old fort hospital. Follow this old road, steadily climbing on grassy tread beneath towering spruces. The

Old-growth Sitka spruce on Scarborough Hill

way bends left to pass an old observation station and a nice view overlooking the fort compound.

The way then swings right, reaching a junction (elev. 475 ft) with the Scarborough Trail at 0.6 mile. Go left. You'll be returning from the right. Following another old grassy roadbed, the trail soon heads north at an old junction with an abandoned trail that comes from the fort. Now on single-track tread, wind through rows of spruces and alders. Admire the glaucous sheen of the alders' smooth trunks contrasted against the spruces' scaly purple bark. At 1.2 miles, return to the Military Road Trail (elev. 780 ft) near Scarborough Hill's forested summit.

The trail left continues another 0.5 mile to a viewpoint, but the trail is currently closed at 0.2 mile due to a massive blowdown. Better to turn right and head down the Military Road Trail. On a gentle descent, pass the Scarborough Trail junction in 0.6 mile and reach the trailhead in another 0.6 mile. Be sure to allot some time to explore the historical fort grounds before leaving the park.

Long Beach Peninsula and Willapa Bay

Consisting of a rugged headland, complex dunes, and fine sandy beaches, the Long Beach Peninsula extends over 20 miles from the mouth of the Columbia River to the mouth of Willapa Bay. Ever since Captain William Clark wandered these beaches in November 1805, tourists have been flocking here. In the late nineteenth century, well-heeled Portlanders boarded paddle ships

"OCIAN IN VIEW!"

Any hiker taking to the trails and beaches of southwest Washington will be bombarded not only with beautiful scenery but also with history. In essence, the state's "modern" history began here. In the late 1700s, Vancouver, Meares, Gray, Cook, and others sailed up and down the coastline, mapping, exploring, and trading with Native peoples.

It was Captain John Meares, a British sea merchant, who in 1788 named Cape Disappointment. He was disappointed at not finding the "River of the West." He thought that the mouth of the Columbia was merely a bay. Today, hikers who take to the rugged headlands of Cape Disappointment certainly won't be.

Lewis and Clark spent several wet November days in the region in 1805. Captain William Clark thought he sighted the Pacific near present-day Skamokawa, exclaiming "Ocian in View!" The river mouth that Meares mistook for a bay, Clark mistook for the ocean. Clark was one of the area's first recorded hikers, climbing over North Head at Cape Disappointment and on to Long Beach. Today you can trace his journey on the paved and gravel Lewis and Clark Discovery Trail that leads from Ilwaco to Long Beach (Hike 5). Be sure to also visit the 0.3-mile wheelchair-accessible interpretive trail at Middle Village/Station Camp near Fort Columbia.

Willapa Bay, once known as Shoalwater Bay, helped feed the forty-niners of San Francisco (the gold-rushers, not the football players) with its succulent oysters. But while Europeans and Americans of European and Asian descent were settling and shaping what would become Pacific, Wahkiakum, and Grays Harbor counties, Native peoples had little to say about this change. On July 1, 1855, at the mouth of the Chehalis River near Grays Harbor, Washington's first territorial governor, Isaac Stevens, brought together coastal tribes to sign a treaty stipulating that they relinquish their land. The tribes didn't capitulate—it wouldn't, however, be Stevens's last attempt.

You can reflect on the state's fascinating and sobering human history while hiking the beaches and trails of southwest Washington.

destined for the peninsula's beach towns downriver: Seaview, Long Beach, and Ocean Park. Oystermen settled the peninsula's northern reaches in Nahcotta and Oysterville, once one of the richest communities in Washington.

Today, beachcombers still enjoy the Long Beach Peninsula, and oyster harvesting is still a viable part of the local economy. For hikers, the peninsula offers two prime destinations: Cape Disappointment on the southern end, with its rugged headlands and old-growth forests; and Leadbetter Point on the northern end, consisting of some of the state's wildest coastline and best bird habitat. Sadly, the state still allows vehicles to maraud the peninsula's beautiful beaches (note to legislators: the beaches are no longer needed for mail and goods delivery; State Route 103 does just fine), but at Leadbetter Point and Cape Disappointment you and the resident wildlife are able to wander free from motors.

Willapa Bay is the second-largest estuary on the Pacific coast—only San Francisco Bay is larger. But unlike that California estuary, which is home to over seven million people, Willapa Bay is practically deserted. And though settlements along Willapa's shores are among the oldest in the state (Oysterville was founded in 1854), much of the 260-square-mile estuary looks as it did when British captain John Meares first sighted and named it Shoalwater Bay in 1788.

In 1937, President Franklin D. Roosevelt established the Willapa National Wildlife Refuge, ensuring that a large portion of this prime and productive estuary would remain a healthy ecosystem. The refuge consists of three main parcels (management units): Leadbetter Point; the Lewis and Riekkola units; and the Long Island Unit, which protects the largest estuarine island on the West Coast.

You can hike the Willapa Bay refuge all year, but note that it's popular with elk and bird hunters. Plan your hikes accordingly and respect these users—they help fund public-land acquisition and most of them have high conservation ethics. Visit the refuge headquarters along US Highway 101 (near milepost 24) for a map and more information.

3 Cape Disappointment State Park: North Head

RATING/ DIFFICULTY	ROUNDTRIP	ELEV GAIN/ HIGH POINT	SEASON
***/2	3.6 miles	400 feet/ 210 feet	Year-round

Map: Adventure Maps NW Coast Trail Map and Guide; **Contact:** Cape Disappointment State Park; **Notes:** Discover Pass required. Dogs permitted on-leash; **GPS:** N 46 17.157, W 124 03.814

Hike along a rugged headland through a salt-sprayed maritime forest to Cape Disappointment's dramatic North Head Lighthouse. From the high headland and its 1898 lighthouse, take in breathtaking views that include thundering waves, windswept dunes, and scores of shorebirds skimming the crashing Pacific surf.

GETTING THERE

From the Astoria–Megler Bridge, follow US Highway 101 for 11 miles north to Ilwaco and the junction of State Route 100. Follow SR 100 (it's a loop; bear left on the Robert Gray Drive section) to Cape Disappointment

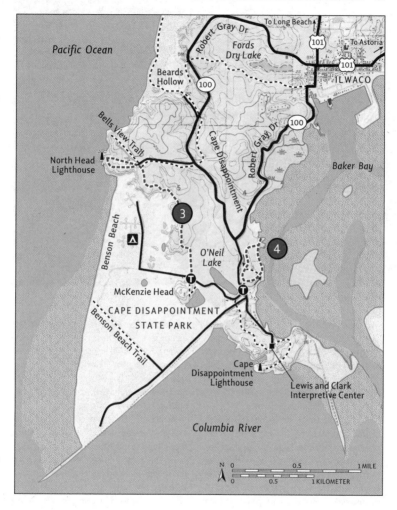

State Park and a junction at 1.7 miles. Turn left and continue 0.4 mile on SR 100-Spur to a four-way stop. Turn right, pass the park entrance station, and in 0.2 mile turn right again. In 0.4 mile, park at the McKenzie Head trailhead (elev. 20 ft), on the left.

ON THE TRAIL

There are over 8 miles of hiking trails in 1882-acre Cape Disappointment State Park. Once the location of Fort Canby, a military reservation established in 1852 (before Washington statehood), the state park

Looking north from the North Head Lighthouse

was created in the 1950s. Home to a large campground and two lighthouses, including the oldest in the state, Cape D is a popular place. The 1.5-mile North Head Trail along a rugged headland draped with moisture-dripping old-growth Sitka spruce forest offers a respite from the crowds.

Locate the trailhead on the north side of the road and begin hiking across a flat marshy area before heading up a rugged ridge. When Lewis and Clark visited this area, the ridge was a headland protruding into the Pacific. After the North Jetty was built in 1917, this marshy forested area formed through accretion (trapped sand and silt accumulation). The land mass and beaches of Cape Disappointment are growing. (Mark Twain was wrong—they are making more land!)

On muddy and at times rooty tread, climb above the old coastline of the former headland (elev. 200 ft). Then descend 150 feet on an up-and-down route before climbing again. Giant Sitka spruces keep you well shaded, while gaps in the forest canopy offer splendid views down to the "new" beach. Continue through a lush jungle, noting copious frogs and newts along the way.

At about 1 mile, rejoice upon reaching well-built tread and boardwalks, which make the hike much easier. Drop into a small ravine to cross a creek before making the final climb to a parking lot (elev. 210 ft) at 1.5 miles. Yes, you could have driven to this point—but why? Exercise and nature are good for your body and soul! Now hike the 0.3-mile old service road down to the North Head Lighthouse for one of the finest maritime settings in all of Washington. Return to the North Head Trail via the 0.3-mile light keeper's walkway.

EXTENDING YOUR TRIP

From the lighthouse parking area, walk the paved 0.3-mile Bells View Trail to a great overlook of the Long Beach Peninsula. Back at the McKenzie Head trailhead, hike the 0.6-mile roundtrip up McKenzie Head. From this old World War II battery, admire the mouth of the Columbia River and the Cape Disappointment Lighthouse—completed in 1856, it's the state's oldest. You can hike to this lighthouse too via a 0.6-mile trail from the park's Lewis and Clark Interpretive Center.

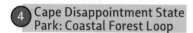

4 Cape Disappointment State Park: Coastal Forest Loop

RATING/ DIFFICULTY	LOOP	ELEV GAIN/ HIGH POINT	SEASON
**/1	1.4 miles	260 feet/ 140 feet	Year-round

Map: Adventure Maps NW Coast Trail Map and Guide; **Contact:** Cape Disappointment State Park; **Notes:** Discover Pass required. Dogs permitted on-leash; **GPS:** N 46 17.066, W 124 03.269

Travel through a tranquil old-growth Sitka spruce and western hemlock forest perched on a bluff at the treacherous mouth of the Columbia River. And admire sweeping views of the fishing community of Ilwaco on Baker Bay, set against the rolling backdrop of the cloud-cloaked Bear River Range.

GETTING THERE

From the Astoria–Megler Bridge, follow US Highway 101 for 11 miles north to Ilwaco and the junction of State Route 100. Follow SR 100 (it's a loop; bear left on the Robert Gray Drive section) to Cape Disappointment

A hiker dwarfed by a giant Sitka spruce

State Park and a junction at 1.7 miles. Turn left and continue 0.4 mile on SR 100-Spur to a four-way stop. Turn left for the trailhead (elev. 10 ft), located in large parking lot west of the boat launch.

ON THE TRAIL

Lined with alders and sword ferns, the trail immediately begins climbing, soon coming to a junction. Head right, you'll be returning on the left. At 0.2 mile, come to a junction that offers a shorter loop (0.5 mile) option. Continue right instead, coming to impressive Sitka spruces, a tree that primarily grows along a narrow stretch of the Pacific coast from Northern California to southern Alaska.

Hiking along a 100-foot bluff, look out at Coast Guard buildings, spoil islands, and old pier posts in the river. The trail drops into a grove of massive trees, coming to a junction at 0.6 mile. Head right on the spur to a small bluff (watch children) that provides excellent viewing across Baker Bay and out to Cape Disappointment.

Return to the junction and continue right, passing more monster trees and climbing a 140-foot hill. Stay right at the shortcut junction and descend. Catch views of McKenzie Head and O'Neil Lake through the trees before coming to the first junction. Bear right to return to the trailhead.

EXTENDING YOUR TRIP

Consider hiking some of the park's other short and scenic trails. Hike to Cape D via the ranger station on a 1.2-mile trail that includes a stop at the Lewis and Clark Interpretive Center. Or hike the 0.5-mile Benson Beach Trail for extended beach wandering.

5 Lewis and Clark Discovery Trail

RATING/ DIFFICULTY	ONE-WAY	ELEV GAIN/ HIGH POINT	SEASON
***/2	8.2 miles	200 feet/ 140 feet	Year-round

Maps: Online at visitors bureau, Adventure Maps NW Coast Trail Map and Guide; **Contact:** Long Beach Peninsula Visitors Bureau; **Notes:** Open to bicycles. Dogs permitted on-leash; **GPS:** N 46 18.369, W 124 02.266

This hike replicates the route of Captain William Clark's famous hike of 1805. Travel a mostly paved path from the Port of Ilwaco over a bluff through maritime forest to coastal wetlands and waves of dunes along the Pacific Ocean. Stop at historical displays along the way, including a gray whale skeleton and magnificent bronze sculptures commemorating the Corps of Discovery's epic journey.

GETTING THERE

Southern trailhead: From the Astoria–Megler Bridge, follow US Highway 101 for 11 miles north to Ilwaco. Turn left onto Elizabeth Avenue and after two blocks, turn right onto Howerton Avenue and park on this street. The trail begins on Waterfront Walkway between Advent and Pearl avenues. Restroom available. **Northern trailhead:** From the junction of US 101 and State Route 103 in Seaview, drive north on SR 103 for 2.9 miles (passing through Long Beach) and turn left onto 26th Street to trailhead parking at The Breakers.

ON THE TRAIL

You can access this trail at ten different locations, including from the Bolstad Arch in Long Beach, making for plenty of shorter hiking options. Any section will do, but try to arrange for a car shuttle to do the whole trail in one sweep. Strong hikers and runners won't have any problem doing the complete trail out-and-back.

Starting from the California condor (which once ranged this far north) monument on the Ilwaco waterfront, walk the Waterfront Way west past shops and businesses to 1st Avenue. Turn left on Main Street, walk one block, carefully cross 2nd Avenue, and continue straight on a steep paved drive. At 0.6 mile, reach the beginning of the actual Discovery Trail (no parking here) and continue on an up-and-down but generally up route, skirting the extensive wetlands of Fords Dry

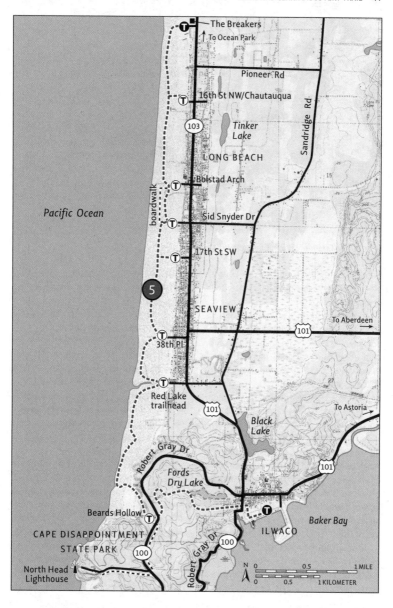

Sculpture of Captain William Clark and big sturgeon

Lake. Watch for newts on the trail—they're prolific, and I imagine quite a few meet their demise under bike tires.

At 1.6 miles, crest a bluff (elev. 140 ft) and carefully cross SR 100. Now in Cape Disappointment State Park, head south along the bluff edge, catching views out to the sea. Under a tower of impressive Sitka spruce, descend steeply on dirt tread to a long boardwalk across Beards Hollow. Accretion has transformed this former cove into a wildlife-rich marsh.

At 2 miles, come to a parking lot and junction. A paved 1-mile trail heads left for the North Head Lighthouse trailhead. The once-again-paved Discovery Trail continues right. Skirt Beards Hollow and head through a gap between basaltic headlands before reaching dunes and beach views. Find good views, too, of North Head towering to the south.

The path now heads north through waves of dunes that mirror the views of ocean waves. At 2.7 miles, cross Beards Hollow's outlet creek on a bridge. Continue across dunes and through colonizing forest and patches of invasive Scotch broom. At 3.9 miles, reach the Red Lake trailhead (30th Street). At 4.5 miles, come to the Seaview trailhead (38th Place; privy available).

Keep heading north on a now much busier trail. At 5 miles, come to the 17th Street trailhead. Pass interpretive panels, a dolphin sculpture, and a beach-access trail for equestrians. At 5.7 miles, come to the busy Sid Snyder Drive trailhead (restrooms available). The trail now parallels Long Beach's boardwalk, coming to the popular gray whale skeleton and sculpture.

The trail soon darts under the boardwalk and reaches the Bolstad Arch trailhead at 6.2 miles. Continue north, soon coming to one of the more intriguing attractions—a sculpture of Captain William Clark and a big sturgeon, along with a basalt monolith commemorating the November 19, 1805, "hike." As you continue north over dunes, crowds thin. At 7.2 miles, reach the Chautauqua trailhead. The way carries on to a 19-foot bronze sculpture replicating "Clark's Tree," where the captain inscribed "William Clark. Nov. 19, 1805. By land from the U. States." From here, he returned to camp on the Columbia River. The Discovery Trail continues and turns east, soon reaching its northern terminus at 8.2 miles at The Breakers trailhead (26th Street NW).

6 Leadbetter Point State Park: Dune Forest Loop

RATING/ DIFFICULTY	LOOP	ELEV GAIN/ HIGH POINT	SEASON
**/1	2.9 miles	100 feet/ 50 feet	Year-round

Map: Adventure Maps NW Coast Trail Map and Guide; **Contact:** Leadbetter Point State Park; **Notes:** Discover Pass required; Dogs permitted on-leash; **GPS:** N 46 36.428, W 124 02.618

Hike an easy loop over old dunes, through quiet maritime forest, and along bird-saturated Willapa Bay on the wild northern tip of the Long Beach Peninsula. Chances are good that you'll sight a bear, deer, or otter along the way. Mosquito encounters are plentiful too, so come prepared for the little buggers.

GETTING THERE

From Kelso, follow State Route 4 west for 60 miles and turn left onto US Highway 101. Continue on US 101 for 14.8 miles. (From the Astoria–Megler Bridge, follow US 101 north for 8.8 miles, bearing right onto US 101-Alt. Continue 0.6 mile to a junction with US 101. Turn left and drive 1.8 miles to Sandridge Road.) Turn right onto Sandridge Road (the turnoff is 0.5 mile east of the junction with

SR 103 in Long Beach) and follow it for 11.3 miles to SR 103 in Nahcotta. Continue north on SR 103 for 7.3 miles (which becomes Stackpole Road) and enter Leadbetter Point State Park. Drive another 1.5 miles to the road's end and trailhead (elev. 40 ft). Privy available.

ON THE TRAIL

Leadbetter Point consists of Washington's wildest coastal lands outside of Olympic National Park. Undeveloped and untrammeled, over 3000 acres of dunes, salt marshes, and maritime forest and more than 8 miles of vehicle-free ocean and bay beaches (except for the short razor-clam season) are protected within a state park and national wildlife refuge.

Over 7 miles of trails traverse Leadbetter Point State Park and the adjacent Leadbetter Unit of the Willapa National Wildlife Refuge, granting access to both the ocean and Willapa Bay, the second-largest estuary on the entire Pacific coast. Leadbetter Point's forests, salt marshes, and mudflats contain some of the best habitat for breeding and migrating birds on the West Coast. While Leadbetter Point's wide, sandy ocean beach (Hike 7) will entice most hikers, the area's real charms lie within its diverse bay and forest ecosystems. The Dune Forest Loop is a great introduction to these wildlife-rich habitats. And if you're looking for a good winter hike, this loop isn't subject to the flooding that keeps the coastal trails under water for half the year.

Start your loop by heading left (west) on the Red Trail, also known as the Dune Forest Loop. On a rolling course, hike through a forest of shore pines. In 0.5 mile, come to a junction with the Blue Trail, which leads 0.8 mile to the Pacific. Continue left, hiking along

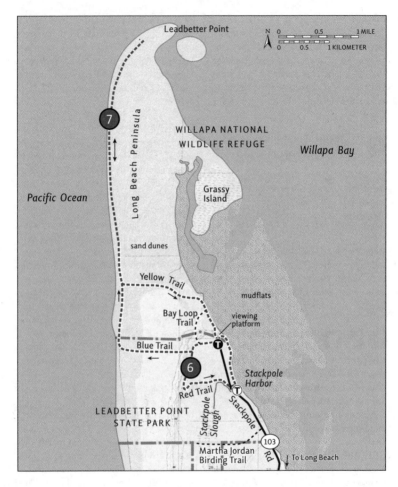

a sand ridge—an old dune that has since been colonized by shore pine, wax myrtle, salal, and bearberry (kinnikinnick). Under a tunnel of salal, evergreen huckleberry, and bearberry and with the faint sound of surf in the distance, continue hiking. At 1.2 miles, the trail bends left to head east over a higher ridge, increasingly dominated by Sitka spruce.

Pass a small wetland area that can flood during heavy rains and wander through groves of impressive big spruces. At 2.1 miles, come to the park road and a trailhead (alternative start). Cross the road, and soon

Quiet sandy beach along Willapa Bay

reach Willapa Bay. The trail now turns north, hugging the shoreline mudflats and beaches of the bay. Enjoy views of the expansive bay against a backdrop of rolling, cloud-hugged hills. Birdlife is profuse. Pelicans, marbled godwits, loons, grebes, mergansers—over a hundred species ply these waters, salt marshes, and mudflats. Eagles often perch on overhanging snags. Mammals are abundant too. If hiking during low tide, scan the mudflats for raccoon, bear, and elk tracks. At 2.8 miles, come to a junction at a viewing platform. Turn left, returning to your start in 0.1 mile.

EXTENDING YOUR TRIP

Combine with the adjacent national wildlife refuge trails (Hike 7) or with the Martha Jordan Birding Trail, which runs for 1.1 miles on a gated dirt road to Stackpole Slough (beyond is the private Sherwood Forest).

7 Willapa National Wildlife Refuge: Leadbetter Point

RATING/ DIFFICULTY	ROUNDTRIP	ELEV GAIN/ HIGH POINT	SEASON
****/2	10.6 miles	100 feet/ 40 feet	May–Oct

Map: Adventure Maps NW Coast Trail Map and Guide; **Contact:** Willapa National Wildlife Refuge; **Notes:** Discover Pass required. Dogs prohibited. Respect plover closure areas Mar 15–Sept 15. Removal of plants or animals from refuge is prohibited. Trails are often flooded Oct–May; **GPS:** N 46 36.428, W 124 02.618

Hike through thick maritime forest and across the state's largest coastal dune complex to the wildest beach south of the Olympic wilderness coast. Then walk along the lonely surf all the way to the

Hiker approaches a deserted Leadbetter Point.

tip of Leadbetter Point. Undeveloped and lacking jetties, Leadbetter's dunes, sandbars, and coastline are constantly shifting as nature intended.

GETTING THERE

From Kelso, follow State Route 4 west for 60 miles and turn left onto US Highway 101. Continue on US 101 for 14.8 miles. (From the Astoria–Megler Bridge, follow US 101 north for 8.8 miles, bearing right onto US 101-Alt. Continue 0.6 mile to a junction with US 101. Turn left and drive 1.8 miles to Sandridge Road.) Turn right onto Sandridge Road (the turnoff is 0.5 mile east of the junction with SR 103 in Long Beach) and follow it for 11.3 miles to SR 103 in Nahcotta. Continue north on SR 103 (which becomes Stackpole Road) for 7.3 miles and enter Leadbetter Point State Park. Drive another 1.5 miles to the road's end and trailhead (elev. 40 ft). Privy available.

ON THE TRAIL

Leadbetter Point's forests, salt marshes, and mudflats are prime scoping grounds for bird-watchers. This wild northern tip of the Long Beach Peninsula contains some of the best breeding and staging grounds on the West Coast for a myriad of species, from snowy owls to snowy plovers. If you want to add some serious hiking to your bird-watching, consider going all the way to the tip of Leadbetter Point. If that's too far, there's a shorter loop option.

Before beginning, take note. The trails to the ocean are subject to flooding from October through May. We're talking knee- to thigh-deep cold water inundating a half-plus mile of each trail. It's possible to wade (I've done it on numerous occasions)—the ground remains pretty firm, and there are no leeches or snapping turtles. Hip waders and long legs are a plus (I have neither). Unless you have a high tolerance for cold water, wait until the trail dries out sometime in late spring.

Starting in the state park, head west for 0.5 mile on the Red Trail (aka the Dune Forest Loop, Hike 6) through shore pines and over old dunes to a junction. Turn right on the Blue (aka Weather Beach) Trail and follow this good and possibly submerged path through low-lying shrubs and thick maritime forest before breaking out onto high dunes adorned in swaying sedges. The trail, now lined with posts, enters the Willapa National Wildlife Refuge (dogs prohibited).

The surrounding dunes are home to nesting threatened snowy plovers (one of only three locations in Washington). Beginning in March, this small wading bird builds its well-camouflaged nest on dry sand in the upper beach and dune areas. Stay on the trail. At 1.3 miles, reach a wide and usually deserted beautiful ocean beach (vehicles are allowed only during the short razor-clam season, in late winter).

Head north to start exploring this large undeveloped sandy strand. Be sure to stay west of the posts denoting closed-to-visitation plover habitat. At 1.8 miles, reach the junction with the Yellow (aka Bearberry) Trail. This is your return route to the trailhead. You can return now, for a 3.6-mile loop, or continue hiking the beach north all the way to Leadbetter Point. It's 3.5 miles to the constantly shifting northern terminus of the Long Beach Peninsula. Along the way, admire (but stay out of) one of the largest undisturbed dune complexes in the state. Reach the tip of the peninsula and scan the wild and treacherous mouth of Willapa Bay. When ready, retrace your steps on the beach back to the Yellow Trail.

Follow this nice path over rows of dunes to a thick forest of shore pines crowded with salal and bearberry (kinnikinnick). As with the Blue Trail, expect over a half mile of submerged tread from October through May. At 1 mile from the beach, the trail reaches glistening mudflats along Willapa Bay's much calmer waters. Look for deer, eagles, and shorebirds. Enjoy views, too, to

Grassy Island to the north and Goose Point to the east.

At 1.3 miles, come to a junction with the Bay Loop Trail. Either way returns to the trailhead, but the preferred route is left along the bay, utilizing beach and marshy tread. At 1.8 miles, the way bends right at a viewing platform, reaching the trailhead shortly afterward.

8 Willapa National Wildlife Refuge: Salmon Art Trail

RATING/ DIFFICULTY	ROUNDTRIP	ELEV GAIN/ HIGH POINT	SEASON
***/2	1.2 miles	200 feet/ 175 feet	Year-round

Map: Adventure Maps NW Coast Trail Map and Guide; **Contact:** Willapa National Wildlife Refuge; **Notes:** Art trail is wheelchair-accessible. Dogs prohibited; **GPS:** N 46 24.863, W 123 56.051

Find salmon in the trees, a chorus line of frogs, colorful birds suspended in the air, and so much more on this delightful duo of trails blending art with nature. Hikers and nature lovers of all ages will delight in this unique path that teaches about the wildlife of Willapa Bay through works of art aesthetically integrated into a natural canvas.

GETTING THERE

From Kelso, follow State Route 4 west for 60 miles to a junction with US Highway 101. Head south on US 101 for 4.8 miles to the Willapa National Wildlife Refuge headquarters and trailhead (elev. 20 ft). (From the Astoria–Megler Bridge, follow US 101 north, using US 101-Alt at 8.9 miles, for 18 miles.) Privy available.

Spinners tell the Salmon Life Story

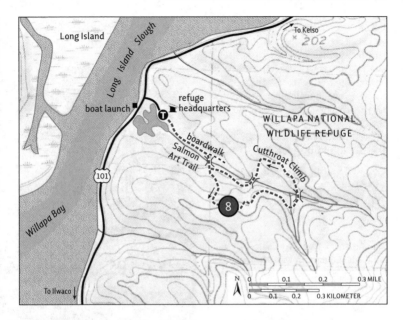

ON THE TRAIL

Stop at the refuge headquarters first and pick up a brochure. Then begin your artsy odyssey on a curving boardwalk above a salt marsh. Aside from looking for real live wildlife, enjoy the artful depictions of native critters. The trail uses commissioned artwork to educate hikers about the refuge and its wildlife. Students from the University of Washington Public Arts Program, under the direction of several professors, created the art, and sponsors and volunteers helped build the trail. It's a short trail, just 0.2 mile, but you'll want to spend plenty of time appreciating the various displays, from the somber (the extinct animals post) to the whimsical (railings adorned with frogs).

Extend your artsy ambling by continuing on the Cutthroat Climb, taking off right. Cross a creek lined with salmon silhouettes

suspended in trees and come to a junction. You'll return on the left, so continue straight, climbing steeply. Unlike the smooth and level art trail, the climb is a little rougher. The highlights of the Cutthroat Climb are the interactive interpretive panels and colorful native birds designed by artist Becca Weiss.

After steeply climbing 150 feet and reaching an elaborate bypass over a fallen tree, the way then descends through mature timber with a few little uphill sections that slow momentum. Cross a salmon-bearing creek, follow an old road, and then traverse a boardwalk over lush bottomland that in springtime fills the air with the pungent fragrance of skunk cabbage. The way then crosses the creek once more, bringing you back to the Cutthroat Climb start at 1 mile. Follow the art trail once more, returning to your vehicle in 0.2 mile.

EXTENDING YOUR TRIP

Not too far north (1.5 miles) on US 101 from the refuge headquarters is the Teal Slough Trail. Hike it 0.8 mile roundtrip to some of the largest, grandest ancient cedars and Sitka spruces (home to marbled murrelets) that remain in coastal southwest Washington.

⑨ Willapa National Wildlife Refuge: Long Island

RATING/ DIFFICULTY	ROUNDTRIP	ELEV GAIN/ HIGH POINT	SEASON
**/3	5.8 miles	500 feet/ 225 feet	Year-round

Map: Adventure Maps NW Coast Trail Map and Guide; **Contact:** Willapa National Wildlife Refuge; **Notes:** Boat needed to access trailhead. Dogs prohibited; **GPS:** N 46 24.722, W 123 56.400

Hike on the largest estuarine island on the Pacific coast. Miles of trails and old woods roads traverse Willapa Bay's 5460-acre Long Island, allowing access to quiet tidal flats, scenic bluffs, hidden sloughs, and old townsites. But the biggest attraction on Long Island is its biggest attraction—a grove of giant cedars almost one thousand years old.

GETTING THERE

From Kelso, follow State Route 4 west for 60 miles to a junction with US Highway 101. Head south on US 101 for 4.8 miles to the Willapa National Wildlife Refuge headquarters and trailhead (elev. 10 ft). Privy available. (From the Astoria–Megler Bridge, follow US 101 north, using US 101-Alt at 8.9 miles, for 18 miles.) Park and launch your watercraft to reach the trailhead on Long Island.

Towering ancient cedars in the Bonker Grove

ON THE TRAIL

The hike to Long Island's ancient cedars isn't overly difficult. It's getting to the trailhead that may be a challenge. There's no bridge to the island. You'll need your own canoe, kayak, or other kind of boat to make the short channel crossing to the trailhead. Be sure to check in at refuge headquarters (located across from the boat launch) for bay conditions. Mudflats and weather can make the crossing tricky at times.

Once on the island, secure your watercraft and get hiking! Home to settlements and sawmills during the past century, most of Long Island has been logged. Amazingly, a 274-acre tract of old-growth western red cedars was spared the chainsaw. In 1986,

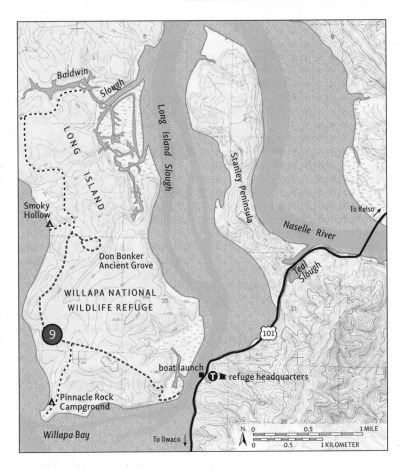

this primeval patch, the last large coastal old-growth forest grove left in Washington, was added to the Willapa National Wildlife Refuge. In 2005, the grove was named in honor of Don Bonker, a former congressman from Vancouver who played a major role in preserving these majestic trees.

The road-trail starts off on a beautiful point with views of Willapa Bay's extensive mudflats to the south. Through second- and third-growth forest, the trail winds its way inland, climbing a couple of hundred feet in the process. Woodland birds like kinglets, juncos, flycatchers, and chickadees flit in the regenerating forest. Long Island is full of life. Bears, elk, deer, and cougars all live here.

At 1.2 miles, come to a junction. The trail left leads 0.7 mile to High Point and the

Pinnacle Rock Campground, one of five campgrounds on the island (first come, first · served except during archery season, when a permit is required). Continue on the main trail, reaching another junction at 2.5 miles. Head right, descending to a small hollow that harbors a creek and the Don Bonker Ancient Grove.

A few big stumps greet you first. Then complete trees! Ancient trees! Giant trees! An old-growth cathedral of trees and more than likely, you're the sole parishioner. The trail loops 0.8 mile along the periphery of this special grove to keep from disturbing this endangered ecosystem. It has defied windstorms and logging. Walk quietly and embrace it.

EXTENDING YOUR TRIP
Consider hiking some of the other trails on the island and staying overnight.

Chehalis River Valley

The Chehalis River forms a big horseshoe in southwest Washington. From the cloud-cloaked Willapa Hills, the Chehalis flows northeast through rural countryside to the small cities of Centralia and Chehalis where, surrounded by lush pastures, the river bends westward, cutting a low divide between the Willapa Hills and Black Hills. As the Chehalis gets closer to its outlet, Grays Harbor, it takes on the characteristics of a southern low-country river, fanning out into a labyrinth of sloughs.

Very little wild country remains along the Chehalis. Logging, farming, and creeping urbanization have taken a toll on the natural communities of this large watershed. Only a few pockets of old growth remain. Very little remains, too, of the biologically diverse prairies and oak savannas that once graced this river's lower reaches.

Most of the Chehalis River valley remains in private ownership. But the few parcels of public lands along this river that do exist help preserve some of the region's rich natural history, as well as introducing hikers to this oft-overlooked part of the state.

10 Rainbow Falls State Park

RATING/ DIFFICULTY	ROUNDTRIP	ELEV GAIN/ HIGH POINT	SEASON
*/1	Up to 3 miles	200 feet/ 475 feet	Year-round

Map: Online at Rainbow Falls State Park; **Contact:** Rainbow Falls State Park; **Notes:** Discover Pass required. Dogs permitted on-leash; **GPS:** N 46 37.812, W 123 13.911

Hike through some of the last remaining old growth in the Chehalis Valley on trails built by the Depression-era Civilian Conservation Corps (CCC). Once finished hiking, admire the small cascade for which this park is named.

GETTING THERE
From Chehalis (exit 77 on I-5), follow State Route 6 west for 16 miles to the trailhead (elev. 275 ft) on the south side of the highway in Rainbow Falls State Park. Park on the north side of the highway.

ON THE TRAIL
This little state park on the upper reaches of the Chehalis River has been attracting visitors since the early twentieth century when it was a community park. Once surrounded by thousands of acres of old-growth forest, this 139-acre park contains the only ancient

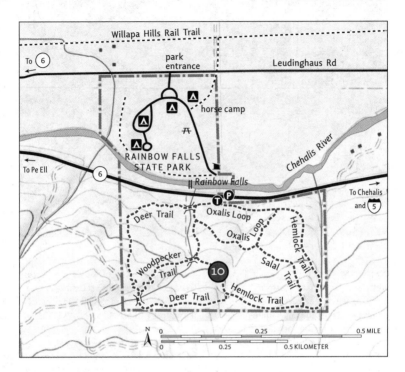

trees left in the region. Rainbow Falls lures most visitors, but the remnant old growth is more impressive.

About 3 miles of interconnecting trails wind through the lush tract of big cedars, hemlocks, Douglas-firs, and the occasional Sitka spruce. Beneath the lofty canopy, moss drapes the alders and oxalis carpets the forest floor. It's a magical fairy-tale forest where chickarees and chickadees frolic and flit like gregarious elves.

From the trailhead, you can set out in several directions and blaze your own course. Trails are signed and you really can't get lost; all trails loop back to the trailhead. The Oxalis Loop passes by some of the larger

trees in the park, while the Woodpecker Trail descends into a small, lush ravine complete with a babbling brook. The Hemlock and Deer trails trace the park's periphery. Hike these trails as a journey, not for a specific destination, and enjoy this special tract of remnant wild country.

EXTENDING YOUR TRIP

After your hike, make sure to check out Rainbow Falls, a small cascade tumbling over basalt ledges. Then consider heading to the northern section of the park to admire the CCC-built structures and perhaps spend the night in the park's campground. You can also access the Willapa Hills Rail Trail from

Old growth forest at Rainbow Falls State Park

the park. Much of the 56-mile trail is still pretty rough, but the eastern 5.2 miles from Chehalis to Adna are paved and make for nice walking, and the 7-mile graveled section west from the park to Pe Ell makes for good hiking, trail running, and mountain biking.

11 Lake Sylvia State Park

Lake Loop

RATING/ DIFFICULTY	LOOP	ELEV GAIN/ HIGH POINT	SEASON
**/1	2.2 miles	50 feet/ 170 feet	Year-round

Creek Loop

RATING/ DIFFICULTY	LOOP	ELEV GAIN/ HIGH POINT	SEASON
**/2	2.7 miles	400 feet/ 225 feet	Year-round

Maps: Online at Lake Sylvia State Park and City of Montesano; **Contact:** Lake Sylvia State Park and City of Montesano; **Notes:** Discover Pass required. First 0.5 mile of creek loop is wheelchair-accessible. Dogs permitted on-leash; **GPS:** N 46 59.821, W 123 35.737

These two delightful short loops are in a 237-acre state park and 5000-acre city forest not far from downtown Montesano. Enjoy an easy hike through mature forest along a sliver of a lake teeming with fish and birdlife. Then amble alongside a babbling creek to appreciate engineers past (those who conducted trains) and engineers present (furry ones who build dams).

GETTING THERE

Exit US Highway 12 in Montesano and head north on Main Street past a traffic light and the scenic county courthouse. Turn left on Spruce Avenue and proceed three blocks. Turn right on 3rd Street, which eventually becomes Sylvia Lake Road, and drive 1.3 miles to Lake Sylvia State Park. At the park entrance booth turn left, cross the bridge, and park at the day-use area near the ranger residence (elev. 140 ft).

ON THE TRAIL

Lake Sylvia State Park packs a lot of history, natural beauty, and recreation within its tight borders. Once an old logging camp, the area was converted into a park in 1936. The narrow lake was created by damming Sylvia Creek, first for rounding up logs and

then for providing Montesano's electricity. Plenty of artifacts and evidence remain in the park from its early days. But hikers will be pleasantly surprised to see how well the area's forests have recovered. Mature trees hover above the lake and creek, providing not only a pretty backdrop but also some rich wildlife habitat.

Lake Loop: This hike consists of two loops originating from the same trailhead. Start out on the lake loop near the boat

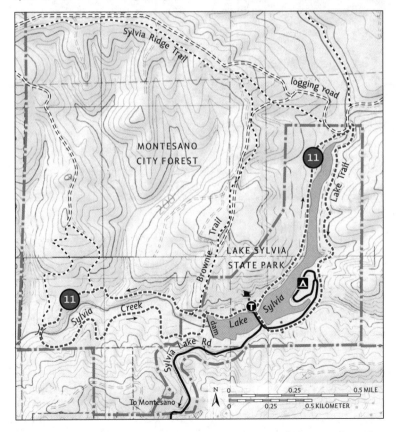

Covered bridge along the trail

launch, hiking north along Lake Sylvia's west shore on a perfectly level path that was once a logging railroad. Gasoline motors are prohibited on the lake, providing paddlers and hikers a peaceful environment. Mature evergreens shade the trail, while large alders drape over the tranquil waters. The northern end of the lake is marshy, giving good cover for ducks, geese, and herons.

In 1 mile, you'll hit a logging road. Turn right, cross Sylvia's inlet stream, and then turn right again, now back on trail, to hike along the lake's eastern shore. The return trail is wilder, climbing over bluffs and

darting in and out of cool side ravines—one housing a covered bridge over a small creek. You'll emerge in the park's attractive campground (a great weekend base). Walk the campground access road a short distance back to the entrance booth, cross the bridge, and return to your start at 2.2 miles.

Creek Loop: Refill your water bottles and then head south along the lake for the second loop, this one along Sylvia Creek. Cross a cove on an old railroad bridge (now a beloved fishing spot) and turn right at the dam, coming to the start of the Sylvia Creek Forestry Trail in 0.2 mile. Entering the adjacent Montesano City Forest, follow this trail (ignoring radiating side trails) into a ravine cradling the creek. In 2012 this trail was greatly improved to include interpretive panels and a half mile of wheelchair-accessible tread.

Hike through a cool forest of maples and cedars, keeping an eye out for more evidence of past human activity (such as old springboard cuts and railroad trestles). Look, too, for signs of animal activity. Beavers are active along this stretch of the creek. At 0.7 mile, the wheelchair-accessible section ends. Cross a creek and climb. At 1.2 miles, the way bends left at a junction, soon crossing Sylvia Creek on a big bridge.

Then climb around an old marshy section of trail and return to creek level, coming to an old mill site complete with scattered

artifacts. The trail climbs again, skirts and crosses a clear-cut, and comes to a junction at 2.4 miles. Go left into a grove of old growth and then cross the old dam that created Lake Sylvia. Turn right on the old railroad bridge to return to the trailhead.

EXTENDING YOUR TRIP
Explore some of the miles of trails and old roads in the Montesano City Forest.

12 Friends Landing

RATING/ DIFFICULTY	LOOP	ELEV GAIN/ HIGH POINT	SEASON
**/1	1.7 miles	Minimal/ 20 feet	Year-round

Map: Online at Port of Grays Harbor; **Contact:** Port of Grays Harbor; **Notes:**

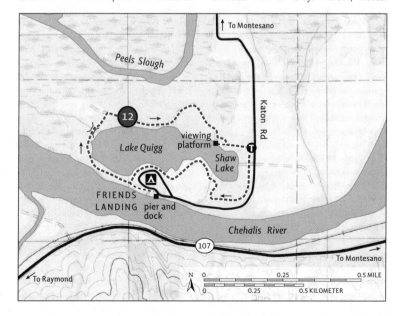

Trail circling Lake Quigg

Wheelchair-accessible. Dogs permitted on-leash. Trail subject to flooding; **GPS:** N 46 56.865, W 123 38.219

Leisurely wander around Lake Quigg in the tidal-influenced Chehalis River Surge Plain on a level paved trail perfect for hikers of all ages and abilities. Once the site of a gravel-mining operation, Friends Landing is now a 152-acre camping and nature park.

GETTING THERE

From Montesano, take the Devonshire Road exit off of US Highway 12. Follow Devonshire Road for 1.2 miles and turn left onto Katon Road. Continue 1.3 miles to the Friends Landing park entrance and trailhead (elev. 20 ft).

ON THE TRAIL

Head clockwise on the paved trail, briefly paralleling the park road before skirting the park's campground and coming to Lake Quigg. Pass a floating dock and the first of several boardwalks and interpretive signs. At 0.6 mile, come to a junction with a short trail leading left to a dock on the Chehalis River and another trailhead (privy available).

Continue right on a narrow treed strip of land between the Chehalis River and Lake Quigg. It's hard to imagine that this pretty scene was once part of a gravel-mining operation. In 1988, the Friend family donated this tract to Trout Unlimited, whose board member David Hamilton designed a park for the disabled community. Trout Unlimited and a group of partners and volunteers then developed Friends Landing around the man-made lake, which now sports quite a healthy fish population. In 2014, the Port of Grays Harbor took over managing the property.

Continue hiking along the lakeshore, passing another floating dock and coming to a bridge spanning the lake's inlet. Try to visit when the tide is coming in, so you can watch waters surge into the lake basin. Watch for birds—eagles, ospreys, kingfishers, and herons are common. At 1.6 miles, come to a junction; a short spur leads right to a viewing platform and popular fishing spot. The main trail continues left, leading back to your start in 0.1 mile.

13 Chehalis River Surge Plain

RATING/ DIFFICULTY	ROUNDTRIP	ELEV GAIN/ HIGH POINT	SEASON
**/1	7 miles	Minimal/ 20 feet	Year-round

Map: USGS Central Park; **Contact:** Washington State Department of Natural Resources, Pacific Cascade Region; **Notes:** Discover Pass required. First 0.5 mile is wheelchair-accessible. Dogs permitted on-leash. Trail subject to flooding; **GPS:** N 46 56.694, W 123 39.021

A "slough" of surprises awaits you on this wonderful interpretive trail within the 3000-acre wildlife-rich Chehalis River Surge Plain Natural Area Preserve. Hike along an old logging railroad through the largest tidal surge plain wetland in the state. Along snaking sloughs and through a tunnel of greenery, at times you may think you're hiking in Louisiana instead of Washington.

GETTING THERE

From Montesano, follow State Route 107 west for 4 miles, turning right onto Preachers Slough Road. **Eastern trailhead:** Reach the eastern trailhead in 0.1 mile (elev. 20 ft). Privy available. **Western trailhead:** Continue west for 1.2 miles on SR 107. Turn right onto Blue Slough Road and reach the

trailhead in 2.4 miles. (From Cosmopolis, the western trailhead is 2.4 miles east of the US 101 junction.)

ON THE TRAIL

From 1910 until 1985, trains chugged through this saturated bottomland of scaly-barked spruce and speckled-bark alder. A few years later, trail crews from the Cedar Creek Correctional Camp helped transform the abandoned line into a great little trail. Hikers can now get onboard for a trip back in time and into the deep recesses of this productive ecosystem. Plan for plenty of stops at viewing platforms and interpretive plaques along this level trail.

Blue Slough

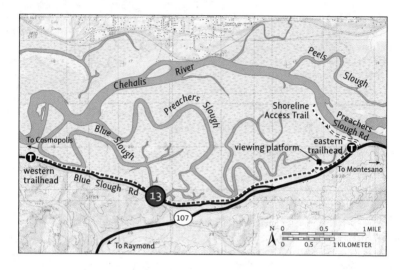

From the eastern trailhead, start by crossing a swampy pool on a firm bridge and then, with all due respect to the late, great Johnny Cash, walk the line. Through a lush understory of vegetation, the trail brushes up against Preachers Slough, named for a young minister who made a wrong turn up this waterway while paddling to congregants. Winter's lack of greenery allows for better viewing and a guaranteed mosquito-free journey. In 0.5 mile, reach a viewing platform that juts out over the lazy waterway. Just a few miles from the Chehalis River's outlet in Grays Harbor, this area is influenced by tides. As the tide comes in, the heavy saltwater sinks, lifting freshwater to the top and forcing it to flood the surrounding bottomlands—hence the name "surge plain."

Next, skirt some homes, cross some side creeks, and pass an active farm. At 1.8 miles, reach a bench at a good slough overlook. The way then continues through rows of alders along a big wetland area teeming with birds—flycatchers, wrens, warblers, and many more. At 3.5 miles, just after passing some big spruces, reach the western trailhead and a good overlook of Blue Slough. Entertain thoughts of kayaking this inviting waterway before hiking back to your car.

EXTENDING YOUR TRIP
From the boat launch near the eastern trailhead, walk the wheelchair-accessible Shoreline Access Trail for a scenic 0.3 mile alongside the Chehalis River.

Grays Harbor

Grays Harbor is Washington's other great coastal estuary. With a surface area of 60,000 acres, it rivals Willapa Bay in both size and ecological importance. But unlike its counterpart to the south, Grays Harbor has been heavily developed. Willapa Bay sports very little human intrusion, has no jetties, and contains thousands of acres of protected shoreline and tideflats—Grays Harbor is a study in contrast.

The eastern reaches of this estuary are highly industrialized. Three cities—Aberdeen, Hoquiam, and Cosmopolis—sprawl where the Chehalis River drains into the estuary. These mill towns were once among the largest providers of forest products in the country. Past and sometimes unsustainable logging practices, coupled with rising globalization that favors cheaper imports, left these once-proud cities economically depressed. A century-plus of intense industrialization has also diminished Grays Harbor's natural communities.

On the estuary's western end, for instance, where it meets the Pacific Ocean, resort development has compromised this great ecosystem. Fortunately for hikers and nature lovers, however, conservationists have been giving this great waterway some much-needed attention. The Grays Harbor Audubon Society has been protecting shoreline along North Bay, near the mouth of the Humptulips River, and the US Fish and Wildlife Service established a 1500-acre national wildlife refuge at Bowerman Basin in 1990.

Grays Harbor is one of the most important staging areas on the Pacific coast for shorebirds. It hosts one of the largest concentrations of western sandpipers, dunlins, and dowitchers south of Alaska. Grays Harbor offers hikers a handful of other great wildlife-observing locales as well.

Hopefully, this region will preserve more areas, providing this important estuary with not only ecological recovery but perhaps also economic recovery in the form of sustainable ecotourism.

14 Westport Light Trail

RATING/ DIFFICULTY	ROUNDTRIP	ELEV GAIN/ HIGH POINT	SEASON
***/1	4.4 miles	Minimal/ 20 feet	Year-round

Map: Online at Westport Lighthouse State Park; **Contact:** Westport Light State Park; **Notes:** Discover Pass required. Wheelchair-accessible. Dogs permitted on-leash; **GPS:** N 46 53.226, W 124 07.323

Walk through dunes alongside an undeveloped beach known among surfers for its great waves. Admire the tallest lighthouse in Washington and an impressive jetty at the mouth of Grays Harbor. And climb to the top of an observation tower to survey what you just walked—and beyond.

GETTING THERE
From Aberdeen, follow State Route 105 west for 18 miles and turn right onto Montesano Avenue (SR 105-Spur). Continue for 2 miles, turning left onto W Ocean Avenue. Follow this road for 0.7 mile (passing the lighthouse) to the parking area and trailhead (elev. 20 ft) at Westport Light State Park. Privy available.

ON THE TRAIL
The Westport lighthouse is not actually in the state park bearing its name. It's an easy 0.2-mile walk by sidewalk to the 107-foot-high lighthouse, built in 1898. After your hike, visit the lighthouse grounds (free) and consider a tour of the lofty structure (check hours and fees at the Westport Maritime Museum).

The lighthouse once sat at the southern entrance of Grays Harbor, but thanks to

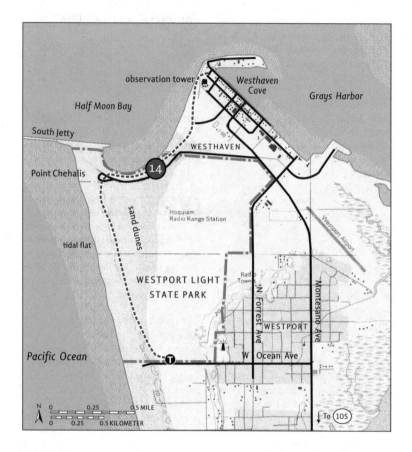

observation tower
Half Moon Bay
Westhaven Cove
Grays Harbor
South Jetty
WESTHAVEN
Point Chehalis
14
sand dunes
Hoquiam Radio Range Station
tidal flat
WESTPORT LIGHT STATE PARK
Radio Tower
N Forrest Ave
WESTPORT
Westport Airport
Montesano Ave
Pacific Ocean
T
W Ocean Ave
N
0   0.25   0.5 MILE
0   0.25   0.5 KILOMETER
To (105)

years of accretion (the opposite of erosion) it now stands a good 0.3 mile away from the shoreline. The massive South Jetty at the harbor's mouth has helped capture shifting sands, creating quite a dune complex near the lighthouse.

The Westport Light Trail (known locally as the Dunes Trail) takes you across the primary dunes (the first line of dunes from the ocean), protected from development within a 626-

acre state park. Follow the concrete path over the rolling dunes, passing interpretive panels, concrete benches, and some viewing platforms along the way. Look out over a wide strand of beach for seabirds, whales, and fishing vessels.

At 1.3 miles, reach Point Chehalis and soon come to privies and a parking lot (alternative approach from Westport). Cross the park access road and continue on trail, now hugging Half Moon Bay, a popular spot for

Westport Light Trail traveling through coastal dunes

stand-up paddlers. The trail then leaves the state park, skirting commercial establishments that line Westport's Westhaven Cove. At 2.2 miles, the trail ends at an observation tower at Westhaven Drive near the marina. Definitely climb the attractive tower, built in 2011, before returning the way you came. You can also walk into town for a cup of chowder and walk the beach back to your start instead of taking the paved trail.

15 Johns River State Wildlife Area

RATING/ DIFFICULTY	ROUNDTRIP	ELEV GAIN/ HIGH POINT	SEASON
*/1	2 miles	Minimal/ 20 feet	Year-round

Map: USGS Hoquiam; **Contact:** Washington State Department of Fish and Wildlife, Region 6 Office, Montesano; **Notes:** Discover Pass required. Partially wheelchair-accessible.

Dogs permitted on-leash. Popular elk- and bird-hunting area; **GPS:** N 46 53.984, W 123 59.739

Walk on a dike along the snaking Johns River into an estuary teeming with birds and elk. The first half of the trail is wheelchair-accessible, offering an easy hike for all.

GETTING THERE

From Aberdeen, follow State Route 105 west for 11.6 miles and, after crossing the Johns River Bridge, turn left onto Johns River Road. In 0.1 mile turn left onto Game Farm Road (signed "Public Fishing"), and in another 0.1 mile turn right into the trailhead parking area (elev. 20 ft). Privy available.

ON THE TRAIL

Developed by the Washington State Department of Fish and Wildlife, this popular trail grants hikers and bird-watchers easy access to the 1500-acre Johns River State

69

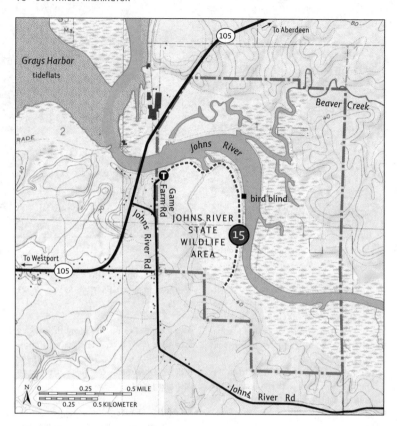

Wildlife Area. The first 0.6 mile is paved and wheelchair-accessible. The pavement also guarantees that the trail won't be muddy during the rainy season, which in Grays Harbor can sometimes be all year.

Hugging this main river of the Grays Harbor basin, the trail traverses an area nearly void of trees. A few lone Sitka spruces and hawthorns punctuate the grasses and reeds of the surrounding estuary. At pavement's end is a bird blind, but quiet hikers shouldn't need it to observe resident birds. Herons, grebes, terns, geese, and sandpipers are usually easily spotted along the way. At the end of the pavement you can also venture right on a grassy dike for a short distance.

The main trail continues straight, now on a grassy surface, reaching the forest's edge at 1 mile. Scan the reclaimed marshland on your right for members of the resident elk herd. If the big beasties themselves aren't present, plenty of evidence of their passing most certainly will be. Return the same way you came.

Level paved section of trail along Johns River

EXTENDING YOUR TRIP

Two miles west on SR 105 (milepost 35) is the Bottle Beach State Park Ruby Egbert Natural Area (Discover Pass required; dogs prohibited). Definitely check out its 0.7-mile wheelchair-accessible trail to three viewing platforms along the Grays Harbor tideflats. In spring, witness thousands of migrating shorebirds.

16 Bowerman Basin

RATING/ DIFFICULTY	ROUNDTRIP	ELEV GAIN/ HIGH POINT	SEASON
***/1	1.9 miles	Minimal/ 20 feet	Year-round

Map: Online at Grays Harbor National Wildlife Refuge; **Contact:** Grays Harbor National Wildlife Refuge; **Notes:** Wheelchair-accessible. Dogs prohibited; **GPS:** N 46 58.438, W 123 55.868

Hike along a boardwalk to views of the expansive mudflats of Grays Harbor's Bowerman Basin. One of the finest places in all of Washington for bird-watching, the basin is inundated with shorebirds from late April until early May. Plan your trip accordingly and witness tens of thousands of migrating western and least sandpipers, dowitchers, black-bellied and semipalmated plovers, and dunlins. Consider visiting during Hoquiam's annual Shorebird Festival in early May.

GETTING THERE
From Hoquiam, follow State Route 109 west for 1.5 miles, turning left onto Paulson Road. Continue for 0.4 mile and turn right onto Airport Way. Follow this road for 0.7 mile to the trailhead (elev. 20 ft), parking at a gate and kiosk (do not drive beyond gate if it's open).

ON THE TRAIL
Start by walking the gated paved airport road west along a row of hangars and a thicket of willows. At 0.4 mile, reach the Sandpiper Trail. This nicely built boardwalk allows easy access to the 1500-acre Grays Harbor National Wildlife Refuge. Established in

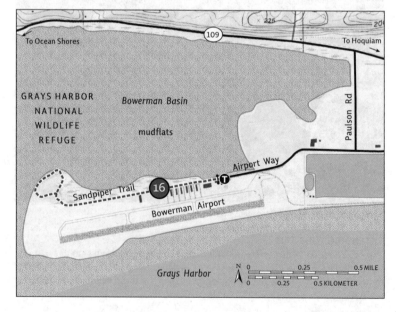

Sandpiper Trail boardwalk loop in Bowerman Basin

1990, the refuge protects Bowerman Basin, one of the most important staging areas on the Pacific coast for migrating shorebirds. The basin also provides excellent habitat for resident birds and a myriad of other wildlife species. Bring your binoculars and take your time.

The trail passes through a tunnel of alders and willows before opening up. Come to several good viewpoints and interpretive displays. At 0.8 mile the trail splits, forming a 0.3-mile loop across Bowerman's extensive tidal and mudflats. Go either direction. Views across the basin and Grays Harbor are excellent. Bird-watching is supreme. If you forgot your scope, there are a couple of fixed ones at the observation decks. Return the way you came.

17 Damon Point

RATING/DIFFICULTY	LOOP	ELEV GAIN/HIGH POINT	SEASON
***/1	4.5 miles	Minimal/10 feet	Year-round

Maps: USGS Point Brown, USGS Westport; **Contact:** Washington State Department of Natural Resources, Aquatic Division; **Notes:** Dogs permitted on-leash on the western 0.5 mile of beach near trailhead. Interior of point closed Mar 1–Sept 15 to protect threatened nesting streaked horned larks and snowy plovers; **GPS:** N 46 56.826, W 124 08.002

Once an island, now a spit, Damon Point keeps growing thanks to sand accretion (the opposite of erosion). Hike around this protruding land mass for sweeping views that include Mount Rainier and the snowy Olympic Mountains. Observe scores of shorebirds (including endangered snowy plovers), harbor seals, and sometimes in winter, snowy owls. Best of all, enjoy over 4 miles of vehicle-free beaches, best hiked at low tide.

GETTING THERE

From Hoquiam, head west for 16 miles on State Route 109, turning left onto SR 115. Continue south for 2.2 miles and turn left at the entrance gate to Ocean Shores onto

Stormy day at Damon Point

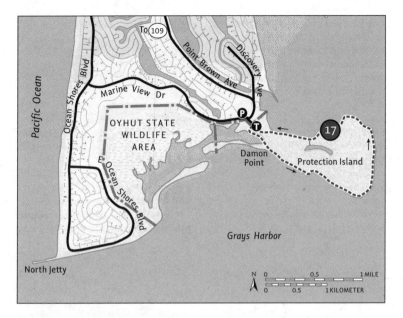

Point Brown Avenue. Follow this road south for 5.1 miles, bearing right onto Discovery Avenue. In 0.2 mile, come to the trailhead (elev. 10 ft) on your left and parking on your right. Privy available.

ON THE TRAIL

Some parks are designed by humans, but nature seems to have had a hand in Damon Point's fate. Named for A. O. Damon, who settled here in 1861, the point has grown to connect with Protection Island, creating a spit over 1.5 miles long and 0.5 mile wide. Washington State Parks then built a road up the middle of the spit. Then nature stepped in, sending a storm to sever the road, providing an outlet for a newly formed pond. In 2007 another storm removed the rest of the road. Will an island reemerge? Maybe—the spit does breach from time to time.

Trailhead access is through an Ocean Shores park, and the spit is managed by the Washington State Department of Natural Resources (DNR) to protect aquatic resources. Please respect all closures to help protect nesting threatened birds.

From the trailhead, follow the short access trail and immediately come to a crashing beach. Head left to begin your 4.5-mile loop around the 61-acre spit.

Enjoy walking a wonderfully wide beach framed with high rolling dunes. Bald eagles frequently perch on big beached logs that line this stretch of beach. Above the dunes is the former state park picnic area, being reclaimed by vegetation, both endemic and invasive. DNR has been aggressively removing the Scotch broom thickets. Walk to the tip of the former Protection Island, enjoying good views of Westport across the way. Then turn left and walk quieter bayside beaches, occasionally hitting soft patches of sand and mudflats. Eventually, beach yields to a small bluff hosting a campground. Turn left before reaching it, hiking a short distance across the spit to return to your starting point.

EXTENDING YOUR TRIP
Walk the sandy beaches of the adjacent 683-acre Oyhut State Wildlife Area to the right (west) of the Damon Point trailhead. Watch for seals offshore and plenty of deer on land. Note snowy plover closures and be aware that the area is open to seasonal hunting.

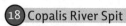

18 Copalis River Spit

RATING/ DIFFICULTY	ROUNDTRIP	ELEV GAIN/ HIGH POINT	SEASON
**/1	4 miles	Minimal/ 25 feet	Year-round

Maps: USGS Copalis Beach, USGS Moclips; **Contact:** Griffiths-Priday State Park; **Notes:** Discover Pass required. Dogs permitted on-leash; **GPS:** N 47 06.882, W 124 10.684

Hike across dunes along a shifting creek to a quiet spit teeming with birdlife. Located just a few miles from bustling Ocean Shores, Griffiths-Priday

Connor Creek is forming a new spit

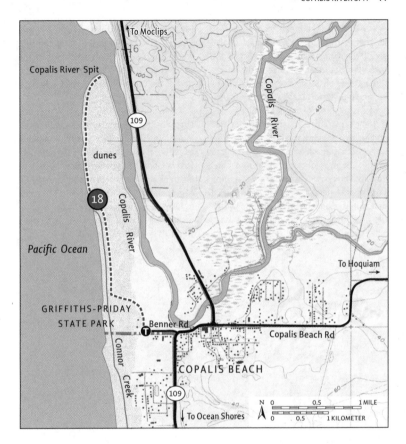

State Park's sandy beach is vehicle-free and often deserted.

GETTING THERE

From Hoquiam, head west on State Route 109 for 20.8 miles to the community of Copalis Beach. At the Green Lantern Tavern, turn left onto Benner Road, proceeding 0.2 mile to the park entrance and trailhead (elev. 20 ft). Water and restrooms available.

ON THE TRAIL

One of the quietest stretches of beach south of the Quinault Indian Reservation, the Copalis River Spit makes for a good hike any time of year. Protected within the 364-acre Griffiths-Priday State Park, this little stretch of beach is as wild as any in the state.

It used to be a 0.25-mile hike to the beach, but in the late 1990s Connor Creek changed course, extending its route to the sea by nearly 0.5 mile. The creek keeps extending its course, creating an increasingly smaller spit. It's now a 0.8-mile hike to get to the surf. But it's a great entrance to the beach, through one of the largest dune complexes in the state. Unfortunately, invasive Scotch broom is colonizing many of the dunes.

Near the picnic shelter, locate the trail and follow the wide path through the dunes. Be sure to stay on the trail so as not to disturb the myriad of birds that nest here. Perhaps someday snowy plovers will return.

Come to a point above Connor Creek and bend right. Continue northward to where the creek turns to empty into the Pacific, where you, too, are free to reach the sea.

Now on a wide, hard-packed sandy beach, hike 1.2 miles north to the tip of the spit, where the Copalis River empties into the ocean. Copalis Rock, a large sea stack and part of the Copalis National Wildlife Refuge, is visible in the distance.

When the tide is out, the spit is often littered with sand dollars, half sand dollars, and quarter sand dollars. The spit is reputed to harbor a few silver dollars too, left over from a long-ago shipwreck. Scan overhanging trees along the north bank of the river for eagles and ospreys. At low tide it's possible to hike along the ocean side of the river for a short ways. Deep mud will let you know when it's time to turn around.

Opposite: A hiker admires a row of giant yellow cedars along the Upper South Fork Skokomish River Trail.

olympic peninsula: south

Wynoochee River Valley

Before World War II the Wynoochee River valley was mainly a wilderness of unbroken old-growth forests. One of the largest watersheds (218 square miles) on the southern flank of the Olympic Peninsula, the Wynoochee has been intensively logged since the 1940s. Miles of trails led through some of its lonely smaller valleys and to some of its scenic peaks. But as the big trees succumbed to chainsaws, most of the trail system was uprooted as well, leaving hikers little reason to visit this once-great valley.

Still, while most of the old trails were destroyed, an excellent new one was built when the river was dammed for flood control. And now that logging in Olympic National Forest has been greatly reduced, the Wynoochee is slowly healing. Hikers can still follow fragments of some of the great trails. Perhaps part of this vast area's recovery will include reopening former trails, reintroducing hikers to the region and instilling a new sense of stewardship for this long-neglected part of our natural heritage.

19 Wynoochee Lake

RATING/ DIFFICULTY	LOOP	ELEV GAIN/ HIGH POINT	SEASON
***/3	13.2 miles	1500 feet/ 1075 feet	Late July–Oct

Map: Green Trails Grisdale No. 198; **Contact:** Olympic National Forest, Hood Canal Ranger District, Quilcene; **Notes:** Trail open to mountain bikes. Loop requires ford of Wynoochee River, only safe during low flows, typically in late summer. Alternative loop with bridge crossing adds 4.1 miles; **GPS:** N 47 23.044, W 123 36.342

Hike an up-and-down route around the forested shores of man-made Wynoochee Lake. From quiet coves, look out across clear waters to craggy peaks and scrappy hills. Traverse groves of old-growth forest harboring huge Douglas-firs. Look for deer, bears, and elk, the latter abundant in this valley. This loop is long, but multiple access points off Forest Road 2270 allow for shorter, kid-friendly, and winter-hiking options.

GETTING THERE

From Montesano, travel north on the Wynoochee Valley Road, which becomes Forest Road 22 at 17 miles. Continue on this paved road another 16.2 miles, turning left at a major intersection. Still on FR 22, proceed for 0.3 mile and turn right onto Wynoochee Dam Road (FR 2294). Continue 0.8 mile to the trailhead (elev. 775 ft) near a bridge. (An alternative start is at the dam day-use area 0.4 mile farther.)

ON THE TRAIL

Start by walking west on a sidewalk across the bridge that spans a gorge on the Wynoochee River below the dam. The Army Corps of Engineers dammed the river in 1972 for flood control, and Tacoma Power manages current lake levels. The lake almost appears natural, lined with tall timber and surrounded by rugged hills. The Forest Service developed the loop trail shortly after the lake's creation.

Emerge on the west side of the dam and follow a paved path, skirting the large day-use area with its picnic tables and swimming areas (privies also available). Pass some

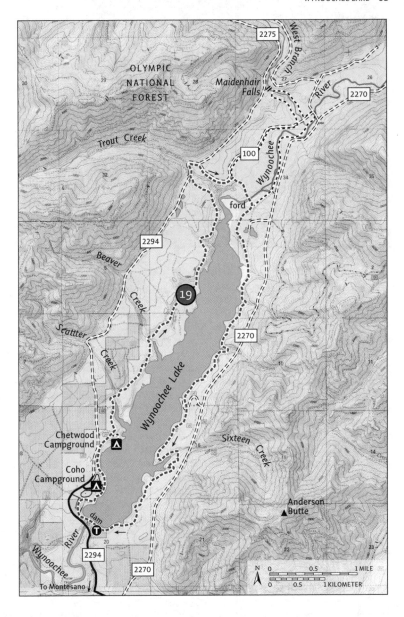

Wynoochee River near trail ford

yurts and cross the boat ramp access road. Then skirt the lovely Coho Campground, coming to the Working Forest Nature Trail at 0.9 mile. This 0.5-mile path veers to the left and rejoins the lake loop in 0.2 mile.

Continue right on the lakeshore trail through thick timber on a level terrace. At 1.2 miles, bear left at a junction with a side path that heads to the right, to the Chetwoot Campground, accessible only by foot and watercraft.

Soon afterward, drop into the first of many ravines to cross a creek, and then climb back out. Get used to this pattern—it'll repeat a dozen times, contributing to a cumulative elevation gain well over 1500 feet. At times the trail follows old logging roads. Undulate between thick second growth and mature groves of towering hemlocks and firs. Oxalis carpets the forest floor.

Traverse alder-lined Beaver Flat, a marshy and gravelly bottomland. Make several bridged creek crossings and pass

some giant cedars and firs, including a big cedar with a hemlock growing on it. Over 140 inches of rain fall on the Wynoochee annually, making it no wonder why so many giants grace this valley.

Reach the upper end of the lake, hiking close to river level. The way then climbs a high bluff above Trout Creek, with excellent views of the lake below and of the upper Wynoochee River valley to the north. Mount Church and Capitol Peak stand out in the east.

At 5.8 miles, come to FR 2294 (elev. 1050 ft). Turn right and walk the road, crossing crashing Trout Creek. Soon afterward bear right onto FR 2275, and soon after that bear right again to continue on quiet FR Spur 100 through old-growth forest. At 6.6 miles, come to a junction. The nonfording option continues left on the road (see Extending Your Trip). To ford the river, go right, once again on trail. Descend and reach the Wynoochee River (elev. 800 ft) at 7.1 miles. Scout the wide gravel bar for a safe place to ford the river. Look for a shallow spot to make the crossing. If it can't be done safely, either head back to the trailhead or take the alternative loop, adding 4.1 miles to your already long hike.

Once across, bear right at a junction and head south along the generally more attractive eastern shore through large pockets of old growth, across steep ravines of crashing creeks, and by good lake-viewing gaps in the forest. Maintenance has been sporadic here, so expect to encounter some brushy sections and big blowdowns.

The way goes up and down, darting into side ravines. At 10.4 miles, come to a spur road that leads to the shore. Turn left here, picking up the trail again in 0.2 mile. Climb to a bench high above the lake. Once again on good trail, drop to a bridged crossing of Sixteen Creek—your last ravine dip. Steeply climb back up to the bench, coming to the dam at 13 miles. Enjoy a good lake view before following a paved path 0.2 mile back to your start.

EXTENDING YOUR TRIP

For the long loop, at the ford trail junction continue left on the FR Spur 100, coming to its end at the West Branch Wynoochee River in 1.2 miles. Turn left on trail and follow alongside the river in a nice grove of old growth, eventually climbing above the river. At 1.8 miles, cross a bridge over a deep chasm where Maidenhair Falls plunges into a punch bowl. Then follow the trail right, downriver, passing spurs to an old road and reaching FR 2270 (an alternative start to the falls) at 2.4 miles. Walk right on the road and cross the Wynoochee River on a bridge, soon afterward picking up trail once again on your right. Now paralleling FR 2270, walk a brushy trail along the river, passing

unofficial roadside campsites, before reaching the ford junction on the east side of the river at 4.1 miles.

20 Wynoochee Pass and Lake Sundown

RATING/ DIFFICULTY	ROUNDTRIP	ELEV GAIN/ HIGH POINT	SEASON
****/4	11.8 miles	3150 feet/ 3820 feet	Mid-July– Oct

Maps: Green Trails Mt Christie No. 166, Custom Correct Enchanted Valley–Skokomish; **Contact:** Olympic National Forest, Hood Canal Ranger District, Quilcene; Olympic National Park, Wilderness Information Center; **Notes:** Dogs prohibited beyond park boundary; **GPS:** N 47 30.740, W 123 32.709

Follow a lightly used trail over a rugged pass and descend into the Graves Creek valley. It's then a steep climb to heather meadows, berry patches, and a beautiful sparkling lake tucked in an emerald basin at the edge of rugged Six Ridge.

GETTING THERE

From Montesano, travel north on the Wynoochee Valley Road, which becomes Forest Road 22 at 17 miles. Continue on this paved road another 16.2 miles to a major intersection. Proceed straight on graveled FR 2270, bearing right at 5.7 miles, bearing left at 9.4 miles, and reaching a junction at 11.5 miles. Turn right on rough FR Spur 400 and follow it for 1.3 miles to its end at the trailhead (elev. 2500 ft).

ON THE TRAIL

Hike east on the old spur, soon coming to a huge slide. As you walk across the slide, contemplate why clear-cut logging was ever permitted on such a high, steep slope—which consequently caused this ecological blemish on the mountainside. The Wynoochee Valley was heavily logged in the past; this trail once traveled for miles through some of the most magnificent ancient forests in the Olympics.

At 0.4 mile, at a switchback, come to the preslide trailhead. Head right, now on real trail, into old-growth forest. At 0.7 mile, enter Olympic National Park. At about 1.3 miles, cross the first of several creeks rushing down rocky little gullies. When rainfall is heavy, these crossings can be somewhat tricky.

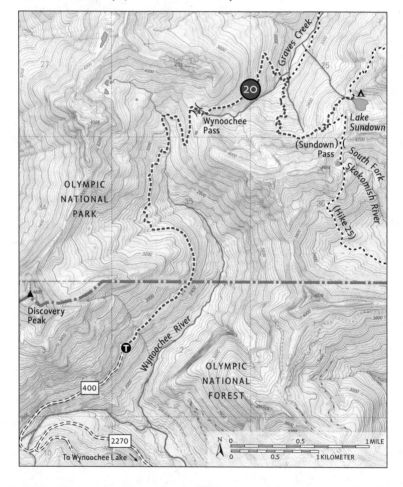

Remote and lightly visited Lake Sundown

The trail traverses steep slopes shrouded in big trees high above the Wynoochee River. At about 2.2 miles, cross the Wynoochee (elev. 3200 ft)—a crashing creek here, sporting a pair of showy waterfalls. The way now gets steeper and more rugged; the trees—giant yellow cedars and pistol-butted hemlocks—more impressive.

At 2.8 miles, reach 3600-foot Wynoochee Pass and a couple of grassy-shored shallow ponds surrounded by subalpine forest. Pass a shortcut (not recommended) to Lake Sundown and steeply descend through gorgeous old-growth forest. At 4.2 miles, just after crossing the upper reaches of rocky Graves Creek (which may be flowing underground), come to a junction (elev. 2700 ft). The trail left leads 6 miles to the East Fork Quinault River (Hike 121) and includes a potentially difficult ford of Success Creek.

You want to go right and immediately start climbing. Traversing parkland meadows and subalpine forest granting limited views, the trail works its way out of a steep basin. At 5.5 miles, shortly after crossing the cascading headwaters of Graves Creek, reach a junction (elev. 3775 ft). The lightly used trail right heads to the South Fork Skokomish River valley (Hike 25). Continue straight through clusters of mountain hemlock, meadows, and huckleberry patches. Cross a small creek and climb a little. Then descend a little, ascend a little before reaching the hidden, semi-open basin that cradles peaceful Lake Sundown (elev. 3810 ft) at 5.9 miles.

There are a couple of good campsites by the lake's outlet, and a way path along the lake's northern shore leads to flowering meadows. With its outlet positioned west at the edge of the ridge, the lake is indeed a good place for sunsets. It's also a great place for afternoon naps.

LOGGING THE ANNALS OF HISTORY

About 1 mile south of Wynoochee Lake, a large sign on the side of Forest Road 22 marks where Camp Grisdale once stood. Developed in 1946 by the Simpson Timber Company, Grisdale was unlike other logging camps—it was designed to stay in one place. Over fifty fully serviced homes, a school, bowling alley, and baseball field comprised the complex. In 1986, after forty years of operation, Simpson closed Grisdale. It was the last residential logging camp in the continental United States, and its closure was the end of an era in Pacific Northwest history.

Nothing remains of Grisdale. Douglas-firs nearly thirty years old occupy the site. You can see a scale replica of the camp on display at the Mason County Historical Museum in Shelton. While it's easy to romanticize this colorful part of Northwest history, the age when timber was king in Washington certainly left its mark on the landscape, and in particular on the southern flank of the Olympics.

These forests need rejuvenation, and so do the economies of the communities that once relied on the timber from these hills. Perhaps it's time to enter a new era, one of sustainable timber harvesting based on ecologically sound principles and friendly to recreation. Perhaps, too, new camps can be established in these parts, employing men and women to help rehabilitate the surrounding scarred forests and mountains and maybe even revive a trail or two.

South Fork Skokomish River Valley

Like the Wynoochee Valley, this valley on the southern flank of the Olympics has been heavily cut over. In 1946, with little regard to recreation and preservation, the Forest Service signed an exclusive agreement with the Simpson Timber Company, granting it a ninety-nine-year lease to log and manage a huge portion of public land (our land)—in essence, turning the area into a private tree farm.

It's easy to lament the loss of thousands of acres of primeval forest, and hundreds of miles of trails, but fortunately a few fragments of trail and uncut tracts survive. Now, with a substantially lower timber cut and new environmental laws that favor

protecting roadless areas, there's hope for preserving what little wildlands remain in the South Fork Skokomish River drainage. The area offers a lot of potential for expanded recreation too—from restoring abandoned trails to converting decommissioned logging roads into new trails. And the upper reaches of this valley contain some of the finest old growth remaining in Olympic National Forest. Protecting it within an expanded Wonder Mountain Wilderness would ensure that these trees remain a part of our natural heritage.

21 Spider Lake

RATING/ DIFFICULTY	LOOP	ELEV GAIN/ HIGH POINT	SEASON
**/1	2 miles	200 feet/ 1400 feet	Year-round

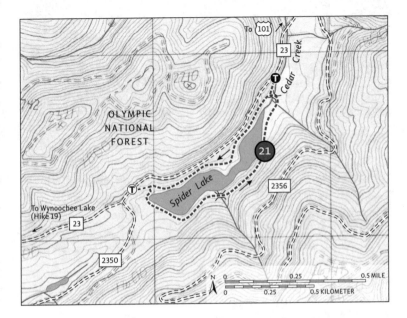

Map: Green Trails Mt Tebo No. 199; **Contact:** Olympic National Forest, Hood Canal Ranger District, Quilcene; **GPS:** N 47 24.881, W 123 25.715

Saunter around a small lake snugly tucked within a narrow valley on the Skokomish–Satsop River divide. Surrounded by hillsides of regenerating forests, Spider Lake's tranquil shores are graced with exceptional groves of ancient giants. Pleasant any time of year, this hike glows pearly white in early summer when blossoming dwarf dogwood and queen's cup blanket the forest floor.

GETTING THERE

From Shelton, travel north on US Highway 101 for 7 miles, turning left (west) at milepost 340 onto the Skokomish Valley Road (signed "Skokomish Recreation Area"). Follow it for 5.6 miles, bearing right at a V intersection onto Forest Road 23. Continue for 9.3 miles (pavement ends at 1 mile and resumes again at 2.5 miles), and bear left at a Y junction with FR 2353. Continuing on FR 23 (pavement ends), follow this good gravel road for 7 miles to the trailhead (elev. 1260 ft), on the left. Parking is on the right.

ON THE TRAIL

In the mid-1990s, trail builders resurrected a portion of an old trail that once traveled up the Cedar Creek valley and constructed brand-new tread to form a 2-mile loop around little Spider Lake. Trail-building aficionados may find the loop's three bridges noteworthy for their durability and aesthetics. Bird-watchers will enjoy the wildlife-rich lake.

Placid Spider Lake

Starting from Trail No. 879's unassuming trailhead, immediately enter cool old-growth forest. In 0.1 mile, come to a junction. Turn right (although either direction will work), crossing the outlet stream. Soon reach Spider's western shoreline. Pass big trees, good fishing spots, and viewpoints of the placid lake. Gaze up at the surrounding ridges. The intensively logged hillsides offer quite a contrast to the virgin groves that circle the lake.

At 1 mile, cross a small creek and come to a junction. The trail right steeply climbs a short distance to an alternative trailhead. Continue left instead, ambling above the green waters of the lake and beneath the emerald canopy of ancient behemoths. Along the eastern shoreline, the trail climbs a bit across a steep slope. Cross an impressive high log bridge, and soon afterward descend back to lake level, passing a sitting bench along the way. Cross an inlet stream in a marshy area and return to the first junction at 1.9 miles. Head right 0.1 mile to return to your start.

22 Pine Lake

RATING/ DIFFICULTY	ROUNDTRIP	ELEV GAIN/ HIGH POINT	SEASON
***/2	5.8 miles	700 feet/ 1830 feet	Year-round

Map: Green Trails Mt Tebo No. 199; **Contact:** Olympic National Forest, Hood Canal Ranger District, Quilcene; **Notes:** FR 2361 closed Oct 1–Apr 30 to protect wildlife; **GPS:** N 47 26.270, W 123 25.678

This hike to a pleasant little lake will leave you pleasantly surprised. Thank the Forest Service for the aesthetically pleasing road-to-trail conversion. And the lake? It's a beauty surrounded by ancient forest. But not pines—you won't find one at this misnamed lake.

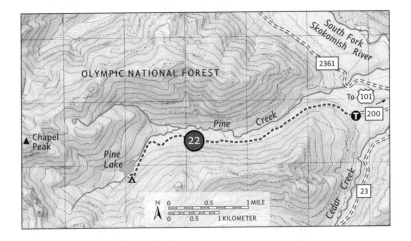

GETTING THERE

From Shelton, travel north on US Highway 101 for 7 miles, turning left (west) at milepost 340 onto the Skokomish Valley Road (signed "Skokomish Recreation Area"). Follow it for 5.6 miles, bearing right at a V intersection onto Forest Road 23. Continue for 9.3 miles (pavement ends at 1 mile and resumes again at 2.5 miles), and bear left at a Y junction with FR 2353. Continuing on FR 23 (pavement ends), follow this good gravel road for 4.3 miles and bear right onto FR 2361. Continue for 1.2 miles, turning left onto unsigned FR Spur 200. Follow it 0.7 mile to its end and the trailhead (elev. 1200 ft).

ON THE TRAIL

Many road-to-trail conversions simply involve closing the road and trenching a few culverts, making for an unappealing hike. Not this one. The well-designed trail curves along the old roadbed, and the roadbed has been restored to original contours in places. Someday soon, it will be tough to see that this trail was once a logging road.

Old growth forest reflecting in Pine Lake

From the trailhead, start through second-growth forest, traversing slopes high above Pine Creek. At about 1.3 miles, encounter a patch of invasive Scotch broom, a plant that crowds out native vegetation in disturbed areas (like cuts and roadbeds). The Forest Service and Washington Conservation Corps crews have done a good job at Pine Lake restoring native vegetation. Hopefully, they can soon attack the broom before it sweeps across the valley.

At around 2 miles, the way cuts through cool old growth. Then the fairly gentle grade ratchets up a little. At 2.8 miles, leave the old roadbed to the right and enter a grove of big trees. Then pass some campsites and descend to Pine Lake. Be careful not to trample restored vegetation along the shoreline of this pretty lake, which reflects the surrounding hillsides and Chapel Peak. Stay for a while and enjoy the avian residents.

23 Church Creek and Satsop Lakes

RATING/ DIFFICULTY	ROUNDTRIP	ELEV GAIN/ HIGH POINT	SEASON
***/3	6.4 miles	2300 feet/ 3200 feet	June–Sept

Maps: Green Trails Grisdale No. 198 and Mt Tebo No. 199; **Contact:** Olympic National Forest, Hood Canal Ranger District, Quilcene; **Notes:** FR 2361 closed Oct 1–Apr 30 to protect wildlife. FR Spur 600 is rough, requires high-clearance vehicle; **GPS:** N 47 26.928, W 123 29.437

Hike a forgotten but restored trail through some of the biggest trees this side of the Hoh River. Church Creek epitomizes why the southern flank of the Olympics was cherished (and nearly completely cut over) by the big timber companies. Towering Douglas-firs reach dizzying heights, and wide-girth cedars and hemlocks hundreds of years old line the trail from end to end. The Satsop Lakes make a satisfying destination—peaceful and scenic—but the forest is the star of this hike.

GETTING THERE
From Shelton, travel north on US Highway 101 for 7 miles, turning left (west) at milepost 340 onto the Skokomish Valley Road (signed "Skokomish Recreation Area"). Follow it for 5.6 miles, bearing right at a V intersection onto Forest Road 23. Continue for 9.3 miles (pavement ends at 1 mile and resumes again at 2.5 miles), and bear left at a Y junction with FR 2353. Continuing on FR 23 (pavement ends), follow this good gravel road for 4.3 miles and bear right onto FR 2361. Proceed for 3.4 miles, turning left onto FR Spur 600. Follow this rough road 2.2 miles to its end and the trailhead (elev. 1850 ft).

ON THE TRAIL
Church Creek Trail No. 871 once extended from the South Fork Skokomish River all the way to the Wynoochee River, but logging has whittled it to a fraction of its former length. By the late 1990s, the Forest Service had abandoned it. But the trail was resurrected and restored in 2005 thanks to the Olympia Mountaineers. From its unimposing trailhead, immediately enter a cathedral forest of buttressed cedars and spires of fir. Cascading Church Creek, audible but not visible, adds a soothing aria to this sanctuary. Named not for a house of worship, but in honor of Frederic Church of the 1890 O'Neil Expedition, the alternate meaning is nevertheless apropos for this truly sacred place.

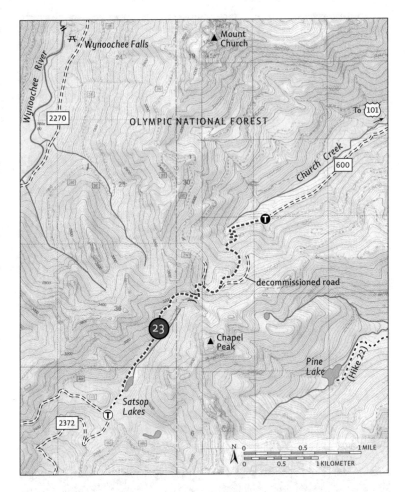

As you walk beneath a lofty canopy supported by gigantic beams, your attention will be diverted upward for most of this hike. Good thing, too, for these old-growth giants will take your mind off of the stiff climb when a series of switchbacks kicks into gear. The trail comes close to Church Creek on several occasions, but the plummeting waterway remains hidden in a deep ravine.

The forest understory soon unfolds into a boundless huckleberry patch—visit in August to reap the bounty. In early summer, fawn lilies, calypso orchids, and marsh marigolds brighten this emerald world. Hop

Upper Satsop Lake

over a handful of small creeks and after 1.3 miles, reach a decommissioned road (elev. 2850 ft). This entire basin was once slated for the mills. Today it's getting close to being permanently protected (see the "Untrammeled Olympics" sidebar on page 118).

Turn right for 0.1 mile, once again picking up the trail. Through a more open forest that grants views to Mount Church, continue climbing, reaching the 3200-foot divide between the South Fork Skokomish and Satsop rivers at 2 miles. A huge double-pistol-butted hemlock stands sentry.

Next, steeply descend through a forest of silver firs. Pass a lovely cascade as it fans into a steep ravine, and again encounter giant cedars and Douglas-firs as the trail levels out. At 3.2 miles, and after losing over 900 feet of elevation, emerge in a grassy opening housing the upper Satsop Lake (elev. 2250 ft). A gravel outwash area makes for a good lunch spot. Keep your eyes on the lake for surfacing newts—the lake is home to thousands of them. Trout too. Roam around the lake and notice no outlet. Water seeps to the Satsop River via a cavernous basalt basin. Three of the other four Satsop lakes are located off of FR 2372, and another lies in the forest south of you. Save some energy for the climb back.

EXTENDING YOUR TRIP

The trail continues another 0.5 mile under more giant trees, ending at FR 2372, an alternative trailhead from the west.

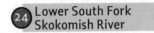

24 Lower South Fork Skokomish River

RATING/ DIFFICULTY	ROUNDTRIP	ELEV GAIN/ HIGH POINT	SEASON
***/3	10.2 miles	950 feet/ 900 feet	Year-round

Maps: Green Trails Mt Tebo No. 199, Custom Correct Mount Skokomish–Lake Cushman; **Contact:** Olympic National Forest, Hood Canal Ranger District, Quilcene; **Notes:** NW

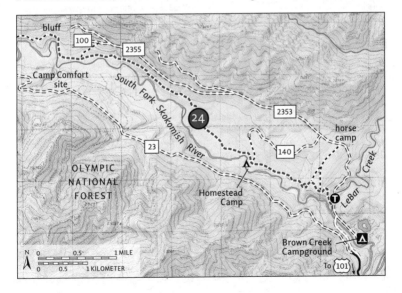

South Fork Skokomish River from high bluff

Forest Pass or Interagency Pass required. Open to stock and mountain bikes; **GPS:** N 47 25.122, W 123 19.756

🚶‍♂️🦴🌲 *Big trees, a big river, and a big chance—especially during the wet winter months—of seeing some big elk are what you can expect on this well-maintained trail. Follow alongside the free-flowing South Fork Skokomish through groves of big maples and firs, being constantly soothed by the river's churning and rippling.*

GETTING THERE

From Shelton, travel north on US Highway 101 for 7 miles, turning left (west) at milepost 340 onto the Skokomish Valley Road (signed "Skokomish Recreation Area"). Follow it for 5.6 miles, bearing right at a V intersection onto Forest Road 23. Continue for 9.3 miles (pavement ends at 1 mile and resumes again at 2.5 miles), bear right at a Y junction with FR 2353. In 0.6 mile, come

to a junction upon crossing the South Fork Skokomish River. Turn left, continuing on FR 2353 and reaching the trailhead (elev. 575 ft) in 0.2 mile. Privy available.

ON THE TRAIL

South Fork Skokomish River Trail No. 873 immediately gets down to business, making a steep little climb of about 325 feet. Rounding a high bluff above the roaring river below, the trail enters a magnificent old-growth grove of Douglas-firs, some over five hundred years old. In 0.4 mile, as you're nearing the crest of the bluff, a spur trail heads right to the LeBar Creek Horse Camp. In another 0.1 mile, another path leads right. Stay left to a series of short, steep switchbacks, dropping back to the valley floor. After hopping across a cascading side creek, traverse a beautiful glade of mossy maples and alders.

Soon come to more old fir giants, as well as a few stumps of cedar giants that were sent to the mills many years ago. At

1.5 miles, reach a bluff with a great river view—a good destination for a shorter hike. Continue upriver, crossing a side creek in a big-timbered ravine. After walking across a boardwalk (no more mud thanks to the Washington Trails Association), come to a junction with a trail leading to FR Spur 140. Almost immediately afterward, at 2.3 miles, reach Homestead Camp, once the site of an old ranger guardhouse. A half mile farther you may get your feet wet crossing a side creek in a large outwash. The next creek crossing however, comes with a nice bridge.

Venturing slightly up and away from the river, you'll pass some old slides before dropping back again toward the roaring waterway and more old growth. Encounter several more creek crossings—most nicely bridged—and a nice cascade, and then at 4.5 miles come to a junction. The trail right leads to FR Spur 2355-100. The short spur left leads to the former site of Camp Comfort (elev. 690 ft), washed away from flooding in 2007. Continue straight, soon coming to a nice river view.

At 5.1 miles, reach an incredible overlook (elev. 790 ft) of the river on a bluff high above a big bend, where the river has taken away bluff and trail in the past. Be careful admiring the view, and then start your return journey back to the trailhead.

EXTENDING YOUR TRIP

Beyond the bluff, the trail is lightly traveled and a little brushy in spots. On an up-and-down course, the trail reaches a ford of the South Fork Skok (safe only in low flows) at 8.6 miles. The way then comes to the Church Creek shelter and trail. From here, tread improves and the trail continues upriver, passing inviting Laney Camp and the spur to the Camp Harps Shelter and reaching its upper trailhead (elev. 1100 ft) on FR 2361 at 10.6 miles. Arrange for a pickup and do the entire trail one-way. At Brown Creek Campground near the original trailhead, check out the very nice 0.8-mile family-friendly nature trail around wildlife-rich Brown Creek Pond.

25 Upper South Fork Skokomish River

RATING/ DIFFICULTY	ROUNDTRIP	ELEV GAIN/ HIGH POINT	SEASON
****/5	16.4 miles	3700 feet/ 4125 feet	July–Sept

Maps: Green Trails Mt Tebo No. 199, Mt Christie No. 166, and Mt Steel No. 167, Custom Correct Enchanted Valley–Skokomish; **Contact:** Olympic National Forest, Hood Canal Ranger District, Quilcene; Olympic National Park, Wilderness Information Center; **Notes:** Dogs prohibited beyond park boundary. FR 2361 closed Oct 1–Apr 30 to protect wildlife. Hike requires two fords, only safe during low flows, typically in late summer; **GPS:** N 47 28.765, W 123 27.125

Venture on a rarely traveled trail up a wild valley to lonely meadows and subalpine pools set in a bowl at the headwaters of the South Fork Skokomish River. Then steeply climb a pass and descend through parkland meadows and berry patches to a pretty little subalpine lake. The trees are huge along the way—among the biggest and oldest on the peninsula.

GETTING THERE

From Shelton, travel north on US Highway 101 for 7 miles, turning left (west) at milepost 340 onto the Skokomish Valley Road (signed "Skokomish Recreation Area"). Follow it for

Meadows along the Upper South Fork Skokomish River Trail

5.6 miles, bearing right at a V intersection onto Forest Road 23. Continue for 9.3 miles (pavement ends at 1 mile and resumes again at 2.5 miles), and bear left at a Y junction with FR 2353. Continuing on FR 23 (pavement ends), follow this good gravel road for 4.3 miles and bear right onto FR 2361. Proceed for 5.1 miles to the road's end and trailhead (elev. 1100 ft).

ON THE TRAIL

From the large parking area, the Upper South Fork Skokomish River Trail heads north and the Lower South Fork Trail takes off south (see Hike 24). Head north, following an old roadbed 0.6 mile to the still-signed old trailhead. Then continue on bona fide trail, soon emerging on a narrow shelf—the river thunders but it's nowhere

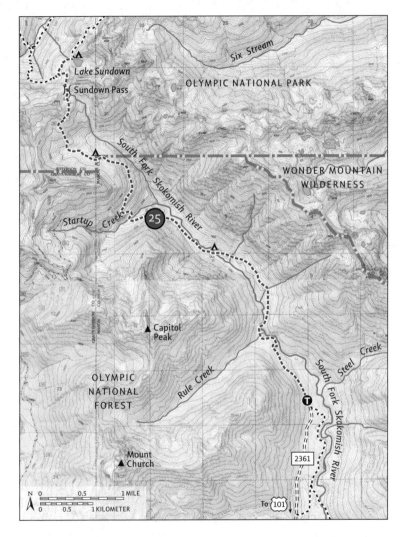

in view. Carefully creep to the edge of the trail and peer straight down. Directly below you, the South Fork Skok careens through a tight chasm, its booming waters occasion-ally interrupted by the high-pitched call of a rapids-loving dipper.

At 1.2 miles, cross Rule Creek on a big log bridge. Shortly afterward, come to your first crossing of the South Fork Skok (elev. 1400 ft). Gone is the big bridge that once spanned it, but a large fallen cedar can be used (with caution) to cross. The trail then climbs 300 feet above the tumultuous waterway, weaving through a procession of old-growth giants that'll leave your neck sore from constantly cocking it upward. This area was left out of the 1984 Washington Wilderness Act due to pressure from timber interests, and the Wild Olympics campaign is hoping to correct this environmental injustice (see the "Untrammeled Olympics" sidebar on page 118).

Cross numerous side streams (plan on wet feet in early season) before coming to camps and the second crossing (elev. 1600 ft) of the South Fork Skok at 2.6 miles. In late summer the ford is usually a mere rock hop. In early season and rainy periods it can be tough, requiring extreme caution. Once across, continue up the valley through mossy glens and tranquil flats alongside the riverbed, but not always along the river, as sections of it often flow underground late in the season.

The trail eventually pulls away from the river and begins climbing. The tread gets rockier and brushier. At 4.4 miles, come to Startup Creek (elev. 2000 ft), which can be tricky to cross when it's flowing well. The way then begins to climb in earnest, making a long, sweeping switchback before getting down to business. At 5.3 miles, reach the national park boundary (dogs prohibited beyond). Soon afterward, come to a camp at the first of a series of pretty meadows where tread is absent. Angle to the northwest and you shouldn't have trouble finding your way. Look for elk.

Once you're back in the forest, good tread returns. The way crosses a small creek and then steeply climbs to a small open basin graced with wildflowers and sparkling tarns, the headwaters of the South Fork Skok. The way then reenters forest and steeply climbs once more to reach forested Sundown Pass (elev. 4125 ft) at 7.4 miles.

Next, descend, traversing meadows that offer good views of Wynoochee Pass and the Graves Creek drainage. Mount Olympus hovers in the distance. At 7.8 miles, come to a junction (elev. 3775 ft). Left leads to Wynoochee Pass (Hike 20) and the East Fork Quinault River (Hike 121). Go right, through a pretty basin, reaching Lake Sundown (elev. 3810 ft) at 8.2 miles. Good swimming. Good resting. Good camping (park permit required). Good workout. Return to the trailhead when you're recharged.

olympic peninsula: east

North Fork Skokomish River Valley

Like its southern counterpart, the North Fork Skokomish River has seen its share of human meddling—namely, intensive logging and a hydro dam. But the upper watershed, protected within Olympic National Park, is pure wilderness. Owing to the presence of Lake Cushman and close proximity to Olympia, Shelton, and Bremerton, this valley sees a fair amount of recreational use. Trails to the Staircase Rapids and Mount Ellinor can get downright busy. But there are plenty of options for solitude seekers, such as Dry Creek and Copper Creek.

The North Fork Skokomish offers diverse hiking options. Choose from challenging peak bagging to lazy river jaunts. Head to quiet backcountry lakes or along crashing, cascading creeks. Hike trails trodden by prospectors and explorers, elk and cougars. While parts of this valley have succumbed to modern development, most of it remains as wild as when Lieutenant Joseph P. O'Neil led one of the first exploratory missions across this region in 1890.

26 Big Creek

RATING/ DIFFICULTY	LOOP	ELEV GAIN/ HIGH POINT	SEASON
**/2	4.3 miles	850 feet/ 1850 feet	Year-round

Maps: Green Trails Olympic Mountains East No. 168S, Custom Correct Mount Skokomish–Lake Cushman; **Contact:** Olympic National

Bridge over Skinwood Creek

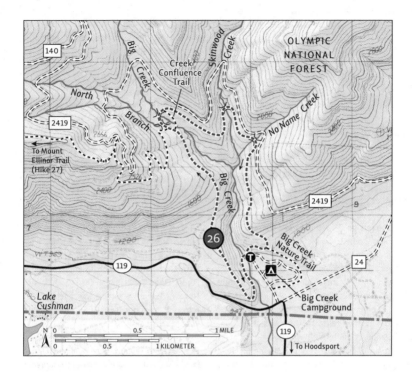

Forest, Hood Canal Ranger District, Quilcene;
Notes: NW Forest Pass or Interagency Pass
required; **GPS:** N 47 29.599, W 123 12.661

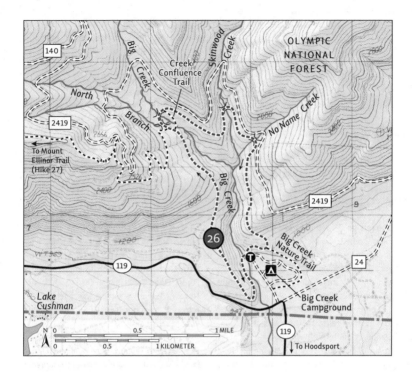 *Venture within the shadow of
Mount Ellinor on an enjoyable
circuitous route around the Big Creek drainage, and savor the sweet serenity of cascading
water. There's no need to hurry—there are
plenty of spots for resting and contemplation
along the way.*

GETTING THERE

From Shelton, travel north on US Highway
101 for 15 miles to Hoodsport. Turn left
(west) onto State Route 119 and proceed 9.3
miles west to a T intersection with Forest
Road 24. Turn left and then immediately
turn right into the Big Creek Campground,
proceeding a short distance to the day-use
area and trailhead (elev. 1000 ft). Privy
available.

ON THE TRAIL

Save this hike for a hot summer day when
shaded glens offer respite from the mid-
day rays. Forested all the way, and always
within earshot of tumbling water, the Big
Creek Trail makes a fine rainy-day hike
too—especially when stream flow is high,
intensifying the many cascades on this
hike. Utilizing old roads and new tread,

an all-volunteer crew built this loop that's guaranteed to make you appreciate the beauty of cascading waters.

Starting from the rebuilt and expanded Big Creek Campground, follow Upper Big Creek Loop Trail No. 827.1 to a junction. For this loop, clockwise is the preferred direction for an easier-on-the-knees descent. Cross Big Creek on a sturdy bridge and briefly walk downstream before making a U-turn and ascending above the creek. Mileposts, signed features, and resting benches grace the way. After 1 mile, the grade gets steeper. Mount Washington hovering above occasionally appears through gaps in the forest canopy. At 1.8 miles, come to a junction. To the right is an interesting side trip on the Creek Confluence Trail, dropping to the confluence of Big and North Branch creeks, where you'll find good lunch rocks.

Continuing on the main loop, soon come to a junction (elev. 1850 ft) with the Mount Ellinor connector trail, which leads 1.4 miles to the Mount Ellinor Trail. This is the long and challenging way to this popular peak. Continue straight, crossing North Branch Creek on a good bridge. A few steps ahead, encounter another good bridge, this one spanning Big Creek above a gorgeous cascade. The loop then begins descending, skirting some big boulders and granting good views of roaring Big Creek.

At 2 miles, the Creek Confluence Trail meets back up with the main loop. Stay left, now following an old road, and work your way back to the campground. En route, cross scenic Skinwood and No Name creeks, pass a few giant firs that loggers forgot, and catch a glimpse of Mount Ellinor rising above the watershed. At 4.2 miles, come to a junction with the Big Creek Nature Trail, which loops around the campground for 0.8 mile, if you want more exercise. Otherwise, continue right for 0.1 mile to the trailhead.

EXTENDING YOUR TRIP
Nearby Hoodsport Trail Park (milepost 3 on SR 119) offers 2 miles of quiet, forested, interlocking trails near Dow Creek.

27 Mount Ellinor

RATING/ DIFFICULTY	ROUNDTRIP	ELEV GAIN/ HIGH POINT	SEASON
*****/4	6.6 miles	3270 feet/ 5944 feet	July–Oct

Maps: Green Trails Olympic Mountains East No. 168S, Custom Correct Mount Skokomish–Lake Cushman; **Contact:** Olympic National Forest, Hood Canal Ranger District, Quilcene; **Notes:** NW Forest Pass or Interagency Pass required for upper trail; **GPS:** N 47 30.397, W 123 13.928

An Olympic classic, Mount Ellinor delivers one of the most supreme views this side of the Hood Canal. From the jagged summit, peer deep into the heart of the Olympic wild-erness or out across Lake Cushman and Puget Sound to the Cascades spanning the eastern horizon. All of this comes at a price however—this is one steep hike.

GETTING THERE
From Shelton, travel north on US Highway 101 for 15 miles to Hoodsport. Turn left (west) onto State Route 119 and proceed 9.3 miles to a T intersection. Turn right onto graveled FR 24, drive 1.6 miles, and turn left onto FR 2419. After 4.6 miles, come to the lower trailhead (elev. 2675 ft). (For the upper trailhead, continue on FR 2419 for 1.6 miles.

Hiker approaches Ellinor's summit as clouds ring Mount Washington.

Then turn left on rough and rocky FR Spur 014 and follow it 1 mile to the trailhead at 3500 feet. Privy available.)

ON THE TRAIL

Starting at Trail No. 812's upper trailhead shortens this hike by over 3 miles and knocks off 800 feet of elevation. If you're intent on getting to the view as fast as possible, head to that starting point. Otherwise, take the longer route and get a chance to warm up, enjoy fine old-growth groves, and find a little solitude at a very popular destination.

Begin by immediately entering a cool forest of old-growth hemlocks and Douglas-firs with a rhododendron understory. At 0.2 mile,

stay right at a junction. The way left leads downhill 1.4 miles to the Big Creek loop (Hike 26) utilizing part of the original route to Ellinor from Lake Cushman.

Skirt the edge of an old clear-cut, enjoying teaser views of what lies ahead. Then steadily ascend a heavily forested ridge to a junction (elev. 3600 ft) at 1.6 miles. The trail right leads 0.3 mile to the upper trailhead. Stay left, soon coming to another junction (elev. 3850 ft) at 1.9 miles. The trail right—the most popular portal to Ellinor, descends 350 feet to the upper trailhead (elev. 3500 ft) in 0.3 mile.

Now joining plenty of other hikers, head left on well-trodden tread and steeply climb. Skirt a giant outcropping that calls

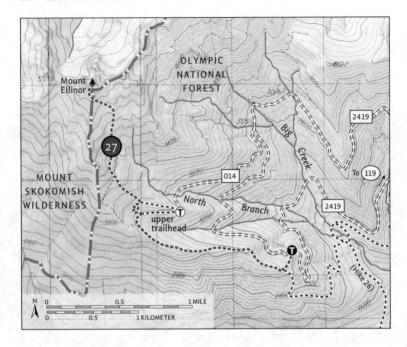

for some inspecting. At 2.4 miles, bear left where the winter route (elev. 4300 ft) leads right. Trees soon yield to meadows and rocky gardens. Years ago, going beyond this point was a tricky scramble. But thanks to the Mount Rose Trail Crew, a trail now carves into the steep mountain face, making the ascent much safer and manageable. Look for a monument honoring these trail blazers.

Continue huffing and puffing, sometimes on steps, ascending an incredibly steep slope. Pause to admire carpets of flowers and an amazing view unfurling before you. Traverse beneath the summit block, and then bend left and clamber up a rocky ridge to Ellinor's 5944-foot summit at 3.3 miles (1.7 miles from the upper trailhead).

Minding the precipitous drop-offs, feast on some stunning views. Nearly one vertical mile below is shimmering Lake Cushman. Just beyond, Hood Canal and Puget Sound sparkle against a Cascades backdrop dominated by Mount Rainier and Mount Saint Helens.

Turn your attention north and west to a diorama of jagged Olympic peaks. Washington, Pershing, and Stone, like a lineup of generals, flank Ellinor to the north. Lincoln, Cruiser, Gladys, and Copper guard her to the west. Icy Olympus lingers in the distance. Be sure to gaze down into the vertigo-inducing Jefferson Creek valley and spot an inviting but isolated pond. Ellinor's nonnative mountain goats may make an alpine appearance as well. Keep a safe distance.

EXTENDING YOUR TRIP

If you're a purist or want a real challenge, ascend Ellinor from the Big Creek Campground (Hike 26). Hike the Big Creek Trail 1.8 miles to the Mount Ellinor connector trail and follow it another 1.4 miles to the Mount Ellinor Trail. From there, it's 3.1 miles to the summit. The complete trip from top to bottom is 12.6 miles roundtrip and 4950 feet of elevation gain.

28 Mount Rose

RATING/ DIFFICULTY	ROUNDTRIP	ELEV GAIN/ HIGH POINT	SEASON
***/5	6.7 miles	3500 feet/ 4301 feet	June–Oct

Maps: Green Trails Olympic Mountains East No. 168S, Custom Correct Mount Skokomish–Lake Cushman; **Contact:** Olympic National

Lake Cushman from Mount Rose's summit

Forest, Hood Canal Ranger District, Quilcene; **Notes:** Wilderness rules apply; **GPS:** N 47 29.731, W 123 16.051

⚙️ *With all due respect to the Bard, what's in a mountain? That which we call Mount Rose by any other name would still be as steep. This is a challenging hike—one of the steepest trails in the Olympics. Consider Rose a quiet alternative to Mount Ellinor. And Rose offers a few scenic rewards too, including a knockout view of Lake Cushman from 3500 feet directly above it.*

GETTING THERE

From Shelton, travel north on US Highway 101 for 15 miles to Hoodsport. Turn left

(west) onto State Route 119 and proceed 9.3 miles to a T intersection. Turn left and continue 2.7 miles to the trailhead (elev. 800 ft) (the pavement ends and the road becomes FR 24 at 1.7 miles).

ON THE TRAIL

Start on Trail No. 814 by crossing a cascading creek on a bridge and heading up an old road. Enjoy it, for it's the only level walking you'll see on this hike. Then begin the grind. On good tread, start switchbacking to the heavens. Yes, the grade is steep, but it used to be worse before a dedicated volunteer trail crew reconfigured much of the route.

A carpet of salal lines the trail. Uniform second growth and a few remnant giants

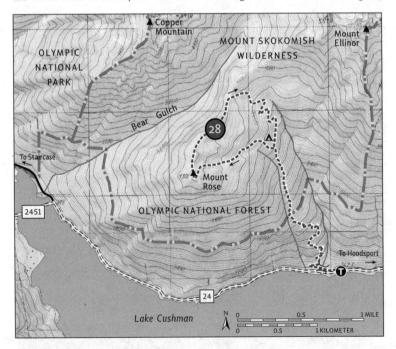

(survivors of early twentieth-century fires) offer needed shade. At 0.5 mile, pass through a pair of towering Douglas-firs that act as a gateway. Despite the roar of a distant creek, the slope is dry, as evidenced by the few madronas and manzanita bushes.

At 1.2 miles and after 1000 feet of climbing, a bench with a limited view of Lake Cushman invites a break. Catch your breath and continue. Soon afterward enter the Mount Skokomish Wilderness. Ironically, the trees are now smaller and less impressive. Perhaps it's due to thinner soils, for the way gets even steeper. Enter a cool forest of hemlocks where the trail splits in two, soon to reunite as one again.

At 1.9 miles, at a small campsite, reach the summit loop junction (elev. 3000 ft) and a small plaque honoring the crew that built this trail. Take the left trail—it's shorter and steeper—leaving the longer and more gradual option for the descent, relieving your knees.

The summit loop climbs 1300 feet in just over 1 mile through a 2006 wildfire burn and remnant pockets of old growth. At 3.1 miles, reach the 4301-foot forested summit. Don't despair—a small vertigo-inducing rock outcropping juts out of the forest, providing a panoramic payoff. Directly below, waters sparkling, is Lake Cushman. Lightning Peak and Timber Mountain rise majestically behind it. Wonder Mountain and Church Peak are just off to the right. The Skokomish delta, Black Hills, Willapa Hills, and Mount Rainier are all visible from this pulse-raising promontory. Through silver snags and white pines, catch a glimpse of the deep valley of the North Fork Skokomish.

After your rosy outlook, continue on the loop. Along a forested ledge, the trail makes a saner 1.7-mile return to the loop junction.

Enjoy glimpses of Copper Mountain, but the real point of interest is a colonnade of four silver firs about halfway down the trail. They have grown so close together they appear fused. At the familiar junction, turn left and put your trekking poles to the test, careening 1.9 miles down the mountain.

29 Dry Creek

RATING/ DIFFICULTY	ROUNDTRIP	ELEV GAIN/ HIGH POINT	SEASON
***/4	12.6 miles	2800 feet/ 3600 feet	June–Nov

Maps: Green Trail Mt Tebo No. 199, Custom Correct Mount Skokomish–Lake Cushman; **Contact:** Olympic National Forest, Hood Canal Ranger District, Quilcene; **Notes:** Trail begins on a private road—respect adjacent private property and stay on trail. Ford at Dry Creek can be difficult and dangerous except during low flows, typically in late summer; **GPS:** N 47 30.096, W 123 19.212

Hike a lightly traveled trail along the rocky and stump-lined shoreline of man-made Lake Cushman. Then follow an old logging road through second-growth forest to misnamed Dry Creek. If you can safely ford it, gorgeous tracts of old growth and a nice view of the lake below await your discovery. It's a stiff climb, but solitude is almost assuredly guaranteed.

GETTING THERE

From Shelton, travel north on US Highway 101 for 15 miles to Hoodsport. Turn left (west) onto State Route 119 and proceed 9.3 miles to a T intersection. Turn left and continue 5.4 miles to a junction (the pavement ends and the road becomes Forest Road 24

Giant Douglas-fir and western red cedar

hundreds of acres of prime old growth were cut and the area flooded.

Soon climb a small bluff that offers a good vantage of Mount Rose across the lake's reflective waters. Then start pulling away from the lake and climb. At 1.4 miles, reach a junction (elev. 950 ft) with a spur trail that heads left to a campsite on Dry Creek at its outlet into Cushman—a good turnaround point for those intent on enjoying more of the lake than the creek valley.

The Dry Creek Trail climbs steadily on an old road, the creek within earshot but not in view. After about a mile of uphill grunting, the trail levels out under a canopy of alders. In spring this portion is lined with thousands of trilliums, bleeding hearts, and violets.

At 3.5 miles, the trail finally comes upon Dry Creek (elev. 1600 ft). The old footlog spanning it was wiped out years ago, and to continue requires a ford. Dry Creek, as you can see, is far from dry, and depending on flow level (especially in early season), crossing it can be treacherous. But if you can safely cross, the best of this trail awaits your bootprints.

Once across, follow tread much less trodden. Transition into luxurious ancient forest and begin hiking away from and above Dry Creek. Steadily ascend a ravine, crossing several creeklets along the way. Pause at a few window views of Dry and Timber mountains. The trail steepens. The trees become more impressive. Marvel at a massive coupled Douglas-fir and cedar. In season, reap a bountiful berry harvest.

Attain a ridge crest with nice albeit waterless camps, and after a short reprieve from climbing, steeply ascend once again. Traverse a few brushy avalanche slopes beneath Dry Mountain and come to the edge of an old clear-cut. Continue and after one

at 1.7 miles). Bear left onto FR 2451 and cross a causeway, coming to the trailhead (elev. 800 ft) on your left in 0.4 mile.

ON THE TRAIL

Start by walking down a private road lined with summer cabins. Be sure to stay on the road and not to trespass on private property. At 0.4 mile Trail No. 872 begins. However, the way still travels through private parcels, including one sporting a very elaborate tree house. After 1 mile, leave the cabins behind and begin walking along Lake Cushman. The lake was enlarged in the 1920s when the city of Tacoma built a dam on it for power;

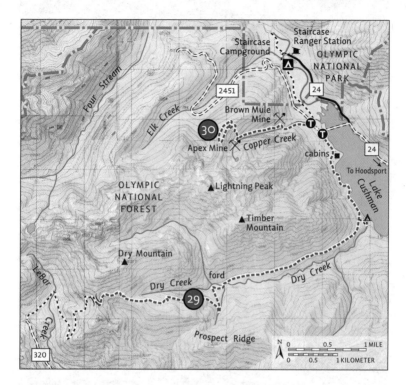

last grunt reach a 3600-foot ridge gap at 6.3 miles. Enjoy the views of Prospect Ridge and Lake Cushman with Kitsap's Green and Gold mountains in the background.

EXTENDING YOUR TRIP

The trail continues, steeply descending in old timber and reaching a decommissioned logging road at 0.7 mile. From there you can follow the road-turned-trail, passing several good views of Mount Tebo and the South Fork Skokomish River valley before losing more elevation. The way then fords LeBar Creek, continues on an old roadbed, and terminates at 2.2 miles at an unassum-

ing trailhead (elev. 2600 ft) on FR Spur 320 (reached from FR 2300).

30 Copper Creek

RATING/ DIFFICULTY	ROUNDTRIP	ELEV GAIN/ HIGH POINT	SEASON
***/4	4.3 miles	2400 feet/ 3200 feet	May–Nov

Maps: Green Trails Olympic Mountains East No. 168S, Custom Correct Mount Skokomish–Lake Cushman; **Contact:** Olympic National Forest, Hood Canal Ranger District, Quilcene; **GPS:** N 47 30.325, W 123 19.587

Cascading Copper Creek

Follow a steep trail along-side crashing Copper Creek through a deep and narrow ravine. Explore a couple of old mine sites, and then continue onward through primeval forest to a high and narrow shoulder of Lightning Peak.

GETTING THERE

From Shelton, travel north on US Highway 101 for 15 miles to Hoodsport. Turn left (west) onto State Route 119 and proceed 9.3 miles to a T intersection. Turn left and continue 5.4 miles to a junction (the pavement ends and the road becomes Forest Road 24 at 1.7 miles). Bear left onto FR 2451 and cross a causeway, coming to the trailhead (elev. 800 ft) on your left in 0.8 mile, just after crossing Copper Creek.

ON THE TRAIL

Built originally in 1915 by prospectors searching for copper and manganese, this long-abandoned Trail No. 876 was rebuilt in the early 2000s by volunteers. Integrating some of the original tread, the new trail is just as steep and challenging as the original. It's just as wild and beautiful too. Although miners clambered along the vertical slopes above Copper Creek, loggers fortunately shunned these slopes, leaving plenty of big old trees in place.

Immediately start climbing, entering a narrow and dark ravine cut by Copper Creek. In 0.2 mile, cross the crashing waterway on a good bridge. Just below, look over on the west side of the ravine wall to spot a shaft from the Brown Mule Mine. Use caution if you wish to explore it.

The way now gets steeper. Take a break from the toil to admire a cascading tributary plummeting from high above. Working your way up an increasingly narrow ravine, you'll be hard-pressed to hear anything above the roaring creek pummeling the earth by your feet. When you think the trail can't get any steeper, it does. A series of tight switchbacks climbs above the creek on the western slope of the ravine.

In a grand forest of giant cedars and Douglas-firs, the trail eases a bit. At 1.4 miles, come to a junction (elev. 2300 ft). The trail left leads 0.1 mile to Copper Creek and the site of the old Apex Mine. Check it out. Then return to the junction and continue steeply climbing, reaching another junction (elev. 2900 ft) at 1.7 miles. The trail now loops. Head right—you'll be returning from the left. On a rougher path, continue climbing, attaining a 3200-foot narrow shoulder of Lightning Peak. Views are limited on the forested ridge, but you'll get a few dizzying glimpses of Lake Cushman and the Elk Creek basin as well as a decent view of Wonder Mountain. Close the loop at 2.4 miles and brace yourself for a knee-burning descent back to your vehicle.

31 Wagonwheel Lake

RATING/ DIFFICULTY	ROUNDTRIP	ELEV GAIN/ HIGH POINT	SEASON
**/5	5.8 miles	3175 feet/ 4050 feet	Mid-June– Nov

Maps: Green Trails Olympic Mountains East No. 168S, Custom Correct Mount Skokomish–Lake Cushman; **Contact:** Olympic National Park, Wilderness Information Center; **Notes:** National park entrance fee. Dogs prohibited; **GPS:** N 47 30.969, W 123 19.669

Silver snag on a knoll above Wagonwheel Lake

The trailhead sign warns (or boasts) that this is one of the steepest trails in Olympic National Park. Gain over 3000 vertical feet in less than 3 miles. Utilizing tight switchbacks and no switchbacks at all, the grade is brutal. And once you get to Wagonwheel Lake, you'll find a tiny forest-ringed pond with nary a good place to soak your feet. But if you can muster some energy to climb the ridge behind the lake, this hike goes to four stars and all that sweat and pain will be worth it.

GETTING THERE

From Shelton, travel north on US Highway 101 for 15 miles to Hoodsport. Turn left (west) onto State Route 119 and proceed 9.3 miles to a T intersection. Turn left and continue 5.4 miles to a junction (the pavement ends and the road becomes Forest Road 24 at 1.7 miles). Turn right and drive 1.2 miles, turning right at the Staircase Ranger Station for trailhead parking (elev. 875 ft). Water and privy available.

ON THE TRAIL

Despite its grueling statistics, little Wagonwheel Lake gets its fair share of visitors—rather, its attempted share. Many hikers comprehend 2.9 miles, but not 3175 vertical feet. It's an insane combination, bringing many an unconditioned hiker to their knees and back to the trailhead unfulfilled. If you're ready for the challenge, carry on!

Through a lush understory of shoulder-high ferns and salal, the trail eases into the climb. At about 0.4 mile, pass an old mining bore (elev. 1225 ft) on your right (which is more interesting than an old, boring miner). Then, on a series of short, tight switchbacks, relentlessly climb the steep slopes. In the mostly second-growth firs, a

few white pines and rhododendrons break the monotony of the forest. The monotony of the climb, however, is rarely broken. At about 1.7 miles, near a small ledge (elev. 2800 ft) with a limited view of the valley, enter a cooler forest of hemlocks.

The trail then gets even steeper; long gone are the switchbacks. Hikers like me who grew up scaling the peaks of the Northeast will feel right at home. After what feels like forever, the trail miraculously levels out. Now through old-growth firs and hemlocks, skirt a steep slope and break out onto a brushy avalanche chute. Work your way across slumping tread, enjoying views of Mount Lincoln and Sawtooth Ridge.

Reenter cool evergreen forest, cross Wagonwheel's outlet creek, and finally, after 2.9 miles, arrive at the little lake (elev. 4050 ft). A small sunny bench above the lake makes for a good place to collapse.

EXTENDING YOUR TRIP

If you have any oomph left, locate a primitive path taking off from the main trail at the lake. It goes 0.5 mile straight up the 4700-foot knoll to the north. From its meadows punctuated with silver snags, enjoy a breathtaking panorama of peaks: Pershing, Washington, Ellinor, Copper, Lincoln, Skokomish, Wonder, and the Brothers. Even little Wagonwheel looks great from up here.

32 Staircase Rapids

RATING/ DIFFICULTY	LOOP	ELEV GAIN/ HIGH POINT	SEASON
***/1	2 miles	225 feet/ 1000 feet	Year-round

Maps: Green Trails Olympic Mountains East No. 168S, Custom Correct Mount Skokomish–

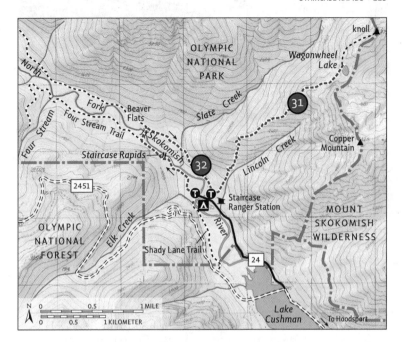

Lake Cushman; **Contact:** Olympic National Park, Wilderness Information Center; **Notes:** National park entrance fee. Dogs prohibited. Staircase access road closed in winter—park at picnic area and hike 1 mile up road or hike 0.8 mile on Shady Lane Trail (trailhead just past Copper Creek trailhead); **GPS:** N 47 30.931, W 123 19.767

Stand in awe watching the swift-moving waters of the North Fork Skokomish River barrel and thunder over a series of cascades. This is a great hike any time of year, but Staircase Rapids are especially impressive during spring runoff. Hikers of all ages and abilities will be delighted to experience this easy and captivating loop.

GETTING THERE

From Shelton, travel north on US Highway 101 for 15 miles to Hoodsport. Turn left (west) onto State Route 119 and proceed 9.3 miles to a T intersection. Turn left and continue 5.4 miles to a junction (the pavement ends and the road becomes Forest Road 24 at 1.7 miles). Turn right and drive 1.2 miles, turning right at the Staircase Ranger Station for trailhead parking (elev. 875 ft). Water and privy available.

ON THE TRAIL

The trek to Staircase Rapids is a heck of a lot easier today than it was in 1890 when Lt. Joseph P. O'Neil, accompanied by a group of scientists, led an army expedition here. The O'Neil Party was intent on

North Fork Skokomish River

traversing the Olympic Peninsula. Lacking the wonderful trails that now grace the region, O'Neil and company cut a mule trail up the North Fork Skokomish River to help transport supplies to base camps along the way. Among the many findings that the O'Neil Party would bring back was that this wild area deserved protection. In his trip report, O'Neil wrote that the Olympic interior would serve admirably as a national park. Nice forward thinking, Lieutenant O'Neil; I salute you.

From the main parking area, cross the North Fork Skokomish on a solid bridge to begin this hike following part of the original O'Neil mule trail. Immediately come to a junction with the Shady Lane Trail (see Extending Your Trip), which heads left downriver. Continue straight and soon come to a side trail leading left to the small hydro plant that powers the ranger station. Just beyond, come to another side trail. This short path leads left to what was once an incredibly large standing cedar. Today it leads to an incredibly large

windfall. The old cedar yielded to a winter storm in the late 1990s.

The main trail gently climbs, soon coming to the riverbank. March alongside the frothy river, passing big boulders and a series of roaring rapids. Follow the thundering river from one mesmerizing spot to another, coming to a junction (elev. 1000 ft) at 0.9 mile. The trail straight ahead leads to Four Stream (see Extending Your Trip). The loop continues right to a sturdy, fairly new suspension bridge spanning the wild waterway.

Shortly beyond the bridge, reach the North Fork Skokomish River Trail. Head right, downriver. On a wide trail (once an old road), traverse lush riparian flats. Cross fanning Slate Creek, and then soon afterward climb a little to bypass a large slide. Then descend, returning to the parking area at 2 miles.

EXTENDING YOUR TRIP

If this wonderful loop is a tad short for your hiking tastes, consider these two options for extending the splendor.

Extension 1: From the south end of the suspension bridge, continue upriver on the lightly hiked Four Stream Trail, soon coming to Beaver Flats, a nice spot to soak feet in the refreshing river. Next, pass through a forest of silver and charred snags, thanks to a wildfire sparked by a careless camper in 1985. Greenery is growing in, so the views of Mount Lincoln rising over the valley won't be around much longer.

The trail reenters mature forest to follow alongside a river that is now much calmer. The way then heads up a bluff, skirting a recent slide. Then descend, reaching Four Stream at 1.1 miles from the bridge. An old section of trail and campsites lie beyond, but you must ford Four Stream to reach them. This is a good spot to turn around for most folks.

Extension 2: Follow the Shady Lane Trail 0.8 mile downriver to its end at FR 2451. The way passes an old mine and hobbles over some riverside ledges, providing exceptional views of the river. And it traverses impressive forest groves that contain some of the biggest and oldest trees in the Staircase area.

33 North Fork Skokomish River and Flapjack Lakes

Big Log Camp

RATING/ DIFFICULTY	ROUNDTRIP	ELEV GAIN/ HIGH POINT	SEASON
***/2	11 miles	775 feet/ 1550 feet	Mar–Nov

Flapjack Lakes

RATING/ DIFFICULTY	ROUNDTRIP	ELEV GAIN/ HIGH POINT	SEASON
****/4	15.4 miles	3050 feet/ 3850 feet	Mid-June– Oct

Maps: Green Trails Olympic Mountains East No. 168S, Custom Correct Mount Skokomish–Lake Cushman; **Contact:** Olympic National Park, Wilderness Information Center; **Notes:** National park entrance fee. Dogs prohibited. Staircase access road closed in winter—park at picnic area and hike 1 mile up road or hike 0.8 mile on Shady Lane Trail (trailhead just past Copper Creek trailhead). Backcountry camping requires permit.; **GPS:** N 47 30.968, W 123 19.691

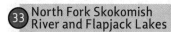 *Your choice: An easy all-day hike along a roaring wild waterway embraced by coniferous giants, or a very long all-day hike to a pair of subalpine lakes in the shadow of the jagged Sawtooth Ridge. Neither hike is particularly difficult, but both are long. Even so, expect company. The North Fork Skokomish River valley has been attracting legions of hikers ever since Lt. Joseph P. O'Neil and his boys passed this way shortly after Washington statehood.*

GETTING THERE

From Shelton, travel north on US Highway 101 for 15 miles to Hoodsport. Turn left (west) onto State Route 119 and proceed 9.3 miles to a T intersection. Turn left and continue 5.4 miles to a junction (the pavement ends and the road becomes Forest Road 24 at 1.7 miles). Turn right and drive 1.2 miles, turning right at the Staircase Ranger Station for trailhead parking (elev. 875 ft). Water and privy available.

ON THE TRAIL

Starting on the North Fork Skokomish River Trail, follow this popular route alongside the river, which before it was dammed by Tacoma Power in the 1920s was one of the largest salmon-bearing streams on the

Sawtooth Ridge provides a rugged backdrop to the Flapjack Lakes.

peninsula. The trail follows part of the O'Neil Party's 1890 exploratory route. Several months after the famous Press Expedition, which traversed the Olympic interior from north to south, Lieutenant O'Neil led a group of scientists and soldiers across the Olympics from east to west.

On an old roadbed (decommissioned in the early 1970s), head upstream, rounding a washout and then slightly descending. Cross a couple of side creeks (bridged) and travel through a luxuriant bottomland of big cedars, Douglas-firs, and moss-cloaked big-leaf maples. Stay right at a junction with

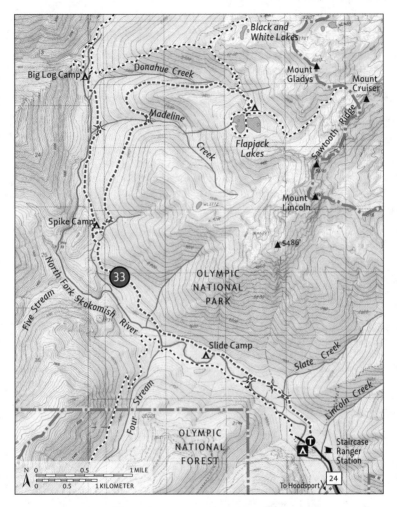

the Staircase Rapids Loop at 1 mile, and soon come within earshot and eyesight of the tumbling North Fork Skok.

At 1.6 miles, pass the Slide Camp access, leading to good camp and picnic sites on the river. Then traverse the Beaver Fire of 1985, caused by an illegal campfire during a drought, resulting in 1400 acres of old growth going up in flames. Through big snags and feisty undergrowth, the trail

UNTRAMMELED OLYMPICS

While much of Olympic National Forest has been heavily roaded and logged, nearly 90,000 of the its 633,000 acres (15 percent) are protected as federal wilderness. Bowing to a rising public environmental consciousness, Congress passed the Wilderness Act in 1964 (by a vote of 373–1), one of the strongest and most important pieces of environmental legislation in our nation's history.

Recognizing that parts of our natural heritage should be altered as little as possible, the Wilderness Act afforded some of our most precious wild landscapes a reprieve from exploitation, development, and harmful activities such as motorized recreation. Even bicycles are banned from federal wilderness areas. Wilderness is "an area where the earth and community of life are untrammeled by man," states the act, "where man himself is a visitor who does not remain."

Only Congress can designate an area as wilderness. While Olympic National Forest had no shortage of qualifying lands back in 1964, not one single acre was protected. A powerful timber industry with friends in both political parties made sure all of Olympic National Forest remained on the chopping block. Finally, in 1984, a sweeping wilderness bill was signed into law, creating five wilderness areas in Olympic National Forest:

Wonder Mountain, 2349 acres
Colonel Bob, 11,961 acres
Mount Skokomish, 13,105 acres
The Brothers, 16,682 acres
Buckhorn, 44,258 acres

Conservationists argued (rightfully) that these new areas were too small to afford ample protection for imperiled species like the spotted owl. Old-growth logging continued in the Olympics, leaving very little of the national forest in an untrammeled condition. But now, with old-growth logging no longer occurring on federal forestland on the Olympic Peninsula, it's time to add the last remaining roadless areas of Olympic National Forest to the wilderness system—places like Moonlight Dome and the upper South Fork Skokomish River valley.

The Wild Olympics coalition (www.wildolympics.org) has been instrumental in seeing that the last Olympic wildlands and wild rivers receive protection. In 2019 their efforts led to Senator Patty Murray and Representative Derek Kilmer reintroducing the Wild Olympics Wilderness and Wild and Scenic Rivers Act. The act calls for the permanent protection of more than 126,500 acres of Olympic National Forest as wilderness and nineteen rivers and their major tributaries as Wild and Scenic Rivers.

The Wild Olympics Wilderness and Wild and Scenic Rivers Act has broad support and has been endorsed by a wide array of businesses leaders, elected officials, sportsmen and women's groups, recreation interests, conservation groups, and this author.

gradually moves away from the river. At 3.6 miles, reach a junction (elev. 1450 ft) just before Spike Camp. Decision time.

Big Log Camp: Head straight, soon returning to the riverbank and more impressive old growth. At 5.5 miles, arrive at a junction. Big Log Camp is to your left, a great place to while away the afternoon by the river.

Flapjack Lakes: Head right, climbing out of the valley. After a few switchbacks, the trail turns north, traversing a slope and gradually gaining elevation. After passing through a marshy area of big cedars, arrive at Madeline Creek (elev. 2100 ft) cascading through a narrow ravine at 5.4 miles. Cross it via a sturdy bridge. Traverse another hillside and then work your way up the Donahue Creek ravine. The way, now considerably steeper, parallels the cascading creek. At 7.1 miles, the climb eases and you reach a junction with the trail that heads to Black and White Lakes and Smith Lake.

Continue right and after 0.6 mile, reach the two Flapjack Lakes (elev. 3850 ft). Ringed by subalpine forest and framed by the rugged spires of Sawtooth Ridge, the lakes serve up a hearty helping of views. Sit and savor them or amble around the western shore on an 0.8-mile path. In this popular place, please help mitigate environmental degradation by practicing Leave No Trace principles.

EXTENDING YOUR TRIP

Strong day hikers might want to continue beyond the lakes for another 1.4 miles to 5000-foot Gladys Divide beneath the impressive summit of 6104-foot Mount Cruiser. Strong hikers might also consider an alternative return, first via the 1.3-mile trail to Black and White Lakes (elev. 4475 ft) and then, after a lake visit, backtracking 0.2 mile

and heading 2.2 incredibly steep miles down to Big Log Camp. From there it's 5.5 miles back to the trailhead.

Hamma Hamma River Valley

According to legendary guidebook writer Robert Wood, Hamma Hamma is a Native word meaning "big stink," in reference to the smell of thousands of rotting carcasses left behind by spawning salmon. Other sources say Hamma Hamma refers to a Twana village named Hab'hab that once sat at the river's mouth. Hab'habs are reeds (probably horsetails) growing along the river.

There are certainly abundant reeds in this valley—and beautiful forests and a handful of lakes with wonderful hiking trails leading to them. Most of this valley succumbed to heavy logging and forest fires during the twentieth century, but the upper reaches are as wild and rugged as any place in the Olympics. And two federal wilderness areas ensure that the remote corners of the Hamma Hamma Valley and the river's tributaries will remain untrammeled.

34 Living Legacy Trail

RATING/ DIFFICULTY	LOOP	ELEV GAIN/ HIGH POINT	SEASON
***/1	1.8 miles	125 feet/ 700 feet	Year-round

Maps: Green Trails Olympic Mountains East No. 168S, Custom Correct Mount Skokomish–Lake Cushman; **Contact:** Olympic National Forest, Hood Canal Ranger District, Quilcene; **Notes:** First 0.25 mile wheelchair-accessible; **GPS:** N 47 35.691, W 123 07.412

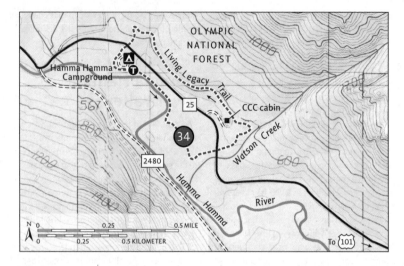

 Enjoy a peaceful walk along the Hamma Hamma River and to a historic guard station built by the Civilian Conservation Corps (CCC). This delightful family-friendly—and surprisingly lightly traveled—loop provides good river views and interpretive panels that offer a peek back into history.

GETTING THERE

From Hoodsport, travel north on US Highway 101 for 13.7 miles, turning left at milepost 318 onto Hamma Hamma River Road (Forest Road 25). (From Quilcene, travel south on US 101 for 23.5 miles, turning right onto FR 25.) Continue west for 6 miles and turn left into the Hamma Hamma Campground. Proceed for 0.1 mile to the trailhead (elev. 600 ft), near campsite 12.

ON THE TRAIL

From the campground, head east on a section of tread renovated in 2015 by the Mount Rose Trail Crew to accommodate wheelchairs. Stop at the interpretive panels that recount the role of the Depression-era Civilian Conservation Corps in this corner of Olympic National Forest.

The trail hugs a bank above the Hamma Hamma River, affording excellent views of the pretty waterway. Look for dippers year-round. In spring look for harlequin ducks that nest here after returning from the Salish Sea. After about a half mile, the trail turns north to cross FR 25. Then follow the trail along cascading Watson Creek, climbing about 100 feet to a bench overlooking the creek.

The way then turns west, soon reaching the CCC cabin that is the Hamma Hamma Guard Station. You can rent this eloquently rustic structure for overnight stays. Please respect any current guests by not walking on the grounds.

Continue west on the loop, crossing a small creek and ambling through some

The author's wife and son on the Living Legacy Trail

mature second growth. The way then descends into a ravine before recrossing FR 25. Pass some big old trees and reach the campground loop road near campsite 6. Turn right and walk the road a short distance back to your start.

35 Elk Lakes

RATING/ DIFFICULTY	ROUNDTRIP	ELEV GAIN/ HIGH POINT	SEASON
**/2	4.9 miles	400 feet/ 1200 feet	Year-round

Maps: Green Trails Olympic Mountains East No. 168S, Custom Correct Mount Skokomish–Lake Cushman; **Contact:** Olympic National Forest, Hood Canal Ranger District, Quilcene; **Notes:** Trail damaged in 2018 Maple Fire, check with ranger station for status; NW Forest Pass or Interagency Pass required at FR 2401 trailheads; **GPS:** N 47 34.759, W 123 07.222

Hike along a sunny canyon and through primordial old growth to two little lakes bursting with ducks and herons. The Elk Lakes are easily accessible off of Jefferson Creek Road (Forest Road 2401), explaining their popularity with weekend anglers. But this "back way" guarantees you a quiet journey and plenty of big cedars and firs to admire along the way.

GETTING THERE

From Hoodsport, travel north on US Highway 101 for 13.7 miles, turning left at milepost 318 onto Hamma Hamma River Road (Forest Road 25). (From Quilcene, travel south on US 101 for 23.5 miles, turning right onto FR 25.) Continue west for 6.4 miles (passing the campground) and turn left onto FR 2480. Cross the Hamma Hamma River, and in 0.2 mile turn right onto unsigned FR 2421. Follow this rough but drivable road 1.6 miles to a pullout on your left where the road makes a sharp turn right. Park here;

Tranquil Elk Lake

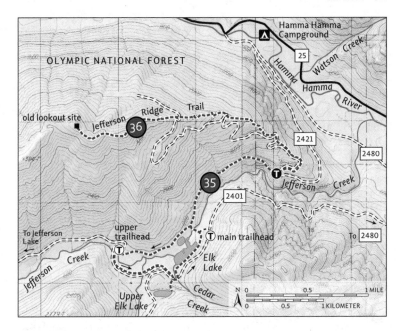

this is the trailhead (elev. 1050 ft) for the "back way" to Elk Lakes. (If FR 2421 is too rough and you still want a lake trip, stay on FR 2480 for 3 more miles, turn right onto FR 2401, and proceed 2.5 miles to the popular main trailhead.)

ON THE TRAIL

On a remnant of an old trail that once spanned the entire valley, start hiking west through a tunnel of second-growth greenery. Within minutes emerge on a dry hillside, several hundred feet above roaring Jefferson Creek. Born in the snowfields of Mount Ellinor and her rugged neighbors, the creek crashes through a steep, narrow canyon before draining into the Hamma Hamma River.

In early summer you'll admire wildflowers painting the landscape as you traverse the sun-kissed canyon wall. Rhododendrons add to the array of colors, and a few flaky-barked madronas add a nice touch as well. The way then enters old-growth forest, makes a few ups and downs, and climbs about 150 feet. It then slightly descends, reaching a junction (elev. 1100 ft) at 1.1 miles. You'll be returning from the left, so head right, through a grove of monster cedars to Elk Lake. Depending on the season, the lake may be a wet grassy swale or a pretty reflecting pool. Regardless, there will be plenty of birdlife.

Continue along the shore, stopping occasionally to inventory the quiet lake's residents. The mostly level trail follows Jefferson Creek through more impressive old growth. At 1.9 miles, reach FR 2401 and an upper trailhead. You can retrace your steps, but I prefer making a loop by following the road left for 0.8 mile, picking up the trail again just after crossing Cedar Creek. But first, just before the creek, head right for 0.2 mile to pretty little Upper Elk Lake (elev. 1150 ft). Then retrace your steps, cross the road, and follow the trail as it drops back down to the lower lake.

Pass big trees and some nice shoreline lounging spots. At 0.6 mile from the road, reach a junction. Right leads 0.1 mile to the main trailhead (privy available). Head left, soon crossing Jefferson Creek on rocks. In spring and other periods of high water, this may be difficult (you may want to do this loop in reverse at those times, in case you need to turn around here).

Just beyond the crossing, come to a familiar junction. Turn right for the 1.1-mile return hike to your vehicle.

36 Jefferson Ridge

RATING/ DIFFICULTY	ROUNDTRIP	ELEV GAIN/ HIGH POINT	SEASON
**/4	6.6 miles	2800 feet/ 3850 feet	June–Nov

Maps: Green Trails Olympic Mountains East No. 168S, Custom Correct Mount Skokomish–Lake Cushman; **Contact:** Olympic National Forest, Hood Canal Ranger District, Quilcene; **Notes:** Trail damaged in 2018 Maple Fire, check with ranger station for status; Road beyond Elk Lake trailhead is rough, requires high-clearance vehicle; **GPS:** N 47 34.759, W 123 07.222

Climb through a patchwork of old clear-cuts and old growth to a lonely ridgetop, site of a long-gone fire lookout. It's a steep hike up an old logging road and old trail, but you'll be rewarded with solitude and good views of Hood Canal and Lena Lake. And if you come in early summer, blossoming bear grass and rhododendrons add to the mix.

GETTING THERE
From Hoodsport, travel north on US Highway 101 for 13.7 miles, turning left at milepost 318 onto Hamma Hamma River Road (Forest Road 25). (From Quilcene, travel south on US 101 for 23.5 miles, turning right onto FR 25.) Continue west for 6.4 miles (passing the campground) and turn left onto FR 2480. Cross the Hamma Hamma River, and in 0.2 mile turn right onto unsigned FR 2421. Follow this rough but drivable road 1.6 miles to a pullout on your left where the road makes a sharp turn right. Park here (elev. 1050 ft).

ON THE TRAIL
The Elk Lake and Jefferson Ridge trails are remnants of much longer trails all but obliterated during the logging frenzy of the 1960s and 1970s. Fortunately, portions of both remain—and they're portions worth hiking and rehabilitating. While it's possible to drive farther to begin this hike, the road beyond here is extremely rough.

Start hiking up FR 2421, steeply climbing up a ridge spine. At 0.8 mile, look for old tread (elev. 1625 ft) heading right. If you miss it (easy to do), keep hiking up the road another mile to the official trailhead. If you located the old tread, continue steeply climbing along the ridge spine through old-growth forest. The tread is fairly discernible, but expect a few brushy spots through salal patches.

At 1.4 miles, come to FR 2421 (elev. 2250 ft) once more. Continue right, immediately picking up the trail again. This is the

Lower Lena Lake and The Brothers from Jefferson Ridge

official trailhead. Sign the register and ask the Forest Service to maintain the lower portion. Then continue hiking on much better-defined tread. The way continues to ascend steeply, skirting old growth and an old cut. Views emerge of Mount Rainier and Kitsap County's Green Mountain.

At 2 miles, cross FR 2421 (elev. 2900 ft) again—the road here is a rocky mess. Now the fun begins. Continue steeply climbing up more tight switchbacks. Pass through young forest and rhody groves, eventually attaining the ridge crest. Then hike along the crest enjoying excellent views of Mounts Washington, Pershing, Jupiter, Bretherton, and Lena and Lena Lake in an emerald valley beneath the Brothers. This is a neat perspective of the popular lake.

The way then enters old growth, passing view-granting ledges and skirting a couple of knolls. At 3.3 miles, reach the end of the trail at the remains of the old fire lookout (no views) that once graced this summit (elev. 3850 ft). It's an anticlimactic finish, so

retreat to your favorite viewpoint along the ridge for your lunch before making the steep descent back to your vehicle.

37 Lena Lakes

Lower Lena

RATING/ DIFFICULTY	ROUNDTRIP	ELEV GAIN/ HIGH POINT	SEASON
**/2	6 miles	1225 feet/ 1925 feet	Apr–Nov

Upper Lena

RATING/ DIFFICULTY	ROUNDTRIP	ELEV GAIN/ HIGH POINT	SEASON
****/5	14 miles	4100 feet/ 4600 feet	July–Oct

Maps: Green Trails Olympic Mountains East No. 168S, Custom Correct Mount Skokomish–Lake Cushman; **Contact:** Olympic National Forest, Hood Canal Ranger District, Quilcene and Olympic National Park, Wilderness Information Center; **Notes:** NW Forest Pass

Upper Lena Lake and Mount Lena

or Interagency Pass required. Dogs prohibited at park boundary. Camping (no fires) at Upper Lena requires permit; **GPS:** N 47 35.984, W 123 09.055

Take an easy kid-friendly hike or choose a challenging grunt. Lower Lena Lake is flanked by old growth, easy to hike to, accessible most of the year, and one of the most popular backcountry destinations in the Olympics. Upper Lena Lake sits in a stunning high basin surrounded by alpine meadows and rocky peaks; it's reached by a steep, rocky, root-tangled trail. But that rough approach keeps the crowds away—not so at Lower Lena, especially on a sunny weekend.

GETTING THERE

From Hoodsport, travel north on US Highway 101 for 13.7 miles, turning left at milepost 318 onto Hamma Hamma River Road (Forest Road 25). (From Quilcene, travel south on US 101 for 23.5 miles, turning right onto FR 25.) Continue for 7.5 paved miles to the trailhead (elev. 700 ft). Privy available.

ON THE TRAIL

The day hike to Lena Lake is one of the most popular in the Olympics. As one of the easiest trails to a backcountry lake, and with developed campsites, it attracts throngs of backpackers too, especially neophytes. And while this good-sized body of water nestled among old-growth firs and cedars is fairly scenic, it sees its share of neglect from less-than-enlightened visitors. Be sure to practice Leave No Trace ethics, and help educate others along the way.

The trail takes off in second-growth timber, along a gentle and carefree climb. Lena Creek can be heard crashing in the distance. After about a mile, come to impressive old

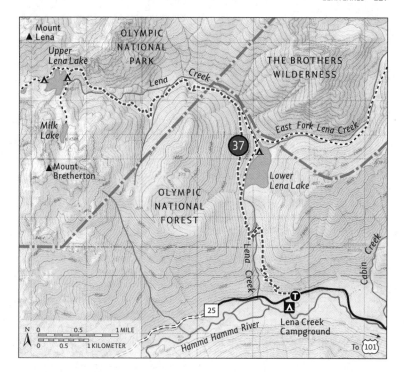

growth. As the trail crosses Lena Creek, you may be in for a surprise: standing on a bridge over missing waters. The creek often goes underground here, leaving you standing high and dry over a mossy, rocky draw. After the bridge, wind around and below a ledge, climbing high above Lower Lena Lake and reaching a junction (elev. 1925 ft) at 3 miles.

Lower Lena Lake: Venture right, and within a few hundred feet encounter an inviting sunny ledge that provides a resting spot and a wonderful view of Lena Lake 100 feet below. Call it quits here, or continue descending to the shoreline, passing well-used campsites.

At 0.4 mile from the junction, cross Lena Creek and come to another junction. The trail left leads 0.2 mile to Upper Lena Lake Trail. The trail right passes shoreline camps and picnic spots before heading toward the Brothers.

Upper Lena Lake: Continue left from the original junction, now on much lighter tread. After a short climb and drop, reach a junction (elev. 1975 ft) with the old trail (now a connector to the lower lake) at 3.5 miles. Bear left and follow alongside Lena Creek through a spectacular primeval forest. At 4.1 miles, enter Olympic National Park (elev. 2350 ft). Dogs are prohibited from this point on.

Elevation gain continues to be minimal as the way parallels Lena Creek in an increasingly tighter valley marred by avalanches on its north slopes. At 5 miles, cross a tributary on a log bridge (elev. 2650 ft), after which the way gets downright nasty! Begin an insanely steep climb up a rocky, rooty, brushy course. In wet weather the route can be treacherous. After you carefully negotiate a ledge and clamber up a steep bed of big rocks posing as trail, the climbing eases somewhat.

At 6.2 miles, cross Lena Creek (elev. 3900 ft), which may be flowing underground. Continue through open forest and attractive old-growth groves before once again climbing steeply, this time across abrupt slopes above Lena Creek. At 7 miles, crest a ridge (elev. 4600 ft) that cradles Upper Lena Lake and look back at Mount Rainier in the distance. Day use and good soaking spots are a short distance to the right. Enjoy a classic backdrop view of 5960-foot Mount Bretherton rising above and reflecting in the lake. Good camps (permits required) are just beyond, along the lake's eastern shore and on the lake's western shore.

EXTENDING YOUR TRIP

From Upper Lena, a 0.5-mile trail leads to beautiful Milk Lake (elev. 4718 ft), set beneath a small glacier on Mount Bretherton.

From Lower Lena, the Brothers Trail heads along the oft-subterranean East Fork Lena Creek through the Valley of the Silent Men in the Brothers Wilderness. You'll encounter a lot of old growth, as well as a few climbers on their way to and from the Brothers, one of the most recognized Olympic peaks from the Seattle waterfront. It's a 3-mile journey to the Brothers Camp (elev. 3000 ft), beyond which only prepared and experienced climbers should venture.

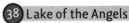

38 Lake of the Angels

RATING/ DIFFICULTY	ROUNDTRIP	ELEV GAIN/ HIGH POINT	SEASON
****/5	7.4 miles	3350 feet/ 4950 feet	Late July– mid-Oct

Maps: Green Trails Olympic Mountains East No. 168S, Custom Correct Mount Skokomish–Lake Cushman; **Contact:** Olympic National Forest, Hood Canal Ranger District, Quilcene and Olympic National Park, Wilderness Information Center; **Notes:** Dogs prohibited at park boundary. Camping (no fires) at lake requires permit; **GPS:** N 47 35.016, W 123 14.083

Cupped in a high cirque on snowy, craggy Mount Skokomish, Lake of the Angels in the Valley of Heaven is one of the prettiest alpine lakes in the Olympics. But reaching this divine destination is a passage through hell. The trail is brutally steep in places, requiring use of hands in one short section over a headwall. It's not dangerous, but hikers skittish on ledges may want to opt for another trail. For those who work hard to get to this celestial setting, expect one of the most dramatic backdrops in the Olympics as your reward.

GETTING THERE

From Hoodsport, travel north on US Highway 101 for 13.7 miles, turning left at milepost 318 onto Hamma Hamma River Road (Forest Road 25). (From Quilcene, travel south on US 101 for 23.5 miles, turning right onto FR 25.) Continue for 11.8 miles (the first 8 miles of which are paved) to the trailhead, (elev. 1600 ft), on the right.

ON THE TRAIL

Named in honor of Carl Putvin (his grave is along the trail), an early pioneer, trapper,

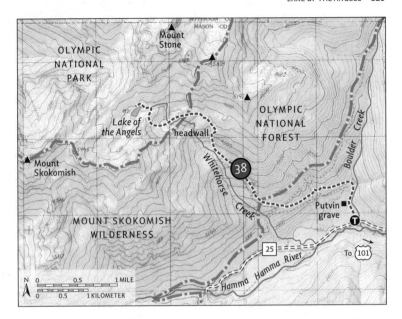

and explorer, the Putvin Trail No. 813 is as rugged and daring as its namesake. The first 1.2 miles, however, are relatively easygoing, traveling along tumbling Boulder Creek and crossing two narrow ravines before emerging on an old roadbed (elev. 2400 ft). From this point, the trail climbs more than 2000 feet in 1.7 miles.

Pass the old roadbed, soon enter the Mount Skokomish Wilderness, and waste no more time heading to the heavens. With Whitehorse Creek crashing trailside, it's up, up, and away. At 3500 feet, enjoy a brief respite from climbing, traversing a brushy avalanche chute at the base of a large headwall.

As Whitehorse Creek plummets over the sheer wall in a series of breathtakingly beautiful cascades, the trail looks for a way to get over the obstacle. Angling to the northeast,

it ascends a series of ledges, some requiring handholds or a sturdy anchored root to thrust you up to the rim of the headwall. Once you've subdued the wall, enjoy an alpine world flush with wildflower-bursting meadows and frog-fortified tarns, high on a bench above the Hamma Hamma Valley. Enjoy views, too, especially of imposing Mount Pershing across the valley and Hood Canal and the Cascades in the distance.

At 3 miles, enter Olympic National Park (elev. 4500 ft). Negotiate a crossing of Whitehorse Creek, and then make one final steep grunt over a snowfield and through thick greenery, reaching heavenly Lake of the Angels (elev. 4950 ft) at 3.7 miles. The lake is perched in an open basin scoured by ice and snow. Cascading waters fed by perpetual snowfields stream down polished rock faces and over terraced ledges.

Lake of the Angels in the Valley of Heaven

Resident marmots pierce the mountain air with their warning whistles, and nonnative mountain goats frequent the lake basin. It's quite spectacular.

EXTENDING YOUR TRIP

Lake of the Angels is sublime, and it's easy to while away the day in here. But if the hike in didn't beat you up, follow scramble paths higher up the slopes of 6434-foot Mount Skokomish and 6612-foot Mount Stone. Just the slopes, though, not the summits—those are climbers' domains. And be sure to avoid tramping across fragile heather meadows.

39 Mildred Lakes

RATING/ DIFFICULTY	ROUNDTRIP	ELEV GAIN/ HIGH POINT	SEASON
***/5	9 miles	2925 feet/ 4100 feet	July–Oct

Maps: Green Trails Olympic Mountains East No. 168S, Custom Correct Mount Skokomish–Lake Cushman; **Contact:** Olympic National Forest, Hood Canal Ranger District, Quilcene; **Notes:** NW Forest Pass or Interagency Pass required; **GPS:** N 47 34.517, W 123 15.672

Three beautiful backcountry lakes in a hidden valley surrounded by craggy summits await you at the end of this arduous hike. A boot-beaten path that'll leave you beat, the Mildred Lakes Trail was forged by tenacious fishermen and masochistic hikers. An entanglement of roots and rocks, along an up-and-down course that defies logic, this trail is notorious as one of the nastiest in the Olympics. This hike is all about the destination, not the journey.

GETTING THERE

From Hoodsport, travel north on US Highway 101 for 13.7 miles, turning left at milepost 318 onto Hamma Hamma River Road (Forest Road 25). (From Quilcene, travel south on US 101 for 23.5 miles, turning right onto FR 25).

Continue for 13.3 miles (the first 8 miles are paved; the last 1.5, rough) to the trailhead (elev. 1900 ft). Privy available.

ON THE TRAIL

Never officially constructed, the second half of this trail is little more than a way path. It's extremely steep in places, with very difficult tread—not recommended for children and beginning hikers. Starting near a dramatic gorge and waterfall (did you peek over the bridge before the parking lot?), Mildred Lakes Trail No. 822 immediately enters the Mount Skokomish Wilderness.

The first mile or so is easy enough as it winds through recovering wilderness that was logged decades ago. But once you cross a large avalanche chute and enter old growth, you'll commence with the misery. Around fallen logs, over fallen logs, and straight up rocky and rooty slopes, the trail climbs a 3200-foot ridge. Mount Pershing looms in the southeast.

Then through hemlock and huckleberry, the trail hightails it off the ridge, descending into a cool forested glen graced by rushing Huckleberry Creek (elev. 3000 ft). Skirt the creek and some camps, coming to a questionable log crossing at 2.3 miles. Teeter on the log or wade across, and soon come to another creek crossing, this one much easier.

Now the way gets tricky and tough. Ascend a steep ridge and come to a tight ravine. Using roots as handholds, drop 25 steep feet into a dank draw before resuming a taxing climb. After clambering over rock, root, and ledge—and gaining 1000 feet in elevation in less than 0.7 mile—the insanity ends on a 4100-foot heather-draped ridge crest. Wander along the open ledge, enjoying excellent views of Mount Cruiser and Sawtooth Ridge, but no lakes.

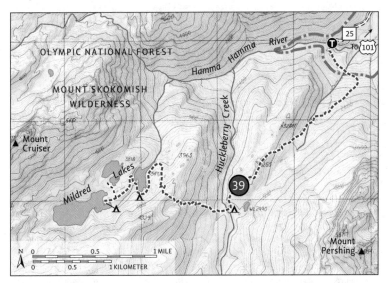

Middle Mildred Lake

Duckabush River Valley

From its origins in the glaciers and alpine lakes near O'Neil Pass, far within Olympic National Park, the Duckabush River cuts one of the great, deep valleys of the Olympics' eastern slope. But unlike the Hamma Hamma, Skokomish, and Dosewallips rivers, which have roads alongside them for miles, the Duckabush frees itself from civilization after only 6 miles. That leaves more than 20 miles of wilderness river valley unpenetrated by roads, accessible only by foot or on horseback.

While deep forays into the Duckabush Valley require backpacking, day hikers can still enjoy this ripe-with-rapids tumbling blue-green river. A couple of short hikes lead to a spectacular waterfall and a secluded chasm, respectively. Or enjoy a wilderness experience by sauntering just a few miles up the 20-mile Duckabush River Trail. And for strong hikers looking for a challenge, the Mount Jupiter Trail provides an eagle's-eye view of nearly the entire watershed—from its snowy mountainous origin to its terminus in Hood Canal.

Your punishment isn't over yet. Drop 250 feet through marshy, mosquito-breeding grounds before finally coming to the first lake (elev. 3750 ft). Set in deep old timber with a backdrop of rugged summits, the scene is serene and it's all yours—you deserve it. Scramble over more root and rock to the far side of the lake for good fishing, resting spots, and campsites. Share the abundant trout with the resident osprey.

Then head to Upper Mildred Lake (elev. 3825 ft), one of the largest backcountry lakes in the Olympics. Cross Lower Mildred's inlet stream and follow a rough path through heather meadows for 0.3 mile. To reach the rocky-island-dotted Middle Mildred Lake, follow a rudimentary path northwest that takes off from the upper lake path about 0.1 mile before reaching the upper lake.

40 Mount Jupiter

RATING/ DIFFICULTY	ROUNDTRIP	ELEV GAIN/ HIGH POINT	SEASON
*****/5	14 miles	3950 feet/ 5701 feet	Mid-June– Oct

Maps: Green Trails Olympic Mountains East No. 168S, Custom Correct the Brothers–Mount Anderson; **Contact:** Olympic National Forest, Hood Canal Ranger District, Quilcene; **Notes:** Road subject to changes and closures due to logging on adjacent private

REALLY GETTING MY GOAT

Name a nonnative invasive species in the Olympic Mountains: how about Scotch broom, purple loosestrife, Robert geranium, and mountain goats? Yes, mountain goats, those furry alpinists and members of the cattle family (*Bovidae*). They don't belong here. The mountain goat, indigenous to the Cascades and Rockies, was never native to the Olympic Mountains, isolated as they are by the Puget Trough. In the 1920s, before the establishment of Olympic National Park, a dozen goats from Canada were introduced to the Olympics for hunting purposes. Then in 1938, the national park was established, prohibiting hunting in much of the Olympic range. The goat population exploded, reaching 1500 by the early 1980s.

Foraging on plants endemic to the Olympics (which had never adapted to munching mountain goats), the furry invasives threatened the fragile alpine ecosystems, and the Park Service called for their removal. Big problem, though: the public loved watching the critters at Hurricane Ridge. Park plans for the goats' removal were often controversial and contentious, including such measures as allowing a hunt and sterilizing the animals. Ultimately, a removal program began in which over four hundred goats were tranquilized and helicopter-evacuated.

The program, while successful in its objective (mountain goat removal), fell under budget cuts and some loud (and often misguided) criticism and backlash. In 2018, the park service once again began removing and relocating goats and plans to continue for the next five years, making the park goat free. Now, let me make this clear. I love mountain goats, too, but in their natural environment. Current estimates for invasive goats in the Olympics are around 700 and growing. Meanwhile, the native goat population in Washington's Cascades has plummeted from 9000 in 1960 to around 3000 today. To me, it seems like two problems could be solved pretty easily. Hey you, Olympic goats! There's a whole wilderness area named after you in the Cascades. How about we help you move? The views are great and the meadows simply succulent.

lands. Road closed for wildlife management mid-Oct–May 1. Do not park in front of gate; **GPS:** N 47 41.049, W 122 57.414

This is a long, bone-dry, and at times steep trek to a former fire lookout site atop Mount Jupiter—but the views are worth the effort! Feast on them, from prominent eastern-slope Olympic peaks to Hood Canal, Mount Rainier, and a procession of Cascade peaks. Situated between Mount Constance and the Brothers, Jupiter also provides an eagle's-eye perspective of the Duckabush and Dosewallips valleys, two of the Olympics' great green portals into its hinterlands.

GETTING THERE

From Quilcene, drive south on US Highway 101 for 15 miles to Mount Jupiter Road (Road 92004), located on the right, exactly 2.5 miles beyond the Dosewallips State Park entrance. (If you're coming from the south, the turnoff is 0.5 mile north of the Duckabush Road junction.) Follow the gravel road for 3.1 miles to a junction and gate. If the gate is closed, park here (do not block gate). If the gate is open, bear left onto Road 92006.

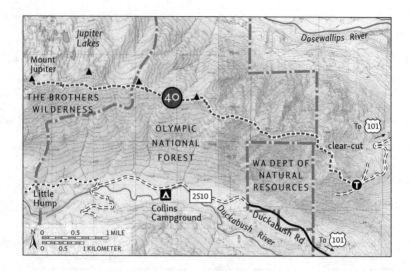

Then, following Road 92006, bear right at 0.4 mile and left at 1.4 miles. In another 0.8 mile, reach the signed trailhead (elev. 2050 ft) near a road junction in a recent clear-cut.

ON THE TRAIL

Starting on private timberland, Trail No. 809 switchbacks up a ridge through a recovering clear-cut. At 1 mile, traverse a steep slope harvested in 2013. Shortly afterward, reach standing timber at the Olympic National Forest boundary (elev. 2950 ft).

Next, enjoy fairly easy walking along a ridge crest draped with thick forest. In early summer, rhododendrons add splashes of color to the emerald cloak. Undulating between the Dosewallips and Duckabush watersheds (though there's no water along the trail), the way makes a few minor ups and downs as it progressively gains elevation.

At 3.3 miles, drop into a 3000-foot saddle. Then begin climbing more earnestly, rounding first a 3500-foot knob and shortly

afterward another knob that grants a view down to the Duckabush Valley. After a few more mild descents and ascents (which will seem major on the return), the trail ratchets up the climbing.

Through a thinning forest canopy and across open ledges, growing views convince you to carry on. At 5 miles, enter the Brothers Wilderness (elev. 3900 ft) and start getting down to business. Steeply and relentlessly, switchback up and across ledges (some blasted for trail construction) and dry open slopes. In early summer, wildflowers brush these forbidding slopes with dazzling colors.

At 7 miles, reach the 5701-foot rocky and open summit. Kick back and enjoy the incredible views in every direction: Waves of craggy Olympic peaks to the west and waves of saltwater in the Puget Sound basin to the east. Seattle's skyline shimmers in the afternoon sunlight. A series of remote tarns and the Jupiter Lakes sparkle in north-facing

Hiker admires Hood Canal from Jupiter's summit.

cirques far below. While Mount Jupiter is nowhere near being one of the Olympics' highest summits, its position along the eastern slope and its isolation from other peaks gives it a bit of distinction. Perhaps the Roman god who lent his name to this summit even prefers the views from here rather than from the remote, chilly, and oft-cloud-shrouded Mount Olympus.

41 Ranger Hole

RATING/ DIFFICULTY	ROUNDTRIP	ELEV GAIN/ HIGH POINT	SEASON
**/1	1.9 miles	250 feet/ 375 feet	Year-round

Maps: Green Trails Olympic Mountains East No. 168S, Custom Correct the Brothers–Mount Anderson; **Contact:** Olympic National Forest, Hood Canal Ranger District, Quilcene; **Notes:** NW Forest Pass or Interagency Pass required; **GPS:** N 47 40.882, W 122 59.670

From a historical ranger station—the oldest in the Olympics—travel back to the early days of the Olympic National Forest. Then amble under moss-draped trees to an isolated fishing hole in a thundering chasm on the Duckabush River.

GETTING THERE

From Quilcene, drive south on US Highway 101 for 15.5 miles, turning right at milepost 310 onto Duckabush Road. (From Shelton, drive north on US 101 for 37 miles, turning left onto Duckabush Road.) Drive 3.6 miles to the trailhead (elev. 300 ft) at the Interrorem Cabin. Water and privy available.

Duckabush River thundering in the Ranger Hole

ON THE TRAIL

This short, oft-overlooked trail leads to, not along, the Duckabush, stoking your anticipation as it cuts its way through a dense and dank forest and delivers you to a sunny ledge above the tumbling and churning river. But before you make a beeline to the river, a little history lesson is in order. Start by admiring the Interrorem Cabin. Built in 1907, this structure is the oldest Forest Service dwelling on the Olympic Peninsula. Interrorem served as a ranger station, a base for Works Progress Administration and Civilian Conservation Corps workers, and a fire guard station. The Forest Service now rents it out for overnight stays (www.recreation.gov). Respect the privacy of any guests.

The first overnighter at Interrorem was Ranger Emery Finch. Mr. Finch, an avid fisherman, was responsible for building Ranger Hole Trail No. 824—an 0.8-mile path to his favorite fishing hole on the Duckabush. Through mature second growth (cut circa Finch's tenure), the good path climbs a little hump (elev. 375 ft) and then makes a slow descent toward the river. In April hundreds of trilliums line the way. As the Duckabush's roar becomes more audible, the trail makes a steep drop, skirts a recent washout, and then emerges at the famed fishing spot (elev. 200 ft).

While the fishing isn't what it used to be, you'll still catch some good views of the river. The Duckabush crashes through a narrow chasm here. Frothy gurgling waters crash up against the narrow cleft. Be sure to keep children and dogs nearby while admiring this landmark. On your return, take the 0.3-mile interpretive loop for more information on the Interrorem Cabin and the Ranger Hole.

42 Duckabush River and Big Hump

RATING/ DIFFICULTY	ROUNDTRIP	ELEV GAIN/ HIGH POINT	SEASON
***/3	10.6 miles	2150 feet/ 1700 feet	Year-round

Maps: Green Trails Olympic Mountains East No. 168S, Custom Correct the Brothers–Mount Anderson; **Contact:** Olympic National Forest, Hood Canal Ranger District, Quilcene; **Notes:** NW Forest Pass or Interagency Pass required. Open to horses; **GPS:** N 47 41.100, W 123 02.393

The Duckabush River Trail travels more than 20 miles into the heart of the Olympic Peninsula, but a trip of 3, 4, or 5 miles up this well-maintained path delivers ample scenery, solitude, and opportunities for spotting bears or elk. Marvel

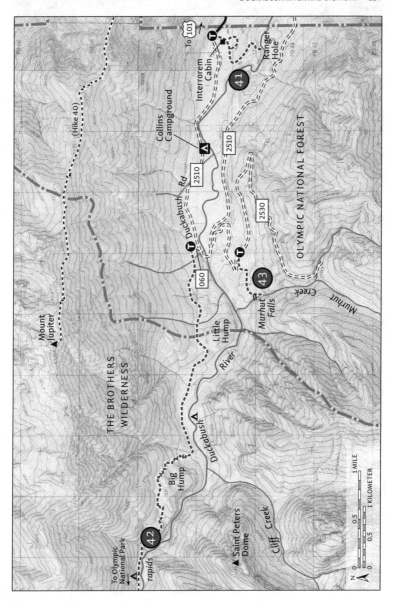

Mossy overhanging branch along the Duckabush River

at the wild river as it tumbles over giant boulders and squeezes through narrow rocky clefts, and stand atop ledges on Big Hump surveying the wild valley.

GETTING THERE

From Quilcene, drive south on US Highway 101 for 15.5 miles, turning right at milepost 310 onto Duckabush Road. (From Shelton, drive north on US 101 for 37 miles, turning left onto Duckabush Road.) Follow Duckabush Road for 6 miles; it becomes Forest Road 2510 (and gravel) at 3.6 miles. Pass a horse-unloading area and turn right onto FR Spur 060, proceeding 0.2 mile to the trailhead (elev. 425 ft). Privy available.

ON THE TRAIL

Duckabush River Trail No. 803 begins on an old roadbed, gently climbing through uniform second-growth firs. At 1.2 miles, the trail enters the Brothers Wilderness at a gap (elev. 900 ft) near Little Hump. Now on bona fide trail, descend 250 feet and then follow an old logging railroad grade, cutting through a mossy wonderland on an almost perfectly flat path. A few remnant old firs greet you along the way.

Pass a campsite and at about 2.3 miles, the river finally comes into view. At 2.6 miles, come to an absolutely gorgeous spot where giant emerald cedars and firs hang over churning white water. This mesmerizing spot is a good place to turn around if you don't want to make the steep 1000-foot climb up Big Hump.

If you're hankering to hike the Hump, continue, passing some good camps in an old-growth grove before commencing to switchback. Soon, fire-scarred trees greet you. Climbing higher, the trail traverses a large area scorched by wildfire 2011 (from a careless camper). Avoid this area during high winds, as burnt snags are prone to toppling.

At about 3.1 miles, emerge onto a ledge (elev. 1100 ft) with a spectacular view east down the river valley and out to the Cascades. The impressive Saint Peters Dome hovers to the south. More spectacular than the view is the spring floral show. Come in April for fawn lilies. In May, rhodies flaunt their blossoms. This is a good spot to turn around. But if you want to keep hiking, resume climbing, encountering another outcropping before cresting the Hump (elev. 1700 ft) at 3.9 miles.

Then, through burnt forest and remnant old growth, the way descends toward the river. At 5.3 miles and after dropping 600 feet, the trail finally reaches the river again at a well-used camping area near a series of impressive rapids—a great spot to call it quits. Enjoy the view. Watch for darting dippers. And rest up for your return back over the Hump.

EXTENDING YOUR TRIP

Feeling energetic? Continue upriver, traversing a talus slope before passing a nice camping area and waterfall. Then traverse ledges along and above the river. Leave the burn zone for good and hike through beautiful old-growth groves, reaching the Olympic National Park boundary at 6.7 miles (elev. 1240 ft; dogs prohibited). Beyond, the trail continues another 15 miles to Marmot Lake.

43 Murhut Falls

RATING/ DIFFICULTY	ROUNDTRIP	ELEV GAIN/ HIGH POINT	SEASON
**/1	1.6 miles	300 feet/ 1050 feet	Year-round

Maps: Green Trails Olympic Mountains East No. 168S, Custom Correct the Brothers–Mount Anderson; **Contact:** Olympic National Forest, Hood Canal Ranger District, Quilcene; **Notes:** NW Forest Pass or Interagency Pass required; **GPS:** N 47 40.616, W 123 02.360

Follow a short and easy trail to a beautiful 130-foot, two-tiered waterfall set in a tight ravine. Come in May and marvel at blooming Pacific rhododrons along the way.

GETTING THERE

From Quilcene, drive south on US Highway 101 for 15.5 miles, turning right at milepost

Murhut Falls

310 onto Duckabush Road. (From Shelton, drive north on US 101 for 37 miles, turning left onto Duckabush Road.) Follow Ducka-bush Road for 6.3 miles to a junction just beyond a bridge over the Duckabush River (the road becomes Forest Road 2510 and gravel at 3.6 miles). After the bridge, bear right onto FR 2530 and continue for 1.3 miles to the trailhead (elev. 800 ft). Park on the left in a small pullout.

ON THE TRAIL

Trail No. 828 starts by following an old logging road converted to trail. It was the logging in this area that led to the discovery of Murhut Falls, hidden in a narrow ravine.

It's understandable why early traipsers missed these falls.

Follow the good trail for a short climb of about 250 feet, rounding a ridge. Then on single-track trail, descend about 50 feet into a ravine, catching a glimpse or two through the trees of Mount Jupiter across the Ducka-bush Valley. At this point, the roar of Murhut Falls is quite loud. Continue into the damp, dark, cedar-lined ravine, and at 0.8 mile behold the falls crashing before you. The upper waterfall drops more than 100 feet; the lower one crashes about 30. Save this hike for spring when snowmelt adds to the falls' intensity and flowering rhododendrons line the trail.

Dosewallips River Valley

One of the great passages into the heart of the Olympic interior, the Dosewallips River cuts a deep, narrow valley through the range's eastern front and is fed by three main forks. The middle one, Silt Creek, origi-nates high on Mount Anderson at Eel Glacier, the largest glacier in the eastern Olympics.

Flowing within the shadow of some of the loftiest peaks on the peninsula, the Dosewal-lips is surrounded by supreme alpine beauty. Long a haven for backpackers, this wild valley also offers day hikers a few choices. But the river is prone to raging tantrums—its periodic floods often claim tread, bridges, and the access road. Since 2002 the valley has been off-limits to all but the strongest day hikers because of a devastating road washout (see the "All Washed Up" sidebar). Day hiking around the river's terminus at Hood Canal, however, remains inviting and accessible to all hikers.

44 Dosewallips State Park

RATING/ DIFFICULTY	LOOP	ELEV GAIN/ HIGH POINT	SEASON
**/2	3.6 miles	550 feet/ 425 feet	Year-round

Maps: Green Trails Olympic Mountains East No. 168S, state park map at ranger station; **Contact:** Dosewallips State Park; **Notes:** Discover Pass required. Dogs permitted on-leash; **GPS:** N 47 41.380, W 122 54.184

 *The 425-acre Dosewallips State Park, well-known for family-friendly camping and great shell fishing on Hood Canal, offers good hiking too, unbeknownst to many visitors. Over 5 miles of trail lead along the Dosewallips River, crossing tumbling creeks and traversing quiet stands of tall timber. Relics of the area's bygone logging days add historical perspective to peaceful rambling.*

GETTING THERE

From Quilcene, drive US Highway 101 south for 12 miles to the state park campground entrance at milepost 307. (From Shelton, follow US 101 north for 40 miles.) Turn right (west) into the park, proceed 0.3 mile, and park near the ranger station (elev. 25 ft). Privy and water available.

ON THE TRAIL

Legend has it that Dos-wail-opsh was a Twana Indian who was turned into a mountain, forming the source of the Dosewallips River. From his lofty position in the Olympic wilderness, this transformed Native American created one of the peninsula's most wild and scenic rivers—enjoy some of its grandeur and bounty with ease here at Dosewallips State Park.

Start by walking the dirt road (signed for Maple Valley Trail) that heads northwest from the ranger station. Walk past the Meadow Group Camp and reach the Maple

Phantom Creek Bridge on the Maple Valley Trail

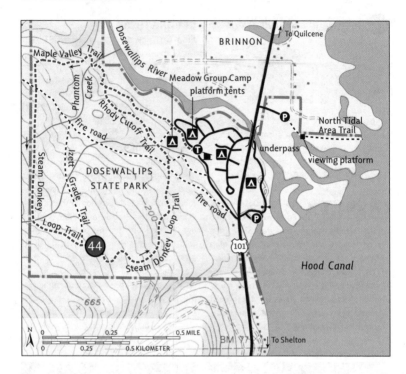

Valley trailhead in 0.1 mile. Soon after, come to the river. Hike through a forest of cedars, cottonwoods, and of course maples, both big-leaf and vine. In fall, the canopy is a radiant gold.

The trail hugs a steep slope above a river channel, coming to a junction with the Rhody Cutoff Trail at 0.4 mile. You'll be returning from the left, so head right, gently descending to a bridged crossing of cascading Phantom Creek. The way then climbs a bluff and moves away from the river, passing benches for those who need a break. Then in fir forest and skirting an old cut along the park's boundary, the trail bends left and reaches a fire road (elev. 220 ft)

at 1 mile, providing a shortcut back to the campground. To continue on the loop, go straight on the Steam Donkey Loop Trail along the park's western periphery. Gently climb through maturing second growth, once again crossing Phantom Creek. Then cross a creek with a colorful name describing an embarrassing incident.

After crossing another cascading creek, crest the ridge (elev. 425 ft) and begin a long descent on an old woods road through maturing timber. At 1.8 miles, the Izett Grade Trail takes off left on an old logging railroad grade for 0.5 mile back to the fire road. Continue right on a downhill course, eventually skirting a small dammed pool, whose waters powered the steam donkeys this trail was named for. Loggers used these machines in the early twentieth century to power winches for yarding and loading large logs at a railway landing.

Shortly afterward, at 2.5 miles, intersect the fire road again. Continue straight, passing part of the old railroad bed that was decommissioned in 1913. Then descend, staying left at a junction onto the Rhody Cutoff Trail (right goes to the park road). Cross a bridge spanning a cedar-studded creek (elev. 50 ft) and bear left again (right goes to a group camp). Climb a ridge (elev. 150 ft) rife with rhododendrons before descending and meeting back up with the Maple Valley Trail at 3.2 miles. Turn right, retracing familiar steps 0.4 mile to your start.

EXTENDING YOUR TRIP

Dosewallips State Park's campground, complete with platform tents and cabins, makes a good base for exploring nearby Olympic National Park and Forest. The Dosewallips River drains into Hood Canal at the park, creating a productive delta and estuary perfect for exploration. Follow the 0.3-mile North Tidal Area Trail to a viewing platform in the delta and look for seals and abundant birdlife.

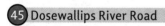

45 Dosewallips River Road

RATING/ DIFFICULTY	ROUNDTRIP	ELEV GAIN/ HIGH POINT	SEASON
**/3	11 miles	1300 feet/ 1600 feet	Year-round

Maps: Green Trails Olympic Mountains East No. 168S, Custom Correct the Brothers–Mount Anderson; **Contact:** Olympic National Forest, Hood Canal Ranger District, Quil-

cene, and Olympic National Park, Wilderness Information Center; **Notes:** Dogs permitted on-leash. Open to mountain bikes; **GPS:** N 47 44.346, W 123 04.373

Severed by a washout, Dosewallips Road has been closed to vehicles since 2002. While its fate is still being disputed, thanks to a reroute around the slide you can hike the road (or bike it). Much of the way is a slog, but there are some highlights, including a couple of nice riverside stretches and a beautiful thundering waterfall.

GETTING THERE

From Quilcene, drive south on US Highway 101 for 11 miles to Brinnon, turning right at milepost 306 onto Dosewallips Road. (From Shelton, drive north on US 101 for 41 miles and turn left, 1 mile beyond Dosewallips State Park.) Proceed 8.5 miles to a rough area prone to washouts. You might have to park here; if the way is passable, continue another 1.2 miles to the trailhead (elev. 600 ft) at the 2002 washout.

ON THE TRAIL

Walk west past the road barrier and immediately come to the large 2002 washout that closed the rest of this road to vehicle traffic. It's unclear if the upper road will be reopened (see the "All Washed Up" sidebar). But thanks to the Washington Trails Association, which constructed a bypass around the huge slide, hikers and cyclists can travel the road upriver.

Head right, onto the bypass, steeply climbing 100-plus feet on the riverbank above the slide. Then descend 100 feet, reaching the roadbed at 0.4 mile. Walk the road along the churning river, noticing how quickly vegetation has reclaimed the

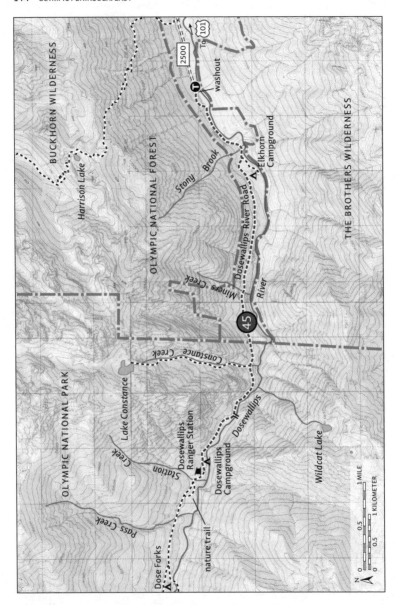

roadbed. The road soon pulls away from the river, reaching a junction (elev. 700 ft) at 1.3 miles. The road-trail left leads a short distance to the Forest Service's Elkhorn Campground—one of two once-popular car campgrounds that now serve as backcountry camps (no fee or permit).

Head right and climb, the river now far below in a canyon, out of sight but not out of sound. Pass beneath some ledges and cross a cascading creek. Then enter the scorched remains of a forest from a 2009 lightning-caused fire. Soon afterward, at 3.9 miles, enter Olympic National Park (elev. 1300 ft). Dogs prohibited beyond this point.

Cross Constance Creek and then come to the Lake Constance Trail. Continue climbing, passing a big overhanging boulder. The way then drops about 100 feet, skirting beneath a big ledge before coming to the base of a dramatic 100-plus-foot waterfall. Steeply climb beside the raging cascade, admiring its hydrological force—especially during autumn and winter rains.

The road-trail then follows a gentler course as it enters a hanging valley. The river flows more gently here too. At 5.5 miles, after a slight descent, reach the Dosewallips Campground (elev. 1550 ft), another former car campground now a backcountry camp (no fee or permit). Set in a grassy flat shaded by big-leaf maples and frequented by docile deer, this is a great spot for lunch, a nap, or to call it quits.

EXTENDING YOUR TRIP

Walk through the campground 0.2 mile to the old Dosewallips trailhead near the ranger station. Strong day hikers can easily add the 1.1-mile Dosewallips Terrace Nature Trail Loop and/or continue up the rhododendron-lined Dosewallips River Trail 1.4 miles to a

Dramatic waterfall on the Dosewallips River

junction, from where it's 0.2 mile to the Dose Forks bridge and backcountry campsites (permit required).

Strong day hikers who bike Dosewallips Road can ditch their bikes at the campground and hike several miles up the West Fork Dosewallips River Trail or attempt the challenging and rewarding 12-mile roundtrip from the old trailhead to Sunnybrook Meadows (with 4000 feet of elevation gain).

46 Lake Constance

RATING/ DIFFICULTY	ROUNDTRIP	ELEV GAIN/ HIGH POINT	SEASON
***/5+	12.6 miles	4300 feet/ 4800 feet	Late June–Oct

Maps: Green Trails Olympic Mountains East No. 168S, Custom Correct Buckhorn Wilderness; **Contact:** Olympic National Park, Wilderness Information Center; **Notes:** Dogs prohibited. Requires scrambling and routefinding skills. Fire in 2009 wreaked serious damage, creating many obstacles and hazards; **GPS:** N 47 43.777, W 123 08.504

This secluded tarn is tucked in a cleft high on Mount Constance, a mind-blowing setting. Turquoise waters reflect sheer cliffs that spiral to the heavens. But getting here is arduous. The climbers' path requires stamina, sure footing, and use of hands. The elevation gain is insane: 3400 feet in 2.2 miles. And to make things even more difficult and long, a fire laid waste to half the trail and the access road is washed out. Only the most dogged and skilled hikers should attempt this trip.

GETTING THERE

From Quilcene, drive south on US Highway 101 for 11 miles to Brinnon, turning right at milepost 306 onto Dosewallips Road. (From Shelton, drive north on US 101 for 41 miles and turn left, 1 mile beyond Dosewallips State Park). Proceed 8.5 miles to a rough area prone to washouts. You might have to park here; if the way is passable, continue another 1.2 miles to the trailhead (elev. 600 ft) at the huge 2002 washout.

ON THE TRAIL

Since 2002, Dosewallips Road has been washed out at mile 9.7, requiring a 4.1-mile walk or bike ride to reach the Lake

Lake Constance sits in a high rocky basin.

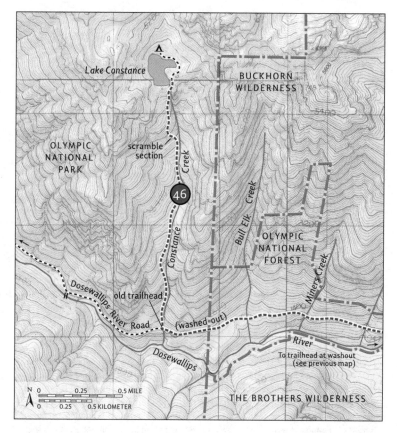

Constance trailhead. Start by walking west past the road barrier and heading to the right on a bypass trail around the huge slide. Climb 100-plus feet on the riverbank above the slide, and then descend 100 feet to the roadbed at 0.4 mile. Walk the old road and bear right at 1.3 miles. Steadily climb above the river, now far below in a canyon. Pass beneath some ledges and cross a cascading creek. Then enter the scorched remains of a 2009 lightning-caused fire. Enter Olympic National Park, cross Constance Creek, and at 4.1 miles reach the Lake Constance Trail (elev. 1400 ft), which may be unsigned.

In burnt forest, immediately climb—and steeply. Fallen blackened trees, eroded tread, and choking brush make for difficult hiking and possibly tough routefinding. But though this is the hardest trail in the national park, Lake Constance is a fairly popular destination for bivouacking alpinists and a substantial number of tenacious hikers.

ALL WASHED UP

Most hikers probably agree that far too many roads mar our national forests. Most hikers also probably support decommissioning many of these past relics of the age of unsustainable logging, perhaps converting a handful of them to trails. But what most hikers don't agree on is what to do after a washout or series of washouts renders a major access road to a favorite trailhead impassable.

Such is the case with Dosewallips Road. The winter of 2002 walloped the road with a 300-foot washout. Repairing the road would require serious capital—hard to come by in these days of cash-strapped forest and parks budgets. And a new road would also need some realignment—which could mean losing some mature trees and possibly increasing sedimentation in the river.

Conservationists and some hikers, seeing a silver lining in the washout, point out that critical salmon habitat—degraded when the road was first designed—could be properly restored. They see Dosewallips Road as ripe for becoming an all-season, low-country hiking trail, with the bonus of restoring the valley to a wilderness state.

Other hikers disagree. They argue that the road can be repaired with minimal impact to the environment and that the cost is justified by the valley's popularity. This would restore two well-loved car campgrounds and a beloved trailhead that once provided easy access to a remote corner of Olympic National Park, now unnecessarily off-limits to thousands of recreationists. Most people, the road proponents say, lack the time and physical energy now required to access this popular area.

The Forest Service supports rebuilding the road. Local communities support rebuilding the road, saying that Jefferson County has lost its only eastside access to the national park. Some environmental groups, on the other hand, support converting the road to a trail. The washout has done more than just sever the road. It has divided the hiking community.

This guidebook author supports reopening the road, and I believe it can be done with minimal environmental impact. Dwindling access to public lands is a serious problem in this state—exacerbated by our growing population. If the tax-paying public can't access their lands, will they continue to vote to support them? So much of Olympic National Park is already off-limits to day hikers. Sure, you can hike or mountain bike the road to the old Dosewallips trailhead—parts of the road trip are pretty. But much of it is a slog, and the extra mileage is beyond many day hikers' physical limits.

When the hiking community becomes deeply polarized on issues such as rebuilding Dosewallips Road, how will it come together to support much larger (and in my opinion more important) habitat-protecting initiatives such as new wilderness legislation?

Head up the extremely narrow draw cut by Constance Creek, clambering over root, rock, and downed trees along the crashing, bashing creek. The straight-up route defies gravity. Pass numerous picturesque cascades—many are fine destinations in themselves if you find yourself questioning continuing. Giant boulders litter the forest floor, including a couple of mini Rocks of Gibraltar. After gaining 1600 feet in just over 0.75 mile, the trail grants a reprieve. The relief is brief, though; the trail soon resumes its mountainside attack with even more fury. Fortunately, a cool canopy of old growth welcomes you after the burn zone.

As the valley closes in, the trail has no choice but to go directly up the creekbed. It's a rocky, brushy affair and, depending on water flow, also wet. The worst of this gauntlet is next. The route leaves the creek, ascending straight up the wall of the narrow draw. It's steep but not exposed. Using your hands and Spidey strength, scramble up the abrupt slope. Occasionally look back at the Brothers hovering in the distance. Finally, at the brink of exhaustion, after probably the hardest 2.2 miles of your hiking career, enter the hidden basin housing Lake Constance (elev. 4800 ft). Its beauty should take away what little breath you have left.

Despite this rugged setting beneath the Olympics' third-highest summit, the lakeshore is fragile. Please walk lightly and respect areas closed for restoration. Consider walking 0.3 mile on a trail along the eastern lakeshore to an open area of talus and boulders, for a good place to sit in the sun above the lake. Nurse those knees for the descent.

Quilcene River Valley

A rugged area of easily accessible trails, the Quilcene River valley offers a wide array of hiking options, from easy to challenging. Blessed with mild temperatures and moderate annual precipitation, the valley is a good choice for year-round adventures.

Much of the surrounding steep ridges succumbed to the chain saw in the past,

but the forests began recovering after the timber industry went into a deep decline on the Olympic Peninsula. Mount Walker and Quilcene Ridge, both once heavily logged, now offer delightful hiking through unbroken forest.

The upper reaches of both the Big and Little Quilcene rivers lie within the 44,000-acre Buckhorn Wilderness, the largest protected area in Olympic National Forest. The Tunnel Creek and Marmot Pass trails take hikers into the Buckhorn, to some of the wildest and prettiest forest and alpine zones in the eastern Olympics.

47 Mount Walker

RATING/ DIFFICULTY	ROUNDTRIP	ELEV GAIN/ HIGH POINT	SEASON
**/3	5 miles	2050 feet/ 2804 feet	Year-round

Map: Green Trails Olympic Mountains East No. 168S; **Contact:** Olympic National Forest, Hood Canal Ranger District, Quilcene; **Notes:** Road gated in winter—park away from gate and walk 0.3 mile to trailhead; **GPS:** N 47 46.554, W 122 54.854

Hovering over the glacial trough known as Hood Canal, Mount Walker is the easternmost peak in the Olympic Mountains. From its two summits you can gaze out over the Puget lowlands to the Seattle skyline or cast your eyes westward to jagged, mighty Mount Constance. In May and June, rhododendrons transform Walker into a purple mountain majesty.

GETTING THERE

From Quilcene, drive US Highway 101 south for 5 miles. (From Shelton, follow US 101

Hood Canal from the South Summit

north for 47 miles.) Just north of milepost 300, turn left (east) onto Mount Walker Road (Forest Road 2730) and proceed 0.3 mile to the trailhead (elev. 850 ft), on the right.

ON THE TRAIL

Washington's state flower, the Pacific (or coast) rhododendron, grows in profusion along the steep, dry slopes of Mount Walker. For much of the year, the rhodies merely add a layer of dark green to the forest understory. But come late spring, this hardy shrub adds its rosy-purple bouquets to the surrounding firs and hemlocks. By June, vibrant violet bell-shaped blossoms ring throughout the emerald forest. Mount Walker is one of the best places in the state to witness this floral show. If you can't come for the blossoms, Mount Walker also makes for a great winter hike. With the summit road closed, you won't have to worry about sharing those far-flung Puget Sound views.

Start on hiker-only Mount Walker Trail No. 894—it's short and steep but well main-tained. Immediately begin climbing through a tunnel of rhodies under a uniform canopy of second-growth cedars and hemlocks. Look up occasionally to see if you can locate any of the old wire and insulators that once serviced a fire tower on the summit. After about 1.5 miles, small ledges begin to break the forest monotony and tease with limited views.

The grade eases slightly, and after 2 miles and nearly 2000 feet of climbing you emerge at the North Summit viewpoint, the site of a fire lookout from 1931 to 1967. Enjoy good but limited views to the west and north. Then head to the South Summit (dogs must be leashed at the summits), reached by walking the graveled Summit Road for 0.4 mile and then following a 0.1-mile trail to a breathtaking panoramic view of Puget Sound. Stare straight down to Dabob Bay and the Toandos Peninsula. Behind, Green and Gold mountains rise on the Kitsap Peninsula and Mount Rainier adds a snowy backdrop. And if you're here in June, the

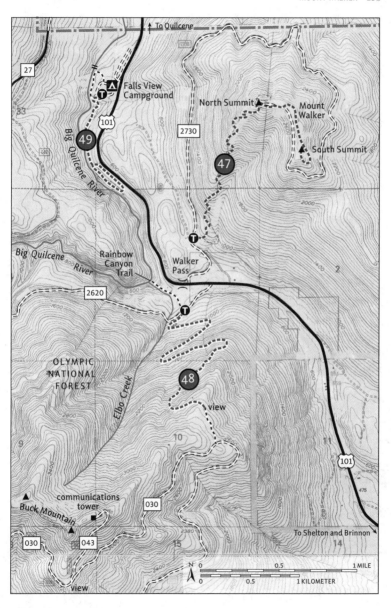

To Quilcene

27

33

Falls View
Campground

North Summit

Mount
Walker

101

Big Quilcene River

2730

49

47

South Summit

Big Quilcene River

Rainbow
Canyon
Trail

Walker
Pass

2

2620

OLYMPIC
NATIONAL
FOREST

48

view

Elbo Creek

9

10

11

101

communications
tower

Buck Mountain

030

030

043

view

15

2380

14

To Shelton and Brinnon

N   0   0.5   1 MILE
    0   0.5   1 KILOMETER

whole scene will be framed with fragrant purple boughs.

If the road is closed (winter), consider returning on it. It loops 3.9 miles around the mountain, offering more views of the surrounding territory.

48 Elbo Creek

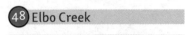

RATING/ DIFFICULTY	ROUNDTRIP	ELEV GAIN/ HIGH POINT	SEASON
**/3	4.6 miles	1770 feet/ 2600 feet	Year-round

Map: Green Trails Olympic Mountains East No. 168S; **Contact:** Olympic National Forest, Hood Canal Ranger District, Quilcene; **GPS:** N 47 46.263, W 122 55.000

Uniform second-growth forest along the Elbo Creek Trail

 *This abandoned trail up Buck Mountain was recently reopened by the Washington Trails Association. Views are limited, but so are crowds, making this peaceful hike perfect on an overcast winter's day or during late spring when a host of blossoming rhododendrons brighten the way.*

GETTING THERE

From Quilcene, drive US Highway 101 south for 5.2 miles, turning right (west) onto Rocky Brook Road (Forest Road 2620), just south of milepost 300 and Mount Walker Road. (From Shelton, follow US 101 north for 46.8 miles and turn left.) Continue west on FR 2620 for 0.2 mile to the trailhead (elev. 830 ft).

ON THE TRAIL

Technically, this trail starts at the abandoned Rainbow Campground, but most folks begin from FR 2620, where parking is better. The Civilian Conservation Corps first constructed the trail in the 1930s, and it once went all the way to Buck Mountain. But logging in the 1960s and 1970s obliterated much of the route. When the Washington Trails Association reopened the trail, we gained another year-round hiking option.

Trail No. 892.1 steadily ascends a ridge, switch backing through second-growth Douglas-firs and hemlocks. Salal and rhodies line the well-constructed tread. Elbo Creek is out of view in the ravine below, but you can hear it cascading downslope.

On a good grade, continue climbing, eventually leaving the old trailbed at around 2 miles. The way then heads east and terminates in a large blowdown area (elev. 2600 ft) at 2.3 miles. Enjoy a view out to Mount Walker and the Quilcene Ridge and valley before heading back to your vehicle.

EXTENDING YOUR TRIP

From the windfall, you can easily continue hiking on a well-defined boot-beaten path 0.2 mile to FR Spur 030 (elev. 2700 ft). Turn right and walk this lightly driven road 1.5 miles to a 3300-foot gap between Buck Mountain and Mount Turner for an excellent view of Jupiter Mountain, Mount Constance, and the Dosewallips River valley.

From the trailhead, you can follow a trail north 0.2 mile to the abandoned Rainbow Campground. Then walk 0.5-mile Rainbow Canyon Trail No. 892 down into the Big Quilcene River gorge (elev. 450 ft).

49 Falls View Canyon

RATING/DIFFICULTY	ROUNDTRIP	ELEV GAIN/HIGH POINT	SEASON
**/1	1.5 miles	400 feet/450 feet	Year-round

Map: Green Trails Olympic Mountains East No. 168S; **Contact:** Olympic National Forest, Hood Canal Ranger District, Quilcene; **Notes:** NW Forest Pass or Interagency Pass required; **GPS:** N 47 47.367, W 122 55.698

From a popular campground off a busy highway, escape the commotion in a hidden little canyon along the Big Quilcene River. Enjoy the serenading rapids and in springtime a floral show of blossoming lilies, honeysuckle, and rhododendrons. And as the canyon name suggests, there's a waterfall too.

GETTING THERE

From Quilcene, drive US Highway 101 south for 3.6 miles to Falls View Campground. (From Shelton, follow US 101 north for 48.5 miles.) Enter the campground and turn left,

Big Quilcene River in Falls View Canyon

proceeding 0.3 mile to the trailhead (elev. 450 ft) in the day-use picnic area. Privy available. When the campground is closed, park at the gated entrance.

ON THE TRAIL

Plunging from the get-go, Trail No. 868 loses nearly 200 feet of elevation in 0.1 mile. Frothing white water comes into view as the trail leads to a ledge alongside the thundering Big Quilcene River. Here, deep within the chasm, the river's roar amplifies, ricocheting off the guarding walls.

Next, cross a side creek on a bridge, under a canopy of maples veiled with mosses, and follow the rushing river upstream. Stop periodically to be mesmerized by the churning, turning, chugging waters. At 0.5 mile, come to a junction (elev. 325 ft). Head either way—it's a loop. To the right, the trail continues a short distance alongside the Big Quilcene, passing more rapids before climbing about 75 feet and descending back to the junction. Then head back to your car, remembering that a small climb awaits you at the finish.

EXTENDING YOUR TRIP

What about the falls of Falls View? Before or after your canyon ramble, walk the adjacent (wheelchair-accessible) 0.1-mile Falls View Loop Trail No. 848. It leads to a promontory above the canyon, where you can gaze straight down to the roiling Big Quilcene River. Cast your attention straight across the canyon, too, to an unnamed creek cascading 100 feet into the cleft.

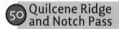

50 Quilcene Ridge and Notch Pass

RATING/ DIFFICULTY	ROUNDTRIP	ELEV GAIN/ HIGH POINT	SEASON
**/4	8.4 miles	2800 feet/ 2400 feet	Apr–Nov

Map: Green Trails Olympic Mountains East No. 168S; **Contact:** Olympic National Forest, Hood Canal Ranger District, Quilcene; **GPS:** N 47 49.579, W 122 56.316

Through a pass high on Quilcene Ridge, retrace an ancient Native American route. In the 1930s, Roosevelt's Tree Army—the Civilian Conservation Corps—constructed a good trail over the centuries-old route. By the 1960s, however, the trail was abandoned. Then in the 1990s, a Forest Service wilderness crew, the Quilcene Ranger Corps, and a Washington Trails Association work party restored and reopened it. The way is steep, and there aren't many views, but a hike through Notch Pass is a quiet walk back in time.

Bridge over Townsend Creek

GETTING THERE

From Quilcene, drive US Highway 101 south for 1.5 miles. (From Shelton, follow US 101 north for 50.5 miles.) Turn right (west) onto Penny Creek Road. After 1.5 miles, bear left onto Big Quilcene River Road (Forest Road 27). Proceed 1 mile, taking a right on an unmarked dirt road (FR Spur 010). Continue 1.3 miles to the trailhead (elev. 700 ft), where there's limited parking on the right shoulder.

ON THE TRAIL

In my home state of New Hampshire, mountain passes are called notches. So to me Notch Pass sounds redundant. And this "pass pass" will feel like two too, after you've made the steep climb. This notch in your hiking belt is going to cost you 1700 vertical feet in just over 2 miles.

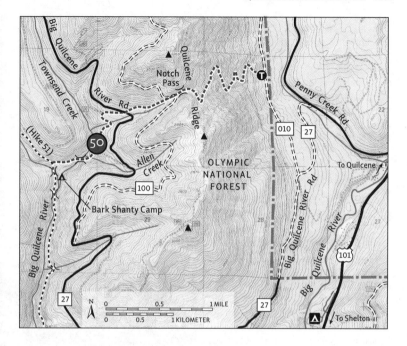

Trail No. 831 immediately starts off steep. Via long switchbacks, work your way up a salal-, rhododendron-, and fir-covered slope. Much of Quilcene Ridge went up in flames in the 1930s. Fire-scarred cedars and charred stumps and snags attest to the past conflagration. Continue climbing through thick forest, occasionally broken with limited views out to Mount Walker. After 1 mile, cross a sometimes-flowing creek, the only water source on this side of the ridge.

After the relentless elevation gain, enter the dark notch of a pass at 2.1 miles. Now high on Quilcene Ridge (elev. 2400 ft), pass through a tunnel of scrappy, tightly packed trees. At 2.2 miles, emerge in daylight on reaching an old logging road. It's kind of anticlimactic, but the best is yet to come if

you don't mind losing 900 feet of elevation and regaining it all on your return. Cross the road and descend through a scree-covered and ledgy mininotch. At 2.7 miles, come to FR 27 (elev. 2100 ft), an alternative trailhead with limited parking.

The trail resumes across the road, a few hundred feet to the right. Walk the road a couple of hundred feet more for some good views of Mounts Townsend and Constance. Then resume hiking on trail, descending into the Townsend Creek valley through a mixture of new and old growth adorned with rhodies. At 3.5 miles, marvel at the Mosquito Rock erratic before crossing cascading Allen Creek.

Just beyond, in a lush ravine crowded with ancient conifers, reach Townsend Creek.

Cross it on a sturdy bridge. Then climb 100 feet above its banks before descending 100 feet to meet the Lower Big Quilcene River Trail (elev. 1500 ft) just above the Bark Shanty Bridge at 4.2 miles. Take a break along the Big Quil before making the up-and-over return to your start.

EXTENDING YOUR TRIP

Amble up or down the Lower Big Quilcene River Trail (Hike 51), or arrange a car shuttle for a one-way hike over Notch Pass and out the Big Quil.

51 Lower Big Quilcene River

RATING/ DIFFICULTY	ROUNDTRIP	ELEV GAIN/ HIGH POINT	SEASON
***/2	10.2 miles	800 feet/ 2000 feet	Apr–Nov

Maps: Green Trails Olympic Mountains East No. 168S, Custom Correct Buckhorn Wilderness; **Contact:** Olympic National Forest, Hood Canal Ranger District, Quilcene; **Notes:** NW Forest Pass or Interagency Pass required. Open to mountain bikes, horses, motorbikes; **GPS:** N 47 47.008, W 122 57.903

Big Quilcene River Trail No. 833.1 to Marmot Pass (Hike 53) is one of the most popular trails in Olympic National Forest. What many hikers don't realize is that it was once twice as long. The road to the trailhead severed it in two. But the entire trail still exists, the eastern 6.5 miles are now known as the Lower Big Quilcene River Trail. Much of the route runs through a rugged canyon cloaked in patches of primeval forest—a perfect destination when clouds cloak the upper trail.

GETTING THERE

From Quilcene, drive US Highway 101 south for 1.5 miles. (From Shelton, follow US 101 north for 50.5 miles.) Turn right (west) onto Penny Creek Road. After 1.5 miles, bear left onto Big Quilcene River Road (Forest Road 27), which eventually becomes paved. Bear right at 3 miles, continuing on FR 27, and after 0.4 mile turn left onto FR Spur 080. Follow this gravel road 0.4 mile to the trailhead (elev. 1400 ft). Privy available.

ON THE TRAIL

Starting at 1400 feet, Lower Big Quilcene River Trail No. 833 climbs a mere 1200 feet in its entire 6.5-mile journey. Besides making for an easy trek, the low elevation is ideal for

Bridge near Bark Shanty Camp

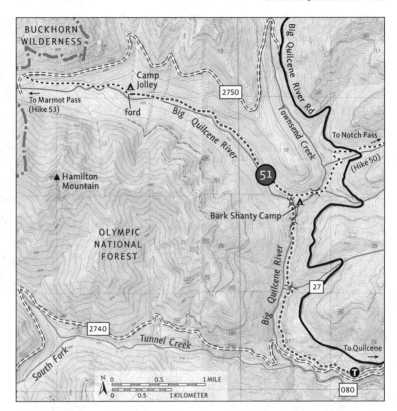

an early-season hike. And if you wait until late spring, you'll be rewarded with blooming rhododendrons. The trail passes by old camp and shelter sites, testaments to when there was no shorter option to Marmot Pass. A good day-hike objective is Camp Jolley at 5.1 miles. But the 2.7-mile trip to Bark Shanty Camp makes a fine day hike too. No matter how far you venture, the Lower Big Quilcene offers one of the best low-country valley hikes in the eastern Olympics.

The trail starts high above the river on an old roadbed, and the walking is fast and easy

on this well-groomed and well-graded path. After a descent of about 100 feet in the first mile, the trail enters a steep-walled canyon. Climb and drop 100 feet again, coming to a bridged crossing of the Big Quilcene River at 2.5 miles. Then hike along the river through towering old growth, soon reaching Bark Shanty Camp, a great place to stare at the rapids or cut some z's under an ancient tree.

The trail continues, however, recrossing the river on a sturdy bridge (elev. 1500 ft) and coming to the western terminus of the Notch Pass Trail (Hike 50) at 2.8 miles.

Continue left along the river, undulating between old, rapidly recovering clear-cuts and primeval groves of virgin timber. Try to keep your boots dry across a series of side creeks, but fording Jolley Creek (elev. 2000 ft) at 5.1 miles will be tricky. Camp Jolley is on the west bank. Ford the creek and reach the camp, or call it a hike before crossing over. Take a break by the bubbling creek before happily making your way back to the trailhead.

EXTENDING YOUR TRIP

The trail continues for 1.4 miles, climbing away from the river and through gorgeous old growth to reach an upper trailhead (elev. 2500 ft) at FR 2750. If you can arrange a car shuttle, consider making a one-way hike. Another option is to saunter from Bark Shanty up the first 0.5 mile of the Notch Pass Trail to a beautiful, lush gorge along Townsend Creek.

Tunnel Creek at trail crossing

52 Tunnel Creek

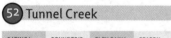

RATING/ DIFFICULTY	ROUNDTRIP	ELEV GAIN/ HIGH POINT	SEASON
***/3	9.4 miles	2650 feet/ 5050 feet	Apr–Nov

Maps: Green Trails Olympic Mountains East No. 168S, Custom Correct Buckhorn Wilderness; **Contact:** Olympic National Forest, Hood Canal Ranger District, Quilcene; **Notes:** Open to horses. Wilderness rules apply; **GPS:** N 47 46.892, W 123 03.127

Located within the 44,000-acre Buckhorn Wilderness, Tunnel Creek is one of the quieter trails in the Olympic rain shadow. Perhaps because it doesn't lead to a major lake or peak, this trail escapes the attention of many goal-driven hikers.

GETTING THERE

From Quilcene, drive US Highway 101 south for 1.5 miles. (From Shelton, follow US 101 north for 50.5 miles.) Turn right (west) onto Penny Creek Road. After 1.5 miles, bear left onto Big Quilcene River Road (Forest Road 27), which eventually becomes paved. At 3 miles, bear left onto graveled FR 2740 and follow it for 6.9 miles to the trailhead (elev. 2400 ft) at the road's end.

ON THE TRAIL

For nearly 3 miles, delightful Trail No. 841 follows the South Fork Tunnel Creek through towering old-growth hemlocks and firs. This hike is perfect on a misty morning

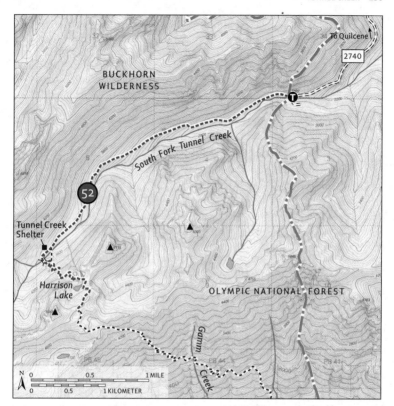

or a sweltering afternoon, as the ancient trees do a good job of regulating the temperature, keeping you either warm or cool. At 3.3 miles, come to the restored Tunnel Creek Shelter (elev. 3900 ft), a good destination for a shorter hike.

Beyond, the trail splits: stock left, hikers right. Cross the cascading creek on a sturdy bridge and then steadily and steeply climb. Clamber over some ledges and pass a small pond before reaching tiny Harrison Lake (elev. 4700 ft) at 4.3 miles. Continue just a little bit more to take in an up-close-and-

personal view of Mount Constance's impressive vertical east face. At 4.7 miles, the trail crests a ridge, maxing out at 5050 feet. You can scramble along the rocky ridge a little ways to better appreciate Constance's towering presence. Take a break and head back.

EXTENDING YOUR TRIP

If you can arrange a car shuttle, consider continuing on the trail. From the ridge it makes an insanely steep drop of more than 4300 feet in 3.6 miles to a trailhead on Dosewallips Road, 9 miles from US 101 (limited parking).

The trail is brushy in spots and easy to lose 0.4 mile from the ridge. Otherwise it's in decent shape as it heads down steep slopes and through old growth. There's a nice waterfall at Gamm Creek, after which the trail's grade eases considerably.

53 Marmot Pass

RATING/ DIFFICULTY	ROUNDTRIP	ELEV GAIN/ HIGH POINT	SEASON
*****/4	10.6 miles	3450 feet/ 5950 feet	July–Nov

Maps: Green Trails Olympic Mountains East No. 168S, Custom Correct Buckhorn Wilderness; **Contact:** Olympic National Forest, Hood Canal Ranger District, Quilcene; **Notes:** NW Forest Pass or Interagency Pass required. Open to horses. Wilderness rules apply; **GPS:** N 47 49.672, W 123 02.466

If for some terrible reason you're only allowed one hike in the Olympics in your lifetime, this should be it. The trail to Marmot Pass captures the very essence of what makes the Olympics so special, and so darned pretty. Towering old growth, a tumbling pristine river, resplendent alpine meadows, and horizon-spanning views that include majestic snow-clad craggy spires are all part of this amazing hike. And it gets even better—being in the Olympic rain shadow, Marmot Pass is often kissed with sunbeams while nearby ridges swirl with clouds.

GETTING THERE

From Quilcene, drive US Highway 101 south for 1.5 miles. (From Shelton, follow US 101 north for 50.5 miles.) Turn right (west) onto Penny Creek Road. After 1.5 miles, bear left onto Big Quilcene River Road (Forest Road 27), which eventually becomes paved. Continue on FR 27 for 9.3 miles, turn left onto graveled FR 2750, and drive 4.7 miles to the trailhead (elev. 2500 ft). Privy available.

ON THE TRAIL

Upper Big Quilcene River Trail No. 833.1 gains 3450 feet in its 5.3-mile journey to Marmot Pass, but the climb is quite agreeable. The grade is mostly moderate, the tread smooth, and the scenery is spectacular throughout the hike, enabling you to easily overlook any discomfort along the way.

Immediately enter the Buckhorn Wilderness and a magnificent stretch of primeval forest. For 2.5 miles, the trail winds through hulking hemlocks and colossal cedars and firs hundreds of years old, all while the Big Quilcene River keeps you company. Mossy overhanging boulders and numerous gurgling side creeks greet you now and then.

At 2.6 miles, reach Shelter Rock Camp (elev. 3800 ft). Then part ways with the Big Quil, making a short and steep ascent away from the valley floor. Forest soon yields to open avalanche chutes and scree slopes fanning down from Buckhorn and Iron mountains. Enjoy breathtaking views of the rugged surroundings from these exposed slopes, which are hot in the sun. Rocky knobs sit on the steep ridge above like gargoyles on a medieval cathedral, while slender stalks of fireweed dance in the gentle breezes whisking down from the pass. The way then enters groves of yellow cedars and subalpine firs and at 4.6 miles reaches inviting (and busy) Camp Mystery (elev. 5400 ft), with its dual springs.

Next, break out into a meadowed corridor painted in season with red, white, and purple flowers and pockmarked with

Looking west from just beyond Marmot Pass

marmot burrows. Skirt beneath a steep rock face, emerging at a small hanging valley just below the open pass. One final push and—voilá!—at 5.3 miles you're standing on 5950-foot Marmot Pass, one of the supreme viewing spots in the Olympics. Gaze east to Hood Canal, Puget Sound, and the Cascades. The Dungeness Valley spreads out below to

the west, flanked by a wall of some of the highest summits in the Olympics—Mystery, Deception, and Walkinshaw.

The high mountains are dry and open here, like the Cascades' eastern slopes, the rainshadow environment allows lodgepole and whitebark pines to grow here. Clark's nutcracker, a jay-like bird, roosts in the sub-

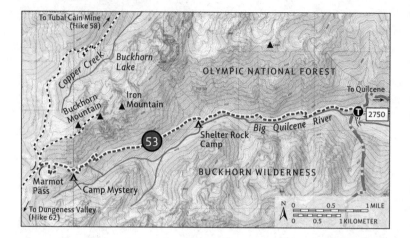

alpine forests, feeding on pine nuts. Listen for their raucous calls, a rare sound in the Olympics.

EXTENDING YOUR TRIP

There are plenty of exploring options from this lofty outpost. Follow a scramble path north for 1 mile, climbing more than 1000 feet to the 6998-foot summit of Buckhorn Mountain. Views are stupendous, especially of Mount Constance. Or if you can arrange a car shuttle, continue north across barren alpine tundra and hike out the Silver Creek valley via the Tubal Cain Mine Trail (Hike 58). Or, another one-way option, hike south (after dangerous snowfields have melted) to Boulder Camp and down the Dungeness Valley (Hike 62).

Opposite: Buckhorn Mountain from the Tubal Cain Mine

olympic peninsula:
northeast

The Rain Shadow

You'll find some of the Olympic Peninsula's best weather in its extreme northeast—and some of its best hikes. Thanks to rings of mountains to the west trapping clouds and marine air, this region enjoys a rainshadow effect. The Buckhorn Wilderness and adjacent areas of Olympic National Park often see sunny skies while valleys and peaks to the west are soaked in moisture.

But it's not just sunny weather that makes this region shine. An abundance of good trails lead to ancient forests, alpine lakes, and lofty peaks exploding with flowering meadows and expansive views. And because trailheads generally start at higher elevations here than in other regions of the Olympics, getting to such special places takes a little less pain.

You'll also hike through the best terrain in Washington for observing the state flower, the Pacific rhododendron. Flower buffs and other botanically inclined hikers will appreci-

ate the wide array of other wildflowers too (including all of the Olympics' endemics) and forests reminiscent of the east slopes of the Cascades.

54 Mount Townsend

RATING/ DIFFICULTY	ROUNDTRIP	ELEV GAIN/ HIGH POINT	SEASON
*****/4	8.2 miles	2980 feet/ 6280 feet	June–Nov

Maps: Green Trails Olympic Mountains East No. 168S, Custom Correct Buckhorn Wilderness; **Contact:** Olympic National Forest, Hood Canal Ranger District, Quilcene; **Notes:** Open to horses. Wilderness rules apply; **GPS:** N 47 51.385, W 123 02.153

Easy road access, a long hiking season, and unparalleled views of Puget Sound and the eastern half of the Olympics make Mount Townsend one of the most

Looking northwest from Townsend's alpine tundra summit

climbed peaks in the Olympics. Of the three trails to its summit, Trail No. 839 is the route most taken. It's not the shortest way, but it's highly scenic and one of the best built and maintained trails in the Buckhorn Wilderness.

GETTING THERE

From Quilcene, drive US Highway 101 south for 1.5 miles. (From Shelton, follow US 101 north for 50.5 miles.) Turn right (west) onto Penny Creek Road. After 1.5 miles, bear left onto Big Quilcene River Road (Forest Road 27), which eventually becomes paved. Continue on FR 27 for 13.7 miles, ignoring the sign at 12.5 miles for the Mount Townsend Trail (that's the lower trail via Sink Lake). Then turn left onto FR Spur 190 and reach the trailhead (elev. 3300 ft) in 0.7 mile.

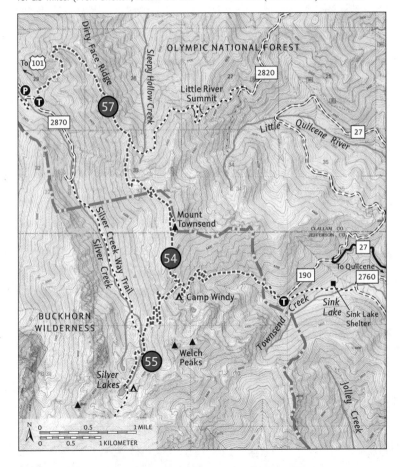

ON THE TRAIL

The well-worn path climbs steadily through a stately grove of firs and hemlocks adorned with Pacific rhododendrons. In 0.5 mile, the trail enters the Buckhorn Wilderness. Soon afterward the terrain opens up and the views begin. Through flower gardens and by cascading creeks, the trail pushes toward the clouds. Over two dozen switchbacks will keep you heading in the right direction: up!

At 2.6 miles, come to a small pine and fir grove nestled on a knoll, where tiny (and in season, buggy) Windy Lake hides just off the trail. Continue onward, bearing right at a junction with the Silver Lakes Trail (Hike 55) at 3 miles (elev. 5500 ft). Leaving the trees behind, continue ascending to Townsend's summit plateau, an expanse of alpine tundra. Ground-hugging juniper and brilliant clumps of cinquefoil and phlox carpet this high country.

At 4 miles, reach a junction. The main trail continues left 1.6 miles, descending to the Little Quilcene River Trail (Hike 57). Instead, take the trail right 0.1 mile to Townsend's highest point (elev. 6280 ft). You can continue on this path a short distance to the mountain's northern 6212-foot summit if you'd like.

The views are great from anywhere along the open peak: Puget Sound and its labyrinth of islands, bays, and channels sprawls below. Watch ferries ply azure waters. Gaze out at the Seattle skyline to glass and metal twinkling in the afternoon sunlight. A fortress of Cascade peaks, punctuated by snowy volcanoes, occupies the eastern horizon. To the north lie Dungeness Spit, Discovery Bay, the San Juan Islands, and Vancouver Island. To the west, nothing but pure Olympic wilderness—jagged peaks and deep green valleys. It should be apparent why Townsend is so well loved.

EXTENDING YOUR TRIP

Most hikers intent on reaching Townsend's 6280-foot open summit opt to begin from the upper trailhead, as described here. This saves 2 miles and 500 feet of elevation gain but misses beautiful old growth, a historical shelter, and Sink Lake, which absorbs tumbling Townsend Creek. Consider making the longer hike to enjoy these intriguing and little-visited features. If you can arrange a car shuttle, try hiking out the Little Quilcene River Trail via Little River Summit, reaching FR 2820 (elev. 4100 ft) at 3.7 miles from the Townsend summit. Reach this trailhead by driving 3.5 miles on FR 2820 from its junction with FR 28 at Bon Jon Pass.

55 Silver Lakes

RATING/ DIFFICULTY	ROUNDTRIP	ELEV GAIN/ HIGH POINT	SEASON
****/4	10.8 miles	3275 feet/ 5675 feet	Mid-June– Nov

Maps: Green Trails Olympic Mountains East No. 168S, Custom Correct Buckhorn Wilderness; **Contact:** Olympic National Forest, Hood Canal Ranger District, Quilcene; **Notes:** Wilderness rules apply; **GPS:** N 47 51.385, W 123 02.153

Cradled in a remote cirque on a lofty ridge, Silver Lakes see a fraction of the hikers that nearby Mount Townsend does. Reaching the lakes involves a challenging hike up and over a shoulder of Townsend. There is a shorter and somewhat

Shallow and serene upper Silver Lake

easier "backdoor" approach, but the longer, preferable route travels a well-built trail loaded with views and seasonal wildflowers.

GETTING THERE

From Quilcene, drive US Highway 101 south for 1.5 miles. (From Shelton, follow US 101 north for 50.5 miles.) Turn right (west) onto Penny Creek Road. After 1.5 miles, bear left onto Big Quilcene River Road (Forest Road 27), which eventually becomes paved. Continue on FR 27 for 13.7 miles. Then turn left onto FR Spur 190 and reach the trailhead (elev. 3300 ft) in 0.7 mile.

ON THE TRAIL

Begin by following Mount Townsend Trail No. 839 (Hike 54) for 3 miles, steadily climbing to a junction (elev. 5500 ft). From this point most hikers continue right to Townsend's lofty summit. You want to go left on much less trodden Trail No. 842, climbing through open forest and soon reaching a small gap (elev. 5675 ft) on Townsend's southern shoulder. Before descending, look back east for a great view of Windy and Sink lakes directly below. To the west, enjoy a sweeping view of the Silver Creek valley. The lakes, however, are not visible. They're hidden behind a small forested knob.

Descend into the valley on a couple of long switchbacks across a steep, barren slope (except in early summer when flowers paint it brilliant colors). At 4.6 miles, reach an unmarked junction (elev. 5000 ft) in a high forested valley. This is the backdoor route (see Extending Your Trip). Continue straight, now climbing again, and soon cross Silver Creek. Its sparkling and cascading waters invite you to follow it to its source. Continue ascending, reaching the larger of the two lakes at its outlet (elev. 5400 ft) at 5.4 miles. Scout the shores for a warm rock to rest on, and enjoy the lake's tranquility, broken only by trout jumping in pursuit of a morsel.

EXTENDING YOUR TRIP

The smaller lake lies off-trail and is of interest mainly to anglers. Instead, follow a primitive path from the larger lake's outlet through campsites, and steeply climb 0.5 mile to a 5800-foot gap on a high ridge above the Big Quilcene River. There are good roaming and views left or right along the ridge.

For the backdoor route to the lakes, find the trailhead for the Silver Creek Way Trail on FR 2870, 1.1 miles beyond the Tubal Cain Mine trailhead (Hike 58). Never officially built, this rough trail is brushy in places (but easy to follow) and steeply climbs alongside cascading Silver Creek, making two wet-boot crossings of it before reaching Trail No. 842 at 2.3 miles.

56 Mount Zion

RATING/ DIFFICULTY	ROUNDTRIP	ELEV GAIN/ HIGH POINT	SEASON
***/3	4.8 miles	1535 feet/ 4278 feet	May–Nov

Maps: Green Trails Olympic Mountains East No. 168S, Custom Correct Buckhorn Wilderness; **Contact:** Olympic National Forest, Hood Canal Ranger District, Quilcene; **Notes:** NW Forest Pass or Interagency Pass required. Open to mountain bikes, horses, motorbikes; **GPS:** N 47 55.368, W 123 01.564

Hike to an isolated peak on the fringe of the Olympics to a series of ledges. Then look out upon a promised land of sweeping views from lofty Mount Townsend to glistening Puget Sound. Make a pilgrimage here in June and be rewarded with a resplendent kingdom of brilliantly blooming rhododendrons.

GETTING THERE

From Quilcene, drive US Highway 101 north for 1.5 miles, turning left (west) onto Lords Lake Loop Road. In 3.4 miles, turn left onto FR 28 at Lords Lake (a public water supply). Then bear right in 4.3 miles and drive another 1.3 miles to Bon Jon Pass (9 miles total from US 101). Bear right at the pass, still on FR 28, and reach the trailhead (elev. 2800) in 2 miles. Privy available.

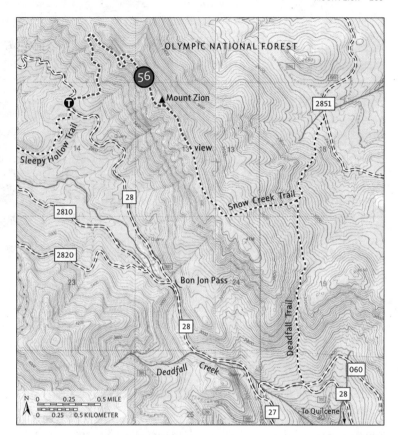

ON THE TRAIL

Start on the well-built Mount Zion Trail No. 836, first heading east and soon angling north. This trail and adjacent Sleepy Hollow Trail No. 852 are part of the Pacific Northwest Trail (see the "North by Northwest" sidebar). As you steadily climb, steeply at times, pass through a dry forest dotted with salal and rhododendrons. Mount Zion ranks as one of the Olympics' supreme rhody hikes.

In maturing timber, big blackened snags are reminders of the large-scale fires that swept this corner of Olympic National Forest decades ago. After marching up a ridge, the trail sweeps east and continues gaining elevation. Negotiate a short series of switchbacks before skirting a series of basalt ledges.

At 1.8 miles, arrive on the rocky summit (elev. 4278 ft). A fire tower perched here until 1975. The surrounding forest has slowly been encroaching on the view, blocking

The author enjoying views from Zion on an overcast day

much of the once-supreme vista. You can still see Mount Baker, the San Juan Islands, Puget Sound, and Quimper Peninsula over the tops of tenacious conifers. But for the premiere showing, carry on a little farther.

Follow Snow Creek Trail No. 890 southeast from the summit. Pass a spring that once provided water for the fire-lookout personnel. Continue on good tread and after 0.6 mile of fairly level hiking, emerge on a huge outcropping (elev. 4220 ft), your portal to panoramic pleasures. Using caution, climb a little onto the open ledge, and then enjoy the view. Mount Townsend dominates the southern horizon, while the rocky high wall of Gray Wolf Ridge commands the western sky. It's a heavenly view—what you'd expect from a mountain named Zion.

EXTENDING YOUR TRIP

If you can arrange a car shuttle, continue east on the Snow Creek Trail for 1.4 miles,

steeply descending in dark forest to a junction (elev. 2900 ft). The Snow Creek Trail continues left for 0.8 mile to FR 2851 (elev. 2340 ft). Go right instead on Deadfall Trail No. 849, cresting a 3300-foot ridge before steeply descending in mixed forest for 1.7 miles to reach FR Spur 060 (elev. 2350 ft) near a junction with FR 28 (3.8 miles east of the Mount Zion trailhead).

57 Dirty Face Ridge

RATING/ DIFFICULTY	ROUNDTRIP	ELEV GAIN/ HIGH POINT	SEASON
****/4	7.8 miles	3030 feet/ 6280 feet	June–Nov

Maps: Green Trails Olympic Mountains East No. 168S, Custom Correct Buckhorn Wilderness; **Contact:** Olympic National Forest, Hood Canal Ranger District, Quilcene; **GPS:** N 47 53.141, W 123 05.386

NORTH BY NORTHWEST

During the backpacking boom of the 1970s, transplanted New Englander Ron Strickland was struck with a novel idea. How about adding another classic long-distance hiking trail to our country's stock? One to accompany and rival the likes of the Appalachian, Pacific Crest, and Colorado Divide trails. Thus began his quest to build the Pacific Northwest Trail (PNT), a 1200-mile path from Cape Alava on the Olympic Peninsula to Montana's Glacier National Park.

Strickland formed the Pacific Northwest Trail Association (PNTA), and soon a slew of tireless volunteers set about promoting, constructing, and maintaining the new trail. Utilizing existing trails along with new tread, the PNT weaves together a good portion of the north Olympic Peninsula. While parts of the trail still follow roads, much progress has been made toward completing the PNT since President Barack Obama signed a bill in 2009 designating it a national scenic trail, a status also held by the Pacific Crest and Appalachian trails.

Several hikes in this book follow portions of the PNT: Mount Zion (Hike 56), Upper Dungeness River (Hike 59), Tubal Cain Mine and Buckhorn Lake (Hike 58), Gold Creek (Hike 63), Elwha River and Lillian River (Hike 95), Appleton Pass and Oyster Lake (Hike 98), Mink Lake and Little Divide (Hike 110), Deer Lake and Bogachiel Peak (Hike 111), Bogachiel River (Hike 113), Third Beach (Hike 131), Hole-in-the-Wall (Hike 132), and Ozette Triangle (Hike 134). Visit the PNTA (www.pnt.org) for more information.

The Dirty Face Ridge hike to Mount Townsend is steep and has a long driving approach, so most hikers shun it for the two easier routes to the summit. That means you'll have plenty of solitude along with the copious good views that help ease the uphill pain.

GETTING THERE

From Hood Canal Bridge, drive State Route 104 to its end, veering north onto US Highway 101. Proceed 16 miles and turn left onto Louella Road, located across from the Sequim Bay State Park entrance. (From Sequim, drive US 101 south for 5 miles to the turnoff.) Drive 0.9 mile and turn left onto Palo Alto Road. Continue for 5.8 miles, bearing right onto graveled Forest Road 2880. After 1.7 steep and twisty miles, bear left onto FR 2870. Then drive 12.6 miles (the last 3 miles can be rough) to the Tubal Cain Mine trailhead parking area (elev. 3250 ft).

ON THE TRAIL

Walk 0.1 mile east on FR 2870 to Little Quilcene River Trail No. 835 and immediately start climbing steeply. Through a tunnel of rhododendrons remarkably reminiscent of the southern Appalachians, you may find yourself humming "Smoky Mountain Sunrise" on the ascent. But after you cross a damp little draw (last available water) and angle up to the ridge and the first viewpoint, it's pure Pacific Northwest mountain scenery.

A succession of viewpoints follow as the trail rapidly gains elevation, heading for the ridge crest. Enjoy precious glimpses of the Silver and Copper creek valleys below. Buckhorn Mountain, with its twin-peaked horns, guards the head of the emerald

Looking south from Dirty Face Ridge

junction at 2.3 miles. The Little Quilcene River Trail continues left, descending 2.1 miles to FR 2820. You want to go right, leaving solitude behind and following a wide path 1.6 miles to Mount Townsend's windswept and tundra-cloaked 6280-foot summit. This former fire-lookout site provides a stunning view of Puget Sound's plethora of islands, peninsulas, bays, and coves.

EXTENDING YOUR TRIP

Make a challenging 10-mile loop by continuing on the Mount Townsend Trail 1 mile to the Silver Lakes Trail. Then follow that path 1.6 miles to the Silver Lakes Way Trail and take it 2.3 miles to FR 2870. Walk the road 1.2 miles back to your start.

58 Tubal Cain Mine and Buckhorn Lake

RATING/ DIFFICULTY	ROUNDTRIP	ELEV GAIN/ HIGH POINT	SEASON
***/3	12.4 miles	2100 feet/ 5225 feet	June–Oct

Maps: Green Trails Olympic Mountains East No. 168S, Custom Correct Buckhorn Wilderness; **Contact:** Olympic National Forest, Hood Canal Ranger District, Quilcene; **Notes:** Open to horses. Wilderness rules apply; **GPS:** N 47 53.173, W 123 05.497

Retrace a packers' trail to a mine dating from the 1890s. Peer into dark forbidding shafts and saunter past relics left over from boomtown settlements that went bust. But the real find is the miles of wildflower-studded meadows beyond the mine. Rhododendrons too—traverse a jungle of them on the trail's lower reaches.

valleys; and Gray Wolf Ridge, with its pack of peaks, paces the western horizon.

At around 1.6 miles, the grade finally eases. Alternating between lodgepole pine groves and crumbling basalt ledges, the trail heads southeast toward Mount Townsend, lupines lining the way. Look for Piper's bellflower, a rare Olympic endemic clinging to several of the rocky outcrops. Junipers creep along the outcrops too; common on the east slopes of the Cascades, this member of the cypress family thrives in this dry corner of the Olympic Peninsula.

At 2 miles, a large ledge (elev. 5200 ft) invites lounging and is a good place to turn around if you've had enough. Otherwise, continue in cool silver fir forest, coming to a

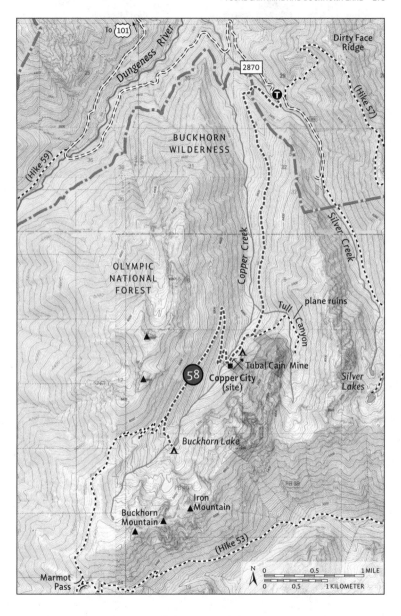

Buckhorn Mountain

GETTING THERE

From Hood Canal Bridge, drive State Route 104 to its end, veering north onto US Highway 101. Proceed 16 miles and turn left onto Louella Road, located across from the Sequim Bay State Park entrance. (From Sequim, drive US 101 south for 5 miles to the turnoff.) Drive 0.9 mile and turn left onto Palo Alto Road. Continue for 5.8 miles, bearing right onto graveled Forest Road 2880. After 1.7 steep and twisty miles, bear left onto FR 2870. Then drive 12.6 miles (the last 3 miles can be rough) to the trailhead (elev. 3250 ft).

ON THE TRAIL

Follow Trail No. 840 south, immediately passing the Silver Creek Shelter and shortly afterward crossing Silver Creek on a log bridge. After entering the Buckhorn Wilderness at 0.5 mile, the way traverses steep slopes high above Copper Creek. Hike through thick stands of second-growth conifers and a luxuriant tunnel of rhododendrons that reign purple in early summer. Occasional breaks in the forest canopy offer previews of the high country ahead.

At 3.2 miles, come to a junction (elev. 4200 ft). The trail left climbs steeply 0.9 mile into Tull Canyon (elev. 4800 ft), an interesting side trip: The trail immediately passes a mine shaft (extremely dangerous to enter) and then climbs into the tight canyon. At 0.7 mile, encounter the remains of a crashed World War II–era B-17 bomber. Just beyond that are the ruins of several cabins—remains of the Tull City mining settlement.

The main trail continues upvalley through dank, scrappy forest, coming to another old mining townsite—Copper City—at 3.7 miles. It's now strewn with campsites and rusted mining relics (some revived, serving the needs of imaginative campers). The Tubal Cain Mine (named for an Old Testament figure said to be the forger of all bronze and iron implements) lies just to the left. It's a private inholding in the wilderness area and is still somewhat active; respect all postings and leave any equipment alone.

Call it a hike here or continue, making a boot-wetting crossing of Copper Creek (elev. 4200 ft). Then begin climbing the valley's west wall via a series of short switchbacks, followed by one long one. Traverse open slopes bursting with wildflowers. Twin-peaked Buckhorn Mountain, with Iron Mountain by its side, hovers over the far end

of the valley. At 5.8 miles, reach a junction (elev. 5225 ft). For Buckhorn Lake, head left across scree and back into forest. Climb a little and then drop, passing good camps and reaching the small lake (elev. 5125 ft) tucked in thick timber at 6.2 miles. The lake isn't much, but Copper Creek cascading into it is pretty.

EXTENDING YOUR TRIP

The Tubal Cain Mine Trail continues another 3.8 miles to 5950-foot Marmot Pass (Hike 53). Continue on it, climbing a high shoulder (elev. 6300 foot) of Buckhorn Mountain, traversing meadows, rock gardens, and alpine tundra. Views are far-reaching and amazing, especially of the Dungeness Valley.

59 Upper Dungeness River

RATING/ DIFFICULTY	ROUNDTRIP	ELEV GAIN/ HIGH POINT	SEASON
***/2	7 miles	600 feet/ 3100 feet	May–Nov

Maps: Green Trails Olympic Mountains East No. 168S, Custom Correct Buckhorn Wilderness; **Contact:** Olympic National Forest, Hood Canal Ranger District, Quilcene; **Notes:** NW Forest Pass or Interagency Pass required. Open to horses. Wilderness rules apply; **GPS:** N 47 52.692, W 123 08.226

A delightful easy hike through ancient timber along the crystal-clear Dungeness River, this trail is ideal for introducing neophytes and youngsters to the backcountry. It's perfect for overcast days too. The handy dandy Camp Handy Shelter provides cover on rainy days, allowing you to enjoy your lunch while droplets run down its cedar shingles.

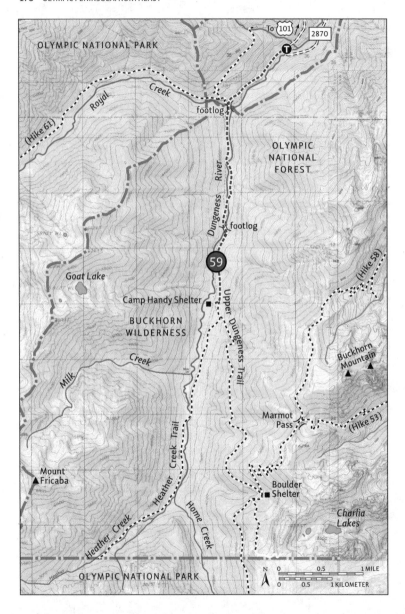

GETTING THERE

From Hood Canal Bridge, drive State Route 104 to its end, veering north onto US Highway 101. Proceed 16 miles and turn left onto Louella Road, located across from the Sequim Bay State Park entrance. (From Sequim, drive US 101 south for 5 miles to the turnoff.) Drive 0.9 mile and turn left onto Palo Alto Road. Continue for 5.8 miles, bearing right onto graveled Forest Road 2880. After 1.7 steep and twisty miles, bear left onto FR 2870. Then drive 8.9 miles to the trailhead (elev. 2500 ft) at a bridge over the Dungeness River. Privy available.

ON THE TRAIL

Upper Dungeness Trail No. 833.2 begins beside the tumbling and crashing river, never letting it out of eyesight or earshot for the entire journey to Camp Handy. The trail is well sheltered by magnificent Douglas-firs that are 200 feet tall and several hundred years old. Embrace the canopy's air-conditioning effects on warm sunny days and its protecting qualities on overcast ones.

Starting on the north side of the bridge, follow the trail west, first climbing a tad and then walking an easy, fairly level course. At 1.1 miles, come to a junction (elev. 2675 ft). The trail right heads to Royal Basin (Hike 61). Bear left instead, crossing Royal Creek on a sturdy footlog bridge, and immediately enter the Buckhorn Wilderness.

Through cool glens of Douglas-firs and hemlocks, across numerous side creeks, and along seeps spawning salmonberries, the trail parallels the majestic river. At 2.6 miles, cross the river on a footlog bridge. Once across, the trail pulls away from the river, the chattering of resident birds no longer drowned out by the thunderous waterway. At 3.4 miles, reach an unmarked junction

Log-bridge crossing over Heather Creek

and head right a short distance to a lovely meadow on the Dungeness River, home to Camp Handy (elev. 3100 ft). If the weather is agreeable, head to the wide gravel bar for views and feet soaking. If it's raining, take to the shelter. Be prepared, however, to fend off snack-sneaking chipmunks.

EXTENDING YOUR TRIP

Want to go farther? Continue up the trail 0.5 mile to a junction. The Upper Dungeness Trail continues left for 2.8 miles, steadily climbing to Boulder Camp and Shelter (elev. 4900 ft) in the shadows of Mount Constance. Lightly traveled Heather Creek Trail No. 863 heads right, reaching riverside meadows and camps in 0.8 mile. It crosses the river on a bridge at 2 miles (elev. 3250 ft) and then steeply climbs through old growth along and above Heather Creek, passing avalanche chutes, viewpoints, and a pretty waterfall. It ends at 3.7 miles, in a meadow (elev. 4300 ft) below 7139-foot Mount Fricaba on the Olympic National Park boundary.

60 Baldy

RATING/ DIFFICULTY	ROUNDTRIP	ELEV GAIN/ HIGH POINT	SEASON
*****/5	10.4 miles	4475 feet/ 6797 feet	Mid-June– Oct

Maps: Green Trails Olympic Mountains East No. 168S, Custom Correct Buckhorn Wilderness; **Contact:** Olympic National Forest, Hood Canal Ranger District, Quilcene; **Notes:** NW Forest Pass or Interagency Pass required. Wilderness rules apply; **GPS:** N 47 52.676, W 123 08.217

What could be more beautiful than hiking into Royal Basin? Hiking above it and looking down into that glacially carved valley flanked by towering spires and icy summits. The hike to Baldy is brutal—one of the steepest trails in the Olympics. One section gains more than 2700 feet in 2.1 miles. But the views are supreme: countless islands and mountains and broad emerald valleys. And at your feet, a brilliant alpine tundra flower garden.

GETTING THERE

From Hood Canal Bridge, drive State Route 104 to its end, veering north onto US Highway 101. Proceed 16 miles and turn left onto Louella Road, located across from the Sequim Bay State Park entrance. (From Sequim, drive US 101 south for 5 miles to the turnoff.) Drive 0.9 mile and turn left onto Palo Alto Road. Continue for 5.8 miles, bearing right onto graveled Forest Road 2880. After 1.7 steep and twisty miles, bear left onto FR 2870. Then drive 8.9 miles to the trailhead (elev. 2500 ft) at a bridge over the Dungeness River. Privy available.

ON THE TRAIL

Start on the gentle Upper Dungeness Trail No. 833.2 through a cool forest of towering firs. Bear right at 1.1 miles, following the trail to Royal Basin. At 1.3 miles, bear right again—a sign points the way to Baldy via Lower Maynard Burn Trail No. 816. Now the fun stops and work begins.

Wildflower meadows on Baldy

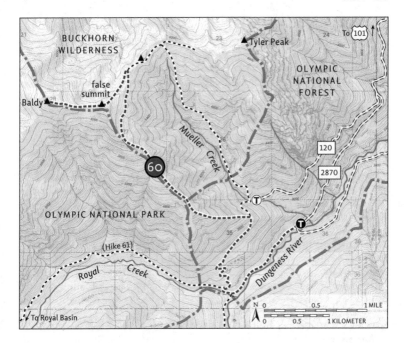

Snake up salal-choked switchbacks as you climb to a former road now cloaked in grasses and daisies. Head left up the grassy road-trail, crossing numerous boggy patches that sport showy orchids and monkey flowers. At 2.3 miles, reach a junction (elev. 3480 ft). The trail right travels 0.6 mile to a trailhead (elev. 3300 ft) on FR Spur 120. It's possible to start your hike from here, saving 1.7 miles of hiking and 800 feet of elevation gain. But you risk compromising your vehicle's tires and paint job.

The trail left takes off for Baldy. Unmarked but well defined, this is the Maynard Burn Trail, created decades ago by the Forest Service as a bulldozed fire-protection lane. It climbs straight up (no exaggeration) a dry steep rib, gaining 2700 feet in 2.1 miles.

Grind your way up the insanely steep grade. At about 3 miles, enter the Buckhorn Wilderness. Straddling the national park boundary, continue more wicked climbing. Gain a reprieve when the trail leaves the Cat track (elev. 5200 ft), and on a saner grade skirt a high slope above the Mueller Creek drainage. Trees thin and views begin as you emerge in an alpine meadow adorned in wildflowers. Asters, lupine, penstemon, and phlox paint the landscape a purple mountain majesty.

Traverse a high bowl, coming to a clump of lodgepole pines. Then follow fading tread into open meadows and reach a 6200-foot saddle at 4.4 miles. Head left on pretty decent tread, cresting a 6537-foot false summit, and then descend on light tread to a 6360-foot saddle. One more push up an open ridge brings you to Baldy's 6797-foot summit at 5.2 miles.

The view, like the hike, will take your breath away. Mount Constance and Warrior Peak dominate the southern horizon over the sweeping, emerald Dungeness Valley. Look northeast over hundreds of islands, American and Canadian. Look north to Sequim, Sequim Bay, Victoria, and Dungeness Spit. To the northwest, Blue Mountain, Elk Mountain, and Mount Angeles fill the viewfinder. Mount Olympus also joins in. And look straight down into Royal Basin. Rest up and prep your knees for the descent.

EXTENDING YOUR TRIP

From the 6200-foot saddle, experienced off-trail hikers can continue on decent tread 0.8 mile to just below a knob west of Tyler Peak. From there, either scramble 6364-foot Tyler Peak, or descend in brutally steep meadows, picking up good tread and following a knee-knocking trail 2.2 miles to the FR Spur 120 trailhead. Then hike west 0.6 mile back to the Lower Maynard Burn Trail.

61 Royal Basin

RATING/ DIFFICULTY	ROUNDTRIP	ELEV GAIN/ HIGH POINT	SEASON
*****/4	14.4 miles	2675 feet/ 5100 feet	Late June–Oct

Maps: Green Trails Olympic Mountains East No. 168S, Custom Correct Buckhorn Wilderness; **Contact:** Olympic National Park, Wilderness Information Center; **Notes:** NW Forest Pass or Interagency Pass required. Dogs prohibited at park boundary; **GPS:** N 47 52.687, W 123 08.219

Hike to a beautiful subalpine lake that's flanked by some of the highest and most craggy snow- and ice-covered peaks in the Olympic Mountains. The trip is long, but much of the way is gentle, through primeval forests up a deep valley and along a crashing, milky creek fed by glaciers high above.

GETTING THERE

From Hood Canal Bridge, drive State Route 104 to its end, veering north onto US Highway 101. Proceed 16 miles and turn left onto Louella Road, located across from the Sequim Bay State Park entrance. (From Sequim, drive US 101 south for 5 miles to the turnoff.) Drive 0.9 mile and turn left onto Palo Alto Road. Continue for 5.8 miles, bearing right onto graveled Forest Road 2880. After 1.7 steep and twisty miles, bear left onto FR 2870. Then drive 8.9 miles to the trailhead (elev. 2500 ft) at a bridge over the Dungeness River. Privy available.

ON THE TRAIL

Start on the popular Upper Dungeness Trail No. 833.2 on a gentle grade through ancient groves of towering firs. At 1.1 miles (elev. 2675 ft), head right at a junction signed for Royal Basin. At 1.3 miles, bear left at a junction. Shortly afterward enter Olympic National Park at 1.5 miles.

Through thick forest carpeted in moss and landscaped with rhododendrons, the trail heads gracefully up the Royal Creek valley. Not always within sight, but always close by, the creek crashes and churns through the deep, narrow vale. You'll need to hop over several tributaries in the first couple of miles, but none pose significant problems.

Heading upvalley, soon cross the first of several brushy avalanche chutes, where the

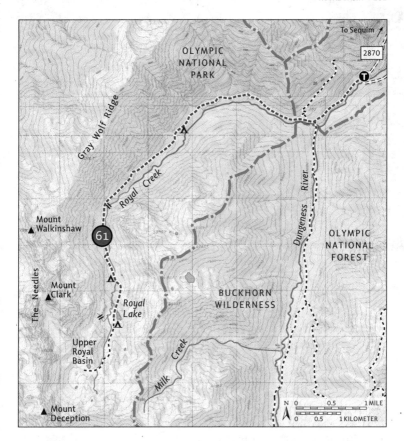

break in tree cover affords a glimpse of the fortress of towering peaks surrounding you. Descend about 75 feet back into old-growth forest reaching, the Royal Creek Camp (elev. 3450 ft) at 3.5 miles. The trail steepens as it ascends rocky and open slopes, granting impressive views both up and down the U-shaped valley while a royal carpet of wildflowers rolls out beneath you.

Climb above a yellow cedar–graced head-wall, Royal Creek furiously cascading over

it. Then follow alongside a much gentler creek, the grade easing as the trail enters the hanging valley of Royal Basin. With the 7000-foot giants of Mounts Clark and Walkinshaw casting their shadows upon you, traverse willow flats and a lovely meadow basin, passing a backcountry camping area (elev. 4700 ft) at 6.3 miles.

Soon cross Royal Creek on a sturdy log bridge. One short climb is your last hurdle before arriving at regal Royal Lake (elev.

Trail heading into Upper Royal Basin

5100 ft) at 7.2 miles. Majestic peaks hold court above the quiet body of water. In early summer the shoreline is adorned in purple regalia, thanks to thousands of blossoming shooting stars. Find a splendid lakeside lunch spot and savor the beauty with the resident deer, chipmunks, and marmots.

EXTENDING YOUR TRIP
The trail continues for another mile, and if you have more energy, the best is yet to come. Follow the trail beyond the lake, passing campsites and reaching the summer ranger station at the edge of a meadow. Here a rough path leads to the right to a spectacular waterfall. The main path continues left, passing a huge erratic and skirting a meadow before steeply climbing to the upper basin. At a creek crossing stay right and continue a short distance, coming to a spectacular tarn (elev. 5700 ft) at the base of a jumble of talus beneath craggy, snow-

and ice-covered Mount Deception (elev. 7788 ft), the second-highest peak in the Olympics. It's one of the most dramatic spots in these mountains.

62 Lower Dungeness River

RATING/ DIFFICULTY	ROUNDTRIP	ELEV GAIN/ HIGH POINT	SEASON
***/3	13 miles	2100 feet/ 2700 feet	Apr–Nov

Maps: Green Trails Olympic Mountains East No. 168S, Custom Correct Buckhorn Wilderness; **Contact:** Olympic National Forest, Hood Canal Ranger District, Quilcene; **Notes:** Open to mountain bikes, horses, motorbikes. Several slides may be problematic or dangerous to cross. As of 2016, part of FR Spur 230 was washed out, requiring walking from FR 2870 or using the upper trailhead.; **GPS:** N 47 56.171, W 123 05.514

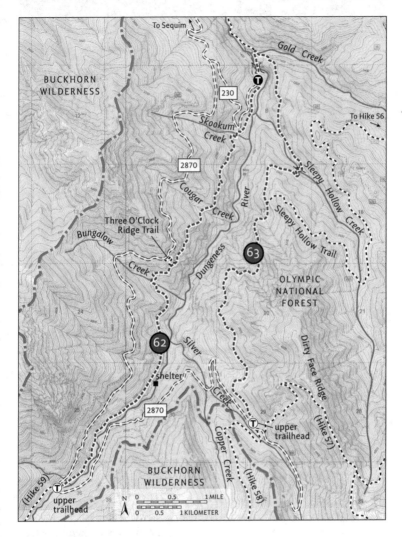

Hike along and above the Dungeness River in an impressive steep canyon. Walk through groves of towering ancient conifers. Visit a historical shelter and admire silvery cascades. This trail through a rugged and lightly traveled landscape is a good choice when higher ground is blanketed in white.

Boardwalk on Lower Dungeness Trail

GETTING THERE

From Hood Canal Bridge, drive State Route 104 to its end, veering north onto US Highway 101. Proceed 16 miles and turn left onto Louella Road, located across from the Sequim Bay State Park entrance. (From Sequim, drive US 101 south for 5 miles to the turnoff.) Drive 0.9 mile and turn left onto Palo Alto Road. Continue for 5.8 miles, bearing right onto graveled Forest Road 2880. After 1.7 steep and twisty miles, bear left onto FR 2870. Then drive 2.5 miles, bearing left on unsigned FR Spur 230. Continue 1.4 miles to the trailhead (elev. 1500 ft).

ON THE TRAIL

Lower Dungeness Trail No. 833.3 starts in beautiful old-growth forest. Hiking upvalley, traverse steep slopes above the crashing river. These unstable grounds are prone to washing out, causing potential trouble spots. Soon pass a path coming in from the right, which leads back to the old trailhead (no parking) on FR Spur 230.

Continue up the narrow and steep valley, crossing Skookum Creek and rounding a ridge that sports sun-loving junipers and provides a good view upvalley. As you traverse increasingly higher and steeper slopes, the river roars far below in a deep canyon—a few ledges offer impressive views of the cleft. At 2.8 miles, come to a junction (elev. 2700 ft) with the Three O'Clock Ridge Trail. This trail steeply climbs 300 feet to reach FR 2870 (no parking) in 0.5 mile. It's used primarily by mountain bikers making a loop with the road.

This is a good spot to turn around for a shorter hike. Otherwise, continue upvalley, starting a long descent. Cross Bungalow Creek and an old burn and reach the valley floor. Then alongside the river, hike through old-growth groves, reaching an old shelter (elev. 2150 ft) at 4.8 miles. The trail continues along the river, passing some impressive ancient trees. Cross boggy areas via a series of boardwalks and pass a couple of pretty cascades as well. At 6.5 miles, reach the upper trailhead (elev. 2500 ft). Return the way you came unless you arranged for a car shuttle.

EXTENDING YOUR TRIP

Strong day hikers or trail runners can make an excellent 17.3-mile loop by heading left up FR 2870 for 3.7 miles and returning 7.1 miles on the Gold Creek Trail (Hike 63).

63 Gold Creek

RATING/ DIFFICULTY	ROUNDTRIP	ELEV GAIN/ HIGH POINT	SEASON
***/4	14.2 miles	2450 feet/ 3250 feet	May–Nov

Maps: Green Trails Olympic Mountains East No. 168S, Custom Correct Buckhorn Wilderness; **Contact:** Olympic National Forest, Hood Canal Ranger District, Quilcene; **Notes:** Open to mountain bikes, horses, motorbikes. As of 2016, part of FR Spur 230 was washed out, requiring walking from FR 2870 or using the upper trailhead.; **GPS:** N 47 56.171, W 123 05.514

Follow a lightly traveled trail to a salmon-bearing creek and then climb up and along the lower Dungeness River canyon. A good hike in late spring when higher options are limited—and trailside rhodies are blooming.

GETTING THERE

From Hood Canal Bridge, drive State Route 104 to its end, veering north onto US Highway 101. Proceed 16 miles and turn left onto Louella Road, located across from the Sequim Bay State Park entrance. (From Sequim, drive US 101 south for 5 miles to the turnoff.) Drive 0.9 mile and turn left onto Palo Alto Road. Continue for 5.8 miles, bearing right onto graveled Forest Road 2880. After 1.7 steep and twisty miles, bear left onto FR 2870. Then drive 2.5 miles, bearing left on unsigned FR Spur 230. Continue 1.4 miles to the trailhead (elev. 1500 ft).

ON THE TRAIL

The old, long way to the Tubal Cain Mine, Gold Creek Trail No. 830 starts first on an old

Dungeness River at crossing

roadbed. Walk it north, descending to a large solid bridge over the Dungeness River; then shortly afterward, at 0.5 mile, come to the old trailhead (elev. 1200 ft). Head right here, on single track, and soon come to Gold Creek. The shelter is gone and so is any bridge across the creek. Look for a log or ford the creek, which teems with spawning salmon come late summer.

The way then steeply climbs the rib of a ridge, passing through old-growth cedar groves. Descend 100 feet to cross Sleepy Hollow Creek (elev. 1900 ft) on a bridge at 2.5 miles. Then resume steadily climbing, traveling through old-burn zones that sport some surviving giant Douglas-firs. At 3.5 miles, come to a junction with the Sleepy Hollow Trail (elev. 2600 ft). This trail (part of the Pacific Northwest Trail) follows recently decommissioned roads and is more of interest to PNT thru-hikers and equestrians than day hikers.

Continue right on the Gold Creek Trail, now also part of the PNT. Climbing higher, the trail traverses the steep and rugged terrain of the east slopes of the deep canyon that cradles the Dungeness River. Round ridge shoulders that grant decent viewing down into the canyon and across it to Three O'Clock Ridge.

Then continue traversing steep slopes, skirting an old clear-cut with good views west to Gray Wolf Ridge. The way eventually levels off, tunneling through young forest and rhododendrons before reaching FR 2870 (elev. 3250 ft) near the Tubal Cain Mine trailhead (Hike 58) at 7.1 miles.

EXTENDING YOUR TRIP

Return the way you came or consider following FR 2870 right for 3.7 miles and taking the Lower Dungeness Trail (Hike 62) 6.5 miles back to the trailhead. If you're interested in hiking the Sleepy Hollow Trail, it heads 8.4 miles east to the Mount Zion trailhead (Hike 56), following old roadbeds on an easy and rolling course. There are some limited views and you'll need to ford both Sleepy Hollow and Gold creeks.

64 Lower Gray Wolf River

RATING/ DIFFICULTY	ROUNDTRIP	ELEV GAIN/ HIGH POINT	SEASON
***/2	7 miles	900 feet/ 1450 feet	Year-round

Maps: Green Trails Olympic Mountains East No. 168S, Custom Correct Buckhorn Wilderness; **Contact:** Olympic National Forest,

Gray Wolf River near Two Mile Camp

Hood Canal Ranger District, Quilcene; **Notes:** Wilderness rules apply; **GPS:** N 47 58.026, W 123 07.649

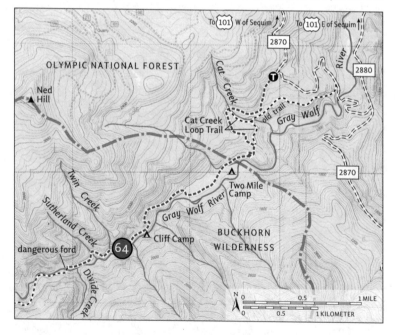 *Hike along the tumbling, churning Gray Wolf River through groves of old-growth conifers and over cascading feeder creeks. This is a perfect winter leg stretcher or spring woodland flower hike, and there's always an excellent chance of spotting a big critter along the way.*

GETTING THERE

From Hood Canal Bridge, drive State Route 104 to its end, veering north onto US Highway 101. Proceed 16 miles and turn left onto Louella Road, located across from the Sequim Bay State Park entrance. (From Sequim, drive US 101 south for 5 miles to the turnoff.) Drive 0.9 mile and turn left onto Palo Alto Road. Continue for 5.8 miles, bearing right onto graveled Forest Road 2880. After 1.7 steep and twisty miles, bear right onto FR 2870 and proceed 1.8 miles to the trailhead (elev. 1450 ft). (Alternatively, from US 101 west of Sequim, turn left/south on Taylor Cutoff Road, turn right on Lost Mountain Road, and then turn left on FR 2870 and drive 5.5 miles to the trailhead.)

ON THE TRAIL

Gray Wolf Trail No. 834 starts by following an old logging road. Descending, take in good views of Maynard Peak and the portal to Gray Wolf Canyon. At 0.7 mile, enter mature forest and come to a junction with the Cat Creek Loop Trail (elev. 1300 ft). This alternative route takes off left, dropping steeply along Cat Creek through an ancient cedar grove, following a portion of the old Gray Wolf Trail, and returning to the main trail in 0.5 mile.

The main trail continues right, leaving the old roadbed and entering a cool old-growth forest of firs and hemlocks. Then it descends to the river, enters the Buckhorn Wilderness, and reaches Two Mile Camp (elev. 1175 ft) at 1.5 miles. Traverse a sun-kissed bottomland that invites naps and snack breaks and then slowly pull away from the river, climbing a steep bluff (elev. 1450 ft) with good river views. Then drop back to river level, reaching Cliff Camp (elev. 1250 ft) at 2.7 miles. Next, hike along the river feeling the cool breezes funneling down the surging waterway. Continue along the river, passing another camp, and then once again climb above it.

Enjoy good views of the Gray Wolf crashing through a tight canyon gorge. Then descend a little, making your way back to the valley bottom (elev.1325 ft) at 3.5 miles. Call it quits here, where the trail ends at a narrow rocky gorge that once housed a high bridge. Noted Olympics guidebook writer Robert Wood once observed, "The bridge was built high enough to preclude its destruction from floods." But a torrent in the early 1990s washed it away.

Fording the river here is extremely dangerous. Nor should you follow the sucker paths leading up nearby slopes. If you want to further explore the Gray Wolf Valley, take the Slab Camp Creek Trail (Hike 66). In the meantime, sit by the lovely waterway, letting its rapids mesmerize and its resident dippers entertain you.

EXTENDING YOUR TRIP

Volunteers recently reopened the old lower part of this trail. From about midway on the Cat Creek Loop Trail, follow the old trail right 1.2 miles to FR 2870 (elev. 1125 ft) near a bridge over the Gray Wolf River (1.2 miles east of the trailhead).

65 Ned Hill

RATING/ DIFFICULTY	ROUNDTRIP	ELEV GAIN/ HIGH POINT	SEASON
*/2	2.2 miles	900 feet/ 3469 feet	May–Nov

Maps: Green Trails Olympic Mountains East No. 168S, Custom Correct Buckhorn Wilderness; **Contact:** Olympic National Forest, Hood Canal Ranger District, Quilcene; **GPS:** N 47 58.081, W 123 11.263

This is a short but steep trip to a historical fire lookout on the edge of the Buckhorn Wilderness, and the views are grown-in. So why go? Solitude, for one. And in early summer, an unbroken tunnel of showy rhododendrons splashes the hillside purple and pink.

GETTING THERE

From Sequim, head west 2.5 miles on US Highway 101, turning left onto Taylor Cutoff Road (just after crossing the Dungeness River). Continue 2.6 miles and bear right onto Lost Mountain Road. In another 2.6 miles, turn left onto dirt Forest Road 2870. Drive 1 mile into Olympic National Forest, and bear right at a junction onto FR 2875. Continue on this road for 3.5 miles to the Slab Camp trailhead and turn left, following FR 2878 for 0.4 mile to the trailhead (elev. 2575 ft), located

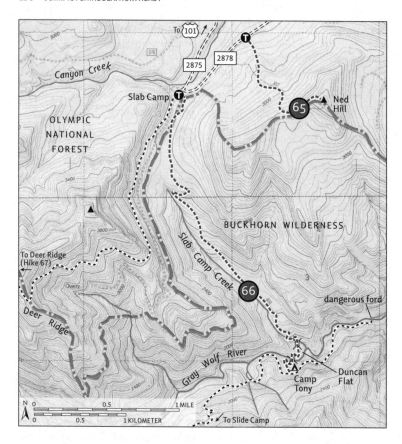

on your right. There is limited parking on the left shoulder just east of the trailhead.

ON THE TRAIL

From its unimposing start, Ned Hill Trail No. 837 takes off on a steep climb through a jungle of rhododendrons, salal, and Oregon grape. This no-nonsense trail was built in the 1930s to service a makeshift fire lookout after much of the area went up in smoke a few years prior. Eventually the forest recovered, the lookout became obsolete, and the trail was abandoned. In the 1990s, longtime Forest Service employee Jim Halvorsm reopened the trail.

Only slightly longer than a mile, this trail may knock the wind out of you with its 30 percent grade in places. Those benches along the route may be quite welcome. On soft tread often covered in moss, work your way up this little peak, a guardian of the Gray Wolf River valley.

Rhododendrons at the old Ned Hill lookout

Blackened and silver snags, testaments to the great fire of yesteryear, periodically punctuate the emerald green canopy of the succession forest. After 1.1 miles, come to Ned Hill's 3469-foot summit and its decaying provisional fire lookout. A gate encloses it. Please stay off of the structure both for your safety and the preservation of this historical relic. Besides, the forest has grown up around it, obscuring the wide views it once granted. If you snoop around Ned a bit, you may get a few peekaboo views of Deer Ridge, Maynard Peak, and Baldy.

66 Slab Camp Creek and Upper Gray Wolf River

RATING/ DIFFICULTY	ROUNDTRIP	ELEV GAIN/ HIGH POINT	SEASON
***/3	5.6 miles	1075 feet/ 2550 feet	May–Nov

Maps: Green Trails Olympic Mountains East No. 168S, Custom Correct Buckhorn Wilderness; **Contact:** Olympic National Forest, Hood Canal Ranger District, Quilcene; **GPS:** N 47 57.909, W 123 11.613

An upside-down trail, start by hiking downhill and get your workout on the return. Descend more than 1000 feet through rhododendrons and ancient forest to the Gray Wolf River. Relax by the churning river—or venture farther up the wilderness valley savoring solitude.

GETTING THERE

From Sequim, head west 2.5 miles on US Highway 101, turning left onto Taylor Cutoff Road (just after crossing the Dungeness River). Continue 2.6 miles and bear right onto Lost Mountain Road. In another 2.6 miles, turn left onto dirt Forest Road 2870. Drive 1 mile into Olympic National Forest, and bear right at a junction onto FR 2875. Continue on this road for 3.5 miles to the Slab Camp trailhead (elev. 2550 ft).

ON THE TRAIL

From a 2550-foot saddle between Deer Ridge and Ned Hill, bear left onto Slab Camp Creek Trail No. 838 and begin a well-graded descent into the Gray Wolf River valley. A mosquito-breeding marsh at the trailhead may have you picking up the pace before you're warmed up. Immediately enter the Buckhorn Wilderness, winding your way through a thick forest of second-growth hemlocks. Much of this area succumbed to major fires early in the twentieth century.

After about 0.5 mile of level walking, begin descending. Through open forest lined with an understory of leathery-leaved rhododendrons, salal, and Oregon grape, catch some good views of Deer and Gray Wolf ridges hovering over the valley.

Bubbling Slab Camp Creek eventually comes into view. As you descend deeper into the Gray Wolf Valley, bigger and older trees become the norm. With the Gray Wolf River now audible but not yet visible, the trail makes a final, somewhat steep drop to the valley floor. Cross cascading Slab Camp Creek on a good bridge on your way down, and emerge in a rich bottomland known as Duncan Flat, with towering cedars. A scattering of campsites along the tumbling and thundering Gray Wolf River make good lunch and nap spots.

A little beyond the flats, the trail crosses the Gray Wolf on a sturdy iron-beamed bridge. Cross it, coming to Camp Tony (elev. 1475 ft) at 2.8 miles. Relax along the river before making the ascent back to the trailhead—or consider the options below.

EXTENDING YOUR TRIP

Follow the trail 0.2 mile to its end at the Gray Wolf Trail (elev. 1575 ft). To the left, you can hike downriver 0.3 mile to ledges high above the Gray Wolf, to where a bridge once spanned the waterway. It's extremely unsafe to ford, so this is as far as you can go.

To the right from the junction, you can follow a good and generally lonely trail high above the river along steep forested canyon walls. Pass some decent views of Grand Ridge, Cameron Divide, and Baldy along the way. Then descend 200 feet, reaching Slide Camp (elev. 2225 ft) on Slide Creek at 2.5 miles. Beyond, the trail descends 200 feet and enters Olympic National Park in 0.5 mile

Bridge spanning Gray Wolf River

(dogs prohibited). It then climbs 400 feet through thick forest before descending 250 feet to meet the Cameron Creek Trail at 5.2 miles. From here, it's 0.4 mile to the right to the Three Forks Shelter (Hike 68).

67 Deer Ridge

RATING/ DIFFICULTY	ROUNDTRIP	ELEV GAIN/ HIGH POINT	SEASON
***/4	9.8 miles	2800 feet/ 5350 feet	June–Nov

Maps: Green Trails Olympic Mountains East No. 168S, Custom Correct Gray Wolf–Dosewallips; **Contact:** Olympic National Forest, Hood Canal Ranger District; Olympic National Park, Wilderness Information Center; **Notes:** Dogs prohibited at park boundary; **GPS:** N 47 57.909, W 123 11.613

You can easily drive to Deer Park via a snaking gravel road from Port Angeles. But here are four good reasons to hike up to it instead. One: access, since the road is often closed until July. Two: profuse wildflowers, both in number and variety. Three: spectacular views of the entire Gray Wolf River valley and its towering peaks. And four: you'll earn it all, something you simply can't do from the seat of your SUV.

GETTING THERE

From Sequim, head west 2.5 miles on US Highway 101, turning left onto Taylor Cutoff Road (just after crossing the Dungeness River). Continue 2.6 miles and bear right onto Lost Mountain Road. In another 2.6 miles, turn left onto dirt Forest Road 2870. Drive 1 mile into Olympic National Forest, and bear right at a junction onto FR 2875.

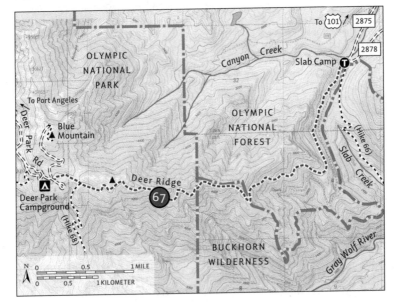

Wildflowers and wilderness views from the Deer Ridge Trail

Continue on this road for 3.5 miles to the Slab Camp trailhead (elev. 2550 ft).

ON THE TRAIL

From the trailhead, bear right onto Deer Ridge Trail No. 846 and follow a decommissioned road-turned-trail for a short while. Then gently climb through a dry forest of Douglas-firs, layered with rhododendrons and carpeted by salal and kinnikinnick. After about 1.5 miles, the easy strolling ends as the way steepens. Pass a spring and consider topping off your water bottle. This is the only water along the trail after the snow melts. At about 2.7 miles, reach an open rib and your first breathtaking views of the Gray Wolf Valley. A bench here memorializes longtime trail volunteer and Sequim resident Phil Hall, a truly great place to be honored.

The trail continues upward through open forest and across dry rocky slopes. At 3.3 miles, enter Olympic National Park (elev. 4800 ft). This is as far as your four-legged hiker can go. Bipeds can continue, hiking through some of the most scenic terrain in this corner of the Olympics. Through parklands, meadows, and basalt outcroppings, the trail weaves its way to Deer Park, delivering breathtaking views at every bend. Gaze out to barren Baldy and Gray Wolf Peak. Admire the jagged summits of Mounts Walkinshaw, Clark, Deception, and Mystery, some of the loftiest summits on the Olympic Peninsula.

Peer down into the emerald valleys of the Gray Wolf River and Grand and Cameron creeks. And at your feet? Flowers! Find arnica, phlox, pearly everlasting, stonecrop, chocolate lily, paintbrush, columbine, yellow violet, wallflower, buttercup, cinquefoil, rockslide larkspur, and many more.

At 4.5 miles, come to a junction with the Three Forks Trail (Hike 68). Continue straight 0.4 mile, reaching Deer Park Campground (elev. 5350 ft) high on a grassy shoulder of Blue Mountain. If the road isn't open yet, it'll just be you and the deer enjoying the scenery.

EXTENDING YOUR TRIP

Walk up Deer Park Road 0.8 mile to the 0.5-mile Rainshadow Nature Trail on the summit of 6007-foot Blue Mountain. Enjoy incredible views, from Vancouver Island to the Cascade Range to Grand Ridge.

68 Three Forks

RATING/ DIFFICULTY	ROUNDTRIP	ELEV GAIN/ HIGH POINT	SEASON
***/5	10 miles	3275 feet/ 5350 feet	July–Oct

Maps: Green Trails Olympic Mountains East No. 168S, Custom Correct Gray Wolf–Dosewallips; **Contact:** Olympic National Park, Wilderness Information Center; **Notes:** National park entrance fee. Dogs prohibited; **GPS:** N 47 56.933, W 123 15.509

This route is primarily used by backpackers to reach the remote Gray Wolf and Cameron Creek valleys—and beyond—but strong day hikers can easily get to Three Forks. It's returning that's a challenge. After admiring the cascading confluence of the Gray Wolf, Cameron, and Grand waterways, brace yourself for one stiff climb back to the trailhead.

GETTING THERE

From Sequim, drive west 12 miles on US Highway 101, turning right onto Deer Park Loop. Continue 0.6 mile and turn right onto Deer Park Road. (From Port Angeles, drive east 5 miles on US 101, turning right onto Deer Park Road.) Follow Deer Park Road 16.4 winding miles to the trailhead (elev. 5350 ft) at Deer Park Campground. Privy available.

Rushing whitewater at the Three Forks

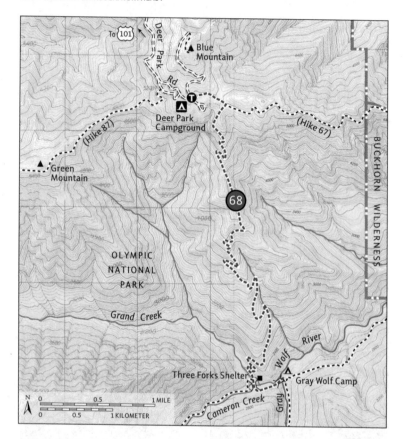

ON THE TRAIL

Walk an easy 0.4 mile on the Deer Ridge Trail to a junction. Turn right onto the Three Forks Trail and steeply descend. Pass through silver snags left over from an old burn and plummet through flowering meadows and the remains of a more recent burn. The grade is steep and the tread rough in places—trekking poles will come in handy.

On the way down be sure to stop and soak in the excellent views—from Gray Wolf Ridge to Grand Ridge and Grand Valley. The grade eventually eases as the trail rounds a shoulder and enters dense forest. The forest then transitions to open and dry as the trail skirts a ravine housing a small creek. Then once again the way steeply descends, reaching the Three Forks Shelter and camps (elev. 2150 ft) at the confluence of Grand and Cameron creeks.

For the third fork, cross Grand Creek on a bridge and stay left at a junction. Then cross

Cameron Creek on a bridge and continue 0.3 mile to the bridged crossing of the Gray Wolf River (elev. 2075 ft) near camps and the junction with the Gray Wolf River Trail. You'll find plenty of great spots to rest and watch mesmerizing rapids before making the arduous return.

EXTENDING YOUR TRIP
Very strong day hikers and trail runners can combine this hike with Hikes 67 (Deer Ridge) and 66 (Slab Camp Creek and Upper Gray Wolf River) for a challenging 18.2-mile loop.

Quimper Peninsula

The northeasternmost point of the Olympic Peninsula, Quimper Peninsula, is bordered by Discovery Bay, Port Townsend Bay, and the Strait of Juan de Fuca. The weather is mild here because of the Olympic rain shadow, with annual precipitation rarely exceeding 20 inches. This small peninsula is also home to the charming Victorian seaport and Jefferson County seat, Port Townsend.

The majority of the county's thirty thousand residents live in communities on the 4-mile-wide by 7-mile-long peninsula. But much of the area is still graced with farms and large green swaths. Several state parks and an active land trust have helped ensure that a good portion of the peninsula remains in a natural state. You'll find miles of good trails and shorelines to explore.

69 Gibbs Lake

RATING/ DIFFICULTY	LOOP	ELEV GAIN/ HIGH POINT	SEASON
**/1	2.8 miles	160 feet/ 450 feet	Year-round

Map: Online at Jefferson County Parks; **Contact:** Jefferson County Parks; **Notes:** Dogs permitted on-leash. Open to mountain bikes, horses; **GPS:** N 47 58.228, W 122 48.640

Gibbs Lake

Hike around a tranquil little lake nestled in the hills south of bustling Port Townsend. Amble through peaceful fir and cedar groves. Watch ducks swim across placid waters while songbirds nesting in shoreline reeds hum sweet melodies. And savor the sweet fragrance of blossoming rhododendrons in the spring.

GETTING THERE

From Hood Canal Bridge, drive State Route 104 west for 9.5 miles and take the Center Road exit, signed "Quilcene, Port Townsend."

(From Sequim, follow US Highway 101 south, bearing right onto SR 104 and continuing 4.2 miles to the exit.) Turn left (north) and follow Center Road for 1.7 miles. Turn left onto Eaglemount Road and in 0.2 mile turn right onto West Valley Road. Proceed for 1.6 miles and turn left onto Gibbs Lake Road, following it for 0.9 mile to the trailhead (elev. 400 ft), on your right.

ON THE TRAIL

Nine miles of trails crisscross more than 650 acres of forested hilly parkland surrounding

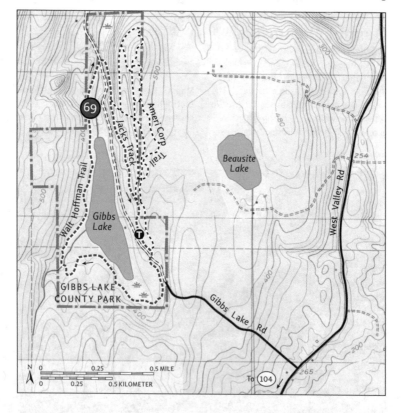

Gibbs and Beausite lakes. But all this could have been stumps without an active citizenry and some enlightened government officials, which resulted in the transfer of this former Washington State Department of Natural Resources plot to Jefferson County Parks. The Quimper Trails Association maintains the trails, and the group continues to plan and build new trails. This loop is a perfect introduction to the park.

You'll be returning on the trail from the left (north), so head southwest from the parking lot on the Walt Hoffmann Trail. Soon come to the park road and cross it. Then skirt a ropes challenge course. The trail is flowy in spots, making it appealing to mountain bikers. Traverse damp forest logged during the Depression years, and catch glimpses of the lake.

The trail pulls away from the lake, crossing several creeks and then ascending drier ground. The lake soon comes back into view as the trail descends toward the lakeshore, passing massive Douglas-firs. Soon encounter more big trees, including a grove of mature cedars. Then work your way through a small wetland. Notice the Sitka spruce, common along the coast but an anomaly in the dry forests of the Olympic rain shadow. After crossing Gibbs's outlet creek, come to the park road at 2 miles

Now pick up Jacks Track across the roadway to the right. The trail makes a steep little climb onto a bluff above the lake. Stay left at a trail fork. At the next junction (elev. 500 ft), where the Escalator Trail veers left, you want to keep right. At 2.6 miles, approach a five-way signed intersection. Head right on the trail (not on the old woods road), emerging in a parking lot after 0.1 mile. Your vehicle is in the next lot. Pick up the trail again, returning to your start at 2.8 miles.

EXTENDING YOUR TRIP

Have fun exploring the generally signed (and popular with mountain biker) miles of trails east of the lake. Hike up to the water tank ruins (elev. 630 ft). Then head south on the Ameri Corp Trail along a ridge of big mature trees that were marked and ready to be harvested before DNR took this pretty parcel off the chopping block.

70 Anderson Lake

RATING/ DIFFICULTY	LOOP	ELEV GAIN/ HIGH POINT	SEASON
**/1	2.3 miles	50 feet/ 310 feet	Year-round

Map: Online at Washington State Parks; **Contact:** Anderson Lake State Park, administered by Fort Flagler State Park; **Notes:** Discover Pass required. Dogs permitted on-leash. Some trails open to mountain bikes, horses. Park closed Nov–Apr, park at gate (do not block); **GPS:** N 48 01.078, W 122 48.224

Set in a quiet valley just 1 mile east of Discovery Bay, Anderson Lake is a peaceful body of water teeming with fish and wildlife. Once the centerpiece to farmland owned by William F. Anderson, the 70-acre lake and surrounding fields and forest are now part of a 476-acre state park. Hike well-maintained and lightly used trails through the old homestead and around the lake within this pastoral park.

GETTING THERE

From Hood Canal Bridge, drive State Route 104 for 5 miles, turning right onto SR 19. Continue north for 10 miles and turn left onto Anderson Lake Road, 1 mile past the

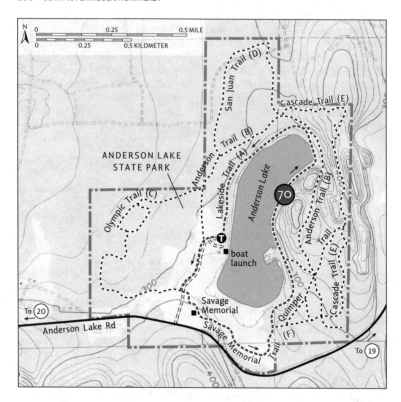

four-way stop in Chimacum. Drive 1.7 miles, turning right into the park. (From Sequim, follow US Highway 101 to SR 20 and turn left. Continue 3.7 miles, turning right onto Anderson Lake Road. Drive 1 mile and turn left into the park.) Continue 0.3 mile to the trailhead (elev. 260 ft) near the boat launch. Privy available.

ON THE TRAIL

More than 8 miles of trails traverse this lovely park. A good introduction is the easy 2.3-mile hike around Anderson Lake. Start by walking 0.3 mile down the gravel access road through rolling pasture to a trail crossing. The trail heading right is the Olympic (C) Trail, a 1.1-mile rolling woodland romp that eventually leads back to the trailhead when linked with the Anderson (B) Trail.

To loop the lake, head left on the Savage Memorial (F) Trail, named for former state and US representative Charles R. Savage of Shelton. On well-built trail, travel through mature stands of firs, cedars, and spruce, making your way to the lake's outlet stream. Cross it on a sturdy bridge and in 0.8 mile come to a junction. Head left on the hiker-only Lakeside (A) Trail. Enjoy a

Anderson Lake

shoreline-clinging journey that undulates through forest and along grassy banks as it rounds the lake. Look for critters small and large who take up residence in this protected habitat.

Tune your senses to the forest too. In spring, trillium and wild strawberry blossoms carpet the forest floor. Honeysuckle and thick stands of waxy-leaved rhododendrons crowd the lofty evergreens. By May, the rhodies' showy flowers burst onto the scene. Cross a bog via a boardwalk at the lake's northern end, and then traverse shoreline groves of cedars before returning to your start at 2.3 miles.

EXTENDING YOUR TRIP

You can easily make your hike longer by adding some of the park's other trails. The 1-mile San Juan (D) Trail and 1.3-mile Anderson (B) Trail follow old woods roads—the latter more interesting, traversing a wetland hollow. The 1.3-mile Cascade (E) Trail climbs a couple of hundred feet along a forested ridge and passes a group of large glacial erratics. It then dips and climbs, crossing a few wetlands along the way.

71 South Indian Island

RATING/ DIFFICULTY	ROUNDTRIP	ELEV GAIN/ HIGH POINT	SEASON
***/1	4 miles	70 feet/ 50 feet	Year-round

Map: Online at Jefferson County Parks; **Contact:** Jefferson County Parks; **Notes:** Dogs permitted on-leash; **GPS:** N 48 01.912, W 122 43.748

Hike through a forest of madronas and Douglas-firs to a long sandy beach with impressive views of Mount Rainier hovering over the horizon. Walk out on a narrow spit, explore a lagoon flourishing with birds, and watch for playful seals plying the waters. The 142-acre Indian Island County Park offers some of the best maritime meanderings on this side of the Olympic Peninsula.

GETTING THERE

From Hood Canal Bridge, drive State Route 104 for 5 miles, turning right onto SR 19. Continue north for 9 miles, turning right at the four-way stop in Chimacum onto Chimacum Road. Drive 1.6 miles and turn right onto SR 116. Then follow SR 116 east for 1.7 miles,

Author enjoys a winter beach hike at South Indian Island.

turning right immediately after crossing the bridge to Indian Island, into the parking area at the trailhead (elev. 50 ft). Privy available. (From Sequim, follow US Highway 101 to SR 20 and turn left. Continue 3.7 miles, turning right onto Anderson Lake Road. Follow it for 2.7 miles and turn left on SR 19. Then proceed 0.6 mile, turning right onto SR 116 and following it 3 miles to the trailhead.)

ON THE TRAIL

Once connected to the Quimper Peninsula by a low stretch of land, Indian Island was cut off in 1913 when Port Townsend merchants had a channel dredged. But it was the US Navy that cut most of this landmass off from the public by establishing an ammunition

storage depot here. Fortunately, a narrow strip along the south shore of the island is a glorious county park.

From the grassy bluff picnic area, follow the Portage Trail east through a tunnel of vegetation along Portage Canal. In late spring enjoy the fragrance and blossoms of primrose and honeysuckle. The trail brushes up against some marshy openings, ideal for seeking out eagles and herons. It then climbs back up a bluff, ending at the park's beach-access road after 0.5 mile.

You can hike left on the road a short distance and then follow the Lagoon Trail for 0.4 mile on a bluff above a big lagoon that teems with birds. But better exploring lies to the right. So walk the road and drop off

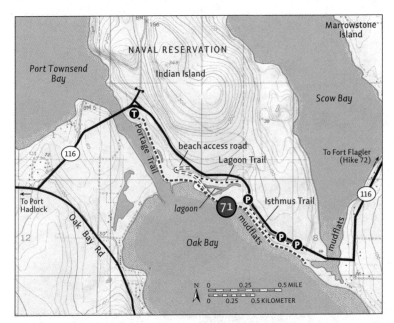

the bluff, reaching an inviting beach at 0.7 mile. If the tide is low, rock hop or wade the small creek draining the lagoon. Then walk east along a sandy spit, one of the finest stretches of beach in the region. At 1.2 miles, pass a parking area (and alternative start if you don't want to cross the creek).

Continue your beach walk around bluffs of glacial till, taking in sweeping views across Oak Bay to Mount Rainier. At 1.7 miles, pass a trail leading left to another parking area and connecting with the Isthmus Trail, which parallels the road and links the park's two eastern parking areas. Continue, now on a narrow rocky strip of beach along marshes connecting Indian and Marrowstone islands. At 2 miles, the public beach ends. Turn around and enjoy your shoreline stroll all over again.

72 Fort Flagler

RATING/ DIFFICULTY	LOOP	ELEV GAIN/ HIGH POINT	SEASON
***/2	5.6 miles	200 feet/ 170 feet	Year-round

Map: Online at Washington State Parks; **Contact:** Fort Flagler State Park; **Notes:** Discover Pass required. Dogs permitted on-leash. Beach sections may be impassable during very high tides; **GPS:** N 48 05.724, W 122 43.386

One of several grand military installations originally established to protect Puget Sound from foreign invaders, Fort Flagler—like the others—never saw combat. In the 1950s these

The author's wife and 3-month-old son hike the Fort Flagler Loop

forts were converted to state parks. At 780 acres, Fort Flagler on the northern tip of Marrowstone Island is the largest, consisting of over 3.5 miles of shoreline. It offers fine beach hiking and miles of trails weaving through quiet forest and historical grounds.

GETTING THERE

From Hood Canal Bridge, drive State Route 104 for 5 miles, turning right onto SR 19. Continue north for 9 miles, turning right at the four-way stop in Chimacum onto Chimacum Road. Drive 1.6 miles and turn right onto

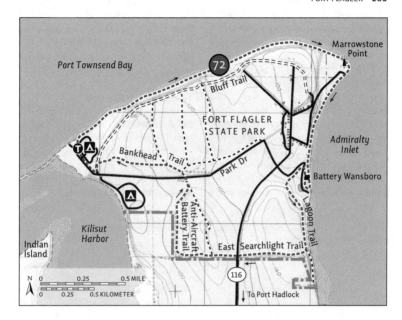

Marrowstone Point

Port Townsend Bay

72

Bluff Trail

FORT FLAGLER
STATE PARK

Admiralty
Inlet

Bankhead Trail

Park Dr

Battery Wansboro

Anti-Aircraft
Battery Trail

Lagoon Trail

Kilisut
Harbor

Indian
Island

East Searchlight Trail

N 0   0.25   0.5 MILE
0   0.25   0.5 KILOMETER

116

To Port Hadlock

SR 116. Then follow SR 116 for 8.7 miles to its end at Fort Flagler State Park. (From Sequim, follow US Highway 101 to SR 20 and turn left. Continue 3.7 miles, turning right onto Anderson Lake Road. Follow it for 2.7 miles and turn left on SR 19. Then proceed 0.6 mile, turning right onto SR 116 and following it 9.8 miles to the state park.) Proceed 0.7 mile into the park and turn left at a four-way intersection. Continue 1.4 miles to the road's end at a large day-use parking area (elev. 10 ft). Water and restrooms available.

ON THE TRAIL

With more than 7 miles of trail and 3.5 miles of coastline, Fort Flagler offers many hiking options. The following loop samples a few of the many facets of this wonderful park. Start your adventure on the wide, cobblestone-strewn beach. Head east, enjoying a grand

view across Port Townsend Bay to the Victorian city of Port Townsend. Admire Whidbey Island's lofty chalky bluffs hovering in the distance. An impressive fortress of bluffs soon begins to tower right above you as well. Gaze up at the tall trees teetering on them—there's a good chance a bald eagle or two will be peering down at you.

Clamber over a few rocks to reach a trail and then walk along a low coastal bluff, rounding Marrowstone Point with its Coast Guard station and lighthouse at 1.9 miles. Enjoy a sweeping view of Admiralty Inlet with Mount Rainier in the distance. Then continue hiking on a wide sandy beach, coming to an old weather-battered pier at 2.6 miles. Now it's time to sample Flagler's interior full of historical structures and interpretive displays. Follow a short trail to a park road and steeply climb to the Battery

Wansboro, perched high on a bluff at 2.8 miles. Then walk left 0.1 mile along the road to the Lagoon Trail.

Hike it, climbing a bluff through mature forest and coming to a junction (elev. 150 ft) and viewpoint at 3.4 miles. The trail straight leads 0.2 mile to a searchlight. The loop continues right on the East Searchlight Trail, reaching the park entrance road at 3.8 miles. Cross the road and follow the Anti-Aircraft Battery Trail, cresting a 170-foot hill and staying left at two junctions. At 4.8 miles, come to Park Drive. Cross it and turn left on the Bankhead Trail. Stay left at two junctions and reach Park Drive again at 5.4 miles. Turn right and walk the road 0.2 mile back to your start.

EXTENDING YOUR TRIP

The 1.5-mile Bluff Trail makes a nice alternative if you'd rather not hike the beach (or can't, because of a high tide), and plenty of other trails connect to the loop described here. Fort Flagler is also a nice place to spend the night, offering snuggly campsites, historical-home rentals, and a hostel.

Opposite: Mount Olympus hovers above the High Divide

olympic peninsula: north

Strait of Juan de Fuca

The 100-mile-long Strait of Juan de Fuca is the portal to Puget Sound, a transition zone between the Pacific Ocean and the Salish Sea's great inland waterways. And like all transition zones, diversity is legion. From dry Douglas-fir forests in the Olympic rain shadow to dew-dripping salty spruce groves at the strait's mouth, Juan de Fuca's landscapes change radically and dramatically east to west. The mood is always maritime, but the alpine zone is nearby—snowcapped Olympic peaks to the south, Vancouver Island's rugged ranges to the north, and the Cascades to the east overlook this long arm of the Pacific.

Though the strait is populated along its eastern fringes, its western reaches are wild and sparsely settled. But this waterway is a busy place, a superhighway for thousands of tankers and vessels plying their way to ports in Victoria, Vancouver, Seattle, Tacoma, and a handful of other destinations. On the trails and beaches of Juan de Fuca, however, it's possible to seek out quieter waters.

73 Miller Peninsula and Thompson Spit

RATING/ DIFFICULTY	ROUNDTRIP	ELEV GAIN/ HIGH POINT	SEASON
**/2	7.7 miles	590 feet/ 375 feet	Year-round

Map: Online at Washington State Parks; **Contact:** Miller Peninsula State Park, administered by Sequim Bay State Park; **Notes:** Discover Pass required. Dogs permitted on-leash. Open to mountain bikes, horses. State-park development under way, expect trail system to change; **GPS:** N 48 03.967, W 122 56.783

Protection Island and Mount Baker

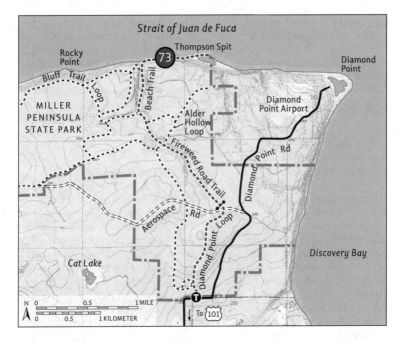

Explore a cool, lush ravine that leads to a remote beach on the Strait of Juan de Fuca. Walk along the shore under towering bluffs to a spit littered with driftlogs and watched over by a battalion of eagles. Take in views of Protection Island, a bird sanctuary at the mouth of Puget Sound. Welcome to the Miller Peninsula, destined to become Washington's next grand state park.

GETTING THERE

From Hood Canal Bridge, drive State Route 104 to its end and veer north onto US Highway 101. Continue for 10.5 miles, turning right onto Diamond Point Road (near milepost 275 at the county line and signed "Airport"). (From Sequim, head east 10 miles on US 101, turning left onto Diamond Point

Road.) Continue for 1.2 miles and turn left into the trailhead parking area (elev. 160 ft). Privy available.

ON THE TRAIL

Once considered a site for a nuclear power plant and golf resort, this former Washington State Department of Natural Resources timberland and magnificent piece of coastal property has not always been revered by state officials. But Washington's citizens came to its aid, and the property was transferred to the state parks division. The Great Recession delayed creation of the planned Miller Peninsula State Park, but the Washington Trails Association, Backcountry Horsemen of Washington, and mountain-biking groups have been busy building and maintaining trails on this sprawling 2800-acre piece of public land. Washington State Parks will soon be unveiling its master plan, which includes building new trails and rebuilding and eliminating some old trails. Expect a lot of changes here over the years, but there's no need to wait to visit.

The hike to Thompson Spit is a great preview of this park. From the parking area (built in 2015), follow the Diamond Point Loop north (staying right at junctions) for 1.1 miles to the dirt Aerospace Road (elev. 375 ft), which accesses Northwest Technical Industries, a private company. Cross the road to a gated old logging road now known as the Fireweed Road Trail. Walk this woodlands byway through a thick stand of second growth, coming to a junction (elev. 300 ft) at 2.1 miles. Here another old road and the continuation of the Diamond Point Loop veer left. You want to go right, continuing on Fireweed Road Trail.

Immediately come to another junction. The Alder Hollow Loop goes right on an old road. Head left, soon passing the Alder Hollow Loop's other junction and at 2.4 miles coming to another junction. The Fireweed Road Trail continues left. You want to go right on the Beach Trail, descending into a narrow ravine graced with rhododendrons and remnant old-growth firs and cedars. Rays of light begin penetrating the forest, and the sound of the surf grows louder. Stay right at a junction with a trail leading to the Bluff Trail Loop, and soon afterward, at 3.1 miles, reach a wildly beautiful beach. If the tide is high, plop your bum on a driftwood log and let the surf serenade you. If the tide is out, walk the cobbled beach right under a fortress of high bluffs capped in thick forest.

Protection Island's chalky bluffs shine across choppy waters. Mount Baker's snowy cone rises above the San Juan Islands. After 0.75 mile of beach strolling, come to the park boundary (don't go any farther) at log-littered Thompson Spit and its bird-rich lagoon. Eagles, buffleheads, geese, herons, and blackbirds go about their business in the brackish waters, while oystercatchers and harlequin ducks ply the shoreline. Enjoy the avian show and then retrace your route to the trailhead.

EXTENDING YOUR TRIP

With a map in hand, consider checking out some of the park's other trails. The Bluff Trail Loop travels 4 miles—half that distance along bluff edges, with occasional views out to the strait. The Sequim Bay Trail diverts from that loop, leading 2.2 miles to a parking area on East Sequim Bay Road that comes from Blyn.

74 Dungeness Spit

RATING/ DIFFICULTY	ROUNDTRIP	ELEV GAIN/ HIGH POINT	SEASON
****/3	11 miles	130 feet/ 130 feet	Year-round

Map: At trailhead kiosk and refuge website; **Contact:** Dungeness National Wildlife Refuge; **Notes:** $3 entry fee per family (or group of four adults; Interagency Pass accepted). Closed at sunset. Dogs prohibited. Hike may be difficult in highest tides; **GPS:** N 48 08.480, W 123 11.395

Hike one of Washington's best saltwater strolls and the longest coastal spit in the continental United States. A narrow strip of sand, dune, and beached logs, Dungeness Spit extends more than 5 miles straight into the strait. It's also the center-

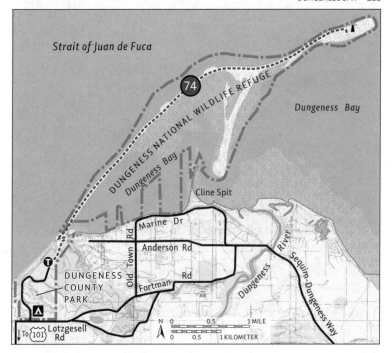

piece of a national wildlife refuge, so expect to see a lot of birds and seals along the way.

GETTING THERE

From Sequim, head west on US Highway 101 for 4.5 miles. (From Port Angeles, drive east on US 101 for 12 miles.) Turn right (north) at milepost 260 onto Kitchen-Dick Road. At 3.3 miles, the road turns sharply right and becomes Lotzgesell Road. In another 0.25 mile, turn left on Voice of America Road (signed "Dungeness National Wildlife Refuge, Dungeness Recreation Area"). Proceed through the Clallam County park and campground, and in 1 mile come to the trailhead (elev. 130 ft). Water and restrooms available.

ON THE TRAIL

The Dungeness Spit was formed over centuries by wind and water currents that forced river silt and glacial till to arch into the Strait of Juan de Fuca. You can hike almost to the tip, where a lighthouse (the second oldest in the state) has been keeping guard since 1857. The very end of the spit, like the Dungeness Bay side, is closed to public entry to protect important wildlife habitat. Because the spit is protected and managed as a wildlife refuge, many recreational activities are restricted. Please respect areas closed to public visitation.

Lying within the Olympic rain shadow, the spit receives less than 20 inches of rain annually, making it a great winter destination

A hiker heads out on Dungeness Spit.

when surrounding areas are socked in. Pack your binoculars too, as the bird-watching is supreme. Over 250 species have been recorded on the spit and in Dungeness Bay, including many that are endangered or threatened. Marbled murrelets, harlequin ducks, and snowy plovers frequent the area.

Follow the refuge trail 0.5 mile through cool maritime forest. Take in sweeping views of the spit from an overlook before descending to the beach. Emerge at the base of tall bluffs, at the start of the spit. It's a straightforward hike to the lighthouse. Pack plenty of water and sunscreen. Be sure to occasionally look back at Mount Angeles towering over the surf. If the 11-mile round trip seems daunting, any distance hiked along the spit will be rewarding.

EXTENDING YOUR TRIP

South from where the trail reaches the shoreline you can wander oft-deserted beaches under golden bluffs. The 630-acre wildlife refuge borders a 216-acre Clallam County park that has a couple of miles of trails too, including one along high bluffs. The park also contains scenic campsites.

75 Robin Hill Farm

RATING/ DIFFICULTY	LOOP	ELEV GAIN/ HIGH POINT	SEASON
**/1	1.9 miles	100 feet/ 270 feet	Year-round

Map: Online at Clallam County Parks; **Contact:** Clallam County Parks; **Notes:** Dogs permitted on-leash; **GPS:** N 48 05.420, W 123 12.834

Take to 3.4 miles of well-groomed trails at this peaceful 195-acre county park not far from busy US Highway 101. Wander through tall timber, across an open field, and beside a wetland. A former farm, Robin Hill now provides outdoor recreation and native plants for revegetating the Elwha River valley, where two dams once stood.

GETTING THERE

From Sequim, head west on US Highway 101 for 5.5 miles. (From Port Angeles, drive east on US 101 for 11 miles.) Turn right (north) onto Dryke Road. Then proceed 0.4 mile, turning right into Robin Hill Farm County Park and driving 0.1 mile to the trailhead (elev. 270 ft). Privy available.

ON THE TRAIL

Equestrians enjoy this park too, but you won't have to worry about them trotting by because the park segregates hikers and horseback riders on their own trails. The trails are well marked and the junctions are signed with numbered posts. For a grand hiker gallop around the park, start on the main trail by a kiosk, soon coming to post 8. You'll be returning on the left, so head right, coming to post 10 in 0.1 mile. A trail veers to the right through attractive forest, winding its way 0.5 mile back to the parking lot—a nice extension to this hike.

Continue straight instead, descending a hilly meadow and passing a couple of horse trails to reach post 5 (elev. 170 ft) at 0.4 mile.

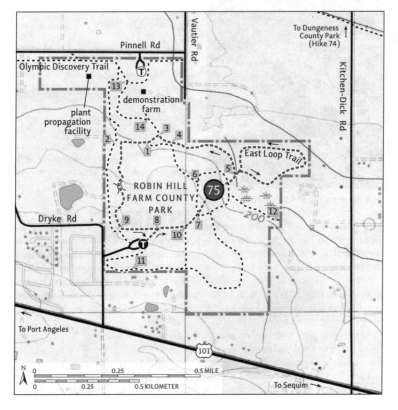

Well-groomed trail at Robin Hill Park

Before continuing left, head right on the East Loop Trail. This delightful path skirts a wetland before circling back through forest and returning you to post 5 in 0.5 mile.

Continue your grand loop on a wide trail through a corridor of tall firs and cottonwoods, coming to post 3 at 1.3 miles. Head left through thick timber. Cross a horse trail and bend left to begin climbing. Pass impressive grand firs, cedars, and Douglas-firs and cross a bridge over a wetland, reaching post 9. Turn left and soon return to post 8 to close your loop at 1.9 miles.

EXTENDING YOUR TRIP
From post 3, continue 0.3 mile through mature trees, coming to the paved Olympic Discovery Trail (see the "Discovering the Olympic Discovery Trail" sidebar) and the Pinnell Road parking area and trailhead. Wander left a short distance to the Olympic National Park plant propagation facility, where native plants are being grown for transplant in the Elwha Valley. Or wander right a short distance to the Washington State University–run demonstration farm complete with cows—kids will love it.

76 Striped Peak

RATING/ DIFFICULTY	ROUNDTRIP	ELEV GAIN/ HIGH POINT	SEASON
**/3	5.4 miles	1150 feet/ 950 feet	Year-round

Maps: Green Trails Joyce No. 102, online at DNR; **Contact:** Salt Creek County Park and Washington State Department of Natural Resources, Olympic Office; **Notes:** Dogs permitted on-leash; **GPS:** N 48 09.733, W 123 41.902

At Striped Peak, two adventures in one await you. Hike to a 1000-foot peak above the Strait of Juan de Fuca. Watch liners and vessels ply this Salish Sea passageway against a backdrop of craggy peaks on Canada's Vancouver Island. Hike directly to the strait via a steep trail down to a remote cliff-enclosed cove.

GETTING THERE
From Port Angeles, follow US Highway 101 west for 5.4 miles, turning right onto State Route 112. Continue for 7.2 miles and turn right at milepost 54 onto Camp Hayden

Remote Hidden Cove on the Strait of Juan de Fuca

Road. Then drive 3.4 miles, turning right into Salt Creek County Park. Continue 0.2 mile to the trailhead (elev. 125 ft), on the right just after the entrance booth. Privy available.

ON THE TRAIL

Port Angeles residents have long known that some of the finest coastal scenery around can be found at nearby Salt Creek County Park. This one-time army post known as Camp Hayden is managed by Clallam County Parks, complete with campground and trails. A 1500-acre Washington State Department of Natural Resources (DNR) tract abuts the park to the east, including 1166-foot Striped Peak. Although heavily logged, the steep northern slopes of the mountain were spared, allowing you to hike amid huge Douglas-firs hundreds of years old.

The trail begins on an old road skirting the park's campground. It then heads through stands of big firs. Hugging the hillside and not far from the coastline, wind through forested flats while listening to

waves splash up against ledge and bluff. Continue deeper into the forest, climbing a bench high above the crashing surf. Enter a primeval grove of towering hemlocks, firs, and cedars. If access weren't so prohibitively difficult, these ancient giants surely would have been logged.

The way then descends about 80 feet before climbing to a small dizzying viewpoint of an isolated cove almost 250 feet below. Be careful while admiring this vista! If you continue, keep skittish dogs and children nearby. The trail rounds the cove high above, coming to a side trail (elev. 200 ft) at 0.9 mile. The rough trail left drops rapidly, reaching the remote cove at the base of a cascade in 0.2 mile. It's worth the effort, so check it out and then return to the main trail to continue ascending Striped Peak.

Head up a damp ravine—a dense fern alley—and then pass a big boulder field. Uniform second growth soon replaces the big trees. Cross numerous side creeks and, after the trail turns south, climb steeply and

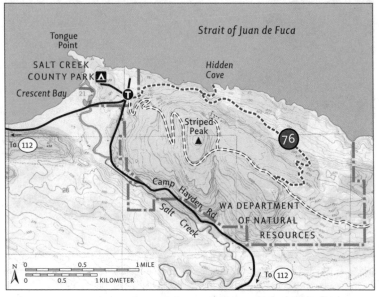

skirt an old cut to emerge on an old dirt road (elev. 950 ft) at 2.4 miles from the trailhead. Follow the road right a short distance to a growing-in viewpoint over a vast expanse of saltwater and Canadian soil. You can make out Vancouver Island's Sooke Harbour across the strait and Salt Spring Island to the northeast. Unfortunately, the summit is anticlimactic, but the workout is good and the forest impressive. As of this writing, WTA is constructing a new trail to create a loop.

EXTENDING YOUR TRIP
It's possible to return to the trailhead via 2.4 miles of DNR roads, but the route is confusing and often not very scenic, so it's best to return the way you came. Back within the county park, sample the short trails to the Tongue Point Marine Sanctuary and the flowerpot sea stacks of Crescent Bay.

77 Cowan Ranch

RATING/ DIFFICULTY	ROUNDTRIP	ELEV GAIN/ HIGH POINT	SEASON
**/1	3 miles	130 feet/ 120 feet	Year-round

Maps: USGS Clallam Bay, USGS Ellis Mountain; **Contact:** Hoko River State Park, administered by Bogachiel State Park; **Notes:** Discover Pass required. Dogs permitted on-leash; **GPS:** N 48 15.502, W 124 21.110

Hike along a salmon-bearing river through an old homestead, now a state park. Where cattle once grazed, elk now browse. Look for eagles, otters, and bears too as you wander an old farm road through a valley in the rain-soaked hills of the state's northwest corner.

Little Hoko River

GETTING THERE

From Port Angeles, follow US Highway 101 west for 5.4 miles, turning right onto State Route 112. Continue for 46 miles to the community of Sekiu. (Alternatively, drive US 101 west to Sappho, follow SR 113 north to SR

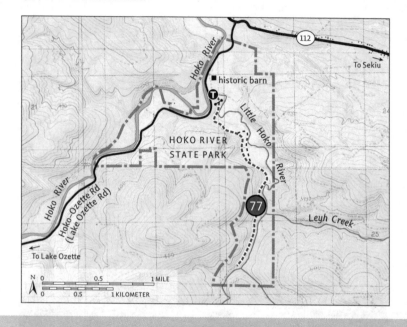

KLAHOWYA TILLICUM

Many place names on the Olympic Peninsula, like in much of the Pacific Northwest, come from the Chinook Jargon, a unique part of our region's heritage. Not an actual language, Chinook is a collection of several hundred words drawn from Coast Salish languages as well as English and French. It was used as a trade language among Native peoples, Europeans, and European-Americans in the Pacific Northwest throughout the nineteenth century. Below are some Chinook words you'll encounter on the Olympic Peninsula.

chuck: water, river or stream
cultus: bad or worthless
elip: first, in front of
hyas: big, powerful, mighty
illahee: the land, country, earth, soil
kimtah: following after, behind
klahanie (klahhane): outdoors
klahowya: greeting, "how are you?"
    or welcome
klootchman: woman

kloshe nanitch: take care, stand guard
la push: the mouth (of a river)
ollalie: berries
potlatch: give, gift
sitkum: half of something, part
    of something
skookum: big, strong, mighty
tenas: small, weak, children
tillicum: friend, people
tupso: pasture, grass

112, and then continue to Sekiu. This way is longer, but not as curvy.) Drive 2.3 miles on SR 112 beyond Sekiu and turn left onto the Hoko-Ozette Road. Proceed for 0.7 mile to the trailhead (elev. 40 ft), on the left just after a bridge over the Little Hoko River.

ON THE TRAIL

Walk around the gate and begin hiking along an old farm road that parallels the Little Hoko River. Across the river lie old barns and pastures, all part of the 522-acre Cowan Ranch Heritage Area. Homesteaded in 1893 and sold to the Cowan family in 1918, the area was ranched until 1984. In 1991 it was sold to Washington State Parks and added to three other prime parcels as part of the 1011-acre Hoko River State Park. Eventually, trails, a campground, and other amenities will be developed here, creating a grand destination park.

Follow the old road alongside gravelly river bars, passing maple glades and alder flats and a handful of big Sitka spruces. Soon enter a pasture with nice views of the scrappy surrounding hills and perhaps a chance to eavesdrop on some elk. The trail splits here near a small creek. Go either way—the two routes soon join up again in another pasture.

Continue farther up the old road, up and over a small wooded hill, passing some big spruces and maples and then returning close to the rippling Little Hoko. At 1.5 miles, the old road ends (elev. 70 ft) in a tangle of brush. Return the way you came.

EXTENDING YOUR TRIP

Head over to Clallam Bay and hike 1.5 miles of beautiful beach at the Clallam Bay Spit County Park. If the tide is low, check out the tide pools east of the spit at Slip Point.

Hurricane Ridge

For many, the Hurricane Ridge region is the créme de la créme of day hiking on the Olympic Peninsula. Nowhere else in these rugged mountains can you access alpine terrain with such ease. Many of the area's hikes start at high elevations and remain high, weaving along lofty ridges flush with flowers and granting sweeping views.

But such notoriety comes at a cost. Many of the trails can get downright crowded, especially on nice weekends (both summer and winter). The Hurricane Ridge Road (Heart O'the Hills Parkway), which enables such easy access to this high country, invites almost anyone. And indeed, more than a few got their first taste of the Olympics because of this popular parkway, gaining a love and respect for this special place.

78 Peabody Creek

RATING/ DIFFICULTY	ROUNDTRIP	ELEV GAIN/ HIGH POINT	SEASON
**/2	5.9 miles	1050 feet/ 1160 feet	Year-round

Maps: Green Trails Port Angeles No. 103, Custom Correct Hurricane Ridge; **Contact:** Olympic National Park, Wilderness Information Center; **Notes:** Dogs permitted on-leash; **GPS:** N 48 05.983, W 123 25.613

One of just a few dog-friendly trails in Olympic National Park, this delightful creekside hike just outside of Port Angeles will appeal to all comers, with or without dogs.

GETTING THERE

From US Highway 101 in Port Angeles, near milepost 249, turn south on Race Street

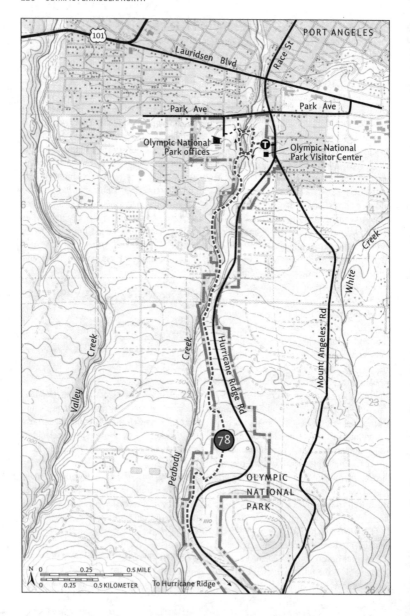

and drive 1 mile to the intersection with Park Avenue. Proceed straight onto Mount Angeles Road and immediately turn right for the Olympic National Park Visitor Center and the trailhead (elev. 390 ft), located on the west side of the parking area. Privy and water available.

ON THE TRAIL

Though this trail takes off from the park's main visitors center, many visitors skip it, opting for hikes higher up on Hurricane Ridge. But Port Angeles residents—especially ones with dogs—make good use of this well-maintained wooded walkway. From the trailhead, enter a lush forest of evergreens and rhododendrons. The way descends into a cool ravine that houses gurgling Peabody Creek. En route you may pass some panels sporting poetry passages. This and other Poetry Walks were conceived by Port Angeles Library manager Noah Glaude and created through a collaboration between the library and national park.

Cross Peabody Creek (elev. 290 ft) on a sturdy bridge, climb some steps, and reach a junction at 0.2 mile. If you're intent on doing just a short 0.5-mile loop, continue right. Then stay right at the next junction (the trail left leads to the park's offices) and cross the creek once again. Then climb out of the ravine and return to the parking lot 300 feet north of where you started.

If you'd like a longer hike, turn left and follow the creek upstream through the ravine. You'd never know you're paralleling the busy Hurricane Ridge Road, as it's not visible or audible for much of the way. At 0.4 mile, cross the creek on a high log bridge. At 0.6 mile, cross the creek again—this time over an old pipeline. You'll cross the creek a couple of more times on your journey.

Trilliums line the Peabody Creek Trail

At 1.2 miles, pass through a powerline swath; then shortly afterward begin climbing out of the ravine. Now high above the creek, hike through mature timber, passing a couple of spurs leading left to the road. The way dips a little, back into the ravine, and crosses a side creek. Then it climbs again, passing a giant fir and ending at 2.9 miles at the Hurricane Ridge Road (elev. 1160 ft) (no parking). Turn around and enjoy the creek downstream, being sure to complete the loop on your way back to the trailhead.

79 Heart O'the Forest

RATING/ DIFFICULTY	ROUNDTRIP	ELEV GAIN/ HIGH POINT	SEASON
**/2	4.6 miles	550 feet/ 1910 feet	Year-round

Maps: Green Trails Hurricane Ridge/Elwha North No. 134S, Custom Correct Hurricane Ridge; **Contact:** Olympic National Park, Wilderness Information Center; **Notes:** National park entrance fee. Dogs prohibited; **GPS:** N 48 02.033, W 123 25.473

A boardwalk cuts through a patch of skunk cabbage

Beginning from the bustling Heart O'the Hills Campground, this well-manicured but lightly hiked trail ventures into the heart of a jungle of ancient conifers. Mosey through rows of giant hemlock, silver fir, and Douglas-fir pillars that hold up a verdant canopy above an equally lush green understory.

GETTING THERE

From US Highway 101 in Port Angeles, near milepost 249, turn south on Race Street and drive 1 mile to the intersection with Park Avenue. Proceed straight for 0.2 mile on Mount Angeles Road and turn right onto Hurricane Ridge Road (Heart O'the Hills Parkway). Continue 5.4 miles, turn left into the Heart O'the Hills Campground (just beyond the park entrance station), and proceed to the trailhead (elev. 1860 ft) located in Loop E. Privy and water available.

ON THE TRAIL

Most campers who find this peaceful little path rarely venture far on it. Start by crossing a creek and walking on a boardwalk through pungent skunk cabbage. Climb about 50 feet, passing impressive cedars and Douglas-firs. The way then slowly descends, blazing across a forest floor of luxuriant undergrowth shaded by primeval giants.

At about 1.1 miles, the forest transitions to mature second growth. The way then follows the rim of a ravine that carries the coursing Lake Creek, born in Lake Angeles far above. Now descending more noticeably, cross a side creek on a bridge and pass through another grove of big old trees. The trail grows rougher and a little brushy as it weaves through a big area of blowdown. Dropping into the ravine, cross another side creek, traverse an old slide, and duck

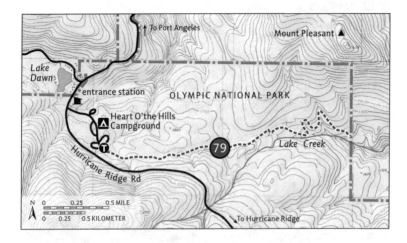

beneath a big fallen fir. The way gets close to—but never reaches—Lake Creek. Come upon a few more big trees before reaching the trail's end (elev. 1360 ft) at the park boundary. Then work your way back to the campground, regaining lost elevation.

80 Lake Angeles

RATING/ DIFFICULTY	ROUNDTRIP	ELEV GAIN/ HIGH POINT	SEASON
***/3	7 miles	2425 feet/ 4225 feet	June–Nov

Maps: Green Trails Hurricane Ridge/Elwha North No. 134S, Custom Correct Hurricane Ridge; **Contact:** Olympic National Park, Wilderness Information Center; **Notes:** Dogs prohibited; **GPS:** N 48 02.345, W 123 25.916

Occupying a glacial cirque below Klahhane Ridge, Lake Angeles is ringed on three sides by steep rocky walls. From high above, the 20-acre lake looks like a teardrop. But you'll be quite happy upon reaching this pretty subalpine body of water fed by tumbling creeks of snowmelt.

GETTING THERE

From US Highway 101 in Port Angeles, near milepost 249, turn south on Race Street and drive 1 mile to the intersection with Park Avenue. Proceed straight for 0.2 mile on Mount Angeles Road and turn right onto Hurricane Ridge Road (Heart O'the Hills Parkway). Continue 5.3 miles, and turn right just before the park entrance station to reach the trailhead (elev. 1800 ft). Privy available.

ON THE TRAIL

The well-worn path immediately sets out climbing, paralleling Ennis Creek, before making a sharp turn east to cross the creek and head over to another drainage. You'll steadily gain elevation on this hike, but the grade is never steep. The way traverses dark, thick forests—successional growth after a fire swept through here more than one hundred years ago.

Lake Angeles flanked by steep cliffs

After crossing a small creek, the way makes a sharp turn back west, crosses the creek again, and begins to climb straight up a rib, the divide between Ennis and Lake creeks. Never easing up, the trail works its way into the deep cirque housing the lake. At close to 3.5 miles, near a backcountry camping area, a sign indicates that the lake is near. Turn left down a short spur and behold, Lake Angeles (elev. 4200 ft), one of the larger backcountry lakes in the Olympics. Cool air rushes down the bare slopes above, rippling the lake surface. Sunlight twinkles off of the small waves. A small island formed by rockfall and adorned with subalpine firs sits in the middle of the emerald lake. It's a soothing scene, but you won't be alone here. Good resting spots along the rugged lakeshore are at a premium.

EXTENDING YOUR TRIP

If the rugged surroundings intrigue you and you're full of energy, the trail continues beyond the lake. Steeply climb 1800 more feet in 2 miles to the open slopes of Klahhane Ridge (Hike 82). You can peer directly down on the twinkling lake and out beyond to the Strait of Juan de Fuca. A grueling 12.5-mile loop can also be made by following the ridge to the Heather Park Trail (Hike 81) and then back to your vehicle. Dangerous snowfields can linger along the ridge into midsummer, so plan accordingly.

81 Heather Park

RATING/ DIFFICULTY	ROUNDTRIP	ELEV GAIN/ HIGH POINT	SEASON
****/4	10 miles	3940 feet/ 5740 feet	Mid-June– Nov

Maps: Green Trails Hurricane Ridge/Elwha North No. 134S, Custom Correct Hurricane Ridge; **Contact:** Olympic National Park, Wilderness Information Center; **Notes:** Dogs prohibited; **GPS:** N 48 02.345, W 123 25.916

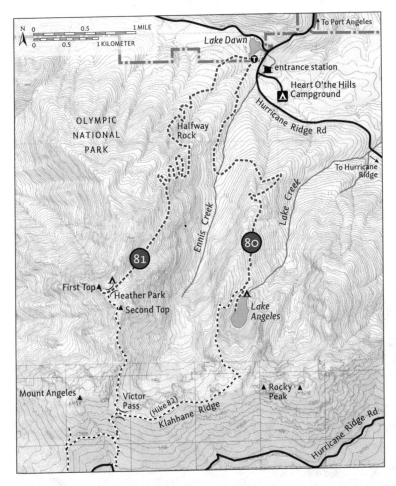

Climb a steep ridge high on the shoulder of Mount Angeles to a prominent pinnacle known as First Top. Enjoy a first-rate panorama that reaches from snowy Mount Olympus all the way to salty Pillar Point on the Strait of Juan de Fuca. And gracing this heavenly haven on the mountain of angels are delightful rock gardens and fields of blooming heather. Divine, yes, but it's a devil of a climb.

GETTING THERE

From US Highway 101 in Port Angeles, near milepost 249, turn south on Race Street and drive 1 mile to the intersection with

Park Avenue. Proceed straight for 0.2 mile on Mount Angeles Road and turn right onto Hurricane Ridge Road (Heart O'the Hills Parkway). Continue 5.3 miles and turn right just before the park entrance station to reach the trailhead (elev. 1800 ft). Privy available.

ON THE TRAIL

The trail starts at the west end of the parking lot. If any cars are parked here, chances are the occupants are on the popular adjacent Lake Angeles Trail (Hike 80). It's a tough hike to Heather Park, but the views and solitude will be worth it. Start hiking through a uniform forest of second-growth Douglas-firs. The original forest burned over one hundred years ago thanks to home-steaders who didn't heed Smokey's sound advice. Through a thick understory, the trail steadily climbs, at times steeply. At 1.5 miles, come to Halfway Rock (elev. 2900 ft), a glacial erratic marking the not-quite-midway point to Heather Park.

The trail then eases somewhat before launching into more switchbacks. Skirting along the northeast slope of First Top, you'll get glimpses through a thinning forest of the amazing views that await you at the summit. Craggy Second Top hovers ahead. The trail soon breaks out into the open, snaking steeply around basalt ledges bursting with blossoming wildflowers.

At 4.2 miles, the way levels out, entering a small basin (elev. 5300 ft) tucked between

Looking west toward the Elwha Range

First and Second Tops. This is the beginning of Heather Park, a subalpine bowl of flowers, boulders, stunted evergreens, and yes, heather. Come upon a small creek and campsites before making a final climb to wind-blasted and sunbaked Heather Pass. Piper's bluebell, cinquefoil, and Olympic onion add colorful touches to the drab shale and scree that litter the pass.

The view is amazing. But it's better from a nearby knob on First Top, 100 feet higher and reached by following a small way path just to the right. From this 5740-foot basaltic shoulder of Mount Angeles, gaze out in every direction for supreme viewing. Port Angeles and the Strait of Juan de Fuca lie to the north 1 vertical mile below. To the east, follow the strait to islands flanked by the snowcapped Cascades. To the west, follow the strait as it parts the peninsula from Vancouver Island and leads to the Pacific. And to the south, take in Mount Angeles, Hurricane Hill, the Bailey Range, and Mount Appleton—all under Mount Olympus's watchful eye.

EXTENDING YOUR TRIP

Strong hikers can continue beyond Heather Pass and make a loop of 12.5 miles. It's a tough but highly scenic hike over loose scree and past some steep, semi-exposed areas. Dangerous snowfields often linger along the ridges beyond Heather Pass well into summer, so plan accordingly. From the pass, continue on the trail for 1.4 miles, dropping about 200 feet below Second Top's cliffs before climbing a 5750-foot shoulder separating Second Top from Mount Angeles. From there the trail drops 300 feet into a high, open basin and then climbs to 5840-foot Victor Pass on Klahhane Ridge (Hike 82). The Lake Angeles Trail (Hike 80) then leads 6.2 miles back to the trailhead.

82 Klahhane Ridge

RATING/ DIFFICULTY	ROUNDTRIP	ELEV GAIN/ HIGH POINT	SEASON
****/4	5.2 miles	1700 feet/ 6046 feet	Mid-June– Oct

Maps: Green Trails Hurricane Ridge/Elwha North No. 134S, Custom Correct Hurricane Ridge; **Contact:** Olympic National Park, Wilderness Information Center; **Notes:** National park entrance fee. Dogs prohibited; **GPS:** N 47 59.225, W 123 27.652

Of the four ways to reach the rugged, rocky, and wide-open Klahhane Ridge, the Switchback Trail is the shortest. Ascending 1400 feet in 1.5 miles, this direct approach wastes no time ruthlessly reaching the high ridge crest. This south-facing ascent guarantees an early-season entry into the high country but also exposes you to plenty of direct sunlight. Pack extra water and sunscreen. And don't forget to stop and smell the flowers—they're profuse.

GETTING THERE

From US Highway 101 in Port Angeles, near milepost 249, turn south on Race Street and drive 1 mile to the intersection with Park Avenue. Proceed straight for 0.2 mile on Mount Angeles Road and turn right onto Hurricane Ridge Road (Heart O'the Hills Parkway). Continue for 14.8 miles to the Switchback trailhead (elev. 4450 ft), on your right.

ON THE TRAIL

Immediately begin climbing open slopes that sport a myriad of wildflowers and provide excellent habitat for deer and chipmunks. Mountain goats frequent this area too, especially the ridge's high crags. At 0.6

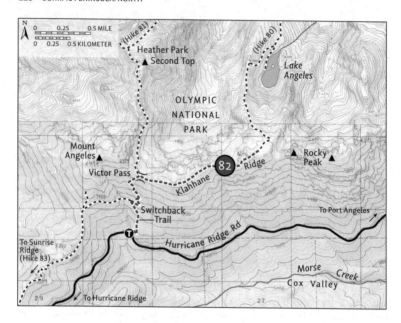

mile, come to a junction (elev. 5050 ft) with the Mount Angeles Trail. This delightful trail travels west 3.1 miles through rolling alpine meadows, past Sunrise Ridge, to Hurricane Ridge (Hike 83).

Proceed right for Klahhane Ridge and some more grueling climbing. There's no question where this trail got its name—a lot of switchbacks indeed. At 1.5 miles, and after 1400 feet of elevation gain, come to Victor Pass (elev. 5840 ft) and a junction. The trail left, often snow covered until midsummer, leads to Heather Park (Hike 81). Take the trail right, the Lake Angeles Trail, to begin an exhilarating stroll over the exposed ledges and precipitous cliffs of Klahhane Ridge. In a few spots, the trail has been blasted directly into the rock, assuring safe passage, though hikers prone to vertigo may want to call it quits at Victor Pass.

Venture east along Klahhane, dipping a little and climbing a little for 1.1 miles to a 6046-foot knoll, a logical turnaround point for day hikers. Beyond, the trail drops mercilessly 1800 feet to Lake Angeles (Hike 80). If you continue a little ways from the knoll, you'll be able to see it, one of the largest backcountry lakes in the Olympics, way down below. Common sense tells you to save Lake Angeles for another day and enjoy the views instead. To the south, Elk Mountain and Grand Ridge dominate the skyline. Craggy, glacier-covered Mount Cameron peeks out behind. The deep green Cox Valley lies directly below in the foreground. To the north are the Strait of Juan de Fuca, Vancouver Island, and British Columbia's Coast Ranges. Mount Baker rises abruptly in the east. Directly below are Port Angeles and Ediz Hook jutting into the strait. *Klahhane* is a Chinook word meaning

A pair of hikers descend on the Switchback Trail.

"outdoors." Upon completing this hike, you'll probably add "great" when describing this prominent ridge.

83 Sunrise Ridge

RATING/ DIFFICULTY	ROUNDTRIP	ELEV GAIN/ HIGH POINT	SEASON
*****/2	5.2 miles	1100 feet/ 5500 feet	Mid-June– Oct

Maps: Green Trails Hurricane Ridge/Elwha North No. 134S, Custom Correct Hurricane Ridge; **Contact:** Olympic National Park, Wilderness Information Center; **Notes:** National park entrance fee. Dogs prohibited; **GPS:** N 47 58.203, W 123 29.702

One of the most view-laden ridge hikes in the Olympics, Sunrise Ridge is also one of the easiest. And it delivers the same jaw-slacking views as Hurricane Hill, but without the asphalt and crowds. Chances are also good that on Sunrise Ridge you'll encounter some resident wildlife. Coyotes, deer, bears, and chipmunks—including the endemic Olympic chipmunk—all make themselves at home along this delightful trail. And wildflowers—they grow in profusion, from magenta paintbrush, to spreading phlox, penstemon, lupine, bistort, and larkspur.

GETTING THERE

From US Highway 101 in Port Angeles, near milepost 249, turn south on Race Street and drive 1 mile to the intersection with

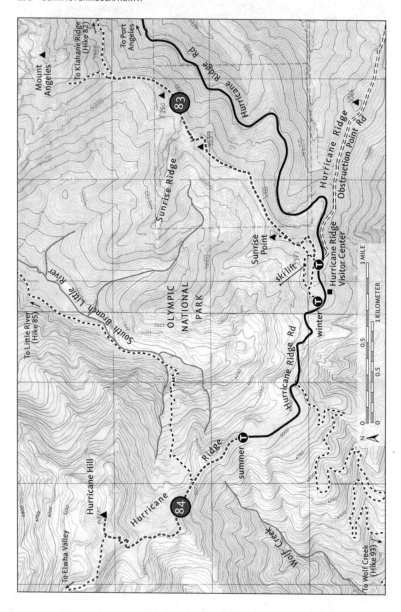

Park Avenue. Proceed straight for 0.2 mile on Mount Angeles Road and turn right onto Hurricane Ridge Road (Heart O'the Hills Parkway). Continue for 17.5 miles to the Hurricane Ridge Visitor Center. Find the trailhead (elev. 5250 ft) on the north side of the large parking area.

ON THE TRAIL

Start by following the 0.3-mile paved High Ridge Nature Trail. Pavement ends after cresting a small knoll (elev. 5471 ft), serviced in winter by a surface ski lift. Just beyond, at 0.3 mile, in a small saddle, come to a junction. The trail left heads back to the parking area and other nature trails. The trail north leads 0.1 mile to Sunrise Point, a 5450-foot viewpoint on the ridge. It's a nice spot, but it gets better on Sunrise Ridge. So head to the right on the Mount Angeles Trail, dropping 200 feet from the saddle and leaving the hubbub of Hurricane Ridge behind.

Undulating between groves of subalpine fir and resplendent alpine meadows, the trail works its way over and around a handful of knolls. Gaze north, out across the Strait of Juan de Fuca to massive Vancouver Island and its scads of mountains. Scan the strait eastward to snowy Mount Baker rising above a myriad of islands and inlets. Turn your attention south to the Olympic interior, to an emerald sea punctuated by craggy summits adorned in ice and snow. Mount Olympus, the centerpiece of this magnificent wilderness setting, dominates the southwest horizon. Of course, it's impossible to ignore the imposing peak in front of you—the one growing taller with each step—6454-foot Mount Angeles.

At 1.2 miles, the way rounds a 5500-foot knoll, after which it steeply drops 350 feet. Then it's easy walking again, coming to a

junction (elev. 5200 ft) at the base of Mount Angeles at 2.6 miles. A climbers' path takes off to the left and the Mount Angeles Trail continues right, skirting the southern slopes of the rocky mountain. This is a good spot to turn around.

EXTENDING YOUR TRIP

The Mount Angeles Trail continues for another 0.5 mile to the Switchback Trail (Hike 82), from where you can continue 0.9 mile left to Klahhane Ridge; or, if you've arranged a car shuttle, descend to the right 0.6 mile to Hurricane Ridge Road for a

Mount Angeles in the distance

one-way trip of 3.7 miles. You can also follow the steep climbers' path a short ways through meadows and subalpine forest. Stop when the trail reaches scree, unless you're trained and prepared to make a class 3 scramble of Mount Angeles.

84 Hurricane Hill

Summer

RATING/ DIFFICULTY	ROUNDTRIP	ELEV GAIN/ HIGH POINT	SEASON
***/2	3.2 miles	650 feet/ 5757 feet	Mid-June– Oct

Winter

RATING/ DIFFICULTY	ROUNDTRIP	ELEV GAIN/ HIGH POINT	SEASON
*****/4	6 miles	900 feet/ 5757 feet	Dec–Mar

Maps: Green Trails Hurricane Ridge/Elwha North No. 134S, Custom Correct Hurricane Ridge; **Contact:** Olympic National Park, Wilderness Information Center; **Notes:** National park entrance fee. Dogs prohibited. Dec–Mar, road open Fri–Sun (and holiday Mondays), weather permitting.; **GPS:** N 47 58.598, W 123 31.065

A paved path leads to an emerald knoll with horizon-spanning views from snowy Olympus and Mount Baker to the azure waters of the Strait of Juan de Fuca. Clogged in the sunny summer months with sauntering tourists, Hurricane Hill has helped introduce folks young and old, local and foreign, to the wonders and delights of the Olympic high country. But when winter spreads its white coat upon these open slopes, it's a whole different adventure—a chance to snowshoe on high in the Olympic Mountains.

GETTING THERE

From US Highway 101 in Port Angeles, near milepost 249, turn south on Race Street and drive 1 mile to the intersection with Park Avenue. Proceed straight for 0.2 mile on Mount Angeles Road and turn right onto Hurricane Ridge Road (Heart O'the Hills Parkway). Continue for 17.5 miles to the Hurricane Ridge Visitor Center, and stop here if it's winter. For summer, continue past the visitors center 1.4 miles to the trailhead (elev. 5100 ft). Privy available.

ON THE TRAIL

Summer: For summertime visits, the way is quite simple and straightforward. Follow the procession of people in front of you on the paved path. At 0.5 mile, pass the Little River Trail (Hike 85) and then climb more earnestly, reaching open grassy slopes. At 1.5 miles, bear right where a trail comes up from the Elwha River valley. At 1.6 miles, reach the 5757-foot pinnacle, where a fire lookout once stood and views still abound. Take in the mountains, from Mount Baker in the Cascades, to Mount Garibaldi in British Columbia's Coast Ranges, to the interior Olympic peaks. Enjoy views of the green cirque below that forms the ridge between Hurricane Hill and Sunrise Point. Wildlife, including bears, are often feeding below. People-friendly deer will probably be loitering on the summit. Don't feed them— they need to fend for themselves if they are to survive the winter. And endemic Olympic marmots frequently lounge near the summit.

Winter: For winter visitors, Hurricane Hill offers one of the most accessible snowshoe routes in the Olympics. Although the route is not overly difficult, windy and icy conditions can make it treacherous. Hurricane Hill is subject to blinding snowstorms and

Winter is a great time to explore Hurricane Hill.

howling, frostbite-inducing winds. Snow along the ridge forms cornices and the steep slopes are prone to avalanches. But when conditions are optimal—stable snow and stable weather—the trek to Hurricane Hill is incredibly rewarding. Always check with the park about conditions before setting out. The park also offers guided snowshoe hikes along the ridge on winter weekends, perfect for introducing novices to snowshoeing.

The winter start (elev. 5250 ft) is from the visitors center, following a snow-shrouded road to a 5000-foot saddle and then climbing to and past the summer trailhead. Along the way enjoy a winter wonderland landscape, with Mount Olympus and the Bailey Range forming a great white wall to the southwest. Venture out on the broad western shoulder of Hurricane Hill for breathtaking views down into the Elwha Valley. In winter, Hurricane Hill is a whole different world.

EXTENDING YOUR TRIP

In the summer, you can reach Hurricane Hill via three different challenging trails from valleys below. The Little River Trail (Hike 85) approaches from the north; the Wolf Creek Trail (Hike 93), from the south. The third route, the Elwha to Hurricane Hill Trail, is the most scenic and challenging and best done one-way downhill to its lower trailhead (elev. 480 ft) near the Elwha Ranger Station. From just below the Hurricane Hill summit, this trail begins by traversing sprawling ridge-crest alpine meadows teeming with marmots, deer, and grouse. After a modest

1.5 mile descent, the trail plummets on a brutally steep course, first across grassy slopes and then through big groves of old-growth forest. It's a lonely and view-filled 6.1-mile journey that loses more than 5100 vertical feet.

85 Little River

RATING/ DIFFICULTY	ROUNDTRIP	ELEV GAIN/ HIGH POINT	SEASON
***/2	7 miles	800 feet/ 1650 feet	Year-round

Maps: Green Trails Hurricane Ridge/Elwha North No. 134S, Custom Correct Hurricane Ridge; **Contact:** Olympic National Park, Wilderness Information Center; **Notes:** Discover Pass required. Dogs prohibited at park boundary; **GPS:** N 48 03.432, W 123 30.063

Hike along the South Branch Little River past mossy and ferny basaltic walls, towering old growth, and a procession of mesmerizing rapids. Hiking this trail all the way to Hurricane Hill is long and tough, but turning around at a little cascade in an elfin gulch before the serious climbing begins makes for a delightful outing.

GETTING THERE

From the Clallam County Courthouse in Port Angeles, follow US Highway 101 west for 1.2 miles and turn right onto the Pine Street Cut-off (the turnoff is 0.2 mile west of the traffic light at Lauridsen Boulevard and Lincoln Street). Proceed a short distance and turn left onto Pine Street (which soon becomes Black Diamond Road), driving 4.5 miles to the junction with Little River Road. Turn left and continue 0.1 mile to the trailhead (elev. 1050 ft), on the right. Parking is on the left.

ON THE TRAIL

This historical trail once led to active mines and a fire lookout on Hurricane Hill, but it fell out of favor with hikers over the years. Recently, volunteers brushed the tread and rebuilt the bridges, and this trail is getting a second look. If you want to hike the entire 8.5 miles, consider a one-way downhill from the upper Hurricane Hill trailhead (Hike 84). The fairly easy trip described here, to a small cascade, is a great way to sample this trail and makes a good early- and late-season hike.

Starting in state forest, follow the trail downhill about 100 feet to a sturdy bridge spanning the Little River. Then steeply regain that 100 feet. The trail then follows old logging roads through second growth, reaching

Hikers admire cascades on the South Branch Little River.

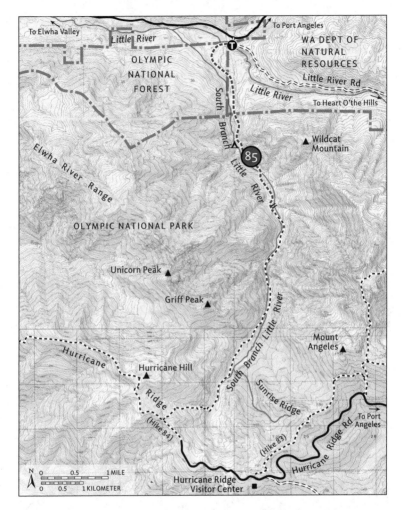

the national park boundary and luxurious old growth at 1.3 miles. Impressive sheer rock walls shrouded in moss and pocked with old mines hem in the valley. You'll soon pass the first of three of what guidebook legend Robert Wood called the Gnome Rocks—giant basaltic boulders. You'll also soon come to the first of seven crossings of the South Branch Little River, all but the last couple on newly built log bridges.

At 2 miles, pass a campsite (elev. 1200 ft) beneath big cliffs and tucked between two close bridge crossings of the river. Heading up the emerald canyon, the trail alternates between blazing through the flood plain and traversing overhanging pillow basalt ledges. You'll pass plenty of gigantic Douglas-firs along the way.

Look for a small waterfall at around 2.7 miles. Cross the river again at around 3 miles. At 3.5 miles, come to another log-bridge crossing (elev. 1650 ft) of the river—this one at the base of a beautiful little cascade framed by mossy and ferny ledges and shaded by a towering ancient forest. Sit and enjoy the serenity before heading back.

EXTENDING YOUR TRIP

Beyond, the trail begins climbing in earnest, passing yet more monstrous firs. At around 4.6 miles, cross another log bridge (elev. 2150 ft) and begin steeply climbing.

Traverse drier forest and a 1990s burn and hop over several side creeks. Cross the river a couple of more times—a mere creek now—and traverse brushy wet meadows (elev. 3800 ft). Then, leaving the river valley, steeply climb via tight switchbacks, transitioning into mountain hemlock forest and reaching the Hurricane Hill Trail (elev. 5100 ft) at 8.5 miles. From here it's 0.5 mile left to the Hurricane Hill trailhead.

86 PJ Lake

RATING/ DIFFICULTY	ROUNDTRIP	ELEV GAIN/ HIGH POINT	SEASON
**/3	1.8 miles	825 feet/ 5020 feet	Mid-July– Oct

Maps: Green Trails Hurricane Ridge/Elwha North No. 134S, Custom Correct Hurricane

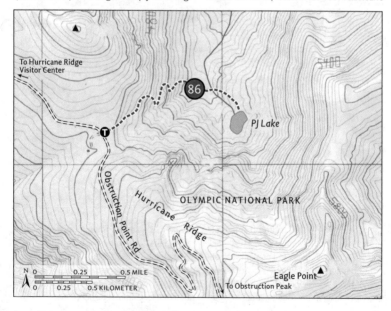

PJ Lake beneath Eagle Point

Ridge; **Contact:** Olympic National Park, Wilderness Information Center; **Notes:** National park entrance fee. Dogs prohibited; **GPS:** N 47 56.750, W 123 25.528

A tiny lake tucked in a hidden bowl on Hurricane Ridge, PJ Lake greets few hikers due to its rough-and-tumble approach. The trail, pockmarked with deer tracks, drops steeply for 650 feet before climbing 175 feet to reach this emerald pool—all in less than a mile! Is it worth it? If you cherish solitude and the opportunity to spot wildlife up close, yes. Wildflowers and a pretty cascade offer a little incentive too.

GETTING THERE

From US Highway 101 in Port Angeles, near milepost 249, turn south on Race Street and drive 1 mile to the intersection with Park Avenue. Proceed straight for 0.2 mile on Mount Angeles Road and turn right onto Hurricane Ridge Road (Heart O'the Hills Parkway). Continue for just shy of 17.5 miles, just before the large parking lot at Hurricane Ridge, and make a sharp left turn on Obstruction Point Road. Follow this very narrow (and harrowing to some) gravel road for 3.8 miles to the Waterhole (elev. 5020 ft), a former picnic area. The trail begins on the left side of the road.

ON THE TRAIL

Start in a stand of subalpine firs and then rapidly drop through open forest, huckleberry patches, and meadow clumps. Watch your footing—critter burrows blemish the tread. When not looking down, gaze out to a window view of the Dungeness Spit. The steep hillside often teems with browsing deer. They have little regard for using the switchbacks.

After dropping 650 feet in 0.6 mile, angle east in a cool glen, crossing two streams. The second one cascades 30 feet over a mossy ledge. Then climb 175 feet, reaching pretty little PJ Lake (elev. 4550 ft) at 0.9 mile, set in a semi-open bowl beneath 6247-foot Eagle Point. The lakeshore is flanked with Alaska yellow cedars, big silver firs, and brushy avalanche chutes and graced with purple

asters and columbine. Jumping trout and frogs break the silence of the basin. A grassy bench near the lake's outlet invites picnicking. If you've hiked in during late summer, allow time for harvesting huckleberries on your way out.

87 Grand Ridge

RATING/ DIFFICULTY	ONE-WAY	ELEV GAIN/ HIGH POINT	SEASON
*****/3	7.4 miles	1200 feet/ 6640 feet	Mid-July– Oct

Maps: Green Trails Olympic Mountains East No. 168S, Custom Correct Hurricane Ridge; **Contact:** Olympic National Park, Wilderness Information Center; **Notes:** National park entrance fee. Dogs prohibited; **GPS:** N 47 55.103, W 123 22.929

The views from this open ridge are grand, the wildflowers are grand, and hiking this trail, the highest in the Olympics is a grand experience. Enjoy nonstop views of craggy, glacier-covered peaks; deep, emerald valleys of unbroken old-growth forest; and miles of wildflower-saturated meadows and alpine tundra.

GETTING THERE

From US Highway 101 in Port Angeles, near milepost 249, turn south on Race Street and drive 1 mile to the intersection with Park Avenue. Proceed straight for 0.2 mile on Mount Angeles Road and turn right onto Hurricane Ridge Road (Heart O'the Hills Parkway). Continue for just shy of 17.5 miles, just before the large parking lot at Hurricane Ridge, and make a sharp left turn on Obstruction Point Road. Follow this very narrow (and harrowing to some) gravel road

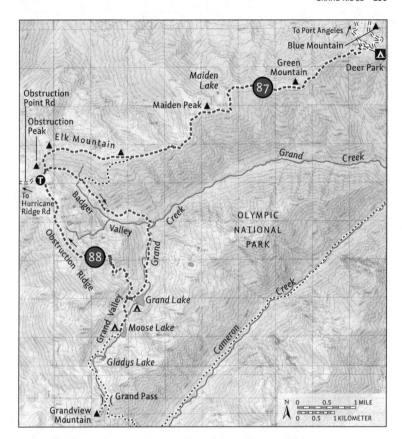

for 7.7 miles to its end at the trailhead (elev. 6140 ft). Privy available.

ON THE TRAIL

The complete trek across Grand Ridge from Obstruction Point to Deer Park is 7.4 miles, with a few good ups and downs. It ranks as one of the all-time great ridge traverses in the Olympics. If you can't arrange for a car shuttle to make this a one-way journey, it's a tough 14.8-mile roundtrip. However, the

5-mile out-and-back to Elk Mountain, the highest point on the ridge, makes for a good day hike.

Starting in wide-open country, head east, gradually descending 0.3 mile to the Badger Valley Trail (elev. 6040 ft) (Hike 88). Your trail angles left, traversing steep slopes below Obstruction Peak. Some years, snow lingers here well into summer, making travel dangerous. If the steep gullies haven't melted out, consider hiking to Grand Valley

Grand views and a grand display of wildflowers

instead (Hike 88). Once the snow is gone, however, it's high and dry on the ridge. Pack plenty of water. Across ledges and loose shale, steadily climb. But don't despair—the grade soon eases.

Traversing alpine tundra, look down and admire the flowers: lupine, columbine, tiger lily, paintbrush, cow parsley, rosehip, penstemon, larkspur, gentian, cinquefoil, and a handful of other showy blossoms. And look for horned larks cleverly camouflaged among the sedges. Take in the views too—they're spellbinding. Spread out before you are some of the highest summits in the Olympics—Mounts Olympus, Cameron, and Deception. And locate the lakes of Grand Valley shimmering below.

The trail reaches a high point of 6640 feet before coming to a junction (elev. 6600 ft) with the Badger Valley Cutoff at 2.1 miles. To the left, you can easily reach Elk Mountain's 6773-foot summit by hiking a short distance off-trail (be mindful of fragile plants). To the right, the way descends to the Badger Valley Trail, an alternate route back to the trailhead (adding 0.6 mile and 600 feet of climbing).

The Grand Ridge Trail continues straight on relatively flat terrain for another 0.5 mile, coming to a spot with good views of the Strait of Juan de Fuca and San Juan Islands. This is a good turnaround point. Otherwise, continue with caution, steeply plunging down a rocky slope to a small col (elev. 6000 ft) and the aptly named Roaring Winds Camp at 3.3 miles. The way then climbs 260 feet to traverse flowering meadows and steep scree slopes just below the 6434-foot summit of Maiden Peak.

Then gradually descend, skirting Green Mountain and transitioning from meadows to pine forest. Reach a 4900-foot saddle and, following an old road, gently ascend to the eastern trailhead (elev. 5225 ft) at Deer Park at 7.4 miles.

88 Grand Valley

RATING/ DIFFICULTY	LOOP	ELEV GAIN/ HIGH POINT	SEASON
*****/4	9.4 miles	2725 feet/ 6425 feet	Mid-July– Oct

Maps: Green Trails Olympic Mountains East No. 168S, Custom Correct Hurricane Ridge; **Contact:** Olympic National Park, Wilderness Information Center; **Notes:** National park entrance fee. Dogs prohibited; **GPS:** N 47 55.102, W 123 22.930

A necklace of sparkling alpine lakes adorn bold mountain faces that span this mile-high valley. Wildflowers, old growth, alpine tundra, deer, bears, marmots—they're all here in this outdoor cathedral, a grand valley indeed. Your ticket into this wild kingdom comes at minimal cost—the trail is mostly downhill. You pay the piper on the way out on a grueling ascent.

Tarn in the Grand Valley

GETTING THERE

From US Highway 101 in Port Angeles, near milepost 249, turn south on Race Street and drive 1 mile to the intersection with Park Avenue. Proceed straight for 0.2 mile on Mount Angeles Road and turn right onto Hurricane Ridge Road (Heart O'the Hills Parkway). Continue for just shy of 17.5 miles, just before the large parking lot at Hurricane Ridge, and make a sharp left turn on Obstruction Point Road. Follow this very narrow (and harrowing to some) gravel road for 7.7 miles to its end at the trailhead (elev. 6140 ft). Privy available.

ON THE TRAIL

The quickest way into Grand Valley is via the Grand Pass Trail, climbing along Obstruction Ridge and then brutally descending to Grand Lake. Consider this loop as an alternative. Sure, it's longer and there's more overall climbing involved, but you'll get to traverse the lightly traveled Badger Valley en route.

Bursting with flowers and teeming with wildlife, this valley is neglected by those in a hurry to get to Grand Valley. Don't expect any badgers, though—it was named after a ranger's horse. There are endemic Olympic marmots, however—close enough.

Start by heading east on the Grand Ridge Trail, coming to the Badger Valley Trail in 0.3 mile. Head right, descending into a wide U-shaped valley, hopping over rivulets and brushing against clumps of fragrant greenery. After passing the Elk Mountain cutoff (elev. 5400 ft) at 1.4 miles, enter subalpine forest. Then, undulating between meadow and forest, cross Badger Creek at 3.4 miles (elev. 4000 ft). Next, alongside Grand Creek, begin a gradual climb to Grand Lake. Cross brushy avalanche chutes and a glacial moraine to reach Grand Lake (elev. 4750 ft) at 5 miles.

Grand Lake is pretty big and quite appealing, but the next lake is much grander.

Continue hiking, now on stone steps and tight switchbacks, coming to a junction (elev. 4925 ft) at 5.3 miles. Your return is via the trail right. But for now, head left, coming to sparkling Moose Lake (elev. 5075 ft) in 0.3 mile. Like Badger Valley, Moose Lake might be misleading. The lake was named for Frank Moose, not the large ruminant that doesn't inhabit the Olympics.

Set amid one of the most spectacular backdrops of any Olympic alpine lake, Moose is surrounded by black-shale pinnacles garlanded with verdant forest. Roam the lakeshore exploring ledges and grassy pockets and consider spending the night at one of the backcountry campsites. When you must relinquish this grand kingdom to its rightful heirs, the deer and marmots, prepare yourself for the excruciating exodus.

Retrace your steps 0.3 mile to the previous junction, and then continue left, climbing

ONLY IN THE OLYMPICS

Because the Olympic Peninsula is in essence a biological island—isolated by eons of glacial ice followed by the "moats" of the Strait of Juan de Fuca and Puget Sound—many of its life-forms are found nowhere else on the planet. The peninsula is home to eight plant endemics and fifteen animal endemics.

Among the region's unique fauna are the Olympic marmot, Olympic yellow-pine chipmunk, Olympic snow mole, Olympic Mazama pocket gopher, Olympic ermine, Olympic torrent salamander, Olympic mudminnow, Olympic grasshopper, arionid jumping slug, and the Quileute gazelle beetle.

Among the peninsula's unique flora are the Olympic Mountain milk vetch (endangered because of introduced mountain goats), Piper's bellflower, Olympic Mountain groundsel, and Flett's violet.

Among original (but not endemic) inhabitants that are missing today from this biologically diverse landscape is the gray wolf. After the wolf was extirpated by early settlers and the Park Service itself (talk about a misguided predator policy), the majestic howl of *Canis lupis* hasn't been heard in the Olympic backcountry since the 1920s. Conservationists hope that this noble creature and important component of the Olympic ecosystem can someday be reintroduced.

1400 steep feet out of the valley. Once you crest Obstruction Ridge (elev. 6425 ft), begin traversing a landscape of alpine tundra, taking in sweeping views over the Lillian River valley to snowy Mount Olympus and the Bailey Range. Grunt 150 vertical feet up a knoll before enjoying a downhill finish to the trailhead at 9.4 miles.

EXTENDING YOUR TRIP
Continue 0.8 mile beyond Moose Lake to little Gladys Lake (elev. 5400 ft), set in a high grassy and moraine-filled bowl. Then hike another 1.5 miles across lingering snowfields to 6400-foot Grand Pass; take a 0.3-mile side trail to 6701-foot Grandview Mountain for a mind-staggering view of glacier-covered Mount Cameron and the remote and gorgeous Lillian Lake.

Elwha River Valley

Comprising nearly 20 percent of Olympic National Park's landmass, the Elwha River is the largest watershed in the park. From its remote point of origin on the rugged southern slopes of Mount Barnes, the Elwha flows 45 miles to the Strait of Juan de Fuca, draining over 300 square miles of surrounding wilderness and passing through one of the largest tracts of old growth left in America. Cutting a deep, green valley in a sea of rugged snow- and ice-capped peaks adorned in alpine meadows, the Elwha consists of some of the finest hiking country anywhere.

While backpackers retrace the historic Press Expedition's 1889–90 traverse across the Olympics—or access routes to remote Hayden Pass or the astonishing Bailey Range traverse—day hikers can reach plenty of spectacular Elwha country too. All along the river's northern reaches, wildlife-rich meadows, remote alpine lakes, forests that have stood for centuries, and miles of stunning landscapes can be explored in a day or less. **Note:** Due to washouts, Olympic Hot Springs Road is closed byond the Madison Falls Trails, 2.1 miles south of US 101. Foot and bike traffic is allowed. Consult ranger station for updates.

89 Cascade Rock

RATING/ DIFFICULTY	ROUNDTRIP	ELEV GAIN/ HIGH POINT	SEASON
**/3	4.5 miles	1850 feet/ 1825 feet	Year-round

Maps: Green Trails Hurricane Ridge/Elwha North No. 134S, Custom Correct Elwha Valley; **Contact:** Olympic National Park, Wilderness Information Center; **Notes:** Campground suffered major flood damage impacting trailhead—check with ranger on current status. See note above about road washout. National park entrance fee. Dogs prohibited; **GPS:** N 48 01.648, W 123 35.295

Viewpoint from trail spur

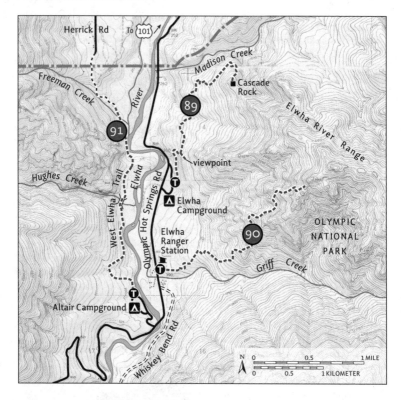

Ascend high above the Elwha River through attractive open forest. While the view from Cascade Rock is limited, the one from an overlook en route is quite nice. And if you come in early summer it's framed by a dazzling floral arrangement.

GETTING THERE

From Port Angeles, follow US Highway 101 west for 8.5 miles. At milepost 240, before the Elwha River Bridge, turn left onto Olympic Hot Springs Road (signed "Elwha Valley"). Continue 3 miles (passing the park entrance station) to the Elwha Campground. The trail

(elev. 325 ft) begins in the campground near a kitchen shelter. Water and privy available.

ON THE TRAIL

Despite beginning in a popular campground, this trail is lightly traveled. Start by crossing a maple-shaded river channel on a bridge. Come to a junction and turn left. The way right is a 0.7-mile nature trail loop worth checking out on the return. Cross another river channel and bear right at an unmarked trail and begin climbing. At 0.3 mile, reach a junction (elev. 500 ft). Definitely head right on the 0.15-mile spur to the valley viewpoint (elev. 650 ft), the best view on this hike. From this flowered opening, look south over the Elwha Valley to Mount Fitzhenry.

Retrace your steps and continue right on the main trail, slightly descending before steeply climbing. The grade then moderates as you traverse slopes of dry open forest. Pass pockets of old growth and madronas and hop over a couple of small creeks. At about 1.2 miles, cross a ledge (elev. 900 ft) with a decent view west over the valley to Mount Baldy. The way then steadily climbs, passing a few window views north and of the Madison Creek valley.

Eventually, bend south and steeply switchback up to a big mossy basalt ledge (elev. 1825 ft) at the trail's end at 2.1 miles. This may or may not be Cascade Rock (some sources say the rock is the previous ledge). Surrounded by firs and madronas, views are limited. The workout to get here, however, was good.

90 Griff Creek

RATING/ DIFFICULTY	ROUNDTRIP	ELEV GAIN/ HIGH POINT	SEASON
***/4	5.6 miles	2800 feet/ 3200 feet	May–Nov

Maps: Green Trails Hurricane Ridge/Elwha North No. 134S, Custom Correct Elwha Valley; **Contact:** Olympic National Park, Wilderness Information Center; **Notes:** See note about road washout, p. 243. National park entrance fee. Dogs prohibited; **GPS:** N 48 00.994, W 123 35.407

Looking west over the Elwha Valley

Ascend a steep and arduous hillside to a couple of sun-kissed ledges granting panoramic perspectives of the wide and wild Elwha River valley, from snow- and ice-covered Mount Carrie down to the newly free-flowing section of river. Griff Creek guarantees plenty of solitude—even when the Elwha Valley is hopping with activity.

GETTING THERE

From Port Angeles, follow US Highway 101 west for 8.5 miles. At milepost 240, before the Elwha River Bridge, turn left onto Olympic Hot Springs Road (signed "Elwha Valley"). Continue 4 miles (passing the park entrance station) to the Elwha Ranger Station. The trail (elev. 400 ft) begins behind the building. Privy available.

ON THE TRAIL

This is not an easy hike. The trail climbs 2800 feet in less than 3 miles. But here's the payoff: though you're likely to run into various critters, chances of encountering a fellow human are slim to none. Despite being named after Griff Creek, the trail travels along a dry ridge high above the waterway. Pack plenty of water.

Begin in a daisy-dotted meadow just behind the Elwha Ranger Station. Traverse a park compound, entering a cool and mature forest of firs and cedars. Griff Creek roars in the distance, but that sound soon becomes a memory. Despite being lightly traveled, the tread is good and the trail is regularly maintained.

At 0.5 mile, cross a seasonal creekbed. The way now wastes no time rising from the moist valley floor to a dry south-facing slope. As you ascend via a series of tight, steep switchbacks, the forest canopy thins, revealing teaser views of what lies ahead. At 1.6 miles, emerge at the base of a dry ledge. Manzanita and madronas

frame a view east to the prominent Elwha River Range pinnacle, Unicorn Peak.

Next, hike one sweeping switchback that delivers you to the top of that ledge. A sign indicates "Rock viewpoint el. 1875 feet." Drop your pack, take a break, and enjoy the view—especially of the former Lake Mills bed above Glines Canyon on the Elwha River directly below. Mount Carrie towers in the distance. Admire the imposing and inhospitable wall of Baldy and Happy Lake Ridge directly across the wide valley, guarding the Hughes Creek drainage.

This is a good turnaround point if you've had enough steepness. Otherwise, keep climbing to another fine viewpoint (elev. 2400 ft) at around 2.3 miles. Beyond that, the trail climbs an insane 800 feet in 0.5 mile on rough and rocky tread to a ledgy terminus (elev. 3200 ft) with an impressive view of Hurricane Hill, Griff Peak, and the Unicorn. Brace your knees for the descent.

91 West Elwha Trail

RATING/ DIFFICULTY	ROUNDTRIP	ELEV GAIN/ HIGH POINT	SEASON
**/3	5 miles	650 feet/ 700 feet	Year-round

Maps: Green Trails Hurricane Ridge/Elwha North No. 134S, Custom Correct Elwha Valley; **Contact:** Olympic National Park, Wilderness Information Center; **Notes:** Campground suffered major flood damage impacting trailhead—check with ranger on current status. See note about road washout, p. 243. National park entry fee. Dogs prohibited; **GPS:** N 48 00.754, W 123 35.600

Follow what was once part of the old Olympic Hot Springs Trail, now truncated by the Olympic Hot Springs Road.

Elwha River from rocky bluff

This delightful trail follows the mighty Elwha River downstream along its west bank, away from roads and away from crowds. En route traverse ancient tree groves and a flowering cliffside above the river.

GETTING THERE

From Port Angeles, follow US Highway 101 west for 8.5 miles. At milepost 240, before the Elwha River Bridge, turn left onto Olympic Hot Springs Road (signed "Elwha Valley"). Continue 4.4 miles (passing the park entrance station), turn right into the Altair Campground, and drive 0.3 mile to the trailhead (elev. 425 ft) near campsite 21. Park at the kitchen shelter. Privy available. If the campground is closed, park at the gate and walk to the trailhead.

ON THE TRAIL

Starting in magnificent old growth, the trail climbs 275 feet up a steep hillside away from the river, tricking unsuspecting hikers into thinking it's leaving the roaring waterway. But it's merely bypassing a tight draw. Cross a couple of side creeks as you traverse steep slopes. Then begin descending, catching a view of the river before reaching lush bottomlands. At 1.5 miles, cross Hughes Creek on a sturdy log bridge (elev. 400 ft). The creek careens out of a canyon draining the steep slopes of Mount Baldy and Happy Lake Ridge.

Then hike through mature second growth, coming to a rocky bluff above the river at 2 miles. Views are good of the rushing river, and the flower show on this sunny bluff is quite nice too. Then descend into a draw of beautiful old growth, reaching unbridged Freeman Creek (elev. 410 ft) at 2.5 miles. This is a good spot to turn around.

EXTENDING YOUR TRIP

If you're a trail purist, continue hiking. The trail climbs steeply and follows an old road through scrappy forest and a Camp Fire Girls Memorial grove, dedicated in 1938. It then traverses private property and reaches Herrick Road (elev. 700 ft) at 3 miles.

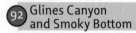

92 Glines Canyon and Smoky Bottom

Glines Canyon

RATING/ DIFFICULTY	ROUNDTRIP	ELEV GAIN/ HIGH POINT	SEASON
***/2	2.2 miles	150 feet/ 600 feet	Year-round

Smoky Bottom

RATING/ DIFFICULTY	ROUNDTRIP	ELEV GAIN/ HIGH POINT	SEASON
**/2	4 miles	525 feet/ 760 feet	Year-round

Glines Canyon at breached dam

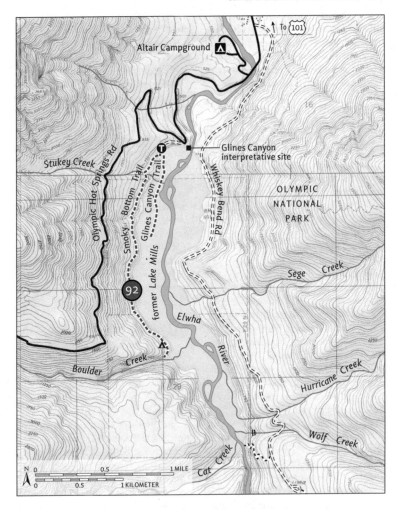

Altair Campground

To 101

Stukey Creek

Olympic Hot Springs Rd

Smoky Bottom Trail

Glines Canyon Trail

T

Glines Canyon interpretative site

Whiskey Bend Rd

OLYMPIC

NATIONAL

PARK

former Lake Mills

92

Sege Creek

Elwha

River

Boulder Creek

Hurricane Creek

Wolf Creek

Cat Creek

N 0   0.5   1 MILE
    0   0.5   1 KILOMETER

Maps: Green Trails Hurricane Ridge/Elwha North No. 134S, Custom Correct Elwha Valley; **Contact:** Olympic National Park, Wilderness Information Center; **Notes:** See note about road washout, p. 243. National park entry fee. Dogs prohibited; **GPS:** N 48 00.117, W 123 36.269

Experience the rebirth of the free-flowing, undammed Elwha River by hiking the former shoreline and lakebed of Lake Mills. Old-growth forest lines the former lake, and the lakebed itself is regenerating to its natural state, with the help of many hard-working conservationists. Transformation has been ongoing and rapid since the removal of the Elwha and Glines Canyon dams encouraging repeat visits to witness the wilderness come alive.

GETTING THERE

From Port Angeles, follow US Highway 101 west for 8.5 miles. At milepost 240, before the Elwha River Bridge, turn left onto Olympic Hot Springs Road (signed "Elwha Valley"). Continue 5.6 miles (passing the park entrance station) and turn left onto a dirt road just beyond the Glines Canyon Spillway Overlook. Continue 0.2 mile to the trail (elev. 600 ft). Privy available.

ON THE TRAIL

Glines Canyon: This new yet unnamed trail starts at a former boat launch, leading across what was once Lake Mills and along the newly free-flowing Elwha River. But first, take a mandatory side trip 0.2 mile left to the overlook at a remnant section of dam and read the many wonderful interpretive panels. Then retrace your steps and descend into the lakebed that held Lake Mills from 1927 to 2012. Lose 100 feet of elevation, hiking across layers of sediment and through trees both naturally and hand-seeded. The area feels a lot like the pumice plain of Mount Saint Helens. And like that disturbed area, nitrogen-fixing plants like lupine are doing their job of preparing the new (old) riverbank for successional flora.

Enjoy excellent views downriver of Glines Canyon and two hulking sections of dam left in place to preserve history and add perspective. The trail drops to a bench above the river, for up-close views of its free-flowing waters. At 0.9 mile from the old boat launch, the trail ends (elev. 550 ft). Retrace your steps to the trailhead and begin your hike along the former lakeshore.

Smoky Bottom: The real charm of the Smoky Bottom Trail is the forest it traverses. Mossy alder groves, a handful of madronas, and plenty of big old firs greet you along the way. There are plenty of ups and downs and a handful of creeks to cross too.

After an easy rolling start, the trail climbs a high bluff (elev. 760 ft) that sports monitoring equipment and grants a good view of the river and former lakebed below. Then begin a descent, followed by some more ups and downs. Hop across a couple more creeks and pass some impressive old-growth trees, coming to a backcountry campsite at 1.9 miles. Proceed for another 0.1 mile to the trail's end at a small bluff (elev. 660 ft) above crashing Boulder Creek. Perhaps someday the Park Service will be able to connect this trail with the Glines Canyon Trail—but until then, retrace your steps to the trailhead.

93 Wolf Creek

RATING/ DIFFICULTY	ROUNDTRIP	ELEV GAIN/ HIGH POINT	SEASON
***/4	16 miles	3800 feet/ 5000 feet	June–Nov

Maps: Green Trails Hurricane Ridge/Elwha North No. 134S, Custom Correct Elwha Valley; **Contact:** Olympic National Park, Wilderness Information Center; **Notes:** See note about road washout, p. 243. National park entrance fee. Dogs prohibited; **GPS:** N 47 58.066, W 123 34.933

It's a long hike from the Elwha Valley to Hurricane Ridge via this old road turned trail. But the grade is moderate, the forest pretty, the views good, the meadows alive with blossoms and animal activity, and the way more than likely void of fellow hikers.

GETTING THERE

From Port Angeles, follow US Highway 101 west for 8.5 miles. At milepost 240, before the Elwha River Bridge, turn left onto Olympic Hot Springs Road (signed "Elwha Valley"). Continue 4 miles (passing the park entrance station) and turn left just beyond the Elwha Ranger Station onto dirt Whiskey Bend Road. Continue 4.5 miles to the trailhead (elev. 1200 ft) at the road's end. Privy available.

ON THE TRAIL

The Wolf Creek Trail follows an old road to Hurricane Ridge. When the Hurricane Ridge Road (Heart O'the Hills Parkway) opened in the 1950s, this road was closed and converted to a trail. Its moderate grade and wide tread makes it ideal for trail running. When the snow level is low, it's also a good choice for cross-country skiing and snowshoeing. It's a long hike, however, so if you can arrange a shuttle, consider doing it one-way downhill.

Pass an old corral and steadily gain elevation on a ridge above Wolf Creek. Some

Deer are often sighted in the subalpine meadows along the way.

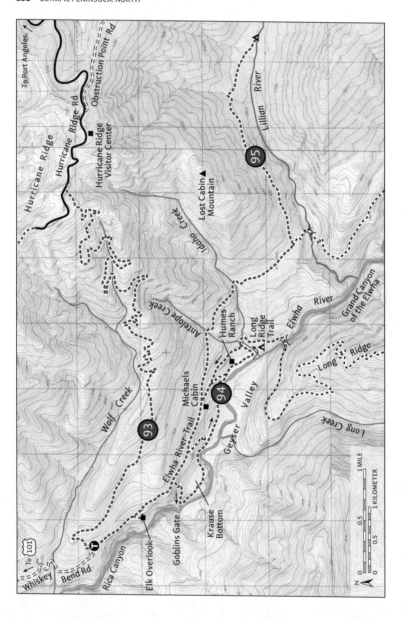

sections of trail are brushy, overtaken by salal, and there are some electrical boxes along the way (not aesthetically pleasing), but the trail is generally in good shape. At about 2.5 miles, you can see Wolf Creek down in a deep ravine. From here, the way steepens, twisting and turning up the ridge. Pass some big firs and madronas. At about 4.4 miles, come to your first viewpoint (elev. 3400 ft). The way then enters the ravine to make the first (elev. 3600 ft) of three crossings of Wolf Creek, at 5 miles.

Now in lush old growth, keep ascending. At about 7 miles, enter a basin (elev. 4500 ft) and begin traversing a series of meadows that explode with flowers, teem with deer and marmots, and delight with sprawling views of the Elwha Valley and Bailey Range. At 8 miles, the trail terminates at a saddle (elev. 5000 ft) on the Hurricane Ridge Road 0.7 mile east of the Hurricane Hill trailhead and 0.7 mile west of the Hurricane Ridge Visitor Center.

94 Geyser Valley

RATING/ DIFFICULTY	ROUNDTRIP	ELEV GAIN/ HIGH POINT	SEASON
****/2	8.1 miles	1000 feet/ 1325 feet	Year-round

Maps: Green Trails Hurricane Ridge/Elwha North No. 134S, Custom Correct Elwha Valley; **Contact:** Olympic National Park, Wilderness Information Center; **Notes:** See note about road washout, p. 243. National park entrance fee. Dogs prohibited; **GPS:** N 47 58.071, W 123 34.951

Stroll alongside the Elwha River's churning waters and lounge on its grassy and rocky banks. Snoop around pioneer homesteads, and scope for elk and bears feeding in surrounding pastures. Wildlife and history spout from the Geyser Valley, but there are no geysers. The Press Expedition of 1889–90—that group of intrepid souls intent on exploring the Olympic interior—either mistook thumping grouse or swirling low clouds when they bestowed their geothermic moniker on this valley.

GETTING THERE

From Port Angeles, follow US Highway 101 west for 8.5 miles. At milepost 240, before the Elwha River Bridge, turn left onto Olympic Hot Springs Road (signed "Elwha Valley"). Continue 4 miles (passing the park entrance station) and turn left just beyond the Elwha Ranger Station onto dirt Whiskey Bend Road. Continue 4.5 miles to the trailhead (elev. 1200 ft) at the road's end. Privy available.

ON THE TRAIL

Start by following the well-trodden Elwha River Trail. This path has been delivering visitors into the Olympic wilds ever since James Christie and company blazed a route across these parts more than 125 years ago. Begin by gently climbing through mature forest and then younger timber (thanks to a series of early twentieth-century fires).

At 0.8 mile, a short spur (elev. 1325 ft) leads to the right to the Elk Overlook, where you can scan the mighty river flowing 500 feet below. The large grassy bend was once part of the Anderson Ranch homestead and is now a favorite grazing ground for resident elk. Back on the main trail, continue through open forest to a junction (elev. 1250 ft) at 1.2 miles with the Rica Canyon Trail. Head right, dropping 500 feet in 0.5 mile to the valley bottom, through a forest damaged by fire in the 1970s. A short 0.1-mile spur right leads to Goblins Gate (elev. 750 ft), a narrow, rocky

Suspension bridge at the mouth of the Grand Canyon of the Elwha

chasm funneling the Elwha's swiftly moving waters. Be cautious with children.

Then work your way upriver on the Geyser Valley Trail. Traverse meadows and fir groves. Rub shoulders with the churning river at wide bends and rocky ledges. At 2.9 miles, come to the Krause Bottom Trail, which leads left, climbing 0.6 mile back to the Elwha River Trail. Head right, traveling above the river and at 3.5 miles reaching the Humes Ranch on a grassy bluff. Inhabited until 1934, a small cabin remains and has been restored by the Park Service. The last inhabitants, Herb and Lois Crisler, used it while filming *Olympic Elk*, which became a Disney classic in the 1950s.

A short trail leads left back toward the Elwha River Trail. You, however, have more valley to see, so continue right, dropping off of the bluff. Pass a campsite by a sprawling meadow and then bend left, following Antelope Creek and coming to a junction (elev. 975 ft) at 4 miles.

Before turning left and heading back to your vehicle, head right along the Long Ridge Trail for 0.6 mile. Climb 75 feet onto a high river bank that grants sweeping views of the river. Then drop 150 feet to the Dodger Point Bridge (elev. 900 ft) at the mouth of the Grand Canyon of the Elwha. This deep, dark gorge is an impressive sight to behold.

Then turn around and retrace your steps 0.6 mile to the last junction and continue right 0.9 mile (passing a trail on the left), back to the Elwha River Trail at Michaels Cabin (elev. 1150 ft), a 1906 homestead. Cougar Mike lived here and made his living hunting predators. Continue left on the Elwha River Trail, ignoring all side trails, to return to your vehicle in 2 miles.

95 Elwha River and Lillian River

RATING/ DIFFICULTY	ROUNDTRIP	ELEV GAIN/ HIGH POINT	SEASON
***/3	13.4 miles	1800 feet/ 2150 feet	Year-round

Maps: Green Trails Hurricane Ridge/Elwha North No. 134S, Custom Correct Elwha Valley; **Contact:** Olympic National Park, Wilderness Information Center; **Notes:** See note about road washout, p. 243. National park entrance fee. Dogs prohibited; **GPS:** N 47 58.071, W 123 34.951

If you're itching for a small taste of the Olympic interior, or looking for a good long winter hike, this trip up the Elwha River Trail to Lillian River should satisfy your restlessness. Leave the busy Elwha Valley and hike a rarely traveled trail along a wild tributary river, soon finding that within the Lillian River valley, the trees are grand—and the solitude is grander.

GETTING THERE

From Port Angeles, follow US Highway 101 west for 8.5 miles. At milepost 240, before the Elwha River Bridge, turn left onto Olympic Hot Springs Road (signed "Elwha Valley"). Continue 4 miles (passing the park entrance station) and turn left just beyond the Elwha Ranger Station onto dirt Whiskey Bend Road. Continue 4.5 miles to the trailhead (elev. 1200 ft) at the road's end. Privy available.

ON THE TRAIL

Follow the Elwha River Trail, gently climbing past the Elk Overlook (elev. 1325 ft) and then gently descending. At 1.2 miles, pass the Rica Canyon Trail (Hike 94). Then pass the Krause Bottom Trail and reach another junction (elev. 1150 ft) at 2 miles, site of Michaels Cabin, a 1906 homestead once occupied by predator hunter Cougar Mike. The resident wildcats have rebounded nicely since Michael's departure.

Continue left and begin to climb, bypassing the narrow gorge known as the Grand

Old growth forest in the Lillian River valley

Canyon of the Elwha. Traverse slopes high above it, and look for a handful of old trees between Antelope and Idaho creeks that bear original ax blazes from the Press Expedition (see "A Pressing Trip," page 262). Through stands of second growth with a lush understory of salal (fires swept the region in the early 1900s), the trail reaches an elevation of 1650 feet.

It dips a little and climbs once more, reaching a junction with the Lillian River Trail at 4.2 miles. Turn left and on at times brushy tread, steadily climb high above the Lillian River. Catch some views through thinning forest, including of Long Ridge to the south. The trail tops out at 2150 feet and then makes a few ups and downs before steeply descending through old-growth forest to a creek (elev. 1960 ft). Steeply climb about 140 feet and descend again

on much rougher tread. Pass through some impressive groves of ancient Douglas-firs and cedars, coming to the trail's end at a campsite (elev. 1875 ft) on a bank above the Lillian River at 6.7 miles. The trail once went farther—no longer. Stay at this tranquil site awhile before making the rough and tumble return.

96 Happy Lake

RATING/ DIFFICULTY	ROUNDTRIP	ELEV GAIN/ HIGH POINT	SEASON
***/4	10 miles	3950 feet/ 5280 feet	Late June– Oct

Maps: Green Trails Seven Lakes Basin/ Hoh River Trail No. 133S, Custom Correct Lake Crescent–Happy Lake Ridge; **Contact:** Olympic National Park, Wilderness Informa-

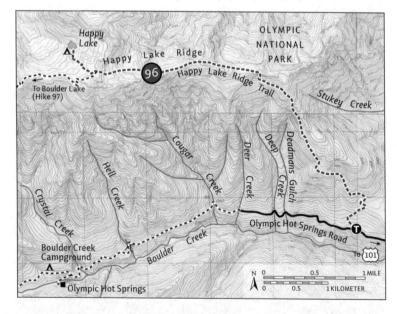

Looking east to Hurricane Ridge and Mount Angeles

tion Center; **Notes:** See note about road washout, p. 243. National park entrance fee. Dogs prohibited; **GPS:** N 47 59.005, W 123 37.540

🌸 *You may have a hard time staying jovial on your way to Happy Lake. Reaching this subalpine lake requires a stiff climb up a high, dry ridge. But once you crest Happy Lake Ridge, a smile is sure to come to your sweaty face. Open forest, quiet meadows, and heather parklands grace the way. Enjoy breathtaking views, too, of the sweeping Elwha Valley and the impressive Bailey Range.*

GETTING THERE

From Port Angeles, follow US Highway 101 west for 8.5 miles. At milepost 240, before the Elwha River Bridge, turn left onto Olympic Hot Springs Road (signed "Elwha Valley"). Continue for 8.7 miles (passing the park entrance station) to the trailhead (elev. 1725 ft), on the right.

ON THE TRAIL

Happy Lake was named by three pioneer bachelors extolling their emotional state in their femaleless society. The fishing must have been pretty darn good! The happy three are long gone, and many women have since visited this lovely little backcountry lake. But don't expect much company of any kind on your trek. You'll probably have the whole place to yourself—happy?

Waste no time gaining elevation. Soon pass a small creek, the last reliable water until the lake. Cutting through thick carpets of salal, the trail next winds its way up Happy Lake Ridge. At 1.5 miles, a small spring may be flowing; big trees and a brushy slope indicate its past irrigations. The climb then stiffens, huckleberry bushes and bear grass now lining the way. Pass a small clearing, getting a good view of Mount Carrie to the south.

After just about 3 miles of unrelenting climbing, the trail reaches the ridge crest (elev. 4500 ft). Head west along the ridge and enjoy much easier going as the the trail ascends a small knoll before leveling out. At 3.5 miles, come upon a stunning view spanning from Appleton Pass all the way to Obstruction Point. Hurricane Hill and Mount Angeles stand out clearly in the east across the deep cut of the Elwha Valley.

Continue along a narrowing crest, taking in views both north and south. The ridge broadens again as you near its highest point. Traversing subalpine forest and heather parkland, the way makes one final climb, topping out at a junction (elev. 5280 ft) at 4.5 miles. Consider walking up one of the adjacent knolls for excellent views; otherwise, head right, down the Happy Lake Trail.

Descend 400 feet and 0.5 mile through lovely subalpine country to the jovial lake (elev. 4880 ft). Situated in a small cirque, the grassy-shored lake is a happy sight. And hungry mosquitoes may be happy to see you. Consider visiting in fall, when the bloodsuckers are gone and the hillside is carpeted in crimson. As far as the fishing goes, it's still pretty good.

EXTENDING YOUR TRIP

The Happy Lake Ridge Trail continues from its junction with the Happy Lake Trail for 5.2 miles to Boulder Lake (Hike 97). Amble just a little ways beyond the junction for some excellent views north into the Barnes Creek basin.

97 Boulder Lake

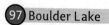

RATING/ DIFFICULTY	ROUNDTRIP	ELEV GAIN/ HIGH POINT	SEASON
***/4	12 miles	2550 feet/ 4350 feet	Late June– Oct

Maps: Green Trails Seven Lakes Basin/Hoh River Trail No. 133S, Custom Correct Lake Crescent–Happy Lake Ridge; **Contact:** Olympic National Park, Wilderness Information Center; **Notes:** See note about road washout, p. 243. National park entrance fee. Dogs prohibited; **GPS:** N 47 59.210, W 123 39.115

Hike to an emerald subalpine lake through miles of magnificent old growth. Come in midsummer and enjoy a swim. Visit in late summer and reap a bounty of succulent huckleberries. Make the trip on a chilly autumn day and look forward to a hot-springs soak on the way out.

GETTING THERE

From Port Angeles, follow US Highway 101 west for 8.5 miles. At milepost 240, before the Elwha River Bridge, turn left onto Olympic Hot Springs Road (signed "Elwha Valley"). Continue for 10 miles (passing the park entrance station) to the road's end and the trailhead (elev. 1800 ft). Privy available.

ON THE TRAIL

This hike starts off fairly easy along an old roadbed, traveling high above Boulder Creek, traversing steep slopes, and crossing cascading creeks. After crossing Crystal Creek on a big suspension bridge, reach a junction (elev. 2100 ft) at 2.2 miles. The trail left crosses Boulder Creek and goes a short distance to the Olympic Hot Springs—a series of inviting pools above the river. Avoid

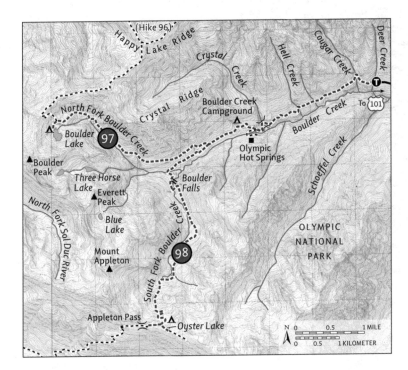

them in the summer (crowded) and welcome them in the winter (satisfying).

You want to continue right, traveling through the former car-now-backcountry Boulder Creek Campground. Bear right where another trail leads left to the springs and saunter via new planking through a wetland area. Then traverse inspiring ancient forest, coming to a junction (elev. 2300 ft) at 3 miles. The trail left leads to Appleton Pass (Hike 98). Go right instead, angling along slopes crowded by coniferous giants. Boulder Creek's crashing and thrashing fades into the distance. Silence.

At about 4.5 miles, the trail approaches North Fork Boulder Creek and steepens,

making a final push to the lake. At 5.9 miles, reach a junction. Boulder Lake (elev. 4350 ft) is a pebble's throw away to the left (the main trail heads right, to Happy Lake Ridge; see Hike 96).

Cross marshy meadows and pass campsites, and reach the lake perched in a semi-open bowl at the base of 5600-foot Boulder Peak. A short distance to the south, find in-viting shoreline ledges that harness the sun's warmth, perfect for a nap or lunch break. Enjoy the green hue of the lake's waters and the silence. Well, not quite silent. Chattering chickarees, busy nuthatches, flittering dragonflies, and surface-breaking fish add some commotion.

Boulder Lake

EXTENDING YOUR TRIP

Strong day hikers can continue beyond the lake and return via the 9.7-mile Happy Lake Ridge Trail and a 1.3-mile road walk back to the trailhead.

98 Appleton Pass and Oyster Lake

RATING/ DIFFICULTY	ROUNDTRIP	ELEV GAIN/ HIGH POINT	SEASON
****/5	15.2 miles	3390 feet/ 5190 feet	July–Oct

Maps: Green Trails Seven Lakes Basin/ Hoh River Trail No. 133S, Custom Correct Seven Lakes Basin–Hoh; **Contact:** Olympic National Park, Wilderness Information Center; **Notes:** See note about road washout, p. 243. National park entrance fee. Dogs prohibited; **GPS:** N 47 59.210, W 123 39.115

This arduous hike through primeval forest leads to one of the most spectacular mountain passes in the Olympics—Appleton Pass, high on the Elwha–Sol Duc divide. Savor stunning vistas of surrounding peaks and deep forested valleys. And marvel at flowered meadows and a sparkling little alpine lake.

GETTING THERE

From Port Angeles, follow US Highway 101 west for 8.5 miles. At milepost 240, before the Elwha River Bridge, turn left onto Olympic Hot Springs Road (signed "Elwha Valley"). Continue for 10 miles (passing the park entrance station) to the road's end and the trailhead (elev. 1800 ft). Privy available.

ON THE TRAIL

Start by following the Olympic Hot Springs Trail 2.2 miles to a junction just beyond the Crystal Creek suspension bridge. The Olympic Hot Springs are a short distance to the left. Consider a soak upon your return from this challenging hike.

Continue right, through campsites and bearing right at another junction. Then cross wetlands and hike through magnificent old growth coming to a junction (elev. 2300 ft) at 3 miles. The trail right leads to Boulder Lake (Hike 97). You want to continue left through imposing ancient firs, cedars, and hemlocks. The forest has a dry feel, as Mount Appleton and the Bailey Range create a bit of a rainshadow effect here on their eastern sides.

At 3.8 miles, cross the North Fork Boulder Creek and begin following the South Fork upstream. At about 4.2 miles, come to two short side trails leading left to pretty little Boulder Falls (elev. 2650 ft), a series of cascades set in a mossy ravine. This is a good destination if you're not intent on going all

A PRESSING TRIP

In February 1890, having made camp at several spots along the lower Elwha River since December, James H. Christie led a group of five rough and ready men, a couple of dogs, and a pack of mules on an arduous three-month journey across the Olympic Mountains. Christie's ambition to explore the last of the uncharted mountain ranges in the continental United States was met with much interest and enthusiasm in the new state of Washington.

Funded by the *Seattle Press* newspaper, Christie's voyage was named the Press Expedition, and upon the party's emergence at Lake Quinault in May 1890, it became the first successful European American north-south crossing of the Olympics. Many of the place names that dot the Olympics today were bestowed by Christie and company: Mount Ferry (for Washington's first governor), Mount Seattle (after the city), Mount Barnes (for an expedition member), the Bailey Range (for the publisher of the *Seattle Press*), and Mount Christie (for Christie himself, no less).

Many modern-day backpackers hike a route that roughly follows the Press Expedition's original course: a 45-mile journey from Whiskey Bend, up the Elwha, over the Low Divide, and out the North Fork Quinault River. What took the intrepid Press Party over three months to complete is now—thanks to manicured trails—easily covered in three to five days.

the way to Appleton Pass. A handful of swimming holes beneath the lower falls may be tempting, but remember, they're no hot springs!

Beyond the falls, the trail crosses the creek and climbs more steeply. As you traverse a deep, rugged valley, forest cover thins, allowing previews of what lies ahead.

Oyster Lake

Bubbling springs and copious huckleberry bushes may entice you to take a few breaks. At about 5.5 miles, the trail enters an open basin, getting rougher while the views get better. Look back at Lizard Head Peak; Mount Appleton looms above. Dazzling wildflowers paint the basin in reds, purples, and yellows, and numerous creeks tumble down the rugged encircling slopes.

The trail makes a few steep and sweeping switchbacks through clumps of mountain hemlocks and sprawling meadows, arriving on a bench (elev. 5100 ft) at 7.5 miles, just east of and above 5050-foot Appleton Pass. The trail continues west to the pass, dropping down into the Sol Duc Valley. You want to go left 0.1 mile on a well-defined path, past camps, to little Oyster Lake (elev. 5190 ft). You earned this beautiful scene.

EXTENDING YOUR TRIP

If time and energy permit, wander beyond the lake on primitive Cat Creek way path to some of the most amazing views in the Olympics.

A RIVER RUNS WILD AGAIN

For millennia the Elwha River ran wild and free. From its origins deep within the Olympic Mountains, the mighty waterway tumbled and flowed 45 miles to its outlet on the Strait of Juan de Fuca. Its legendary salmon runs fed the Klallam people. Hundreds of thousands of the anadromous fish, some weighing 100 pounds, made their way up the Elwha each year. But all that changed in 1911 when a dam was constructed just 5 miles up the river.

The Elwha Dam, the lower of two dams, was built without a fish ladder. Then in 1926 an upper dam was built at Glines Canyon. It, too, was constructed without a fish ladder. After thousands of years, the salmon runs of the Elwha ceased—a blow to a culture, an ecosystem, and a nation. The power generated from the dams was small. To many citizens, conservationists, and anglers, the destruction of one of the greatest salmon runs in the state was not at all justified.

By the 1980s the country's love affair with hydropower projects had begun to change. Many Americans realized that there were real costs involved with this so-called clean energy source. A movement mounted to remove the two dams, and a broad coalition protested the dams' reauthorizations. Then Congress got involved, resulting in the Elwha River Ecosystem and Fisheries Restoration Act of 1992, which authorized the dams' removal. Both dams were finally removed by 2014, the country's largest dam removal to date, and the Park Service continues to rehabilitate the former lakebeds left behind.

The dam removal was a major victory for the river, the salmon, the greater Olympic ecosystem, the Klallam people, and the country. It marked a major shift in policy. Now, more than one hundred years after the mighty river was harnessed, it once again runs free.

Several spots will help you learn more about this historic event and the rebirth of this wild river: Check out the Elwha River Interpretive Center and its nature trails on State Route 112, 1 mile west of the junction with US Highway 101. At the Lower Elwha Klallam Indian Reservation, walk the 0.7-mile Warrior Trail to the Elwha River estuary. And hike the Glines Canyon and Smoky Bottom trails (Hike 92).

Lake Crescent

Lake Crescent, at over 5000 surface acres, is the largest lake in the Olympic Mountains and among the largest natural bodies of freshwater in western Washington. Arched like a crescent, the 9-mile-long lake is known for its crystal-clear waters and stunning mountain reflections. A couple of pockets of private cabins (grandfathered in after the park's creation) line the lake, but the majority of shoreline is undeveloped and managed by Olympic National Park.

Hiking options in the Lake Crescent area range from easy lakeshore wanderings to steep grunts up the surrounding ridges and peaks. Lake Crescent is a great place to set up a base camp for exploring adjacent trails and those in the nearby Sol Duc Valley. Fairholm, a fine national park campground complete with beach and boat launch, sits at the lake's western end, while the Lake Crescent Lodge and Log Cabin Resort offer cushier alternatives. And the lake's alluring waters may have you packing your kayak along with your trekking poles.

99 Olympic Discovery Trail: Adventure Route

RATING/ DIFFICULTY	ROUNDTRIP	ELEV GAIN/ HIGH POINT	SEASON
***/2	7 miles	700 feet/ 850 feet	Year-round

Maps: Custom Correct Lake Crescent–Happy Lake Ridge, online at Olympic Discovery Trail; **Contact:** Olympic Discovery Trail; **Notes:** Dogs permitted on-leash. Open to mountain bikes, horses; **GPS:** N 48 06.351, W 123 33.771

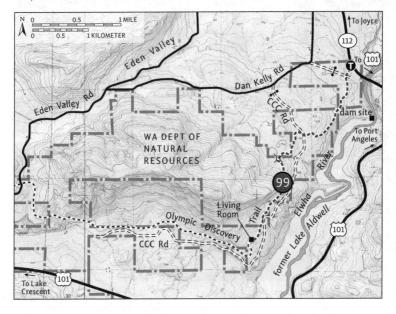

Hike a section of the 25-mile-long Adventure Route of the Olympic Discovery Trail, a favorite destination for area trail runners, mountain bikers, and equestrians. Wind up through working forests and over a ridge to an open hillside known as the Living Room. Then kick back on a bench and watch a showing of the Elwha Valley unfold before you.

GETTING THERE

From Port Angeles, follow US Highway 101 west for 5.4 miles and turn right onto State Route 112. Continue for 1.3 miles (just beyond a bridge over the Elwha River) to the trailhead (elev. 350 ft), on your left.

ON THE TRAIL

Developed and administered by Clallam County and built by volunteers and the Clallam County Sheriff's chain gang, this section of the Olympic Discovery Trail (ODT) (see the "Discovering the Olympic Peninsula Trail" sidebar) offers an adventurous alternative to the well-graded railbed that the ODT primarily utilizes. Traversing a ridge through Washington State Department of Natural Resources and private timberlands, the Adventure Route twists, turns, climbs, and dips through mature second growth and clear-cuts. The first 3.5 miles to the Living Room make for a great day hike.

Pass through the wooden arch and begin

A hiker enjoys the view from the "Living Room."

your adventurous journey on good tread through thinned and mature second-growth forest. Soon cross a gated road—an access point favored by equestrians. The trail steadily climbs, making a few dips along the way. At about 1.4 miles, cross the gravel CCC road. Then continue gently climbing, crossing a creek on a nicely built bridge before switch backing up steeper slopes.

Catch some glimpses east down to the Elwha River and the former bed of Lake Aldwell. At around 2.7 miles, the trail rounds a ridge (elev. 850 ft) and begins to descend. At 3.5 miles, reach the Living Room (elev. 700 ft), an old cut on a hillside that sports a big wooden bench and foot rest. Plop your bum down, kick back, and enjoy the excellent view south of the Elwha River valley. For most day hikers, this spot is a fine objective.

EXTENDING YOUR TRIP

If you can arrange for a car shuttle, consider hiking farther. The trail drops to about 450 feet and then begins a long climb, reaching the Eden Valley Road trailhead (elev. 1000 ft) at about 7.2 miles. From there, the trail continues climbing to about 1350 feet at 9 miles, drops to Bear Creek (elev. 950 ft) at 11.4 miles, and then climbs again. At 12.5 miles, the trail crosses the Joyce Access Road (Discover Pass required) and continues climbing, rounding a ridge at 1450 feet. It meets up again with the Joyce Access Road (Discover Pass required) at 16.1 miles. The trail then contours the ridge, going up and down and reaching the Joyce–Piedmont Road (elev. 700 ft) (Discover Pass required) at 20 miles. At 21.2 miles, the trail follows the fairly level graveled Waterline Road (an old railroad bed), swinging south and paralleling the Lyre River to reach the Spruce Railroad trailhead (Hike 100) at 25 miles.

100 Spruce Railroad Trail

RATING/ DIFFICULTY	ROUNDTRIP	ELEV GAIN/ HIGH POINT	SEASON
***/2	8.2 miles	300 feet/ 720 feet	Year-round

Maps: Green Trails Lake Crescent No. 101, Custom Correct Lake Crescent–Happy Lake Ridge; **Contact:** Olympic National Park, Wilderness Information Center; **Notes:** Dogs permitted on-leash. Open to bicycles; **GPS:** N 48 05.601, W 123 48.172

Hop aboard the Spruce Railroad Trail for a scenic and historical hike along the sparkling shores of massive Lake Crescent—at 9 miles long, over 600 feet deep, and surrounded by steep ridges and peaks, the lake seems more like a fjord. This trail, with its microclimate of drier conditions than areas just a few miles away, is a good choice on an overcast day.

GETTING THERE

From Port Angeles, follow US Highway 101 west for 16 miles to the Olympic National Park boundary. Turn right onto East Beach Road (signed "Log Cabin Resort, East Beach") and continue for 3.2 miles. Just beyond the Log Cabin Resort, turn left onto Boundary Creek Road (signed "Spruce Railroad Trail"). Follow it for 0.8 mile to the eastern trailhead (elev. 620 ft). Privy available.

ON THE TRAIL

Part of the long-distance Olympic Discovery Trail (ODT) (see the "Discovering the Olympic Peninsula Trail" sidebar), the Spruce Railroad Trail is one of the few routes in Olympic National Park that permits mountain bikes and dogs. The trail gains little

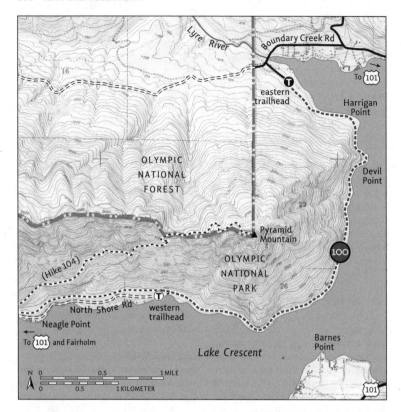

elevation as it hugs the pristine shoreline of Lake Crescent, a lake renowned for its crystal-clear waters. You can peer down over 40 feet into its depths. And when strong breezes are absent, those same pristine waters capture stunning reflections of the surrounding ridges.

On a wide and recently paved path, start hiking through an old orchard graced with big, moss-draped maples. Follow an old roadbed and climb about 100 feet to skirt some cabins. Then drop toward the lakeshore to the old railroad bed, and

begin hiking on the former 36-mile rail line built during World War I to haul Sitka spruce—once coveted for airplane manufacturing—to mills in nearby Port Angeles. Ironically, the Great War ended days before the line was completed. The Spruce Railroad did, however, serve commercial logging interests for thirty-five years. In 1981, the National Park Service converted 4 miles of the railbed to trail, and many more miles have since been transformed into the ODT.

At 1.2 miles, come to the recently renovated McFee Tunnel at Devils Point. Hike

Lake Crescent reflections

through it—or head left on a scenic side trail to Devils Punchbowl. Cross the Punchbowl on a bridge, from which you can admire the lake's impressive depth and the surrounding lofty emerald peaks and ridges. Then return to the railbed, traveling high above the lake. Enjoy sporadic breathtaking views across sparkling waters when the trail breaks out of the canopy of giant firs, hemlocks, and scaly-barked, contorted madronas that line the way. At 2.5 miles, come to the lake's narrowest section at the arch of its crescent. Directly across from you, Barnes Point—formed by river outwash—juts into the lake. Craggy Mount Storm King hovers above it.

At 3.1 miles, round a bluff. The railroad passed through a tunnel here, and it is still discernible (but advisable to stay out of). At 4.1 miles, reach a junction (elev. 700 ft) with a spur leading left to the western trailhead (1.6 miles east of the Pyramid Mountain trailhead; Hike 104). Return to your vehicle or if a shuttle can be arranged consider hiking on the ODT west nearly 6 miles to a trailhead on US 101 near the Sol Duc Road junction.

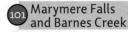

101 Marymere Falls and Barnes Creek

Marymere Falls

RATING/ DIFFICULTY	ROUNDTRIP	ELEV GAIN/ HIGH POINT	SEASON
**/1	1.8 miles	200 feet/ 820 feet	Year-round

Barnes Creek

RATING/ DIFFICULTY	ROUNDTRIP	ELEV GAIN/ HIGH POINT	SEASON
**/3	8 miles	1600 feet/ 2050 feet	Year-round

Maps: Green Trails Lake Crescent No. 101, Custom Correct Lake Crescent–Happy Lake Ridge; **Contact:** Olympic National Park, Wilderness Information Center; **Notes:** Dogs prohibited; **GPS:** N 48 03.492, W 123 47.352

Stately forest along the Barnes Creek Trail

A pretty little waterfall popular with tourists or a lonely valley coveted by those seeking solitude and old-growth splendor—your choice. Mosey up a damp, mossy glen to witness Falls Creek tumbling over Marymere Falls, or hike along Barnes Creek up a secluded valley shrouded in ancient timber. Or hike them both!

GETTING THERE

From Port Angeles, follow US Highway 101 west for 20 miles to Barnes Point at milepost 228 and turn right (signed "Lake Crescent Lodge and Marymere Falls"). In 0.1 mile, turn right and proceed 0.1 mile to a large parking area. The hike begins on the Marymere Falls Nature Trail (elev. 620 ft) near the

Storm King Ranger Station. Picnic site and restrooms available.

ON THE TRAIL

Follow the well-groomed and well-traveled nature trail, passing under US 101 and coming to a junction at 0.5 mile. The trail right follows Barnes Creek to the Lake Crescent Lodge on Barnes Point, a nice alternative return. Turn left instead, following Barnes Creek upstream under a cool canopy of old-growth giants. At 0.6 mile, pass the Mount Storm King Trail (Hike 102). At 0.7 mile, come to another junction (elev. 700 ft).

Marymere Falls: Head right 0.2 mile for the falls, crossing Barnes Creek on a sturdy bridge and then climbing 120 feet to a cool narrow ravine. Marymere Falls plummets 90 feet into this dark, dank slot. A short loop provides several vantages for viewing the cataract. Consider visiting in winter when plenty of runoff promises the most spectacular showing.

Barnes Creek: To venture upvalley, continue straight at the junction and immediately notice the change in tread, from superhighway to quiet byway. Amble alongside the creek in lush bottomlands punctuated by giant conifers. Climb 150 feet up a steep hillside. Then drop steeply 100 feet to the river bottom, reaching a big log bridge at 1.4 miles from the trailhead.

Next, climb 200 feet, traversing steep slopes and bluffs above the wilderness waterway. Cross two creeks—the second via a high log bridge. Amble through delightful maple groves and impressive stands of old growth. The way eventually descends back to the creek before beginning a steep ascent away from it through towering firs and hemlocks.

At 3.6 miles, come to a nice camp along a tributary creek. Then continue climbing,

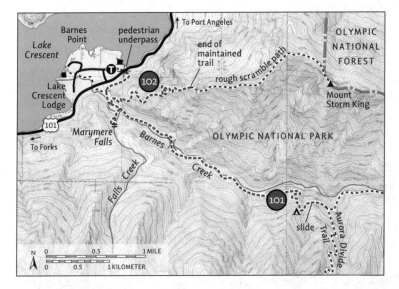

skirting above a huge slide that grants views across the valley to Mount Storm King. At 4 miles, reach a junction (elev. 2050 ft). For most day hikers, this is probably far enough.

EXTENDING YOUR TRIP

Long abandoned beyond this point, the Barnes Creek Trail continues another 5.5 miles to 5000-plus-foot Lookout Dome on Mount Baldy. Volunteers have recently been doing some work to reopen this route, so if you're up for an adventure, keep going! Another option is to turn right and hike up the Aurora Divide Trail on a brutal ascent of 2600 feet in 3.5 miles to Aurora Ridge. A much easier option is to return to the trailhead and stroll the nearby 0.5-mile Moments in Time Nature Trail. It offers stunning views of Aurora Ridge and, across Lake Crescent, of Pyramid Mountain.

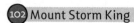

102 Mount Storm King

RATING/ DIFFICULTY	ROUNDTRIP	ELEV GAIN/ HIGH POINT	SEASON
***/4	3.8 miles	1780 feet/ 2400 feet	Apr–Nov

Maps: Green Trails Lake Crescent No. 101, Custom Correct Lake Crescent–Happy Lake Ridge; **Contact:** Olympic National Park, Wilderness Information Center; **Notes:** Dogs prohibited; **GPS:** N 48 03.492, W 123 47.352

Huff and puff up a short, steep trail to an eagle's-eye view of deep-blue Lake Crescent, one of the Olympic Peninsula's most famous landmarks. Despite its difficulty, this trail is popular due to its proximity to the Marymere Falls Nature Trail. Aside from knocking the wind out-of-shape hikers, this

Lake Crescent from a Storm King belvedere

trail can be dangerous because of its exposed ledges. Keep an eye on children and avoid this trip during bad weather.

GETTING THERE

From Port Angeles, follow US Highway 101 west for 20 miles to Barnes Point at milepost 228 and turn right (signed "Lake Crescent Lodge and Marymere Falls"). In 0.1 mile, turn right and proceed 0.1 mile to a large parking area. The hike begins on the Marymere Falls Nature Trail (elev. 620 ft) near the Storm King Ranger Station. Picnic site and restrooms available.

ON THE TRAIL

Start by following swarms of people on the well-trodden Marymere Falls Nature Trail (Hike 101). At 0.6 mile, come to a junction at a giant boulder that came crashing down Storm King many moons ago. Turn left and begin an arduous ascent under a climate-controlled old-growth canopy. As the trail works its way up the south-facing hogback, the dampness dissipates. Madronas and salal soon decorate the way. From here on up, the terrain is dry and the hike can be quite hot during the summer. Get an early start, or consider Storm King as an evening enticement.

As you rise above the Barnes Creek valley and busy US 101, the crash of rushing water and the hum of zooming traffic fills the air. Enjoy a short reprieve from the steepness as the trail traverses a fir-filled bench. Then head into low gear again as the grade intensifies. Occasional window views of Aurora Ridge interrupt the monotony of the grunt.

After 1.4 difficult miles, arrive at a series of belvederes (elev. 2000 ft) on a ledge that drops off precipitously to the north. Enjoy a stunning view of Lake Crescent directly below, Pyramid Mountain hovering over the jewel. Savor the scenery and bask in the sunshine, or carry on. A second viewpoint is another 0.5 mile farther and 400 more feet of elevation gain. There's no lake view from this one, but there's a decent shot of the deep, wide, verdant Barnes Creek valley below.

EXTENDING YOUR TRIP

The trail officially ends at the second viewpoint, but a rugged, steep (rope in places), exposed, and potentially dangerous scramble path continues. Only experienced and sure-footed scramblers should contemplate continuing.

103 Aurora Ridge and Sourdough Mountain

RATING/ DIFFICULTY	ROUNDTRIP	ELEV GAIN/ HIGH POINT	SEASON
***/5	12 miles	4830 feet/ 4625 feet	Late June–Nov

Maps: Green Trails Lake Crescent No. 101, Custom Correct Lake Crescent–Happy Lake Ridge; **Contact:** Olympic National Park, Wilderness Information Center; **Notes:** Dogs prohibited; **GPS:** N 48 03.089, W 123 50.376

Hike one of Olympic National Park's steepest trails to one of its most obscure summits. Sourdough Mountain rises above a busy highway but sees nary a human visitor. Aside from assured solitude and an excellent workout, enjoy miles of ancient forest and a couple of decent viewpoints of Lake Crescent below and Mount Olympus above a wave of emerald ridges.

GETTING THERE

From Port Angeles, follow US Highway 101 west for 22.3 miles to a small turnoff on the right, just west of milepost 226 (2.3 miles past Lake Crescent Lodge and the Marymere Falls turnoff). Park and carefully walk along the road shoulder 0.1 mile to the trailhead (elev. 620 ft).

ON THE TRAIL

Following the Aurora Creek Trail, cross a gully and immediately climb. There's no warming up on this trail, which ascends 3500 feet in 3 miles. Angling east, take in some good lake views. Then angle west into a ravine that cradles cascading Aurora Creek. Pass monstrous Douglas-firs. The way then leaves the creek to begin a brutal ascent up steep slopes.

Toil upward through uniform hemlock forest, pausing occasionally for window views of Pyramid Mountain across Lake Crescent. The trail then attacks a steep ledge, going along, beneath, and over pillow basalt. The seemingly unrelenting climb finally gives way as it skirts a couple of rocky knobs along a narrow ridge. Sourdough Mountain along verdant Aurora Ridge comes into view. Crest the ridge at 4275 feet and then slightly descend into a small gap, reaching a junction (elev. 4225 ft) with the Aurora Ridge Trail at 3.4 miles.

Head right, passing a spring and pocket meadows before steeply descending to a saddle. At 4.5 miles, cross an intermittent stream and small marshy pond (elev. 3875 ft), and then start arduously ascending again! Switch back up a steep slope and swing around a spring teeming with marsh marigolds, coming to a 4300-foot saddle at 5 miles. Then slightly descend to a junction (elev. 4275 ft) at 5.5 miles.

Sourdough Mountain's lonely summit

Head right and soon come to Sourdough Camp in a small meadow. The old shelter is gone and water may be absent too. An unreliable spring is located west and below the camp. For Sourdough Mountain, walk to the eastern edge of the meadow and find fading tread that leads past old privy pits. The trail then switchbacks left, becoming easier to follow.

Approach a meadow under a large ledge. Stay right and hike up a grassy draw before turning left and hiking up a wooded ridge to the rocky, semi-open 4625-foot summit of Sourdough Mountain at 6 miles. Views are good south to Olympus and west over Aurora Ridge to the Sol Duc Valley and beyond. A small tarn is below the summit to the north. You can hike down and explore it and snoop around with caution for some good views north over Lake Crescent.

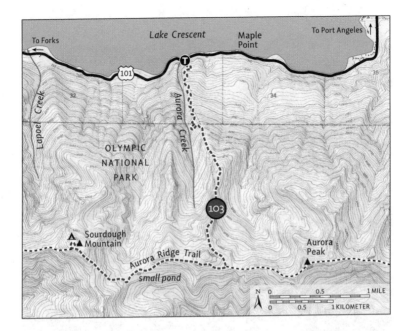

EXTENDING YOUR TRIP

For an easier descent on your knees, arrange a car shuttle and leave Sourdough Mountain by hiking west along Aurora Ridge. Traverse some meadows with good views before moderately descending 2.9 miles along a forested ridge to the Eagle Lakes Trail. From there it's 5.5 miles to the trailhead on the Sol Duc Hot Springs Road (Hike 107).

104 Pyramid Mountain

RATING/ DIFFICULTY	ROUNDTRIP	ELEV GAIN/ HIGH POINT	SEASON
**/4	7 miles	2400 feet/ 3089 feet	Apr–Nov

Maps: Green Trails Lake Crescent No. 101, Custom Correct Lake Crescent–Happy Lake Ridge; **Contact:** Olympic National Park, Wilderness Information Center; **Notes:** Dogs prohibited. **Warning:** Recommended for strong hikers only, not children or those prone to vertigo. Trail crosses a large, unstable, potentially dangerous slide. Tread is narrow and exposed, and a slip can mean serious injury or death; **GPS:** N 48 03.955, W 123 51.562

Hike a prominent peak that hovers over the crystal-clear waters of Lake Crescent. A World War II enemy-airplane spotter cabin still teeters on the precipitous summit. Trees have overtaken the wide views once afforded to lookout personnel, but nearby ledges offer breathtaking glimpses straight down to the lake and out across to Mount Storm King.

Lake Crescent from the landslide on Pyramid Mountain Trail

GETTING THERE

From Port Angeles, follow US Highway 101 west for 27 miles to Fairholm on the western end of Lake Crescent (milepost 221). Turn right on Camp David Junior Road (aka North Shore Road) and proceed for 3.1 miles (the pavement ends at 1.5 miles) to the trailhead (elev. 700 ft).

ON THE TRAIL

Start by following a short paved section of trail, switch backing 0.1 mile to the paved Olympic Discovery Trail, a long-distance rail trail that traverses the peninsula (see the "Discovering the Olympic Discovery Trail" sidebar). Cross the trail and contour along the western ridge of the mountain on an

DISCOVERING THE OLYMPIC DISCOVERY TRAIL

With the backing of a wide array of government officials, trail advocates, and dedicated volunteers, the Olympic Discovery Trail (www.olympicdiscoverytrail.com) is emerging as one of the state's premiere long-distance rail trails. The idea for the trail was born in 1988 along with the Peninsula Trails Coalition (www.peninsulatrailscoalition.org), formed upon the dismantling of a pan-peninsula rail line. Trail work began in 1991 at Sequim's Railroad Bridge Park, and now a hiker-bicyclist trail from La Push on the Pacific all the way to Port Townsend on Puget Sound is becoming a reality.

The Olympic Discovery Trail will ultimately extend 134 miles, spanning the northern half of the Olympic Peninsula. As of 2019, more than 85 mostly paved miles are open in three sections: the Larry Scott Trail on the Quimper Peninsula, Discovery Bay to Port Angeles, and Lake Crescent–Sol Duc. Another 25 miles of nonpaved trail are also open, known as the Adventure Route (Hike 99). Besides offering locals a safe, nonmotorized transportation route, the Olympic Discovery Trail also provides miles of year-round hiking and biking for residents and visitors alike.

easy grade through a dry forest of Douglas-firs, salal, and madronas.

The forest grows more impressive, with big specimens hovering overhead. At 1.5 miles, cross June Creek. Then climb more

steeply, skirting a series of small slides. At 1.8 miles, approach a big landslide area (elev. 1650 ft). Scraped bare of vegetation, the slide is several hundred feet across and highly exposed. Trail tread is only a few

inches wide in spots. The trail was actually rerouted here in 2015, but the new crossing is equally intimidating and just as potentially dangerous as the old one. Do not cross if you are the least bit uncomfortable or if it is raining or snowing. Instead, enjoy the limited views of Lake Crescent from this sunny spot.

If you do cross the slide, you'll find no other obstacles. Now in cool forest, the trail switchbacks and steadily climbs. At 2.7 miles, reach the ridge crest and the edge of an old clear-cut in the adjacent national forest tract. At 3 miles, come to a logging road—since converted to trail and offering a 6.7-mile alternative approach (via Forest Road 3068) to the summit. Then it's a final 0.5-mile push up a steep hillside of old-growth conifers to the 3089-foot summit.

From the forested peak, scout out a ledge to peer straight down to Lake Crescent. Lake Sutherland and the Strait of Juan de Fuca linger in the distance. The old cabin was built in 1942 to spot enemy aircraft intent on reaching Puget Sound. It's one of only two that remain of the original thirteen that once perched on Olympic peaks during World War II. This hiker-historian would like to see it restored as a reminder and a memorial to our servicemen and women.

Sol Duc River Valley

No matter how you spell it—Sol Duc or Soleduck, it still means "sparkling water"—we have early Native inhabitants to thank for its name. One of the longest rivers in the Olympic Mountains, the Sol Duc drains some of its prettiest and most dramatic landscapes: dozens of alpine lakes, deep valleys of old growth, sprawling alpine meadows, rugged ridges, and craggy peaks. Waterfalls, emerald pools, and even hot springs grace this majestic river. Hiking opportunities in the Sol Duc Valley range from gentle to challenging and include some of the best ridge-running trails in the Olympics.

105 Mount Muller

RATING/ DIFFICULTY	LOOP	ELEV GAIN/ HIGH POINT	SEASON
*****/4	12.7 miles	3350 feet/ 3748 feet	May–Nov

Maps: Green Trails Lake Crescent No. 101, Custom Correct Lake Crescent–Happy Lake Ridge; **Contact:** Olympic National Forest, Pacific Ranger District, Forks; **Notes:** NW Forest Pass or Interagency Pass required. Open to mountain bikes, horses; **GPS:** N 48 04.562, W 124 00.789

Lake Crescent from Mount Muller Trail

🔑 *This is a tough climb to one of the best ridge hikes in the Olympics. You'll be rewarded with brilliant wildflower carpets and jaw-slacking views that range from glistening-white Mount Olympus to deep-blue Lake Crescent. And there are plenty of unexpected surprises on this splendid loop.*

GETTING THERE

From Port Angeles, follow US Highway 101 west for 32 miles to an electricity substation at milepost 216 (4.5 miles beyond Fairholm). Turn right on Forest Road 3071 (signed "Mount Muller–Littleton Loop") and proceed 0.3 mile to the trailhead (elev. 1050 ft). Privy available.

ON THE TRAIL

Back in 1975, Forest Service employee Molly Erickson was convinced that Mount Muller and Snider Ridge were the most beautiful places in the Forks Ranger District—and that someone should put a trail on them. Twenty years later, Erickson and a slew of her Forest Service compatriots did just that, designing and building over 20 miles of trail on the long northern ridge above the Sol Duc Valley. They named features along the way, adding a whimsical flair to this rugged ridge. And with the recent opening of the Divide Trail, they continue to expand the trail network.

Do this loop clockwise, tackling the steep climb first. Trail No. 882 starts in a dark, damp glen housing Littleton Creek, your last sure water for 9 miles. The way starts off easy before reaching a series of switchbacks that climb 2000 feet in 2.5 miles. In early summer, twinflower lines the trail like rows of tiny street lights. As you climb, you'll traverse acres of young forest interrupted by big charred stumps.

After 3 long uphill miles, crest the ridge (elev. 3250 ft) at Jims Junction. The trail left leads 3.5 miles to Kloshe Nanitch (Hike 106); the one straight ahead goes 0.5 mile to decommissioned FR 3040. You want to go right, climbing through a stand of silver firs and soon coming to Millsap Meadow (elev. 3400 ft). Embrace a glorious view of the emerald wall of Aurora Ridge and the massive snow and ice heap of Mount Olympus. The trail then descends, bottoming out at Thomas Gap (elev. 3025 ft) before steeply regaining lost ground.

At 4.5 miles, come to a junction (elev. 3425 ft) in Jasmine Meadow. Here, the new Divide Trail drops 2.8 miles to the trailhead, following old logging roads, railroad grades, and new tread. It offers a shorter loop option or a more direct route to Mount Muller. For Muller, continue left through more beautiful meadows. Views of the Sol Duc Valley below grow more impressive. Marvel at all the blossoms: paintbrush, tiger lily, thistle, bleeding heart, vetch, starflower, hawkweed, daisy, bear grass, columbine, lupine, strawberry, bunchberry, queen's cup, and more.

At 5.5 miles, come to a side trail (elev. 3660 ft) leading left for 0.1 mile to the semi-forested 3748-foot summit of Mount Muller. Bag it. Then proceed on the main trail to another side path (take it), this one leading right 0.1 mile to Panorama Point, a series of outcrops in a sea of meadows. If you think the view can't possibly get better, wait until you see Lake Crescent sparkling below. Like sentinels, Pyramid Mountain and Mount Storm King guard the fjord-like lake. Mount Baker hovers in the distance.

After soaking up the view, continue up and down along the ridge crest, dashing behind ledges, passing a balanced rock, and undulating between forest and meadow. From Cahills

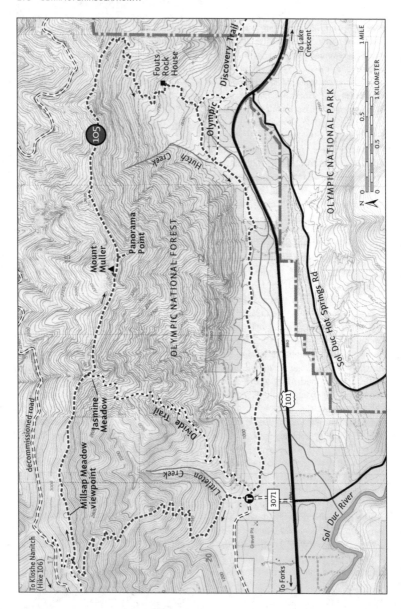

Overlook at 7 miles, drop rapidly to Mosely Gap, a 2800-foot low point on the ridge. After one last uphill struggle of about 50 feet, begin a long descent back to the valley.

At 8.2 miles, check out Fouts Rock House, two giant boulders rubbing shoulders. Then pass a horse camp and trail leading left to the Olympic Discovery Trail (ODT). At 9.4 miles, come to the paved ODT (elev. 1150 ft). Head right on it, crossing Hutch Creek on a bridge. At 9.8 miles veer right, back onto single track, and continue on a mostly level route. Skirt a bog (elev. 950 ft) and cross a new logging road before reaching the trailhead at 12.7 miles.

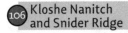

106 Kloshe Nanitch and Snider Ridge

RATING/ DIFFICULTY	ROUNDTRIP	ELEV GAIN/ HIGH POINT	SEASON
***/4	6.4 miles	2410 feet/ 3160 feet	Apr–Nov

Map: USGS Snider Peak; **Contact:** Olympic National Forest, Pacific Ranger District, Forks; **Notes:** Discover Pass required; **GPS:** N 48 04.122, W 124 06.457

Chinook Jargon for "stand guard" or "stand watch," Kloshe Nanitch hosted a striking cupola fire lookout until 1963 and then a beautiful replica of it from 1996 to 2012. Now a viewing platform teeters on this Snider Ridge outcrop high above the glacially carved Sol Duc Valley, allowing you to stand watch over thousands of acres of rugged surroundings.

GETTING THERE

From Port Angeles, follow US Highway 101 west for 37 miles and turn right onto West

A hiker on Snider Ridge pauses for a sweeping view

Snider Road (0.4 mile west of Klahowya Campground, just past the Sol Duc River Bridge). Drive 1 mile to the road's end and trailhead (elev. 750 ft).

ON THE TRAIL

The trail starts on Washington State Department of Natural Resources land (hence the need for a Discover Pass) and follows an abandoned section of US 101. Walk the old road, its asphalt losing ground to moss and shrubbery, along a bend in the Sol Duc River. After 0.2 mile, enter national forest and come to a sign indicating the start of true trail. Through second-growth fir forest carpeted with salal and pipsissewa, Trail No. 882.1 steadily climbs, switch backing up the south side of Snider Ridge. Cross several streams that rush down steep ravines, although by late summer most will be running dry. At

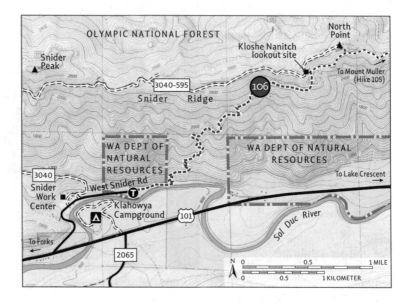

about 2 miles, the grade eases through a stand of hemlocks and then launches into some tight switchbacks (more like Z-backs) before approaching a small ledge that offers a preview of the views ahead.

At 3 miles, after skirting beneath some cliffs, come to a junction (elev. 2980 ft). The trail right travels 3.5 miles along Snider Ridge to connect with the Mount Muller Loop (Hike 105). Head left, breaking out into a wildflower-studded meadow beneath the knob that once supported the lookout. Make one last short, steep climb to arrive at a picnic table, privy, and the lookout site on a ledge at the edge of the long ridge (elev. 3160 ft).

You may have company, as the lookout site can also be reached via rough Forest Road 3040 and FR Spur 595 from the Snider Work Center. More than likely, though, you'll have the viewing platform to yourself.

Scan the Sol Duc Valley from craggy Mount Appleton and the snow-patched High Divide all the way to the Pacific. A blanket of clouds on the western horizon marks the coastline. On a clear day you can see James Island near La Push. That big snow- and glacier-covered mountain to the south is Olympus, of course.

EXTENDING YOUR TRIP

Walk east along FR Spur 595 for 0.4 mile toward North Point. Then follow a trail right that leads 0.2 mile to a junction. Hike right 0.6 mile, skirting cliffs to return to the Kloshe Nanitch Trail. Or hike left 2.9 miles, dropping to a 2850-foot gap before climbing 500 feet to a grassy open knoll. Then it's an up-and-down ridgeline hike through old growth, sprawling meadows, and along cliffs and basalt outcroppings to Jims Junction on the Mount Muller Loop (Hike 105). The views are copious and spectacular.

107 Aurora Ridge and Eagle Lakes

RATING/ DIFFICULTY	ROUNDTRIP	ELEV GAIN/ HIGH POINT	SEASON
***/3	12.2 miles	2765 feet/ 3470 feet	June–Nov

Maps: Green Trails Lake Crescent No. 101, Custom Correct Lake Crescent–Happy Lake Ridge; **Contact:** Olympic National Park, Wilderness Information Center; **Notes:** National park entrance fee. Dogs prohibited; **GPS:** N 48 03.707, W 123 59.661

Despite easy access, Aurora Ridge is one of the least hiked trails in Olympic National Park. Wind through a forested tunnel up this long, lumpy emerald divide between the Sol Duc and Lake Crescent valleys. Then drop into a hidden bowl that cradles the spring-fed, green-tinted Eagle Lakes. While this hike lacks views, it abounds with solitude.

GETTING THERE

From Port Angeles, follow US Highway 101 west for 29 miles and turn left onto the Sol Duc Hot Springs Road (about 2 miles beyond the Fairholm store). Then drive 2.5 miles (passing the park entrance station) to the trailhead (elev. 1300 ft), on the left.

ON THE TRAIL

The way starts on an old logging road lined with alders and often brushy. After about 1 mile, the trail begins to climb more steadily, switch backing through open forest. First primarily hemlocks, then Douglas-firs, the old trees are pretty uniform. The way makes a few dips on its continuous climb. The grade is moderate and the tread is soft, making for enjoyable walking.

While the forest canopy is thick, occasional small breaks provide window views of Mount Muller, Pyramid Mountain, and Lake Crescent. At about 3.5 miles, the trail crests a knob and descends 100 feet into a saddle. It then steeply climbs through ancient forest

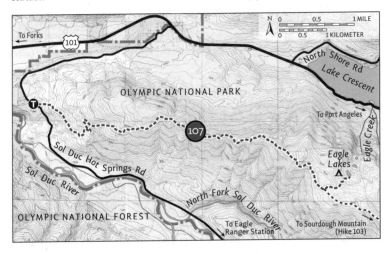

Upper Eagle Lake

groves graced with abundant huckleberry bushes. At 5 miles, round a 3470-foot shoulder. Then drop 120 feet, regain some lost elevation, and come to a junction (elev. 3425 ft) at 5.5 miles.

Go left and climb a little to the edge of the forested ridge. Then steeply descend, coming to a spring that feeds cascading waters into the upper and largest of the three little Eagle Lakes. At 6.1 miles, the trail ends at a campsite (elev. 3050 ft) near the upper lake's inlet. Stay for a while, relishing solitude and staring out over greenish waters to a shoreline of towering old timber. Perhaps the lakes' namesakes will be perched in one of the trees. The other two lakes lie below, deep in the woods—best for woodland critters to explore. Rest up for the return.

EXTENDING YOUR TRIP

For even deeper solitude, keep hiking east on the Aurora Ridge Trail over more knolls shrouded in primeval forest and across a few small meadows granting good views south. In 2.9 miles, reach the spur (elev. 4275 ft) for Sourdough Mountain (Hike 103).

108 North Fork Sol Duc River

RATING/ DIFFICULTY	ROUNDTRIP	ELEV GAIN/ HIGH POINT	SEASON
***/3	12.4 miles	1300 feet/ 2400 feet	Apr–Nov

Maps: Green Trails Seven Lakes Basin–Mt Olympus Climbing No. 133S, Custom Correct Lake Crescent–Happy Lake Ridge; **Contact:** Olympic National Park, Wilderness Information Center; **Notes:** National park entrance fee. Dogs prohibited. Ford required, usually easy by late summer, but potentially dangerous late fall–spring; **GPS:** N 48 00.645, W 123 54.660

A stark contrast from the busy Sol Duc River valley, the North Fork Sol Duc Valley is one of the least hiked routes in the park. An early river ford is part of the reason. But once across, you can traipse through miles of lonely old growth—all the way to a restored shelter if you care to. A handful of elk may greet you along the way.

GETTING THERE

From Port Angeles, follow US Highway 101 west for 29 miles and turn left onto the Sol Duc Hot Springs Road (about 2 miles beyond the Fairholm store). Then drive 8.1 miles (pass the park entrance station) to the trailhead (elev. 1500 ft). Park on the right side of the road; the trail begins on the opposite side.

Hiker at the East Branch Sol Duc River crossing

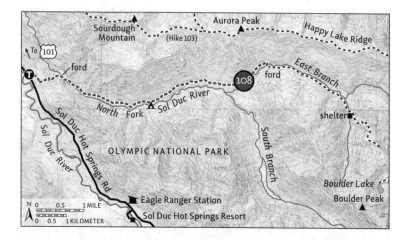

ON THE TRAIL

The trail starts from an overlook above the Sol Duc River. The North Fork is nowhere to be found. It's hidden behind a small ridge. Start by heading up that obstacle through a forest of hemlocks interspersed with a few big Douglas-firs. After a climb of about 300 feet, start descending, reaching the North Fork Sol Duc (elev. 1530 ft) at 0.9 mile.

If the river is not running too high, choose a spot to ford about 1000 feet downstream from the rapids where the river fans out. Once across, resume less nerve-wracking hiking through mossy maple glades, under towering conifers, and along basalt ledges lapped by the river.

At 1.2 miles, cross a careening tributary. Then pass some large Sitka spruces and grassy openings where big game is frequently sighted. At about 3 miles, come to a riverside campsite, perfect for snacking or calling it quits if you prefer a shorter hike.

If wanderlust persists, carry on. After passing a few big mossy boulders, the trail moves away from the riverbank, climbing

above it on a steep slope. The river can now be heard crashing through a canyon, while you traverse a stately forest of Douglas-firs. As you hike deeper into the lonely valley, you'll need to cross numerous side creeks, and a few may leave your boots a tad wet.

At 6.2 miles, the trail drops into a dark, cool ravine and heads back down to the river, now the East Branch North Fork (elev. 2400 ft). You can ford it and continue, but most day hikers will be content turning around here.

EXTENDING YOUR TRIP

Continue upriver, steeply climbing into a tighter canyon. The trail is rough but has received some recent maintenance. You'll need to cross the river three more times—the second crossing easy to miss, the final one via a log. At about 9.2 miles, reach the restored North Fork Shelter (elev. 3000 ft). From here the trail is littered with blowdowns and steeply climbs, terminating (elev. 4100 ft) at about 10.6 miles shortly after passing an old milepost 11. Slated to connect with the Happy Lake Ridge Trail, it was never completed. Experienced off-trail travelers can continue through open forest up steep slopes to reach that trail in about 0.6 mile.

Sol Duc Falls Loop

RATING/ DIFFICULTY	LOOP	ELEV GAIN/ HIGH POINT	SEASON
**/1	5.5 miles	400 feet/ 2000 feet	Mar–Nov

Maps: Green Trails Seven Lakes Basin–Mt Olympus Climbing No. 133S, Custom Correct Seven Lakes Basin–Hoh; **Contact:** Olympic National Park, Wilderness Information Center; **Notes:** National park entrance fee. Dogs prohibited; **GPS:** N 47 58.200, W 123 51.763

This easy loop from the Sol Duc Hot Springs Resort is perfect for hikers of all ages and best done in the spring. Ramble beneath towering old trees to a misty, mossy ravine that the Sol Duc River careens into. Marvel at the thundering falls and watch dippers hunt for insects in the splash zone.

GETTING THERE

From Port Angeles, follow US Highway 101 west for 29 miles and turn left onto the Sol Duc Hot Springs Road (about 2 miles beyond the Fairholm store). Then drive 12 miles (passing the park entrance station) and turn right just beyond the Eagle Ranger Station. Continue 0.1 mile to trailhead parking (elev. 1630 ft) just west of the Sol Duc Hot Springs Resort main lodge.

ON THE TRAIL

The first 0.6 mile of this loop is a social hike through the resort and national park campgrounds. Start by walking the road back toward the ranger station and over a

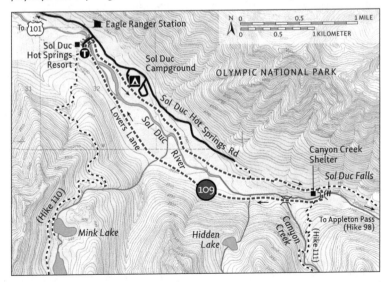

Sol Duc Falls

bridge spanning the Sol Duc (elev. 1620 ft). Then immediately pick up a trail that takes off to the right. Closely following the river, first travel through the resort's RV park and then emerge in the lower loop of the Sol Duc Campground.

Follow the campground loop road a short distance, picking up the trail again and following it to the upper loop of the campground. Then, once again, walk a short distance on pavement to pick up the trail. Now through big timber, saunter 1.3 pleasant miles to a junction. The trail left leads 0.2 mile to a large parking lot—where most of the people you'll now encounter have come from to see the falls.

Continue to the right on a well-trodden, near-level path, coming to a junction (elev. 2000 ft) at a recently restored Civilian Conservation Corps–built shelter at 2.5 miles.

Bear right toward the thundering sound of swiftly moving water barreling over a ledge. Hike down to a mist-sprayed bridge and admire below the fanning Sol Duc Falls crashing 50 feet into a narrow chasm where the sun rarely shines.

After enjoying the spectacle, continue hiking, reaching a junction (elev. 1960 ft) on a small bluff at 2.7 miles. Hang a right onto Lovers Lane, although it's open to all—lovelorn, loveless, and loved alike. Hike along the edge of the chasm hiding the Sol Duc River and soon cross cascading Canyon Creek on a log bridge. Then follow the peaceful path through lush bottomlands and groves of impressive ancient trees, crossing a couple more crashing tributaries. The trail briefly skirts alongside the river before scooting around the resort, where your nose will catch the pungent smell of sulfur. Bear right at a junction to reach the resort and your car.

EXTENDING YOUR TRIP

Beyond the falls, the Sol Duc River Trail travels through deep primeval forest for almost 5 miles (gaining only 1400 feet in elevation) to routes leading to Appleton Pass and the High Divide.

110 Mink Lake and Little Divide

Mink Lake

RATING/ DIFFICULTY	ROUNDTRIP	ELEV GAIN/ HIGH POINT	SEASON
**/2	5.2 miles	1470 feet/ 3100 feet	May–Nov

Little Divide

RATING/ DIFFICULTY	ROUNDTRIP	ELEV GAIN/ HIGH POINT	SEASON
***/4	10.6 miles	2900 feet/ 4225 feet	Late June–Oct

Maps: Green Trails Seven Lakes Basin–Mt Olympus Climbing No. 133S, Custom Correct Seven Lakes Basin–Hoh; **Contact:** Olympic National Park, Wilderness Information Center; **Notes:** National park entrance fee. Dogs prohibited; **GPS:** N 47 58.213, W 123 51.908

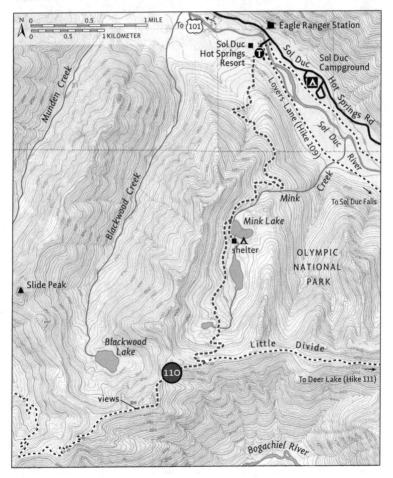

Hike to a quiet backcountry lake ringed with grassy meadows and big trees, or break a sweat to the Little Divide, the loneliest outpost in Sol Duc country. You're far more likely to encounter deer, elk, and bears than fellow hikers in this neck of the Sol Duc.

Mink Lake

GETTING THERE

From Port Angeles, follow US Highway 101 west for 29 miles and turn left onto the Sol Duc Hot Springs Road (about 2 miles beyond the Fairholm store). Then drive 12 miles (passing the park entrance station) and turn right just beyond the Eagle Ranger Station.

Continue 0.1 mile to trailhead parking (elev. 1630 ft) just west of the Sol Duc Hot Springs Resort main lodge.

ON THE TRAIL

Mink Lake: Start in cool second-growth timber, bearing right at a junction. The trail left leads 2.8 easy miles to Sol Duc Falls. Your route follows an old road and then good tread, soon entering mature woods. Winding above the Sol Duc Valley, the trail rounds a knoll and then tags along Mink Creek as it weasels its way to its source. At 2.5 miles, come to a junction (elev. 3100 ft)— a side trail leads left 0.1 mile to campsites, lunch spots, and a historical shelter on Mink Lake's grassy and sunny southern shore. Darting dragonflies provide captivating air shows.

Little Divide: If you're not content to sit by this placid lake, cinch up your pack and continue hiking. Now on much lighter tread, hike past another quiet, grassy-shored lake, this one partially hidden in thick woods. Continue up the trail through thinning forest, which reveals a tiny pool off to the right surrounded by heather.

The way then steeply climbs, leaving the Mink Creek drainage. Look back for a nice view of the lake with Aurora Ridge in the distance. Through heather and huckleberry, the trail attains Little Divide (elev. 4080 ft) at a junction with the Bogachiel River Trail at 4.3 miles. Walk to the right along a hogback ridge, cresting a 4150-foot knoll before dropping to a 4000-foot saddle with window views of remote Blackwood Lake below. Hike a little farther to a 4225-foot knoll at 5.3 miles, where wildflower meadows and good views down to the emerald Bogachiel Valley and out to snowy Mount Olympus should suffice. Beyond, the trail descends, so return the way you came.

EXTENDING YOUR TRIP

From the junction on Little Divide, you can continue east along the Bogachiel River Trail, passing lonely meadows and tarns. The way drops 400 feet, climbs 350 feet, and then drops again to reach Deer Lake (Hike 111)

in 3.6 miles. Then follow the Deer Lake Trail to Lovers Lane and back to your start for a 13.6-mile loop.

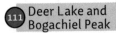

111 Deer Lake and Bogachiel Peak

Deer Lake

RATING/ DIFFICULTY	ROUNDTRIP	ELEV GAIN/ HIGH POINT	SEASON
***/3	7.4 miles	1650 feet/ 3520 feet	June–Nov

Bogachiel Peak

RATING/ DIFFICULTY	ROUNDTRIP	ELEV GAIN/ HIGH POINT	SEASON
*****/5	16.2 miles	3675 feet/ 5474 feet	Mid-July– Oct

Maps: Green Trails Seven Lakes Basin–Mt Olympus Climbing No. 133S, Custom Correct Seven Lakes Basin–Hoh; **Contact:** Olympic National Park, Wilderness Information Center; **Notes:** National park entrance fee. Dogs prohibited; **GPS:** N 47 57.310, W 123 50.103

A moderately difficult hike to a large subalpine lake or an all-day challenging grunt to perhaps the most beautiful viewpoint in the Olympics. This is the famed High Divide country, a land of sparkling alpine lakes, resplendent alpine meadows, and awe-inspiring alpine views. Usually reserved for backpackers, strong and tenacious day hikers can get a small taste.

GETTING THERE

From Port Angeles, follow US Highway 101 west for 29 miles and turn left onto the Sol Duc Hot Springs Road (about 2 miles beyond the Fairholm store). Then drive 14 miles (passing the park entrance station) to a large trailhead parking lot (elev. 1900 ft). Privy available.

ON THE TRAIL

Deer Lake: Start off easy enough on a 0.8-mile nearly level sojourn through spectacular old growth to pretty Sol Duc Falls. Then it's time to work. Cross the Sol Duc, pass Lovers Lane, and commence climbing. On a steep, sometimes rocky path, work your way up the dark ravine housing Canyon Creek. At 1.8 miles, cross high above the tumbling waterway on a sturdy bridge. After another 0.5 mile, the grade eases somewhat.

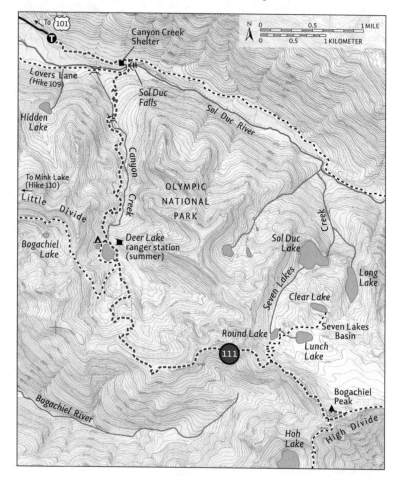

Mount Olympus rising behind the High Divide

Pass three backcountry campsites and then, after another push, cross Canyon Creek once more, this time at the outlet to Deer Lake (elev. 3520 ft). Set in a forested and grassy bowl, the lake's waters reflect a soft green. This is a pretty and serene spot, surrounded by yellow cedars, mountain hemlocks, silver firs, and a thick understory of huckleberries. The lake's namesakes often browse along the shore.

At 3.7 miles, you'll find a backcountry ranger station and multiple campsites. A rough 0.4-mile path circles the lake and reveals a smaller hidden "fawn" lake. Call it a day at the lake or carry on to higher ground.

Bogachiel Peak: Continue past Deer Lake and bear left at a junction. Right leads to Little Divide (Hike 110) and the path around Deer Lake. To the left, head up and wind through open heather fields, through subalpine forest, and past a dozen pothole tarns (aka mosquito incubators). The trail works its way up to the high ridge dividing the Sol Duc and Bogachiel watersheds.

Above the potholes, enjoy far-reaching views across rainforest valleys all the way to the Pacific. As you're hiking, look trailside for what veteran guidebook writer Robert Wood called the snake pit—a cluster of contorted mountain hemlocks resembling a serpentine lair.

The trail soon tops the ridge crest, working its way around a high isolated basin, headwaters of the Bogachiel River. Mount Olympus peeks its icy head over the next ridge, and Bogachiel Peak—still a ways away—beckons. In September, you'll often hear bugling elk from below. And it's not unusual to run into berry-munching bears, so be aware.

At 7 miles, drop into a big rocky depression (elev. 4840 ft). A trail descends left to Seven Lakes Basin, one of the prettiest spots this side of Shangri-la. Continue right, and angle around Bogachiel Basin on steep slopes. Snow often persists well into summer here, making it potentially dangerous to proceed. After a series of tight switchbacks, reach a 5300-foot gap with views into the lake basin. Then at 7.9 miles, come to a junction with the High Divide Trail (elev. 5225 ft).

Head left for 0.1 mile to a junction and then left again 0.1 mile to attain 5474-foot Bogachiel Peak, a former lookout site. The views are beyond breathtaking: The alpine jewels of the Seven Lakes Basin shimmer below. The snowcapped Bailey Range marches off into the eastern horizon. The emerald swath of the Hoh Rain Forest spreads out nearly 1 vertical mile below. And rising above it all, staring you right in the face, is Mount Olympus. Its glaciers and snowfields are blinding on a sunny summer day.

EXTENDING YOUR TRIP

Very strong day hikers can continue east for 2 up-and-down miles on the High Divide Trail and return to the trailhead via the 8.5-mile Sol Duc River Trail, for a grand 18.7-mile loop.

Opposite: Queets River at crossing for Smith Place

olympic peninsula: west

The Rain Forests

Temperate rain forests are one of the Olympic Peninsula's most famous attractions, offering one of the country's most unique hiking experiences. Such forests are found only in Chile, New Zealand, and the Pacific Northwest, and those of Olympic National Park are perhaps the most accessible. Good trails lead to and through all of the major rainforest valleys.

Here you'll hike among some of the largest living organisms in the world. While tropical rain forests rank supreme in biodiversity (number of species), the temperate rain forests of the Olympic Peninsula contain the highest amount of biomass (living matter) on the planet. Giant conifers cloaked in epiphytes and growing upward of 300 feet dominate a forest floor saturated with mosses, ferns, horsetails, and ground pines.

The damp, heavy air of the rain forest teems with spores. Hike into this special environment and you can feel the forest breathe. Sense its pulse. Grasp its fortitude.

And though over 200 inches of rain fall annually in parts of this region, sunshine is not unusual. Days are often dry in August and September—the dry season—and it's not uncommon to get a reprieve from the wet in the middle of winter. Pack sunglasses with your poncho and waterproof those boots—there are miles of trails to explore in this fascinating bioregion.

112 North Snider–Jackson Trail

RATING/ DIFFICULTY	ROUNDTRIP	ELEV GAIN/ HIGH POINT	SEASON
***/3	6 miles	1600 feet/ 1675 feet	June–Oct

Author at Calawah River Ford

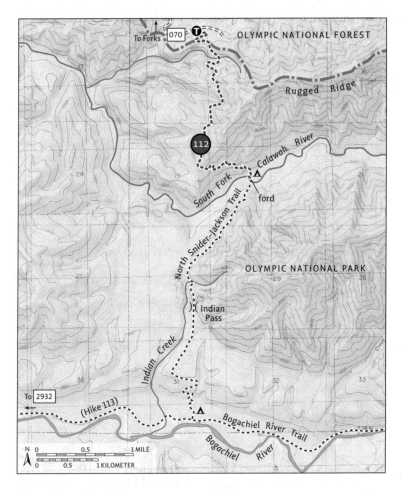

Maps: Green Trails Spruce Mountain No. 132, Custom Correct Bogachiel Valley; **Contact:** Olympic National Park, Wilderness Information Center; **Notes:** Dogs prohibited. Ford at 3 miles may be dangerous or impassable in high water; **GPS:** N 47 56.281, W 124 10.068

Follow a portion of the historical Snider–Jackson Trail that once ran along the Olympic National Forest boundary from Jackson Guard Station (Hoh River) to Snider Guard Station (Sol Duc River). As you hike along appropriately named Rugged

Ridge, marvel at old-growth giants. Then drop deep into a remote valley that embraces the South Fork Calawah River.

GETTING THERE

From Forks, travel north for 1.9 miles on US Highway 101 and turn right just past the State Route 110 junction onto Sitkum–Sol Duc Road (which becomes Forest Road 29). Follow this road 11.1 miles (the pavement ends at 5.4 miles), bearing right onto unsigned FR Spur 070. Cross the Sitkum River on a high bridge and continue 2.2 miles to the trailhead (elev. 1125 ft) at the road's end.

ON THE TRAIL

From the indiscreet trailhead, gently climb through primeval forest and at 0.4 mile enter Olympic National Park. Shortly afterward begin a 100-foot descent into a small ravine, passing some of the biggest and oldest cedars and Douglas-firs anywhere in the park. Cross a creek—one of many along the way—and steeply climb out of the ravine.

The way then stays below the crest of Rugged Ridge, traversing steep side slopes and ledges shaded by luxurious old-growth forest. Dart in and out of ravines, some fed by cascading creeks. Pass monstrous firs, standing and fallen, and one particularly colossal cedar. Note the insulators, hammered into some of the trees, that once carried communications lines along this historical trail.

At about 1.7 miles, the trail crests its high point (elev. 1675 ft) and then begins a steep descent into the South Fork Calawah River valley. Pass more humongous firs and cedars—and spruces too—as you drop farther into the valley. At 3 miles, reach the river (elev. 800 ft) and a couple of camps. For most day hikers, this is far enough. Spend some time on a gravel bar before making the rugged return.

EXTENDING YOUR TRIP

By late summer, the river is usually just ankle-deep, making for an easy ford. The trail resumes across the river, just left of a huge fallen cedar. Then on lightly traveled tread the trail climbs, with a few dips along the way, to an 1100-foot point above low Indian Pass. The forest is open, the spruces are enormous, and elk are abundant. The way then traverses a big flat, passing a large blowdown area. It then descends via switchbacks, reaching the Bogachiel River Trail (Hike 113) at 6.3 miles. If you can arrange a car shuttle, hike the Bogachiel River Trail west 5.8 miles to its trailhead at FR 2932.

113 Bogachiel River

RATING/ DIFFICULTY	ROUNDTRIP	ELEV GAIN/ HIGH POINT	SEASON
***/3	12 miles	550 feet/ 460 feet	Year-round

Maps: Green Trails Spruce Mountain No. 132, Custom Correct Bogachiel Valley; **Contact:** Olympic National Park, Wilderness Information Center; **Notes:** Dogs prohibited at park boundary. Open to horses; **GPS:** N 47 52.931, W 124 16.524

The Bogachiel River snakes through Washington's forgotten rain forest. No main roads run along this major Olympic river, nor do any penetrate its wild valley—all the better to experience the tranquility of towering spruces and firs. Hike all day along the wild waterway for several miles, or wander on a wonderful short interpretive loop.

GETTING THERE

From Forks, travel south for 5.5 miles on US Highway 101. Turn left onto Undie Road (Forest Road 2932), located at milepost 186 directly across from the entrance to Bogachiel State Park. Follow this road for 5.3 miles (the pavement ends at 3.3 miles) to the trailhead (elev. 460 ft). Note: Road is currently closed due to wash-out.

ON THE TRAIL

Start your hike by steeply descending. Then cross Morganroth Creek on a footlog and reach a junction (elev. 325 ft) at 0.2 mile. Ira Spring Wetland Trail No. 825.1 departs left here. Named for one of Washington's greatest trail advocates, this wonderful kid- and dog-friendly interpretive trail skirts a large wetland and meets back up with the Bogachiel Trail in 1.4 miles, to form a 2.9-mile loop.

Bogachiel River Trail No. 825 continues right, coming to another junction at 0.3 mile. Here, Homestead Loop Trail No 825.2 departs right. This 0.3-mile trail passes through the 1890 homestead of Chris Morgenroth, who chronicled his pioneer life in *Footprints in the Olympics: An Autobiography.*

Take the loop or stay left on the main trail, which utilizes an old roadbed. Much of the surrounding forest was logged during the 1940s in the name of national defense. But you'll soon reach old growth and giant spruces. The near-level trail brushes up along the wide river, offering plenty of places to explore—gravel bars and sunny (when it's not raining) riverbanks.

Stay right at the second junction with the Ira Spring Wetland Trail, rock hop over Kahkwa Creek, and reach the national park boundary at 1.6 miles. Then hike alongside channels and across bottomlands. At about 2.8 miles, after passing a horse bypass trail,

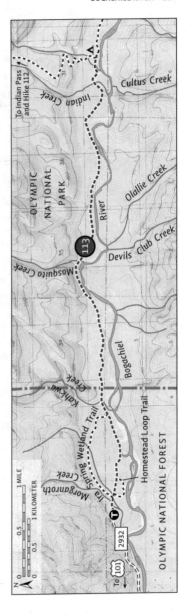

Gravel bar along the Bogachiel River

negotiate a steep bluff (with the help of a rope) to skirt an area claimed by the river. Drop back down to river level and get your feet wet again hopping across Mosquito Creek. Traverse flats of alders and groves of big old trees. Keep your eyes peeled for elk—they're legion in this valley.

Cross small creeks on bridges, in between going up and down small rises in the wide valley. Except for the river's soothing churn and sweet serenades from resident wrens, the primeval forest is quiet. Lichens drape overhead. Fern boughs burst open from the forest floor. Dew-dripping moss clings to everything. Only the glaucous sheen of alder bark breaks the deep green of the rain forest.

At 4.6 miles, hop or wade across Indian Creek. Then traverse a flat teeming with monster spruces and Douglas-firs. At 5.8 miles, come to a post marking the junction with the North Snider–Jackson Trail (Hike 112). Here, a spur path also leads right, to the river. Continue straight instead for another 0.2 mile to the site of the old Bogachiel Guard Station (elev. 450 ft), where you'll find riverside campsites and some great lounging spots. Sit for a while before making the return.

EXTENDING YOUR TRIP

The Bogachiel River Trail continues deep into the Olympic backcountry for another 21.5 miles, giving strong day hikers and backpackers a lot of room to roam.

114 South Snider–Jackson Trail

RATING/ DIFFICULTY	ROUNDTRIP	ELEV GAIN/ HIGH POINT	SEASON
***/4	10.4 miles	3000 feet/ 3200 feet	Apr–Nov

Maps: Green Trails Spruce Mountain No. 132, Custom Correct Bogachiel Valley; **Contact:** Olympic National Park, Wilderness Information Center; **Notes:** Dogs prohibited.; **GPS:** N 47 49.215, W 124 01.324

Hike a steep ridge shrouded in a canopy of ancient timber and experience the world-famous Hoh Rain Forest valley from above. This is a tough hike and views are sparse. But you can marvel at monstrous trees in solitude—something you can't do in the popular valley below.

GETTING THERE

From Forks, travel south on US Highway 101 for 13 miles and turn left onto Upper Hoh Road. (From Kalaloch, head north on US 101 for 20 miles and turn right onto Upper Hoh Road.) Then drive 12.8 miles to a parking area on your right just before the park entrance station (elev. 450 ft). Privy available.

Towering old growth on the South Snider–Jackson Trail

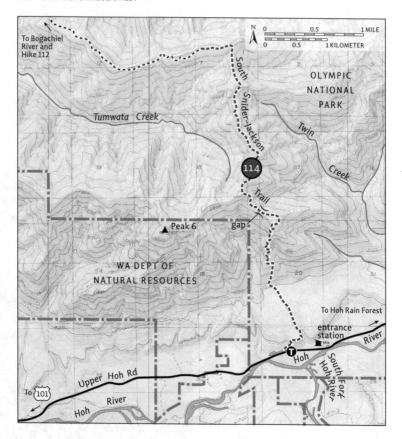

ON THE TRAIL

Carefully walk the road west for 0.1 mile to the trailhead, located on your right (on the north side of the road). Cross a slough and begin to climb. The historical Snider–Jackson Trail once ran from the Jackson Guard Station (now the Hoh Ranger Station) to the Snider Guard Station in the Sol Duc Valley. This route was threatened with abandonment, but the Washington Trails Association helped resurrect it in the early 2000s. Maintenance is light, however, so you may encounter obstacles.

After an initial climb, traverse a broad bench that has several large areas of windfall. Then steeply and steadily climb the ridge complex that divides the Hoh and Bogachiel watersheds. Pass one of the biggest fir snags anywhere and then gigantic complete firs. Gaps in the thick canopy allow some viewing of the valley below and of Mounts Tom and Olympus in the distance.

At around 3 miles, after cresting a shoulder, slightly descend into a 2550-foot saddle, where you'll get limited views west of cutover Peak 6. Then resume steep climbing, first through silver fir forest and then hemlocks. The way angles up a narrow ridge that separates Tumwata and Twin creeks, which you can often hear flowing below. Elk sign is prolific, indicating an abundance of the ungulates here.

Drop 100 feet into another saddle, climb and skirt a knob, and then drop 100 feet again to yet another saddle. Then continue upward on a much gentler trajectory. The way ascends a long, broad ridge and bends left. At about 5.2 miles, the trail reaches its high point (elev. 3200 ft) and begins to descend, making this a good place to call it quits. Turn around and enjoy the descent.

EXTENDING YOUR TRIP
Strong day hikers and backpackers can continue another 4.5 miles on a long descent to the Bogachiel River. From there the trail heads west 2.3 miles along the river, fords it (safe only during low flows), and meets the Bogachiel River Trail 3 miles east of the North Snider–Jackson Trail junction (Hike 112).

115 Hoh Rain Forest and Five Mile Island

RATING/ DIFFICULTY	ROUNDTRIP	ELEV GAIN/ HIGH POINT	SEASON
****/2	10.6 miles	300 feet/ 770 feet	Year-round

Maps: Green Trails Seven Lakes Basin/ Hoh River Trail No. 133S, Custom Correct Seven Lakes Basin–Hoh; **Contact:** Olympic National Park, Wilderness Information

Hoh River

Center; **Notes:** National park entrance fee. Dogs prohibited; **GPS:** N 47 51.628, W. 123 56.063

One of the most popular places in Olympic National Park, the Hoh Valley is where most hikers get their first taste of a temperate rain forest. The visitors center and a couple of well-groomed nature trails attract busloads of admirers from around the world. The Hoh Rain Forest truly is one of the world's most spectacular places, and you only need to hike a few miles upvalley to fully appreciate it.

GETTING THERE
From Forks, travel south on US Highway 101 for 13 miles and turn left onto Upper Hoh

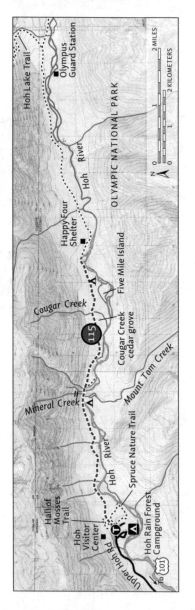

Road. (From Kalaloch, head north on US 101 for 20 miles and turn right onto Upper Hoh Road.) Then drive 18 miles to its end at the Hoh Visitor Center and trailhead (elev. 620 ft). Water and restrooms available.

ON THE TRAIL

This trip to Five Mile Island is far enough to experience the old-growth grandeur and wildness of this valley, yet close enough for most hikers to achieve, whether young or old. The trail is impeccably groomed and virtually level. While most hikers visit the Hoh Valley in the summer and autumn, consider coming in the spring or even winter for a more sedate experience. Aside from far fewer people in the off-season, chances are good of seeing the resident elk herd.

Start by following the paved Hall of Mosses Trail for 0.2 mile to a junction. Then on bona fide tread, begin your journey through primeval forest. Listen for a cacophony of birdsong from wrens, nuthatches, woodpeckers, chickadees, and thrushes, audible over the distant hum of the river. Pass by colonnades of spruces and under awnings of moss-cloaked maples. Licorice ferns and club mosses cling to overhanging trees like holiday decorations on Fifth Avenue in New York. Even in these lush surroundings, the understory is fairly open, thanks to browsing elk that keep the shrubs and bushes well trimmed.

At 1.5 miles, get your first unobstructed view of the river. Gaze out to the emerald High Divide and snowcapped Mount Tom, a peak on the Olympus massif. Pass the Mount Tom Creek campsite at 2.5 miles, and then climb above the river, catching glimpses of deep emerald pools below. Cross Mineral Creek near a lovely cascade. Soon after, another cascade delights. At 2.7 miles, come to a junction with the Mount Tom Trail. If you'd like, follow this path right 0.2 mile to open gravel bars and spectacular valley views.

Veering away from the river, the main path continues upriver. Traverse impressive stands of Sitka spruces and at 4.2 miles come to the Cougar Creek cedar grove. Stand in awe amid these trees, older than the great cathedrals of Europe—and just as inspiring. At 5.3 miles, arrive at Five Mile Island (elev. 770 ft) and its campsites. Formed by river channels, the island is an inviting, grassy bottomland graced with maple glades. Enjoy views up the valley all the way to Bogachiel Peak. If it's raining, the nearby Happy Four Shelter provides cover for your lunchtime break.

EXTENDING YOUR TRIP

The trail continues for 12 more miles to Glacier Meadows at the base of Mount Olympus. That's for backpackers, but strong day hikers may want to continue another 3.6 miles to the historical Olympus Guard Station (elev. 950 ft). And by all means check out the 0.8-mile Hall of Mosses and 1.3-mile Spruce Nature trails on your return, to gain a better appreciation of this fascinating corner of the planet.

116 South Fork Hoh River and Big Flat

RATING/ DIFFICULTY	ROUNDTRIP	ELEV GAIN/ HIGH POINT	SEASON
***/2	8.2 miles	500 feet/ 820 feet	Year-round

Maps: Green Trails Mt Tom No. 133, Custom Correct Mount Olympus Climber's Map; **Contact:** Olympic National Park, Wilderness Information Center; **Notes:** Discover Pass required. Dogs prohibited; **GPS:** N 47 47.954, W 123 57.247

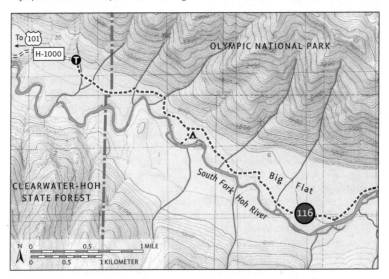

South Hoh River near trail's end

![family icon] ![pinecone icon] *If your idea of experiencing the Olympic rain forest is sans bucketloads of people, cast your attention to the Hoh's little known South Fork. Local fly fishermen and -women are familiar with this wild and lonely valley, but most hikers aren't. Getting to the trailhead can be confusing, but the hike is easy. The payoff is solitude.*

GETTING THERE

From Forks, travel south on US Highway 101 for 15.5 miles and turn left at milepost 176 onto Clearwater Road (aka Hoh Mainline), just beyond a bridge over the Hoh River. Proceed on this paved road for 6.9 miles and turn left onto South Fork Hoh Road. Then drive 2.3 miles and bear right onto Maple Creek Road (H-1000), following signs for the South Fork Hoh Campground. After 5.4 miles (the pavement ends in 0.3 mile), cross the South Fork Hoh River and pass the campground entrance. Continue on H-1000 for another 2.6 rough miles to the trailhead (elev. 780 ft) at the road's end.

ON THE TRAIL

The trail starts on state forest land that has been intensively logged over the decades. Through scrappy trees choked in mosses, descend 100 feet to a flat outwash area. Cross numerous streams and after 0.5 mile reach the national park boundary.

Then hike past old-growth giants as you climb 125 feet onto a bench. Gargantuan Douglas-firs, western hemlocks, and Sitka spruces tower above you like skyscrapers in an ecotopian Manhattan. Drop into a ravine and make a tricky crossing of a rocky creek. Then climb again and begin descending under a canopy of ancient giants.

At 1.4 miles, reach a lush bottomland known as Big Flat (elev. 730 ft), complete with backcountry campsites. A side path diverts right for 0.15 mile to open gravel banks on the South Fork Hoh. The main trail continues left through grassy swales, through maple glades, and alongside colonnades of towering ancient Sitka spruces. At 2 miles, the trail finally greets the river.

Soon afterward, you'll come to a large washout, but the trail has been rerouted around it. Enjoy good views of Owl Mountain in the Clearwater-Hoh State Forest and surrounding peaks in the national park. Then cross a lazy side creek on a sturdy log. Next, enjoy easy walking through spruce flats as the trail pulls away from the river. One gargantuan spruce sports some hitchhiking hemlocks.

The way eventually reaches a grassy open flat and once again approaches the river, offering nice lounging spots. The trail continues a little farther, squeezing through boulders lodged along the riverbank at the base of steep slopes, until it peters out at 4.1 miles (elev. 820 ft). Enjoy the peaceful return.

117 Queets River

RATING/ DIFFICULTY	ROUNDTRIP	ELEV GAIN/ HIGH POINT	SEASON
****/4	10.6 miles	300 feet/ 450 feet	Late July– Sept

Maps: Green Trails Kloochman Rock No. 165, Custom Correct Queets Valley; **Contact:** Olympic National Park, Wilderness Information Center; **Notes:** Dogs prohibited. Queets River ford required, only safe during low flows (typically in late summer) and even then often challenging.; **GPS:** N 47 37.481, W 124 00.881

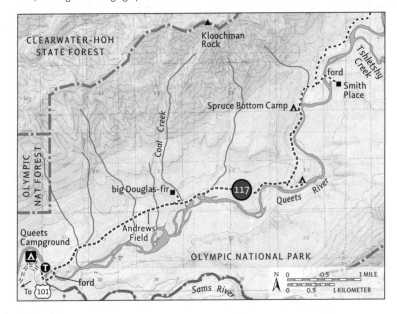

Hiker fording the Queets River

Though the Queets is the peninsula's wildest rainforest valley, many a hiker has never ventured into this enchanting corner of Olympic National Park. The main deterrent is the intimidating and often challenging ford of the Queets River at the trailhead. But for those who venture across this wild waterway, a wilderness valley of abandoned homesteads, mossy maple groves, towering evergreens, and prolific elk await.

GETTING THERE

From Hoquiam, travel north on US Highway 101 for 50 miles. (From Forks, travel south on US 101 for 53 miles.) Turn right onto paved Forest Road 21 and proceed for 8.1 miles, bearing left onto graveled FR 2180. Continue for 1.3 miles and turn left onto FR Spur 011. Follow this road 1.4 miles to Upper Queets Road and turn right. Proceed 3.3 miles to the road's end and trailhead (elev. 290 ft). Privy available.

ON THE TRAIL

From the trailhead, walk 0.1 mile south on the Sams River Trail (Hike 118) to a junction. Head left 0.1 mile, dropping off the riverbank onto a wide graveled outwash and coming to the confluence of the Sams and Queets rivers. It's best to ford the Sams River first and then scout around for a wide ford of the Queets above the confluence. Both crossings can be intimidating, but in the drier months of August and September the rivers are usually only knee-deep. A set of old running shoes for the river's slippery rocks and sturdy trekking poles should help get you across. Do not attempt to cross early in the season or after periods of heavy rain. If the ford looks unfavorable, opt for the Sams River Trail instead.

Once you've crossed the wide river, find the trail and get ready to experience a wilderness Olympic valley the way it should be experienced—crowds in absentia. Giant firs, towering spruces, and humongous hemlocks 200-plus-feet tall and several hundred years old humble your stature and status. Moss-draped maples and lichen-blotched alders line the trail. Boughs of ferns 4 feet tall crowd the understory. Still, though the Queets is a wilderness, humans have been here for centuries. Native Americans have long hunted in this remote valley. A few hardy pioneers homesteaded it.

At 1.9 miles, reach Andrews Field, an old homestead, where a dilapidated barn is quickly fading into the annals of history. Look up at Kloochman Rock, an old lookout site once reached by a trail from this valley. Then traverse the small thistle-sprouting clearing and reenter woods. The trail is in excellent shape having received much-needed maintenance in the summer of 2015 to help firefighters reach the upper portions of this valley.

At 2.6 miles, come to a log crossing of Coal Creek. Just to the west a now almost completely vanished trail leads left 0.2 mile to what was once one of the biggest Douglas-firs in the world until its top was knocked off in a storm. With a trunk 14 feet around, this tree began its life sometime around the first millennium.

The Queets River Trail continues straight through lush bottomlands, through magnificent maple glades, and along the river, coming to a junction at 4.2 miles. A trail right leads 0.1 mile to campsites and a wide gravel bank. The rain forest has reclaimed the former trail on the opposite side of the river.

Back at the junction, the Queets River Trail continues left, eventually climbing 50 feet up a small bluff and then dropping down to reach Spruce Bottom Camp at 5.3 miles (elev. 410 ft), set among some big spruces

near a sandy beach along the river. This is a good place to call it quits for a day hike.

EXTENDING YOUR TRIP

The Queets River Trail continues upriver for more than 10 miles—strictly backpackers' domain, but strong day hikers can continue a short distance for a neat adventure. Continue 0.7 mile, climbing a bluff and crossing a creek and rocky wash to where the trail bends left alongside the river. Ford the river—a wider and much easier crossing than at the trailhead—and hike about 0.2 mile through alders to a grassy opening. Here, find what remains (collapsed timbers and an old bed frame) of Smith Place, a 1920s hunting camp. The trail to Tshletshy Creek no longer exists, so call it a day here, snooping around the historical grounds.

118 Sams River Loop

RATING/ DIFFICULTY	LOOP	ELEV GAIN/ HIGH POINT	SEASON
***/1	2.9 miles	75 feet/ 315 feet	Year-round

Map: Custom Correct Queets Valley; **Contact:** Olympic National Park, Wilderness Information Center; **Notes:** Dogs prohibited; **GPS:** N 47 36.98, W 124 01.904

Enjoy an easy family-friendly loop in the Queets River valley without having to ford the river. Saunter along an open bank above the wild Queets, hike under some of the largest spruce trees in the park, and look for resident elk while traversing old homestead farms. Unlike nature trails at the Quinault and Hoh, you'll have this entire living classroom to yourself.

GETTING THERE

From Hoquiam, travel north on US Highway 101 for 50 miles. (From Forks, travel south on US 101 for 53 miles.) Turn right onto paved Forest Road 21 and proceed for 8.1 miles, bearing left onto graveled FR 2180. Continue for 1.3 miles and turn left onto FR Spur 011. Follow this road 1.4 miles to Upper Queets Road and turn right. Proceed 2.1 miles to the trailhead (elev. 270 ft) at the ranger station.

ON THE TRAIL

Walk across the road and find the trailhead. Then start this loop counterclockwise, saving the best for last. On soft tread frilled with mosses and oxalis, hike across a lush bottomland. This section of trail is often wet and muddy. Pass by wetland pools teeming with crooning frogs. Cross a couple of channeled creeks. Then enter the first of several homestead clearings. Blackberry bushes and apple trees are all that remain. Between the melodic chirps of feasting birds, listen to the voices on the wind speak of the hardships and joys of living in the rain forest. Look for elk sign.

Pick up tread again across the meadow in a grove of mossy maples. Cross another creek and soon come to the banks of the churning Sams River. Climb a small bluff flanked by giant spruces that reach straight for the clouds. Stay left at a junction and reach the Upper Queets Road at 1.6 miles. Turn left on the road, pass the campground entrance, and pick up the trail again at 1.8 miles.

Soon reach a high bluff along the Queets that grants excellent views. Scan the lofty conifers that line the river for perched eagles and kingfishers. Look for dippers in the rapids and sandpipers at the river's

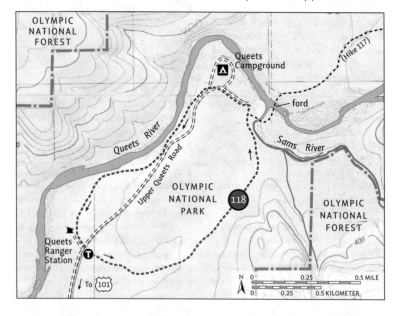

Evening along the Queets River

edge. Continue along the river to another large homestead clearing. Elk evidence is everywhere, from droppings and tracks to flattened clumps of grass. There are some accessible gravel bars along the river at the clearing's edge, perfect for lounging and feet soaking. The trail continues through a stately maple glade, delivering you back to the ranger station at 2.9 miles.

119 Quinault National Recreation Trails

RATING/ DIFFICULTY	LOOP	ELEV GAIN/ HIGH POINT	SEASON
****/2	3.9 miles	500 feet/ 450 feet	Year-round

Maps: Green Trails Lake Quinault No. 197, Custom Correct Quinault–Colonel Bob; **Contact:** Olympic National Forest, Pacific Ranger District, Quinault; **Notes:** NW Forest Pass or Interagency Pass required. Dogs permitted on-leash; **GPS:** N 47 27.594, W 123 51.728

With nearly 10 miles of well-maintained inter-connecting paths, the Quinault National Recreation Trails give you options as varied as spring wildflowers. The mélange leads to campgrounds, a historical lodge, waterfalls, cedar bogs, giant primeval trees, a scenic lakeshore, and along crystal-clear creeks. The loop described here is one suggestion.

GETTING THERE

From Hoquiam, travel north on US Highway 101 for 38 miles and turn right at milepost 126 onto South Shore Road (1 mile before Amanda Park). Proceed for 1.3 miles to the Rainforest Nature Trail Loop trailhead (elev. 240 ft), on the right. Water and restrooms available.

ON THE TRAIL

From the trailhead, hike to the right on a section of wheelchair-accessible trail. Pass a colossal Douglas-fir and emerge on a high bank above Willaby Creek. Search the

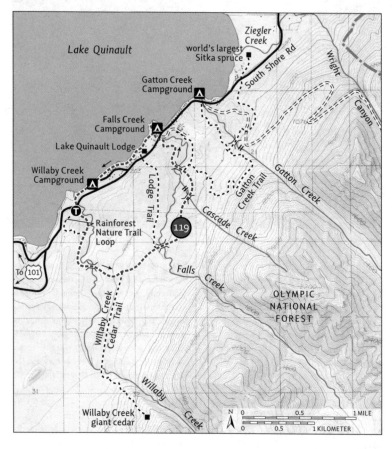

sparkling waters for salmon. Gaze up at the towering forest canopy for eagle nests. Then turn right and begin hiking under a canopy of ancient emerald giants: Sitka spruces, western red cedars, and western hemlocks that were mere saplings when Christopher Columbus set sail for the Americas.

At 0.2 mile, the Rainforest Nature Trail Loop continues to the right and returns to the parking lot in 0.3 mile. You want to continue left on Trail No. 854 and eventually cross Willaby Creek. Then gently climb to a junction at 1.1 miles. The trail right—recently maintained—climbs 600 feet in 1.7 miles to the Willaby Creek giant cedar. To get there, you'll need to ford Willaby Creek, which can be difficult during high flows.

Your loop continues straight, to a cedar bog bursting with pungent patches of skunk cabbage. Traverse this saturated landscape

Section of trail along Lake Quinault

via a boardwalk and come to another junction at 1.8 miles. The trail to your left heads 0.6 mile to the Lake Quinault Lodge; go right instead. Cross Falls Creek and gently climb to a bridged crossing of Cascade Creek at lovely Cascade Falls. Then descend to a junction at 2.4 miles. The trail right goes to Gatton Creek (see Extending Your Trip). Head left and cross Falls Creek again. Then climb a little before descending to South Shore Road at 2.8 miles.

Carefully cross the road and continue hiking. Pass Falls Creek Falls, skirt a campground, and then come to Lake Quinault, one of the largest bodies of water on the Olympic Peninsula. The way then heads west along the lakeshore, passing quiet coves, humble cabins, and the majestic 1926 Lake Quinault Lodge. In times of heavy rainfall, this section of trail is prone to inundation. If that's the case, return via South Shore Road, or head up the Lodge Trail and retrace some of your route.

At 3.7 miles, pass through the Willaby Creek Campground, and the trail resumes,

following Willaby Creek upstream, passing beneath South Shore Road, and returning to the trailhead at 3.9 miles.

The Quinault Valley left a deep impression on President Franklin D. Roosevelt when he visited here in 1937. It inspired him to protect a good chunk of the adjacent lands within a new national park. It should inspire you too.

EXTENDING YOUR TRIP

Follow the Gatton Creek Trail, soon bearing right at a junction where a trail leads left 0.3 mile along Falls Creek. Hike through beautiful primeval forest, climbing 400 feet and passing a junction where a 0.1-mile loop goes to a monster Douglas-fir (and through another one). The main trail then descends to a junction at 1.5 miles. To the left, follow cascading Gatton Creek 0.6 mile to a trailhead near the Gatton Creek Campground. To the right, cross the creek on a bridge near beautiful Gatton Creek Falls and reach the Rain Forest Resort on South Shore Road in 0.7 mile. From there, it's an easy 0.3 mile to the world's largest Sitka spruce.

120 Fletcher Canyon

RATING/ DIFFICULTY	ROUNDTRIP	ELEV GAIN/ HIGH POINT	SEASON
**/3	3.8 miles	1100 feet/ 1400 feet	Year-round

Maps: Green Trails Mt Christie No. 166, Custom Correct Quinault–Colonel Bob; **Contact:** Olympic National Forest, Pacific Ranger District, Quinault; **GPS:** N 47 31.659, W 123 42.387

Venture up a deep canyon into a lonely corner of the 11,961-acre Colonel Bob Wilderness. The hike is steep and rough in places, but it's short and the trees are impressive. Chances are also good of observing elk, cougars, bears, and perhaps even an endangered marbled murrelet in this rugged rift in the Quinault Ridge.

GETTING THERE

From Hoquiam, travel north on US Highway 101 for 38 miles and turn right at milepost

Stately Douglas-firs in Fletcher Canyon

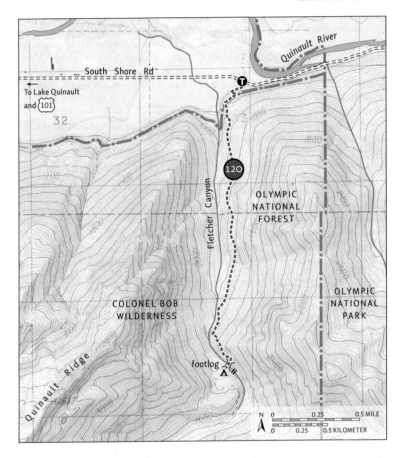

126 onto South Shore Road (1 mile before Amanda Park). Proceed for 11.4 miles (the pavement ends at 7.8 miles) to the trailhead (elev. 375 ft).

ON THE TRAIL

The trail starts near a huge ledge adorned with ferns and lichens. Ignore the kiosk sign that says "Col Bob Trail 4 miles." The trail beyond the 2-mile mark has long been abandoned and is overgrown to jungle proportions—even Sasquatch now avoids it. Immediately start climbing on a sometimes steep, sometimes rocky route. Numerous creeks cross the trail, and it's a challenge to keep your boots dry.

After gaining a couple of hundred feet, the trail rounds a bend and enters the deep canyon, soon after entering the Colonel Bob Wilderness. Continue climbing under an emerald canopy of stately hemlocks and firs as frothing Fletcher Creek crashes in the distance. Waves of sword ferns seem to roll down the vertical canyon walls.

After about 1 mile, the way gets rougher, growing rockier and rootier. Finally, the trail approaches the creek. Enter a magical spot where big mossy boulders corral the feisty waters. Stare across to the sheer vertical wall at the far side of the canyon, where you can see the scars of avalanches and rockslides.

With good tread now a memory, the trail dashes under fallen giants, darts over slick rocks, skirts damp ledges, and wiggles through boulders on a steep course. At 1.9 miles, after a slight descent, break out into a small clearing alongside Fletcher Creek (elev. 1380 ft). A huge cedar log acts as a

bridge over the gurgling waters, and another pretty waterfall is visible just upstream. The trail ends here at a campsite. Sit by the creek and enjoy a corner of the Quinault Rain Forest where few bootprints have been left behind.

121 East Fork Quinault River and Pony Bridge

RATING/ DIFFICULTY	ROUNDTRIP	ELEV GAIN/ HIGH POINT	SEASON
***/2	5 miles	1000 feet/ 1250 feet	Year-round

Maps: Green Trails Mt Christie No. 166, Custom Correct Enchanted Valley–Skokomish; **Contact:** Olympic National Park, Wilderness

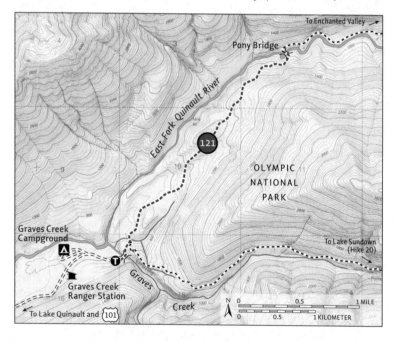

A mesmerized hiker stands on the Pony Bridge.

Information Center; **Notes:** Dogs prohibited. Road from Quinault River Bridge is subject to temporary closures during winter; **GPS:** N 47 34.368, W 123 34.193

Hike along the East Fork Quinault River through a forest of big trees to a narrow waterfall-fed canyon. Explore the same primeval rainforest valley that explorers of the 1890 O'Neil Expedition set out across. And witness a wilderness not unlike the one those intrepid souls experienced.

GETTING THERE

From Hoquiam, travel north on US Highway 101 for 38 miles and turn right at milepost

126 onto South Shore Road (1 mile before Amanda Park). Proceed for 12.9 miles (the pavement ends at 7.8 miles) to a junction at the Quinault River Bridge. Continue right for 6.2 miles to the road's end and trailhead (elev. 600 ft). Privy available.

ON THE TRAIL

The Quinault is one of the grandest of the rainforest rivers. Draining much of the Olympics' southwest corner, the Quinault is comprised of two main branches: the North and East Forks. This hike takes you along the East Fork, through a deep glacier-carved valley.

Start by crossing Graves Creek on a large log bridge. Then bear left at a junction with the Graves Creek Trail at 0.2 mile. The way is wide and well-graded, following an old road. Along a bench, away from the river, traverse moisture-dripping groves of towering hemlocks, spruces, and firs. More than 120 inches of rain annually saturate this valley. In winter scads of hoofprints mar the wet ground; stay alert for elk. The trail meanders over a 1250-foot rise. Scores of creeks and rivulets run under, over, and sometimes down the trail.

At 2 miles, the old road ends. Pass a picnic table that's rapidly losing a fight with the elements and then begin descending to the river. Finally, at 2.3 miles, the East Fork Quinault comes into view. Through a fern-ringed narrow canyon of slate and sandstone, the crystal-clear waters bubble and churn. Walk a little ways to Pony Bridge (elev. 900 ft), which spans this scenic gorge. Enjoy an unobstructed view of emerald pools swirling below and horsetail falls streaking the canyon walls. If you've trekked this way on a rare sunny day, retreat a few

hundred feet on the trail to find a rough path leading down to some lunch rocks along the river.

EXTENDING YOUR TRIP

Continue heading upvalley on an up-and-down course along the river to Fire Creek, 1 mile farther, or all the way to O'Neil Camp at 6.7 miles. Enchanted Valley, at 13 miles, is for backpackers. For solitude, hike 3.5 miles up the Graves Creek Trail through magnificent ancient forest to the Success Creek ford. Beyond the ford, you can continue 4.5 miles farther to Lake Sundown (Hike 20).

122 North Fork Quinault River and Halfway House

RATING/ DIFFICULTY	ROUNDTRIP	ELEV GAIN/ HIGH POINT	SEASON
***/3	10.2 miles	600 feet/ 900 feet	Year-round

Maps: Green Trails Mt Christie No. 166, Custom Correct Quinault–Colonel Bob; **Contact:** Olympic National Park, Wilderness Information Center; **Notes:** Dogs prohibited. North Shore Road is subject to temporary closures during winter; **GPS:** N 47 34.542, W 123 38.889

Hike along a wild river whose big bends and wide gravel bars will make you think you're in Alaska. Massive Sitka spruces, gargantuan western hemlocks, and corridors of mossy maples and speckled alders grace the way. Retrace part of the Press Expedition's 1889–90 route across the Olympics, and visit the former site of a lodge that provided warmth and hospitality to trekkers during the 1920s and 1930s.

North Fork Quinault at Wolf Bar

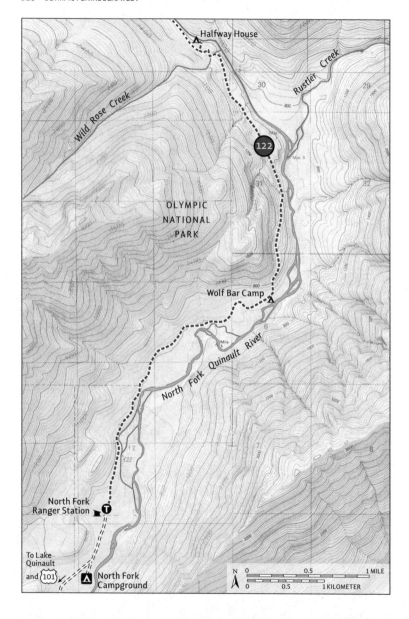

Halfway House

Wild Rose Creek

Rustler Creek

30

29

800

1000

122

Mile 0

31

32

OLYMPIC

NATIONAL

PARK

800

Wolf Bar Camp

6

5

Mile

North Fork Quinault River

8

2

522

North Fork
Ranger Station

To Lake
Quinault
and 101

North Fork
Campground

N

0   0.5   1 MILE

0   0.5   1 KILOMETER

GETTING THERE

From Hoquiam, travel north on US Highway 101 for 38 miles and turn right at milepost 126 onto South Shore Road (1 mile before Amanda Park). Proceed for 12.9 miles (the pavement ends at 7.8 miles) to a junction at the Quinault River Bridge. Turn left and cross the bridge. Then immediately turn right onto North Shore Road and drive 3.5 miles to the road's end at the ranger station and trailhead (elev. 525 ft). Privy available.

ON THE TRAIL

The trail's first 2.6 miles were converted from a road long ago, making for an easy and enjoyable hike to a wide riverbank camping and picnicking spot known as Wolf Bar. Much of the way is directly alongside the roaring river. And as in the past, the river continues to jump its banks, forcing trail rebuilding and reroutes.

About 1 mile from the trailhead, cross the first of several side creeks—easy during the summer, but winter rains can make this and the other crossings difficult. At 1.5 miles, traverse a huge gravel outwash area arranged with boughs of sword ferns and columns of maples swathed in moss. Next, cross a channel bed that may or may not be flowing. Traverse an alluvial island, and then negotiate the channel once more. Next, travel over more outwash, through groves of towering old growth, and along newly exposed riverbanks.

At 2.6 miles, arrive at Wolf Bar Camp (elev. 650 ft), a suitable destination for a shorter hike. Head out on the broad gravel bar for views of the surrounding steep-sided ridges, usually hidden in swirling clouds. Beyond Wolf Bar the trail climbs a terrace, pulling away from the river. On an up-and-down course through thick forest, but always

within earshot of the North Fork, the trail winds up the deep valley.

At 5 miles, come to Wild Rose Creek, requiring a ford that may be dangerous during high water. The Halfway House site (elev. 850 ft) lies just beyond. It's now a backcountry campsite—nothing remains of the old lodge. But the area's charm is still in full swing. Find a piece of ledge to sit on and watch the swirling, gurgling river negotiate a narrow chasm.

EXTENDING YOUR TRIP

The trail continues for another 11 miles to Low Divide. Continue for as far as time and energy allow.

123 Irely Lake and Three Lakes

Irely Lake

RATING/ DIFFICULTY	ROUNDTRIP	ELEV GAIN/ HIGH POINT	SEASON
*/1	2.4 miles	200 feet/ 600 feet	Year-round

Three Lakes

RATING/ DIFFICULTY	ROUNDTRIP	ELEV GAIN/ HIGH POINT	SEASON
***/4	14 miles	2850 feet/ 3175 feet	Late June– Oct

Maps: Green Trails Mt Christie No. 166, Custom Correct Quinault–Colonel Bob; **Contact:** Olympic National Park, Wilderness Information Center; **Notes:** Dogs prohibited. North Shore Road is subject to temporary closures during winter; **GPS:** N 47 34.057, W 123 39.318

Take a leisurely, kid-friendly jaunt to a quiet body of water teeming with wildlife, or make a challenging all-day push through ancient forest to a series of small wildflower-ringed subalpine lakes. Elk are abundant in this verdant valley, while hikers remain scarce.

GETTING THERE

From Hoquiam, travel north on US Highway 101 for 38 miles. Turn right at milepost 126 onto South Shore Road (1 mile before Amanda Park). Proceed 12.9 miles (pavement ends at 7.8 miles) to a junction at the Quinault River Bridge. Turn left and cross the bridge. Then immediately turn right onto North Shore Road and drive 2.7 miles to the trailhead (elev. 500 ft), on the left. Parking is on the right.

ON THE TRAIL

Irely Lake: Begin under a lofty canopy, compliments of a support team of colossal cedars and spruces. After a small climb of 100 feet, come to a flat bisected by Irely Creek. Turn south, following the skunk-cabbage-laced creek. Be careful on the rotten puncheon. Beavers are active along this stretch, and their handiwork causes occasional inundation of the trail.

Cross the small creek on a log bridge, and then head for higher and drier ground. At 1.1 miles, reach a side trail that leads 0.1

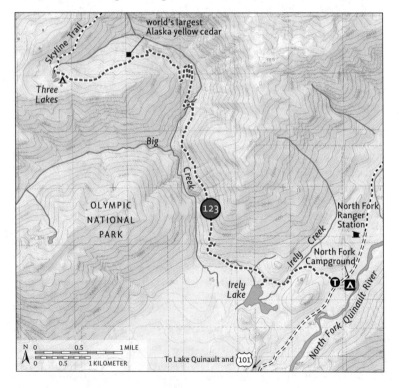

Boggy meadows near Three Lakes

mile down to grassy Irely Lake (elev. 550 ft). The lake, more a big marsh, is a good place to sit still (if mosquitoes aren't present) and scope out birds. Ducks, woodpeckers, blackbirds, and songbirds are present in large numbers.

Three Lakes: Back on the main trail, continue hiking, traversing muddy lowlands and crossing several creeks that often flood during periods of high rain (which is often). The tread gets rougher and rockier, heading deeper into the saturated, verdant forest. Cross a maple flat frequented by elk before beginning a steep climb high above Big Creek. The cedars are enormous along these steep slopes. Several behemoths lay toppled across the trail, victims of strong winter storms. Wind is the number-one agent of succession in the rain forests of the Olympic Peninsula. Strong gusts ensure openings in

the canopy, allowing new growth to compete with the entrenched elders.

Continue up, traversing steep slopes, and then abruptly drop 150 feet toward the crashing creek. With a small cascade on your right, work your way down a short rocky ledge to a sturdy bridge (elev. 1275 ft) spanning the thundering North Fork Big Creek at 4 miles. Then in primeval forest, begin steeply climbing out of the canyon, crossing a tight dry chasm en route. At 6 miles, come to the world's largest Alaska yellow cedar (elev. 2740 ft).

The way continues upward, passing more big yellow cedars, huckleberry patches, and boggy meadows teeming with frogs and blossoms (look for elephant's-head orchids). There are limited views of the surrounding emerald ridges. At 7 miles, come to the Three Lakes (elev. 3175 ft). The largest (although it's quite small) lies along the trail. The other two "lakes" are tucked in boggy meadows to its east. Find peaceful (albeit buggy at times) camps at the first lake and two diverging trails. The faint one heading west is the long since (and unfortunately) abandoned Tshletshy Creek Trail to the Queets Valley. The one continuing north is the famed Skyline Trail, one of the premier backpacking routes in the park.

124 Kestner Homestead

RATING/ DIFFICULTY	LOOP	ELEV GAIN/ HIGH POINT	SEASON
**/1	1.5 miles	30 feet/ 260 feet	Year-round

Maps: Green Trails Kloochman Rock No. 165, Custom Correct Quinault–Colonel Bob;

Contact: Olympic National Park, Wilderness Information Center; **Notes:** Dogs prohibited; **GPS:** N 47 30.310, W 123 49.280

Learn about pioneer life in the saturated Quinault Valley on this delightful kid-friendly interpretive trail. Stroll through the grounds that Anton Kestner claimed in 1889 under the Homestead Act and proceeded to clear for pasture and his domicile. Then finish your visit with a loop through a mossy maple glade.

GETTING THERE

From Hoquiam, travel north on US Highway 101 for 41 miles to Amanda Park and turn right onto North Shore Road. Proceed for 5.7 miles to the national park Quinault Rain Forest Ranger Station and trailhead (elev. 220 ft). Privy available.

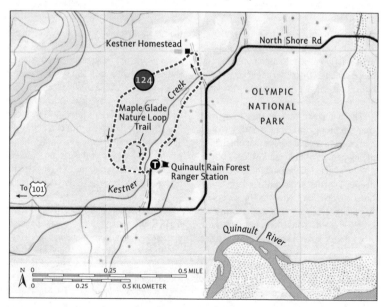

Tractor remains at the Kestner Homestead

ON THE TRAIL

Start this loop by heading north on a wide trail paralleling gurgling Kestner Creek. After walking through a tunnel of maples, spruces, and hemlocks, cross the clear creek and emerge at the more-than-century-old homestead. This valley is rugged, isolated, and receives more than 12 feet of rain a year, and Native peoples have lived here for centuries. But it wasn't until the late 1800s that a few hardy Americans of European descent migrated to this region of big timber and abundant game. The Kestner and Higley families lived on these grounds for decades, and the attractive stream bisecting this homestead and the peak shadowing it bears their names.

Walk through the grounds, inspecting the main home, barn, outbuildings, and various farming relics. Look for elk—frequent visitors, especially during the winter months. After admiring the homestead, continue on the trail and return to the darkness of the forest. In early spring flowering skunk cabbage, nature's swamp lanterns, add light to the dank rain forest. The trail meanders through maple glades and swampy swales and alongside boughs of sword ferns nearly head high.

At about 1.1 miles, the trail intersects with the Maple Glade Nature Loop Trail. Heading straight takes you directly to the trailhead. Turn left instead and wander the wheelchair-accessible nature trail 0.3 mile before returning to the main trail. Then turn left, cross Kestner Creek, and return to your start.

125 Colonel Bob Peak

RATING/ DIFFICULTY	ROUNDTRIP	ELEV GAIN/ HIGH POINT	SEASON
*****/5	14.6 miles	4675 feet/ 4492 feet	Late June– Nov

Maps: Green Trails Grisdale No. 198, Custom Correct Quinault–Colonel Bob; **Contact:** Olympic National Forest, Pacific Ranger Station, Quinault; **GPS:** N 47 29.796, W 123 47.609

 *This challenging hike leads through miles of towering old-growth forest to a prominent peak on the western edge of the Olympic Mountains. From its aerie summit more than 4000 feet above the Quinault Valley, stare down at shimmering Lake Quinault. And when cloud cover is scarce you can see from Mount Olympus to the Pacific.*

GETTING THERE

From Hoquiam, travel north on US Highway 101 for 38 miles and turn right at milepost 126 onto South Shore Road (1 mile before Amanda Park). Proceed for 6 miles to the trailhead (elev. 240 ft), on the right.

ON THE TRAIL

There is a shorter and easier (but not easy) way to this former lookout site (Hike 126), but this route up the Ziegler Creek valley passes through miles of spectacular primeval forest. Closed for several years due to a massive windfall, this trail is once again open thanks to the Washington Trails Association.

From the valley bottom, Trail No. 851 immediately climbs and soon enters the 11,961-acre Colonel Bob Wilderness, passing giant cedars, hemlocks, and Douglas-firs. Staying above Ziegler Creek, climb steadily but moderately and after a couple of switchbacks come to the beginning of a huge blowdown area. Massive trees were toppled, rendering this trail impassable for many years, and a few rough spots remain. The toppled giants have created some new views.

At about 2.5 miles, come to a spring. Pass some big boulders soon afterward and re-enter intact old forest. The way then enters a side valley, eventually crossing a tributary of Ziegler Creek, which may be flowing underground. Then on rougher tread, begin

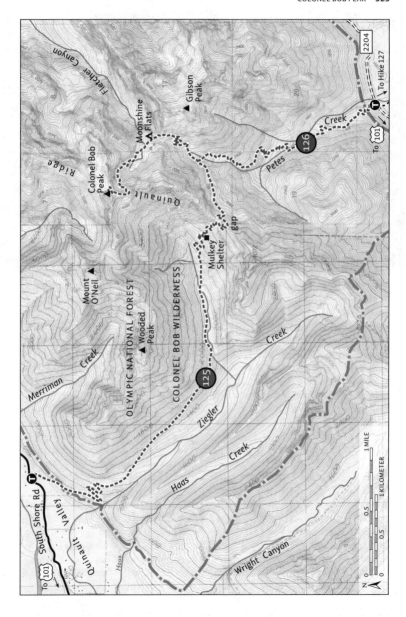

Lake Quinault from Colonel Bob's summit

steeply climbing out of the valley. At 4.5 miles, come to the historical Mulkey Shelter (elev. 2600 ft) near a small creek. The trail continues to ruggedly climb out of the valley, cresting Quinault Ridge at a small gap (elev. 3200 ft) at 4.7 miles.

Then descend a few hundred feet before traversing a brushy slope, which provides good views out to Moonlight Dome to the south. At 5.5 miles, come to a junction (elev. 2840 ft) with the Petes Creek Trail, the shorter approach to Colonel Bob from the south (Hike 126). Head left and steeply climb up an open, brushy, and flowery slope beneath Gibson Peak. Reenter old growth and continue clambering, reaching a gap (elev. 3470 ft) at 6.4 miles where a trail once descended into Fletcher Canyon.

Continue left through berry patches and drop a little to a tarn before climbing through parkland meadows. At 6.6 miles,

cross a creek at Moonshine Flats (campsites), and then prepare for the final push, which ascends nearly 1000 feet in 0.7 mile. Through subalpine forest and skirting basalt cliffs, the rough trail steeply switchbacks to the 4492-foot summit, the final 100 feet on steps blasted into the summit block.

Savor the views. Lake Quinault twinkles 4000 feet below. Mount Olympus glistens to the north. Mount Rainier and Mount Saint Helens hover to the east and south over rows of scrappy hills and ridges. On a clear day you can see Ocean Shores and the Satsop Towers near Elma. And fanning out below is an emerald cloak of luxuriant rain forest draped over forbidding ridges and valleys—a burgeoning kingdom of biomass.

And who was Colonel Bob? Colonel Robert G. Ingersoll was a Civil War veteran, politician, orator, and free thinker who never stepped foot on this peak.

126 Petes Creek and Colonel Bob Peak
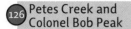

RATING/ DIFFICULTY	ROUNDTRIP	ELEV GAIN/ HIGH POINT	SEASON
*****/4	8.2 miles	3450 feet/ 4492 feet	Late June– Nov

Maps: Green Trails Grisdale No. 198, Custom Correct Quinault–Colonel Bob; **Contact:** Olympic National Forest, Pacific Ranger Station, Quinault; **Notes:** NW Forest Pass or Interagency Pass required; **GPS:** N 47 27.433, W 123 43.905

This shorter and easier route to Colonel Bob Peak via Petes Creek is still a tough climb. But the panorama from this prominent outpost on the Olympics' southwest periphery is worth it, from the rugged Quinault Ridge to Lake Quinault and Mount Olympus to the Pacific.

GETTING THERE

From Hoquiam, travel 25 miles north on US Highway 101. Just past milepost 112, turn right onto Donkey Creek Road (Forest Road 22, signed for Wynoochee Lake). Follow this paved road for 8 miles and turn left onto FR

Flowered meadows below Gibson Peak

2204. Continue for 10.8 miles (the pavement ends in 3 miles) to the trailhead (elev. 1050 ft), on the left. Privy available.

ON THE TRAIL

The hike to this peak is just like the man it was named for: straightforward and to the point. Colonel Robert G. Ingersoll was a Civil War veteran, politician, orator, and free thinker known as the Great Agnostic. He never stepped foot on this peak, but some admiring climbers who did thought the peak should be named for him.

Starting on Petes Creek Trail No. 858, head north and immediately enter ancient forest and the Colonel Bob Wilderness. At about 1 mile, cross Petes Creek, which may be flowing underground. The climb then stiffens as the trail works its way up the west slope of Gibson Peak. Traverse a couple of brushy avalanche slopes that provide views of the Humptulips Valley. Steeply zigzag through rugged terrain, coming to a junction (elev. 280 ft) with the Colonel Bob Peak Trail (Hike 125) at 2.4 miles. Head right, steeply climbing up an open, brushy, and flowery slope beneath Gibson Peak. Reenter old growth and continue clambering, getting a reprieve at a gap (elev. 3470 ft) above Fletcher Canyon.

The trail then heads northwest, dropping a little to a tarn before climbing through parkland meadows. At 3.5 miles, cross a creek at Moonshine Flats (campsites), and then prepare for the final push. which ascends nearly 1000 feet in 0.7 mile. Through subalpine forest and skirting basalt cliffs, the trail steeply switch backs to the old lookout site, the final 100 feet on steps blasted into the summit block.

From the 4492-foot open summit, stare down to Lake Quinault twinkling below.

Mount Olympus glistens to the north, and Mounts Rainier and Saint Helens hover in the east and south, respectively. Directly south lie the unprotected old-growth forests of Moonlight Dome, an area conservationists and this author would like to see protected as wilderness.

127 West Fork Humptulips River

RATING/ DIFFICULTY	ONE-WAY	ELEV GAIN/ HIGH POINT	SEASON
***/3	18.7 miles	Up to 3000 feet/ 3300 feet	Late July–Sept

Maps: Green Trails Lake Quinault No. 197 and Grisdale No. 198, Custom Correct Quinault–Colonel Bob (partial); **Contact:** Olympic National Forest, Pacific Ranger Station, Quinault; **Notes:** NW Forest Pass or Interagency Pass required at Petes Creek trailhead. Multiple river fords required, only safe during low flows; **GPS:** N 47 22.675, W 123 47.658

With spectacular groves of old growth, meadows teeming with wildlife, and views of rugged surrounding peaks, the West Fork Humptulips River flows through one of the most varied of the rainforest valleys. The lightly used trail travels 17 miles from the river's gorge to its headwaters and involves twenty-five river fords! Five trailheads allow several day-hiking options.

GETTING THERE

From Hoquiam, travel 25 miles north on US Highway 101. Just past milepost 112, turn right onto Donkey Creek Road (Forest Road 22, signed for Wynoochee Lake). Follow this paved road for 8 miles and turn left onto FR

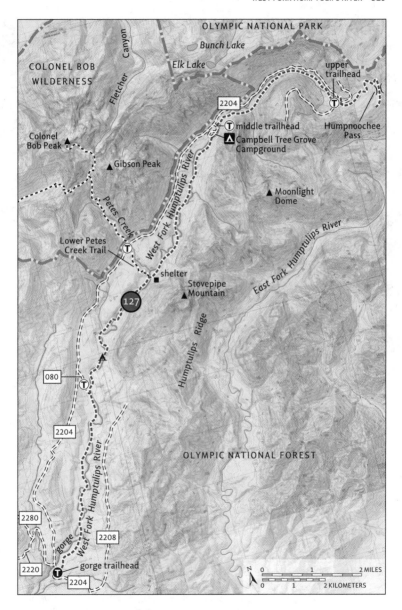

OLYMPIC NATIONAL PARK

Bunch Lake

Elk Lake

Fletcher Canyon

COLONEL BOB
WILDERNESS

2204

upper trailhead

T

middle trailhead

Humpnoochee Pass

Campbell Tree Grove Campground

Colonel Bob Peak

Gibson Peak

West Fork Humptulips River

Moonlight Dome

Petes Creek

Lower Petes Creek Trail

T

shelter

Stovepipe Mountain

East Fork Humptulips River

127

Humptulips Ridge

080

T

2204

OLYMPIC NATIONAL FOREST

West Fork Humptulips River

2280

2208

gorge

2220

T

gorge trailhead

2204

N

0   1   2 MILES

0   1   2 KILOMETERS

Author at one of the numerous fords along the way (Jay Thompson photo)

2204. Continue for 4 miles (the pavement ends in 3 miles) to the gorge trailhead (elev. 550 ft), 10.8 miles to the Petes Creek trailhead (Northwest Forest Pass required), 13.8 miles to Campbell Tree Grove trailhead, and 17 miles to the upper trailhead.

ON THE TRAIL

Built and maintained by the Backcountry Horsemen of Washington, this 17-mile trail sees little hiker use. Yes, there are twenty-five river fords—far easier for horses than humans. But by late summer, much of the river is usually just shin-deep, and the water

soothes on a hot afternoon. Wear lightweight trail-running shoes and take along a set of trekking poles—and have fun! Hike out and back from any of the trailheads, or do sections one-way with a car shuttle.

Gorge to Lower Petes Creek: On a bench high above the West Fork Humptulips River, follow well-groomed Trail No. 806 down to the river, thanks to recent work done by the Washington Trails Association. At about 0.9 mile, come to a bend in the river and the first ford (elev. 475 ft). For this and all subsequent fords, look for wide spots or places where the river has fanned out. And look for markers (usually orange diamonds) on the opposite side of the river for where the trail resumes.

The next ford comes soon afterward; fords 3, 4, and 5 by mile 2. Then enjoy a long dry stretch, passing giant spruces and cedars before reaching ford 6 at 3.9 miles. At 4.5 miles, shortly after ford 7, reach a junction. The short Switchback Trail leads left to a trailhead. The main trail continues right, soon coming to ford 8. Fords 9, 10, and 11 rapidly follow. At 5.2 miles, come to a camp. Cross a boardwalk near a nice old-growth grove before coming to ford 12. Then walk the gravel bar to and just after ford 13. Routefinding may be a little tricky due to fallen trees and flood damage. Cross fords 14 and 15 and then come to a junction (elev. 625 ft) at 7.6 miles. The Lower Petes Creek Trail heads left 1 mile, climbing 400 feet to its trailhead.

Lower Petes Creek to Campbell Tree Grove: This section is perhaps the most scenic, but it's unfortunately the roughest—overgrown stretches and damaged tread are badly in need of maintenance. Soon reach ford 16. Then check out an old cedar-shingled shelter that sits snuggly in a maple grove. Ford 17 soon follows and then ford 18. Views are good of the surrounding rugged peaks: those in the Colonel Bob Wilderness to the west; Stovepipe and Moonlight Dome to the east. The trail next traverses the western edge of the 6000-acre Moonlight Dome Roadless Area, one of the last large tracts of unlogged, unprotected national forest in the rainforest valleys. The Wild Olympics campaign has targeted this tract for wilderness designation.

Between fords 19, 20, and 21, you'll hike through groves of massive spruces and firs and across grassy openings. After ford 22,

enjoy 1.3 miles of dry-foot trekking. At ford 23, you can opt to cross the river on a fallen old-growth giant instead of wading. At 11.6 miles, reach the Campbell Tree Grove (elev. 1050 ft), a lovely stand of old growth that contains one of the most peaceful car campgrounds in the Olympics.

Campbell Tree Grove to Upper Trailhead: From the campground, the trail passes the adjacent middle trailhead and then goes through an impressive maple and cedar flat, reaching ford 24. Pass a waterfall and reach ford 25 at 12.6 miles (elev. 1200 ft)—the final ford! (It actually crosses a tributary of the Humptulips.) The trail then starts climbing, traversing steep slopes above the river. Cross several openings that offer views across the valley. At 14.8 miles, cross the river—a mere trickling creek here (elev. 1875 ft)—without getting your feet wet. Then switch back through ancient timber to the upper trailhead (elev. 2150 ft) at 15.3 miles.

Upper Trailhead to Humpnoochee Pass: Briefly walk east on FR 2204 to a spur on the left. Pick up the trail once more and steadily climb a steep slope shrouded in old growth. Cross a wet meadow and several small creeks—the headwaters of the West Fork Humptulips. Pass big hemlocks and bountiful huckleberry patches before switch backing through second growth to an old logging road. The trail then bends right, following a decommissioned road (now covered in grasses), and reaches Humpnoochee Pass (elev. 3300 ft) at 17 miles. On this divide between the Humptulips and Wynoochee watersheds, enjoy excellent views of the Colonel Bob Wilderness peaks, Moonlight Dome, Three Peaks, and Mount Church. This is the trail's end. Return to the upper trailhead for a one-way hike of the entire trail of 18.7 miles.

MEET THE ROOSEVELTS

That nearly 1 million acres of wildland is protected on the Olympic Peninsula as a national park is primarily the work of two presidents: one a Republican, one a Democrat, both Roosevelts.

Lieutenant O'Neil was one of the first people who called for protection of the area as a national park, back in 1890 after his second scientific and exploratory journey. In 1897, President Grover Cleveland created the Olympic Forest Preserve, but it lacked strong protection. An avid sportsman, President Theodore Roosevelt used the Antiquities Act of 1906 (which he signed into law) to proclaim 600,000 acres as Mount Olympus National Monument, primarily to protect the dwindling elk herds from unregulated hunting. Today the Roosevelt elk bear his name and number over five thousand.

National monuments, however, don't enjoy the same protections as national parks; timber, mining, and development interests began pressuring the government to open the area to exploitation. In 1937, President Franklin D. Roosevelt visited the peninsula, staying at the Lake Crescent and Lake Quinault lodges and prompting him to declare, "This must be a national park!"

In 1938, four weeks before O'Neil's death, FDR signed a bill designating 898,000 acres as Olympic National Park. Most of the coastal strip was added to the park in 1953 with a stroke from President Harry S. Truman's pen (a Democrat). In 1988, Republican president Ronald Reagan signed a bill declaring nearly 95 percent of the park as wilderness, the strongest protection afforded by law. Hopefully, future congresspeople and presidents, both Democrats and Republicans, will continue to follow their predecessors' enlightened examples.

Opposite: Headlands at Rialto Beach

olympic peninsula: coast

Olympic Coast

Majestic sea stacks, secluded coves, deserted strands of smooth sandy beaches, contorted salt-sprayed maritime forests, and tidal pools bursting with urchins, starfish, limpets, barnacles, and all kinds of squishy and crunchy sea critters— this is what you can expect while hiking the Olympic Peninsula's coast.

The Olympic coast is mostly roadless and isolated, offering some of the wildest beaches remaining in the continental United States. Parts of this wild, windswept, and rain-drenched world do require tenacity and determination to visit, but a good amount of this country is relatively accessible.

Nowhere along these pristine beaches that sport sea and river otters, oystercatchers and bald eagles, will you ever have to share the way with motorized vehicles. But it almost didn't happen this way. A coastal highway, oil drilling, and surfside development nearly wreaked havoc on this sacred land of the Makahs, Quileutes, Hohs, and Quinaults. Most of the coastal strip wasn't added to Olympic National Park until 1953, and Shi Shi Beach only joined the protected ranks in 1976.

From Kalaloch's miracle strand of broad sandy beaches to Cape Flattery's towering cliffs over tumultuous currents, there's plenty of good hiking to be had in Washington's wild northwest corner.

128 Kalaloch and Browns Point

RATING/ DIFFICULTY	ROUNDTRIP	ELEV GAIN/ HIGH POINT	SEASON
***/1	4 miles	25 feet/ 25 feet	Year-round

Driftwood logs on Kalaloch Beach

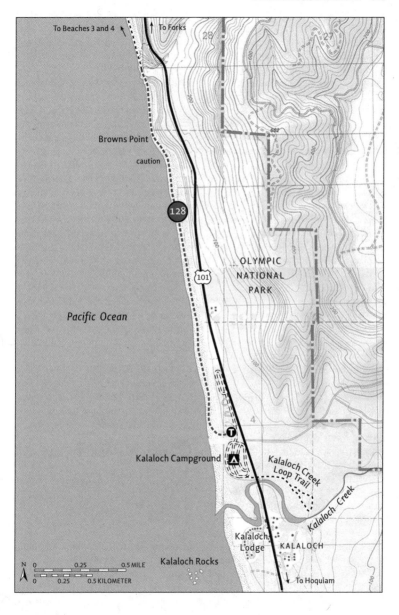

Maps: Green Trails La Push No. 163S, Custom Correct South Olympic Coast; **Contact:** Olympic National Park, Wilderness Information Center; **Notes:** Dogs permitted on-leash. Browns Point can only be rounded during low tides—consult tide chart; **GPS:** N 47 36.771, W 124 22.570

 *The perfect introduction to the wild Olympic coast, this hike leads from Kalaloch's wide, sandy beach to Browns Point over a jumbled collection of rock islands and surf-splashed cliffs. Although the highway is never far, towering bluffs and hidden coves give this area a remote feeling. Spend hours exploring this area's extensive tide pools and headlands—perfect for children and Rover (on-leash) too.*

GETTING THERE

From Hoquiam, travel US Highway 101 north for 70 miles to Kalaloch. (From Forks, travel 34 miles south on US 101.) Turn left into the Kalaloch Campground, just beyond the lodge and ranger station, and park in the day-use area (elev. 25 ft). Water and restrooms available.

ON THE TRAIL

From the picnic area bluff, descend 25 feet, hopping over a tangled pile of driftlogs to reach the beach, and then head north on the wide and smooth expanse of sandy shoreline. Throughout most of the summer, a shroud of fog impairs the view. But on clear fall and spring days, you can see all the way to Hoh Head on the northern horizon. Destruction Island, a 60-acre barren outpost over 3 miles from shore, is also visible when the skies are clear. Uninhabited, it's one of the Pacific coast's most important seabird colonies.

At 1 mile, high grassy bluffs rising to your right increase the feeling of remoteness. At 1.6 miles, a series of ledges and cliffs encroaches upon the surf. If the tide is high, this is as far as you can safely go; turn around and enjoy the 3 miles of beach south of the campground. But if the tide is low, work your way over, around, and even through (there's a small sandstone arch) the rocks and ledges that make up Browns Point. Explore tidal pools and cliffside caves. Admire orange and purple starfish tightly cemented to barnacle-clad rocks. Peer down at spongy urchins and other sea critters in nature's little saltwater baths. But remember, the intertidal zone is a fragile ecosystem. Please don't remove or disturb its inhabitants. That's the job of raucous oystercatchers in search of tasty morsels.

Come to the other side of Browns Point at 2 miles. Beyond, Beaches 3 and 4 offer more wide, sandy stretches. Don't forget to check your tide chart for the return if you decide to go farther.

EXTENDING YOUR TRIP

North of Browns Point, you can hike 4 miles to Ruby Beach (Hike 129). Back at the campground, hike the delightful 1-mile Kalaloch Creek Loop Trail through maritime forest.

129 Ruby Beach

RATING/ DIFFICULTY	ROUNDTRIP	ELEV GAIN/ HIGH POINT	SEASON
***/2	6 miles	80 feet/ 80 feet	Year-round

Maps: Green Trails La Push No. 163S, Custom Correct South Olympic Coast; **Contact:** Olympic National Park, Wilderness Information Center; **Notes:** Dogs permitted

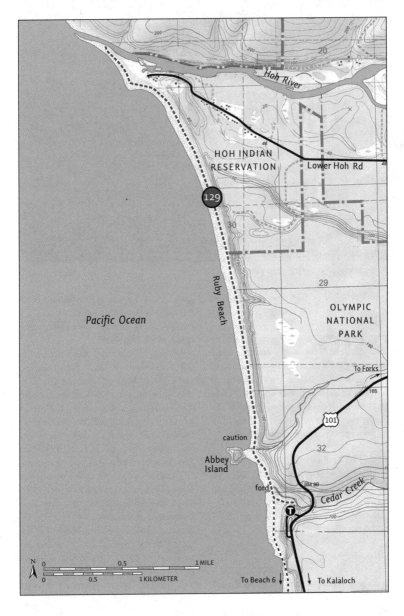

HOH RIVER

HOH INDIAN RESERVATION

Lower Hoh Rd

129

Ruby Beach

Pacific Ocean

OLYMPIC NATIONAL PARK

To Forks

101

caution

Abbey Island

ford

Cedar Creek

T

N

0   0.5   1 MILE

0   0.5   1 KILOMETER

To Beach 6 ↓   ↓ To Kalaloch

Abbey Island offshore from Ruby Beach

on-leash. Avoid in high tide—consult tide chart; **GPS:** N 47 42.591, W 124 24.816

![icons] *Think of Ruby Beach as Olympic wilderness coast lite. You'll get the same great wilderness taste as Cape Alava, Shi Shi Beach, and Third Beach but for a lot less effort. Walk a mere 0.25 mile through salt-sprayed maritime forest to the beach. Then hike a lonely stretch of coastline all the way to the mouth of the Hoh River.*

GETTING THERE

From Hoquiam, travel US Highway 101 north for 77 miles (7 miles north of Kalaloch) and turn left to reach the trailhead (elev. 80 ft). (From Forks, travel 27 miles south on US 101 to the turnoff.)

ON THE TRAIL

Hike 0.25 mile to the sea. Most folks call it quits here, photographing the contorted sea

stacks and Abbey Island just offshore. But if the tide is low and your ambitions are high, consider hiking north for nearly 3 miles to the mouth of the Hoh River.

Check your tide chart. You'll need a low tide to rock hop across Cedar Creek and safely round the small headland just north of it. After that, it's an easy, straightforward hike to the mouth of one of the peninsula's most famous rivers. On a wide, sandy beach, beneath bluffs rising 150 feet, hike all the way to where the rain- and glacier-fed Hoh River empties into the world's largest ocean.

En route you're sure to see bald eagles perched in high snags hanging precariously above the eroding bluffs. You may even encounter a deer or two out on the deserted beach. Spend some time exploring the mouth of the river (which lies within the small Hoh Indian Reservation—respect private property and residents' privacy), and then plan for your return. Don't forget about the tides. Let Abbey Island act like a beacon guiding you back to Ruby Beach. Early settlers of European descent thought the imposing block of an island resembled a cathedral.

EXTENDING YOUR TRIP

During a low tide, you can hike south from the trailhead and round a headland, continuing all the way to Beach 6. Look for small caves carved into the steep bluffs lining the beach.

130 Second Beach

RATING/ DIFFICULTY	ROUNDTRIP	ELEV GAIN/ HIGH POINT	SEASON
****/2	4 miles	310 feet/ 220 feet	Year-round

Maps: Green Trails La Push No. 163S, Custom Correct South Olympic Coast; **Contact:** Olympic National Park, Wilderness Information Center; **Notes:** Dogs prohibited; **GPS:** N 47 53.890, W 124 37.429

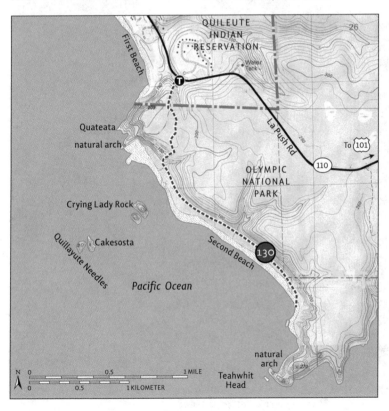

Rugged headlands and sea stacks at Second Beach

👫✨ *Just south of the Quileute village of La Push are three Olympic coast charms: First, Second, and Third Beaches. Each one is sandy and broad and hemmed in by dramatic bluffs and headlands. You can't hike from one to the next because those headlands block the way. First Beach is in the village. Third Beach requires a 1.3-mile slog down a forested trail. Second Beach is just right: reached by a hike just long enough to add a sense of wildness to its stunning beauty.*

GETTING THERE

From Port Angeles, follow US Highway 101 west for 55 miles and turn right onto State Route 110 (signed "Mora–La Push"). (From Forks, the junction is 1.5 miles north along US 101.) Drive west for 7.7 miles to Quillayute Prairie, where SR 110 splits. Bear left (La Push Road) and drive 5.2 miles to the trailhead (elev. 130 ft), on the left just past the Quileute tribal office.

ON THE TRAIL

Well-constructed and well-maintained, the trail starts on the Quileute Indian Reservation. Immediately cross a small creek lined with imposing Sitka spruces before beginning a short climb. At the top of the ascent, enter Olympic National Park and then begin a short, steep descent to the beach, the distant surf growing louder with each step. Soon, start catching glimpses of offshore sea stacks through the surrounding towering spruces. At 0.7 mile, emerge on the log-lined shore.

Time to explore! Hike a short distance along the beach northward to a natural arch. Then retrace your steps and head south. Over 1 mile of scenic sandy beach awaits your footprints. Immediately offshore

is a consortium of battered islets and sea stacks known as the Quillayute Needles. Crying Lady Rock is the largest of the batch. These forbidding landmarks are part of the Quillayute Needles National Wildlife Refuge. Inhospitable to humans, they're productive breeding grounds for thousands of seabirds such as murres, gulls, petrels, cormorants, oystercatchers, and auklets.

Continue wandering and eventually come to an impasse, the headland named Teahwhit Head. But before you turn around and retrace your steps, scan the rugged bluff. Teahwhit Head is also graced with a natural arch. With two arches, a stunning seascape, scores of pelagic birds, and an inviting sandy shoreline, Second Beach just may be second to none.

131 Third Beach

RATING/ DIFFICULTY	ROUNDTRIP	ELEV GAIN/ HIGH POINT	SEASON
***/2	3.6 miles	360 feet/ 300 feet	Year-round

Maps: Green Trails La Push No. 163S, Custom Correct South Olympic Coast; **Contact:** Olympic National Park, Wilderness Information Center; **Notes:** Dogs prohibited; **GPS:** N 47 53.435, W 124 35.941

👫✨ *This is an easy hike to one of the Olympic coast's famed wilderness beaches. Walk the wide, sandy beach to the foot of a waterfall that tumbles from a towering bluff directly into the crashing surf. Feeling more energetic? Leave the crowds behind by grunting over Taylor Point to a secluded beach flanked by steep sea stacks and flowerpot islands.*

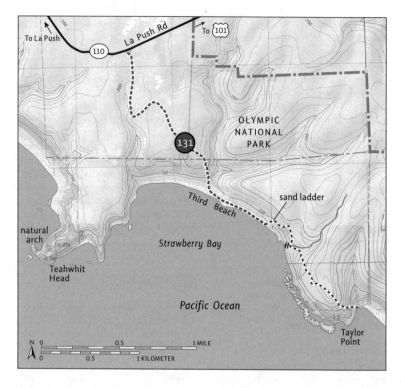

GETTING THERE

From Port Angeles, follow US Highway 101 west for 55 miles and turn right onto State Route 110 (signed "Mora–La Push"). (From Forks, the junction is 1.5 miles north along US 101.) Drive west for 7.7 miles to Quillayute Prairie, where SR 110 splits. Bear left (La Push Road) and drive 3.8 miles to the trailhead (elev. 270 ft), on the left. Privy available.

ON THE TRAIL

The trail starts on an old road through Sitka spruces, hemlocks, and alders. After 0.5 mile, the trail veers left, leaving the old road and entering a more attractive forest. Reach a

300-foot high point, and soon after you'll hear the surf and taste the salty air. Begin a slow descent to the beach at 1.3 miles.

Hemmed in by two imposing headlands, Teahwhit Head and Taylor Point, Third Beach extends for about 1 mile along Strawberry Bay. It's hard to imagine that this wild sweep of coastline was once explored for oil. Luckily for the integrity of the environment and for us hikers, the drillings never proved abundant or profitable.

Hike left (south) 0.5 mile toward the overland trail to admire a waterfall plunging from its heights straight into the pounding waves below.

Dramatic waterfall along the coast

EXTENDING YOUR TRIP

For some really spectacular maritime scenery, continue hiking on the overland trail. Via sand ladders and ankle-twisting terrain, climb 275 feet up Taylor Point. Drop 100 feet into a ravine and cross the creek that feeds the waterfall splashing the sea. Then climb 100 feet through a grove of old-growth Sitka spruces before making a steep descent back to sea level. After a difficult 1.2 miles of overland travel, a quiet and secluded beach is your reward. To go farther requires planning for tides. Find a smooth driftlog and savor the surrounding sea.

132 Hole-in-the-Wall

RATING/ DIFFICULTY	ROUNDTRIP	ELEV GAIN/ HIGH POINT	SEASON
****/1	3.4 miles	None/ Sea level	Year-round

Maps: Green Trails Ozette No. 130S, Custom Correct North Olympic Coast; **Contact:** Olympic National Park, Wilderness Information Center; **Notes:** Dogs permitted on-leash only north to Ellen Creek. Exploration of Hole-in-the-Wall only possible at low tide—consult tide chart; **GPS:** N 47 55.242, W 124 38.282

Hike to a real hole in the wall on the wild Olympic coast: a genuine natural sea arch carved by surf and wind. And while Hole-in-the-Wall is an outstandingly beautiful place, the hike there along Rialto Beach doesn't exactly suffer from a dearth of spectacular scenery. Flanked by sea stacks, lined with giant logs, and strewn with cobblestones, Rialto has all the makings of an Olympic wilderness beach.

GETTING THERE

From Port Angeles, follow US Highway 101 west for 55 miles and turn right onto State Route 110 (signed "Mora–La Push"). (From Forks, the junction is 1.5 miles north along US 101.) Drive west for 7.7 miles to Quillayute Prairie, where SR 110 splits. Bear right (Mora Road) and drive 5 miles to the trailhead (elev. sea level) at the road's end. Water and restrooms available.

ON THE TRAIL

Rialto Beach stretches north from the Quillayute River. But before you bound across the surf-blasted beach, gaze seaward out to high-bluffed, forest-capped James Island. Guarding the mouth of the Quillayute like a sentinel, this island acted as a natural fortress for centuries, protecting the Quileute people from northern invaders.

As you start your hike north, notice the surf-battered logs that line the beach like a giant split-rail fence. Admire their symmetry, but never climb on them during high tides; a wave can easily jostle them loose, trapping and endangering you. A salt-blasted maritime forest rises behind the rows of big beached logs. Look for eagles perched in the higher trees.

At 0.9 mile, come to Ellen Creek, the end of the line for four-legged beach hikers. Crossing Ellen Creek may be tricky. Look for a log, or plod through the tannic and chilled waters. Then pass a couple of impressive "shark teeth" sea stacks before coming to Hole-in-the-Wall, a natural arch at 1.7 miles. During low tides, strut right through it—otherwise, take the steep and short trail over a bluff (elev. 50 ft) around it. The view of Rialto from the crest of the bluff is a classic, endlessly replicated in murals, photos, and memories.

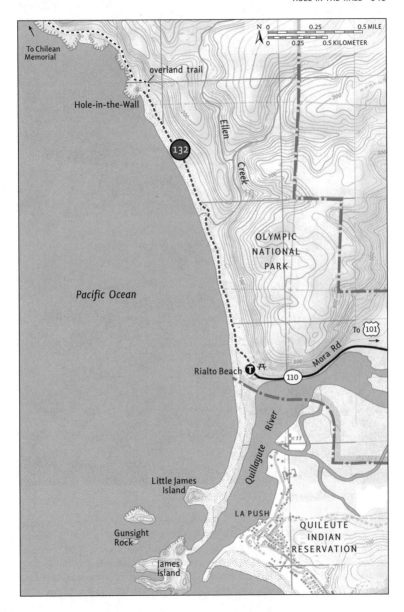

Shark teeth headlands at Rialto Beach

EXTENDING YOUR TRIP

The Chilean Memorial (commemorating a shipwreck) at 4 miles makes a good all-day hike. Heading north from Hole-in-the-Wall, the going gets rockier as the way rounds two small headlands only negotiable during low and medium tides. Offshore reefs, sea stacks, and Dahdayla Island provide a dramatic backdrop. Then enter a quiet, protected island-dotted cove with good views north to Cape Johnson before reaching the small memorial tucked on a bluff in the trees.

133 Quillayute River Slough

RATING/ DIFFICULTY	ROUNDTRIP	ELEV GAIN/ HIGH POINT	SEASON
*/1	1.8 miles	60 feet/ 50 feet	Year-round

Maps: Green Trails La Push No. 163S, Custom Correct South Olympic Coast; **Contact:** Olympic National Park, Wilderness Information Center; **Notes:** Dogs prohibited; **GPS:** N 47 55.089, W 124 36.160

The Quillayute River is famous for its steelhead and salmon fishing. This quiet trail from a popular campground takes you along the river through a rain forest of giant spruces. Hike this trail early in the morning or late in the evening for good wild-life- and bird-watching opportunities.

GETTING THERE

From Port Angeles, follow US Highway 101 west for 55 miles and turn right onto State Route 110 (signed "Mora–La Push"). (From Forks, the junction is 1.5 miles north along US 101.) Drive west for 7.7 miles to Quillayute Prairie, where SR 110 splits. Bear right (Mora Road) and drive 3.3 miles to the Mora Ranger Station. The trailhead (elev. 40 ft) is on the east side of the parking lot. Water and rest-rooms available.

ON THE TRAIL

The Mora Campground is a great base for exploring nearby Rialto Beach (Hike 132), but most campers miss or ignore the Quillayute River Slough Trail that leaves from the camp-ground—all the better for quiet ramblings.

The trail starts out flat and gentle through a forest of scaly-barked spruces carpeted

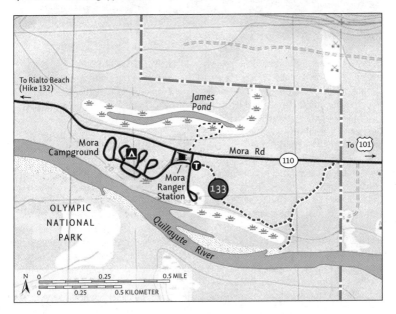

Quillayute River

with mosses. Look for large burls on some of the big trees. After about 0.25 mile, the trail crests a small ridge above one of the many sloughs along the Quillayute. Fed by three major rainforest rivers—the Bogachiel, Sol Duc, and Calawah—the Quillayute snakes and oxbows to the Pacific at La Push. The river takes on an almost southern appearance of a lazy waterway as it cuts through lush bottomlands.

At 0.5 mile, come to a junction. The trail right leads 0.1 mile to the slough, along the way passing a massive old Sitka spruce. The trail left leads 0.3 mile to Mora Road at the national park boundary. Hike them both before returning to the campground. Take your time enjoying the natural riches of this productive environment.

EXTENDING YOUR TRIP

Across the road from the Mora Campground is the James Pond Trail. Hike this short 0.4-mile loop to an oxbow pond teeming with ducks, herons, and eagles.

134 Ozette Triangle

RATING/ DIFFICULTY	LOOP	ELEV GAIN/ HIGH POINT	SEASON
*****/3	9.4 miles	400 feet/ 220 feet	Year-round

Maps: Green Trails Ozette No 130S, Custom Correct Ozette Beach Loop; **Contact:** Olympic National Park, Wilderness Information Center; **Notes:** National park entrance fee. Dogs prohibited. Coastal section can

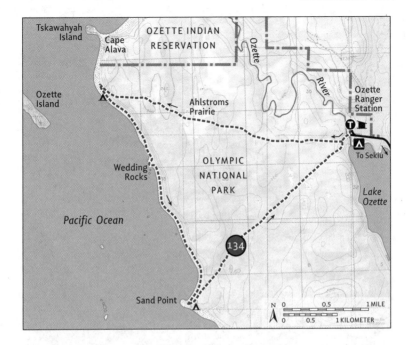

be difficult during high tides; **GPS:** N 48 09.274, W 124 40.132

🧍🦋🌲🏠 *Walk along reefs, tide pools, and also silver strands of spectacular sandy beaches. Scout for whales, eagles, harlequin ducks, and oystercatchers. And admire ancient Native American petroglyphs. The Ozette Triangle (named for the loop's shape) is full of wonders. Sea stacks, sea otters, sea lions, and ocean scenery for as far as you can see.*

GETTING THERE

From Port Angeles, follow US Highway 101 west for 5.4 miles and turn right onto State Route 112. Continue for 46 miles to Sekiu. (Alternatively, take US 101 to Sappho and drive SR 113 north to SR 112 and then on to Sekiu. This way is longer, but not as curvy.) Continue west on SR 112 for 2.3 miles and turn left onto the Hoko-Ozette Road. Follow this paved road for 21 miles to the Ozette Ranger Station and trailhead (elev. 40 ft). Water and privy available.

ON THE TRAIL

Starting from Lake Ozette, one of the largest natural bodies of freshwater in the state, immediately come to an arched bridge crossing of the lazy Ozette River. Then continue 0.2 mile to a junction. You'll be returning left, so go right. The trail travels through a thick forest of western red cedars and Sitka spruces, much of the way on a planked and stepped boardwalk. While this is ideal for

A young hiker admires the Wedding Rocks petroglyphs.

traversing the oft-saturated terrain, it can be pretty slippery during periods of rain. The Park Service is replacing many of the rotting cedar planks with nonslippery plastic ones.

Continue through lush maritime forest drenched in sea mist. Towering ferns and skunk cabbage line the way. After crossing a creek, the trail slowly climbs and reaches Ahlstroms Prairie at about 2 miles, a sprawling grassy bog that was once a homestead site. Pass through another prairie before cresting a 220-foot high point and then steadily descend. At 3.3 miles, reach the wide and wild beaches of Cape Alava. Just offshore, Ozette Island and the Flattery Rocks calm furious breakers intent on crashing the cape.

Walk the shoreline south, past sculpted sandstone ledges. Cast glances out to the sea for seals, whales, and scores of pelagic birds. Look down, too, into tidal pools for starfish tenaciously clinging to barnacle-encrusted walls; and for oystercatchers cruising these open markets. At 4.5 miles, near a short high-tide headland bypass trail, look for Makah petroglyphs etched into the Wedding Rocks, a cluster of shore-hugging boulders at the high-tide line. Respect these historical and sacred artifacts that predate European settlement (but not contact) in the Northwest.

Continue south on rocky wilderness beach, soon coming to a miniature replica of the famous Hole-in-the-Wall of Rialto Beach. Admire scores of other sculpted sea stacks too. At about 5.8 miles, come to another short high-tide detour trail—this one complete with a rope. The way continues along the shelved shoreline, reaching Sand Point at 6.4 miles, which has popular campsites and, to its south, nearly 2 miles of fine sandy beaches.

To close the loop, follow the Sand Point Trail inland. On good tread and extensive boardwalks, traverse expansive cedar bogs and groves of majestic Sitka spruces. Reach a 125-foot high point and then descend, passing a familiar junction and returning to the trailhead at 9.4 miles.

EXTENDING YOUR TRIP

From Cape Alava, walk north 2.2 miles on sandy and scenic beach to the Ozette River. Stay off of Tskawahyah Island, a sacred spot of the Makah people. The area across from the island was once the site of a flourishing Makah village. Artifacts from it are on display in the Makah Museum in Neah Bay.

135 Shi Shi Beach and Point of the Arches

RATING/ DIFFICULTY	ROUNDTRIP	ELEV GAIN/ HIGH POINT	SEASON
****/3	8.8 miles	450 feet/ 250 feet	Year-round

Maps: Green Trails, Cape Flattery No. 98S, Custom Correct North Olympic Coast; **Contact:** Olympic National Park, Wilderness Information Center; **Notes:** Makah Recreation Pass required. Dogs prohibited; **GPS:** N 48 17.623, W 124 39.905

Revered throughout the ages, Shi Shi has its disciples. Many have indelible memories of this magical place—from First Peoples to first-time visitors, naturalists, bird-watchers, hard-core hikers, beach bums, conservationists, and just plain ordinary folk. And Point of the Arches, an assortment of sea stacks extending into the sea, is simply sublime.

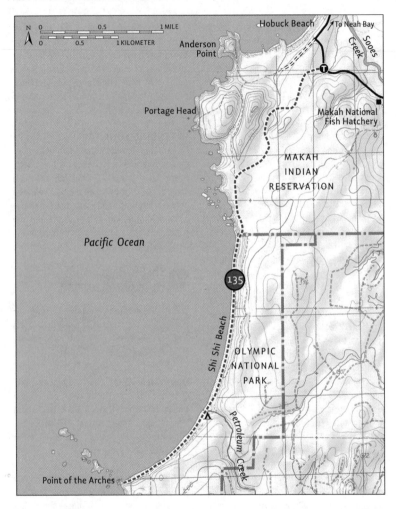

GETTING THERE

From Port Angeles, follow US 101 west for 5.4 miles and turn right onto State Route 112. Continue for 46 miles to Sekiu. (Alternatively, take US 101 to Sappho and drive SR 113 north to SR 112 and then on to Sekiu. This way is longer, but not as curvy.) Continue west on SR 112 for 18 miles to Neah Bay in the Makah Indian Reservation. Drive west on Bayview Avenue for 1 mile, following signs for "Cape Flattery and Beaches." Turn left on Fort Street and in 0.1 mile turn right

Point of the Arches

on 3rd Street. In another 0.1 mile, turn left onto Cape Flattery Road and continue for 2.5 miles to a junction near the tribal center. Turn left onto Hobuck Road and proceed for 4.3 miles (follow signs for the fish hatchery) to the trailhead (elev. 50 ft). Privy available. Note: Overnight parking is allowed only at private lots north of the trailhead, for a fee.

ON THE TRAIL

In 1976 Shi Shi was one of the last additions to Olympic National Park, and its inclusion was met with a fair amount of resistance. Abutting landowners had to be convinced to allow public access. Land developers had to be discouraged from turning the area into an enclave of second homes. And once the Park Service acquired title, it had to remove counterculture squatters and tidy up the mess left behind.

In the last decade, the Makah Tribe developed a new trailhead and built a new trail to the beach—but unfortunately it's not complete, so still expect to encounter Shi Shi's legendary mud holes. The first mile winds through pockets of mature Sitka spruces and rain-saturated bogs via cedar-planked boardwalks and bridges. The new trail then intersects the old road-trail and you must negotiate 0.5 mile of epic mud (hold onto small children). At 2 miles, reach the national park boundary. The only thing separating you from the spectacular beach is a steep trail down a 150-foot bluff.

Brace your knees and emerge at the northern end of the 2-mile-long sandy strand of Shi Shi Beach. Start walking the beach, reveling in the incredible raw beauty of the wilderness before you. Dunes and bluffs hem in the shoreline.

At 3.4 miles, come to Petroleum Creek. Cross it (potentially tricky) and continue 1 mile to Point of the Arches, an amazing array of sea stacks, natural arches, and bluffs jutting into the sea. During low tide, walk exposed shelves to explore the point's tide pools and wind- and water-sculptured landforms. The only thing grander than Shi Shi's natural beauty is its resilience to the forces that tried to deny us from enjoying this national treasure.

EXTENDING YOUR TRIP

Nearby kid- and dog-friendly Hobuck Beach offers 1 mile of wide, sandy shoreline.

136 Cape Flattery

RATING/ DIFFICULTY	ROUNDTRIP	ELEV GAIN/ HIGH POINT	SEASON
***/2	1.5 miles	250 feet/ 300 feet	Year-round

Maps: Green Trails, Cape Flattery No. 98S, Custom Correct North Olympic Coast; **Contact:** Makah Indian Nation; **Notes:** Makah Recreation Pass required; **GPS:** N 48 23.065, W 124 42.940

Rugged Cape Flattery

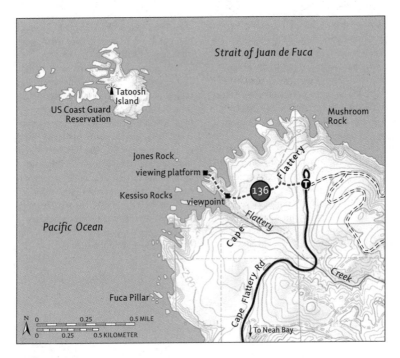

Hike to the northwesternmost point in the continental United States. Here, where the Strait of Juan de Fuca meets the Pacific, Cape Flattery protrudes into a sea of tumultuous waters. A land of dramatic headlands, sea stacks, and deep narrow coves, Cape Flattery exhibits sheer rugged beauty. Scores of seabirds ride the surf and scavenge the sea stacks. Watch for whales and sea lions too. And the sunsets . . . they're simply divine.

GETTING THERE

From Port Angeles, follow US Highway 101 west for 5.4 miles and turn right onto State Route 112. Continue for 46 miles to Sekiu. (Alternatively, take US 101 to Sappho and drive SR 113 north to SR 112 and then on to Sekiu. This way is longer, but not as curvy.) Continue west on SR 112 for 18 miles to Neah Bay in the Makah Indian Reservation. Drive west on Bayview Avenue for 1 mile, following signs for "Cape Flattery and Beaches." Take a left on Fort Street and in 0.1 mile take a right on 3rd Street. In another 0.1 mile, turn left onto Cape Flattery Road. In 2.4 miles pass the tribal center. Proceed for another 5.1 miles to the trailhead (elev. 300 ft). Privy available.

ON THE TRAIL

Thanks to the Makah Indian Nation, the stewards of this land, a well-constructed trail leads to this remote corner of the Northwest.

Start on an old road, descending through a mist-drenched forest of Sitka spruces. The trail soon narrows and continues to descend along boardwalks and steps. Pass a couple of promontories that provide stunning vistas of rugged deep coves and daunting sea stacks. At 0.75 mile, reach the final viewing platform (elev. 50 ft), which teeters on the edge of terra firma.

Admire the cape's abrupt contours of sea stacks, caves, and forbidding sheer cliffs. Look carefully at this hostile environment of strong currents, swift breezes, and frequent storms. And see life! Puffins and guillemots surf the turbulent waters. Murres and gulls nest in the fortress-like cliffs. Oystercatchers probe the tidal pools left behind on offshore reefs. Sea otters, once on the brink of extinction, bob in the protected coves. Whales are often spotted farther out.

People, too, have adapted to this landscape, which is often draped in fog and receives over 100 inches of annual rainfall. Directly offshore is Tatoosh Island. Named for a Makah chief, this 20-acre treeless island once served as a summer fishing camp for the Makahs. The US Coast Guard first constructed a lighthouse on the island in 1857. The current structure is automated. Now only sea lions, seals, and scads of seabirds live on Tatoosh. The Makahs have declared Cape Flattery a nature sanctuary— an enlightened move for this wild world sitting on the brink of the continent.

Appendix I:
Contact Information

CITY AND COUNTY PARKS
City of Montesano,
www.montesano.us/forestry
Jefferson County Parks,
(360) 385-2221, www.countyrec.com
Robin Hill Farm County Park,
(360) 417-2291, www.clallam.net
/Parks/robinhillfarm.html
Salt Creek County Park, (360) 928-3441,
www.clallam.net/Parks/SaltCreek.html

OLYMPIC NATIONAL FOREST
www.fs.fed.us/r6/olympic
Hood Canal Ranger District,
295142 Highway 101, Quilcene, WA,
(360) 765-2200
Pacific Ranger District, 437 Tillicum
Lane, Forks, WA, (360) 374-6522
Pacific Ranger District, 353 South Shore
Road, Quinault, WA, (360) 288-2525

OLYMPIC NATIONAL PARK
www.nps.gov/olym
Wilderness Information Center,
600 East Park Avenue, Port Angeles, WA,
(360) 565-3100

**WASHINGTON STATE DEPARTMENT
OF FISH AND WILDLIFE**
http://wdfw.wa.gov
Region 6 Office, Montesano,
(360) 249-4628

**WASHINGTON STATE DEPARTMENT
OF NATURAL RESOURCES**
www.dnr.wa.gov
Aquatic Division, (360) 902-1786
Olympic Office, (360) 374-2800
Pacific Cascade Region, (360) 577-2025

WASHINGTON STATE PARKS
http://parks.state.wa.us
Bogachiel State Park, (360) 374-6356,
http://parks.state.wa.us/478/
Bogachiel (Hoko River),
http://parks.state.wa.us/321/Hoko
-River (Hoko River)
Cape Disappointment State Park, (360)
642-3078, http://parks.state.wa.us/486
/Cape-Disappointment
Dosewallips State Park,
(360) 796-4415, http://parks.state
.wa.us/499/Dosewallips
Fort Columbia State Park,
(360) 777-8221, http://parks.state
.wa.us/506/Fort-Columbia
Fort Flagler State Park,
(360) 385-1259, http://parks.state
.wa.us/508/Fort-Flagler (Flagler),
http://parks.state.wa.us/240
/Anderson-Lake (Anderson Lake)
Griffiths-Priday State Park,
(360) 902-8844, http://parks.state
.wa.us/516/Griffith-Priday-Ocean
Lake Sylvia State Park,
(360) 249-3621, http://parks.state
.wa.us/534/Lake-Sylvia

Leadbetter Point State Park,
   (360) 642-3078, http://parks.state
   .wa.us/537/Leadbetter-Point
Rainbow Falls State Park,
   (360) 291-3767, http://parks.state
   .wa.us/570/Rainbow-Falls
Sequim Bay State Park,
   (360) 683-4235, http://parks.state
   .wa.us/582/Sequim-Bay (Sequim Bay),
   http://parks.state.wa.us/913/Miller
   -Peninsula-State-Park-Property-Int
   (Miller Peninsula)
Westport Light State Park,
   (360) 268-9717, http://parks.state
   .wa.us/284/Westport-Light

WILDLIFE REFUGES (FEDERAL)
Dungeness National Wildlife Refuge,
   (360) 457-8451, www.fws.gov/refuge
   /dungeness
Grays Harbor National Wildlife Refuge,
   (360) 753-9467, www.fws.gov/refuge
   /Grays_Harbor

**Julia Butler Hansen Refuge for the
   Columbian White-Tailed Deer,**
   (360) 795-3915, www.fws.gov/refuge
   /julia_butler_hansen
Willapa National Wildlife Refuge,
   (360) 484-3482, www.fws.gov/refuge
   /willapa

OTHER AGENCIES AND
PRIVATE ORGANIZATIONS
Adventure Maps,
   www.adventuremaps.net
Long Beach Peninsula Visitors Bureau,
   (800) 451-2542, https://funbeach.com
Makah Indian Nation, (360) 645-2201,
   http://makah.com/makah-tribal-info
Olympic Discovery Trail,
   www.olympicdiscoverytrail.com
Port of Grays Harbor, (360) 482-1600,
   http://friendslanding.org

Appendix II:
Conservation and Trail Organizations

Columbia Land Trust,
www.columbialandtrust.org
Friends of Olympic National Park,
www.friendsonp.org
**Friends of Schafer and Lake
Sylvia State Parks (FOSLS),**
PO Box 642, Montesano, WA 98563,
www.fosls.org
**Friends of Willapa National
Wildlife Refuge,**
PO Box 1130, Ocean Park, WA 98640,
(360) 665-0115,
www.friendsofwillaparefuge.org
Great Peninsula Conservancy,
www.greatpeninsula.org
Jefferson Land Trust,
· 1033 Lawrence Street, Port Townsend,
WA 98368, (360) 379-9501,
www.saveland.org
Klahhane Club,
PO Box 494, Port Angeles, WA 98362,
http://klahhaneclub.org
The Mountaineers,
7700 Sand Point Way NE, Seattle, WA
98115, (206) 521-6001,
www.mountaineers.org

North Olympic Land Trust,
104 North Laurel Street, Suite 114,
Port Angeles, WA 98362, (360) 417-1815,
www.northolympiclandtrust.org
Olympians Hiking Club,
PO Box 401, Hoquiam, WA 98550,
http://theolympianshikingclub.org
Pacific Northwest Trail Association,
www.pnt.org
Peninsula Trails Coalition,
PO Box 1836, Port Angeles, WA 98362,
www.peninsulatrailscoalition.org
Peninsula Wilderness Club,
www.pwckitsap.org
Trout Unlimited,
www.tu.org
Volunteers for Outdoor Washington,
www.trailvolunteers.org
Washington's National Park Fund,
PO Box 4646, Seattle, WA 98194,
www.wnpf.org
Washington Trails Association,
705 2nd Avenue, #300, Seattle, WA
98121, (206) 625-1367, www.wta.org
Wild Olympics,
www.wildolympics.org

Appendix III:
Recommended Reading

Eifert, Larry, and Nancy Eifert. *Olympic National Park Nature Guide*. Port Townsend, WA: Estuary Press, 2001.

Johnston, Greg. *Washington's Pacific Coast*. Seattle: Mountaineers Books, 2015.

Manning, Harvey, Bob Spring, and Ira Spring. *Mountain Flowers of the Cascades and Olympics*. 2nd ed. Seattle: Mountaineers Books, 2002.

McNulty, Tim. *Olympic National Park: A Natural History*. Rev. ed. Seattle: University of Washington Press, 2009.

Olympic Mountain Rescue. *Olympic Mountains: A Climbing Guide*. 6th ed. Seattle: Mountaineers Books, 2006.

Romano, Craig. *Backpacking Washington*. Seattle: Mountaineers Books, 2011.

Whitney, Stephen R., and Rob Sanderlin. *Field Guide to the Cascades and Olympics*. 2nd ed. Seattle: Mountaineers Books, 2003.

Wood, Robert L. *Across the Olympic Mountains: The Press Expedition, 1889–90*. Seattle: Mountaineers Books, 1967.

———. *Men, Mules, and Mountains: Lieutenant O'Neil's Olympic Expeditions*. Seattle: Mountaineers Books, 1976.

———. *Olympic Mountains Trail Guide*. 3rd ed. Seattle: Mountaineers Books, 2000.

Index

1% for Trails
Outdoor Nonprofits in Partnership

Where would we be without trails? Not very far into the wilderness.

That's why Mountaineers Books designates 1 percent of the sales of select guidebooks in our Day Hiking series toward volunteer trail maintenance. Since launching this program, we've contributed more than $14,000 toward improving trails.

For this book, our 1 percent of sales is going to Washington Trails Association (WTA). WTA hosts more than 750 work parties throughout Washington's Cascades and Olympics each year, with volunteers clearing downed logs after spring snowmelt, cutting away brush, retreading worn stretches of trail, and building bridges and turnpikes. Their efforts are essential to the land managers who maintain thousands of acres on shoestring budgets.

Mountaineers Books donates many books to nonprofit recreation and conservation organizations. Our 1% for Trails campaign is one more way we can help fellow nonprofit organizations as we work together to get more people outside, to both enjoy and protect our wild public lands.

If you'd like to support Mountaineers Books and our nonprofit partnership programs, please visit our website to learn more or email mbooks@mountaineersbooks.org.

About the Author

(Photo by Douglas Romano)

Craig Romano grew up in rural New Hampshire, where he fell in love with the natural world. He moved to Washington in 1989 and has since hiked more than 25,000 miles in the Evergreen State. An avid runner as well, Craig has run more than twenty-five marathons and ultra runs, including the Boston Marathon and the White River 50-Mile Endurance Run.

Craig is an award-winning author and co-author of more than twenty guidebooks. His *Columbia Highlands: Exploring Washington's Last Frontier* was recognized in 2010 by Washington Secretary of State Sam Reed and State Librarian Jan Walsh as a Washington Reads book for its contribution to the state's cultural heritage. Craig also writes for numerous publications, tourism websites, and Hikeoftheweek.com.

When not hiking, running, and writing, he can be found napping with his wife, Heather, son, Giovanni, and cat, Giuseppe, at his home in Skagit County. Visit him at http://CraigRomano.com and on Facebook at "Craig Romano Guidebook Author."

OTHER TITLES YOU MIGHT ENJOY FROM MOUNTAINEERS BOOKS

100 Classic Hikes: Washington, 3rd edition
Craig Romano
Gorgeous color photos bring to life
100 of the finest hikes in Washington.

Washington's Pacific Coast: A Guide to Hiking, Camping, Fishing & Other Adventures
Greg Johnston
Expert advice and full-color photos to
help you plan your next visit to the coast.

Urban Trails: Kitsap
Craig Romano
Get out and stay local with this handy
guide to the best trails close to home!

Backpacking Washington
Craig Romano
70 spectacular routes help you
explore Washington's backcountry.

MORE GREAT HIKES—DONE IN A DAY!

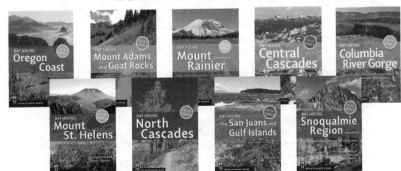

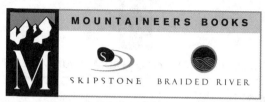

MOUNTAINEERS BOOKS

SKIPSTONE   BRAIDED RIVER

recreation • lifestyle • conservation

MOUNTAINEERS BOOKS is a leading publisher of mountaineering literature and guides—including our flagship title, *Mountaineering: The Freedom of the Hills*—as well as adventure narratives, natural history, and general outdoor recreation. Through our two imprints, Skipstone and Braided River, we also publish titles on sustainability and conservation. We are committed to supporting the environmental and educational goals of our organization by providing expert information on human-powered adventure, sustainable practices at home and on the trail, and preservation of wilderness.

The Mountaineers, founded in 1906, is a 501(c)(3) nonprofit outdoor activity and conservation organization whose mission is "to explore, study, preserve, and enjoy the natural beauty of the outdoors." One of the largest such organizations in the United States, it sponsors classes and year-round outdoor activities throughout the Pacific Northwest, including climbing, hiking, backcountry skiing, snowshoeing, bicycling, camping, paddling, and more. The Mountaineers also supports its mission through its publishing division, Mountaineers Books, and promotes environmental education and citizen engagement. For more information, visit The Mountaineers Program Center, 7700 Sand Point Way NE, Seattle, WA 98115-3996; phone 206-521-6001; www.mountaineers.org; or email info@mountaineers.org.

Our publications are made possible through the generosity of donors and through sales of more than 800 titles on outdoor recreation, sustainable lifestyle, and conservation. To donate, purchase books, or learn more, visit us online:

MOUNTAINEERS BOOKS
1001 SW Klickitat Way, Suite 201 • Seattle, WA 98134
800-553-4453 • mbooks@mountaineersbooks.org • www.mountaineersbooks.org

 Mountaineers Books is proud to be a corporate sponsor of The Leave No Trace Center for Outdoor Ethics, whose mission is to promote and inspire responsible outdoor recreation through education, research, and partnerships • The Leave No Trace program is focused specifically on human-powered (nonmotorized) recreation • Leave No Trace strives to educate visitors about the nature of their recreational impacts and offers techniques to prevent and minimize such impacts • Leave No Trace is best understood as an educational and ethical program, not as a set of rules and regulations • For more information, visit www.lnt.org, or call 800-332-4100.